The Trauma *of* Freud

Also by Paul Roazen

Freud: Political and Social Thought (1968, 1986, 1999)
Brother Animal: The Story of Freud and Tausk (1969, 1990)
Freud and His Followers (1975)
Erik H. Erikson: The Powers and Limits of a Vision (1976)
Helene Deutsch: A Psychoanalyst's Life (1985, 1992)
Encountering Freud: The Politics and Histories of Psychoanalysis (1990)
Meeting Freud's Family (1993)
How Freud Worked: First-Hand Accounts of Patients (1995)
Heresy: Sandor Rado and the Psychoanalytic Movement (with Bluma Swerdloff) (1995)
Canada's King: An Essay in Political Psychology (1998)
Oedipus in Britain: Edward Glover and the Struggle Over Klein (2000)
Political Theory and the Psychology of the Unconscious (2000)
The Historiography of Psychoanalysis (2001)

Edited by Paul Roazen

Sigmund Freud (1973)
Walter Lippmann, *The Public Philosophy* (1989)
Louis Hartz, *The Necessity of Choice: Nineteenth Century Political Theory* (1990)
Helene Deutsch, *The Psychoanalysis of the Sexual Functions of Women* (1991)
Victor Tausk, *Sexuality, War, and Schizophrenia: Collected Psychoanalytic Papers* (1991)
Helene Deutsch: *The Therapeutic Process, the Self, and Female Psychology: Collected Psychoanalytic Papers* (1991)
Walter Lippmann, *Liberty and the News* (1995)

The Trauma of Freud

Controversies in Psychoanalysis

Paul Roazen

Transaction Publishers
New Brunswick (U.S.A.) and London (U.K.)

This book is printed on acid-free paper that meets the American National Standard for Permanence of Paper for Printed Library Materials.

Library of Congress Catalog Number: 2002021768
ISBN: 0-87855-0112-4
Printed in the United States of America

Library of Congress Cataloging-in-Publication Data

Roazen, Paul, 1936-
The trauma of Freud : controversies in psychoanalysis / Paul Roazen.
p. cm.
Includes bibliographical references and index.
ISBN 0-7658-0112-4 (alk. paper)
1. Psychoanalysis—History. I. Title.

BF173 .R5514 2002
150.19'52—dc21 2002021768

In Behalf of the Idealistic Aspirations of Those Pioneers Who Created York University in Toronto

Contents

Preface

Over one hundred years have passed since psychoanalysis was first created by Sigmund Freud in Vienna. As the past century has witnessed the relative decline in the traditional forms of religious faith, people have turned for therapeutic help and moral direction to psychology, believing it to be neutral and scientific. The new profession Freud invented has flourished on the secularization of Western culture, and it is almost impossible to overestimate the influence of various popularizations of aspects of psychoanalytic teachings. By the turn of the twenty-first century, psychoanalytic influence has increasingly extended to some non-Western societies as well. Little has so far been written, for instance, about what kind of impact Freud has had in Russia, Japan, India, and China, yet one suspects that the future take on him that those cultures adopt remains a key aspect of the ultimate fate of his doctrines.

Throughout the years since the first publication of Freud's *The Interpretation of Dreams* in late 1899, and then his beginning to assemble a circle of followers around him in 1902, psychoanalysis has, despite its traditional pretensions to being aloof from ethical questions, attracted to itself an extraordinary degree of sectarian bitterness. Freud both satisfied and at the same time frustrated an urgent modern need for meaning, which helped spawn a series of schisms in his movement. And so there have been, in addition to a small hard core of true believers in Freud's original faith, a series of "heretical" schools that have developed with elaborate theories of their own.

Anyone considering writing on the history of psychoanalysis should have to proceed with an awareness of the existence of Freud's own short 1914 polemical pamphlet "On the History of the Psychoanalytic Movement."[1] Here Freud was trying to draw a firm dividing line between his own contributions and the innovating ideas of his former associates Alfred Adler and Carl G. Jung; this public controversy has acquired almost mythic proportions, and probably deserves to have attracted more attention than any other internal psychoanalytic quarrel.[2] Whether Adler and Jung left Freud, or he threw them out — and no doubt a combination of both alternative possibilities played a part — has never been a successfully settled matter. It is not so much that a large literature arose in connection with these pre-World War I difficulties as that Freud had succeeded in setting the terms of debate for years to come. Thus, whenever trouble arose later within psychoanalysis, it could be possible to tar any original thinkers as so-called dissidents in the field; one cannot underestimate the potential force of the charge of being like these early "renegades." The "mainstream" is supposed alone to retain legitimacy, without specifying how authoritarian in its exclusions any such a metaphor can be. In retrospect it is apt to seem striking that neither Adler nor Jung did much to contest Freud's published views about them, and by default the historiographical field was largely left to accept Freud's own personal viewpoint.[3] But that meant that the accusation of being either Jungian or Adlerian was to be all the more a dreaded possibility.

At least as striking as this early set of quarrels is how, whatever one might think now of the merits of what psychoanalysis has had to contribute to the life of the mind, the history of psychoanalysis throughout the twentieth century was repeatedly punctuated by a whole series of hotly contested controversies. It would be impossible to try to write an account of the saga of what psychoanalysis has amounted to apart from these many difficulties with their accompanying acrimony. The fact that all these rancorous disputes have taken place does not, in my view, in any way detract from the importance of the subject matter itself. On the contrary, that people were willing to engage in such disagreements means to me that something important must have been at issue to make it worthwhile to undertake such differences of opinion. The merits of the case were inextricably mixed up with questions concerning power and ambition, as well as what was perceived to be the future of the "movement." Although it is not always obvious what generates intellectual strife, and all the splintering associated with such passionate argumentation, it should be safe to generalize that live subjects attract debate, whereas stale matters are left ignored. For example, no one would be discussing the rights of serfs after the end of feudalism; and fights about whether socialism can be achieved in only one country, which were once so heated a subject of theoretical views at the time of the Russian Revolution, are unlikely to be revived again. So that the fact that psychoanalysis has been such a source of recent contentiousness means, I think, that it has been central to how we have thought about ourselves.

The purpose of this book is to try to put in some sort of sequence and perspective the most memorable issues that have come up in connection with the history of Freud's school. Perhaps part of what Freud really (unintentionally) established with his 1914 polemic was that this field would continue to be an avidly contested one. He certainly thought that the stakes were high enough then to make public his side of things; and although he never again engaged in any such explicit bit of polemicizing, quarrels did not cease to break out in his lifetime. It has to be noteworthy that he was successful enough in creating a set of doctrines which attracted others so that intellectual blow-ups continued to occur well after his death in 1939. At least a portion of the objective people had in mind was to succeed to the mantle of Freud's authority; the question of legitimate lineage has always been unusually important within psychoanalysis. Analysts have had special problems with being self-created, as biological parenthood could become secondary to who had trained whom; the legitimacy of the offspring of recognized disciples came to acquire special importance.[4] (Even while Freud was still alive his students could argue about who had remained true to the essence of his teachings.) Freud himself had relied on various of his great predecessors in the history of ideas in order to help establish his authority, and on a smaller scale that sort of reasoning about ancestry, although confined within the psychoanalytic canon itself, has continued in the years since his death.[5]

The following chapters cannot hope to be definitive, since even more strenuously debated past problems may yet be uncovered; even if no doubt further contentions are yet to arrive, I think that it is possible now to lay out some of the central issues that have marked the story of psychoanalysis's coming of age. It should not satisfy intellectual historians to allow those who were willing openly to be in contention, as opposed to the ones who preferred to sit on the sidelines, to have the last word on what was being fought over. So that just as it is necessary to look with skepticism at what happened between Freud as opposed to Adler and Jung, it is also incumbent on us to try to evaluate fairly the more recent outbreaks of differences of opinion. The legends that arose necessarily had a certain sort of truth, but mythologizing can be a misleading way to orient ourselves.

Silence can of course become a deadly weapon of argument in itself; any powerful movement proceeds in part by ignoring those it wants to overcome. So part of the job of scholarship has to involve challenging those who might have preferred to let sleeping dogs lie. To take an outstanding example, one of the great historical success stories over the last two decades has been the favorable transformation in the reputation of the Hungarian Sandor Ferenczi. Once he was dismissed as not only wrongheaded but mentally unbalanced, yet at present he seems to be securely established as one of the heroic pioneers in modern psychotherapy.[6] While other bits of commonly received wisdom, connected, for example, with Adler and Jung, have remained relatively constant and unreconsidered, the tide of opinion about Ferenczi has shifted almost completely. Yet it remains memorable that even before his death in 1933 some of his writings were considered too shocking to be safely presented before fellow analysts, or translated into other languages. If he is now considered to have been reliably prophetic of much of today's most up-to-date thinking, then what are we to make of those who tried for so long to discredit him? But to replace the demonization of Ferenczi with the blackening of the reputations of those who once so unfairly assailed him seems to me an unsatisfying way of proceeding. Yet the successful transmutation into Ferenczi's current high standing is one of the single most encouraging signs in this whole area of thinking. And it is hard not to look forward to future changes in how the past of psychoanalysis gets rethought.

Inevitably, then, as the history of psychoanalysis becomes more established as a legitimate subject for discussion, there are going to be an increasing range of different points of view. It should be taken as a sign of sophistication that it is possible to advance rival interpretations about the past of this field. Many others besides Ferenczi have been unjustly treated up to now. The example of what has happened in connection with him is only the most striking case of a complete reversal of what once was considered a standard view. Without anticipating that it is going to be possible to achieve similar rehabilitations of reputations which once were in tatters, I think we can expect that by looking over the issues to be discussed here that we can learn some valuable lessons about how any conventionally accepted thinking is likely to be misleading. My objectives in *The Trauma of Freud: Controversies in Psychoanalysis* will have been fulfilled if it helps lead others in the future to look on all such matters with more of the nuances that a serious historical subject deserves.

Too often people look on psychoanalysis's past in terms of "good" versus "bad" guys. It simplifies things to use broad brushstrokes to categorize people moralistically one way or another, as critical judgments get handed out about who deserves attention. In fact, I think the real attraction of this whole field is the degree to which it should be impossible to come to any such straightforward ways of dividing up the history of the whole area of psychoanalytic thought. The more we understand about the various contrasting purposes that were in play, the more genuinely interesting I think this entire subject becomes. I am not arguing that it is impossible to come to some conclusions about the merits of what have been at various times proposed, but I am trying to encourage more open-mindedness about questions that may seem already settled. Intellectual life can be enriched the more we know about the past, even if that means putting aside traditional partisan allegiances. Although it can be hard to reconsider conflicts that once seemed established matters, I think that the rewards of doing so are considerable. For the history of psychoanalysis can prove an immensely rewarding topic in terms of awakening us to the full variety of options that are possible.

As we shall see, often the bitterness associated with some of these past heated engagements was due not only to the immediate questions of personal loyalty or betrayal, but also to more enduring problems associated with what the good life might be like. For although Freud partly started out as a scientist, inevitably he also had ethical (and even artistic) purposes in mind. And this combination of empirical and moral objectives has helped make the topic of psychoanalysis such an engaging one. For example, Adler was a socialist, and that ideological commitment played its role in his disagreeing with some of Freud's most central beliefs; it also led Adler, however, to take different attitudes toward society, and female psychology, for instance, which encouraged him to say things which at the time Freud considered threatening to the survival of his new movement. I will not be repeating here what I once advanced in my *Freud and His Followers* about the struggles that took place during 1912–13 within psychoanalysis, but the reader should be aware that I think that reconsidering those matters is incumbent on us as intellectuals. Legend-weaving makes for comfort but not good history, and so I have tried to proceed over the years in the path of independent scholarship. The rewards have, I think, been immensely satisfying.

I have not shied away from controversy, and part of the exhilaration that comes from the enterprise of studying the history of psychoanalysis is associated with how it is still possible for intellectual historians to make a mark working in this area. Ideally one might like to think that the world of the intellect ought to be less combative, but contentiousness is in itself not harmful. Vigorous debate is healthy, and probably essential to avoid ill-considered dogmatic self-assurance. If there had all along been more tolerance for different fundamental viewpoints within psychoanalysis, perhaps fewer of the more famous outbursts would have been necessary.

Fanaticism is another matter, and the ideal of toleration — which I will specifically address in my conclusions — has to give us trouble when it comes to handling the phenomenon of psychoanalytic ayatollahs as they arise; liberals who believe in tolerance are bound to be in a bind when confronted with various ideological intolerances. Fighting fire with fire is never a satisfactory solution. Polemicizing rarely leads to the purposes one might like. On the whole I think that even though the path of moderation often proves relatively ineffective, at least in the short run, one has to put one's faith in the possibilities of such sanity for the future, and hopefully the most rationally conducted debate will eventually win out. But there are no guarantees, and a naïve faith in progress would be misguided; since our own actions can shape the contours of discussion, I believe it is necessary to dip oars into even the most troubled waters in order to help steer the discussion in a decent direction. The following essays represent the best of what I have been able to do, and I hope they prove helpful as time passes.

My objective has not been unnecessarily to revive past partisanship, or to perpetuate old rivalries and animosities. I do believe that certain central alternative possibilities were initially raised by outstanding earlier thinkers; such problems as authoritarianism, or subtle pretensions to omniscience, were posed years ago, and are apt to reappear today under new guises. I doubt, for example, that enough attention gets paid now to how the latest scientific-sounding diagnostic classifications are, in fact, disguised forms of moral judgment-making.

It is sometimes astonishing for me to read new psychoanalytic books which simply ignore past ideological differences, as they paper over prior fissures. Occasionally one can hope that this can be taken to represent a genuine advance, in that earlier contentiousness has been replaced by a greater catholicity of viewpoints. These quiet changes can be a sign of greater tolerance. But at the same time I suspect that unless and until we face up to some of the earlier disputes, the identical sorts of ideological decisions are likely to recur once again, even if clothed in different sorts of terminology.

My hunch is that potential zealotry lies just below the surface of even the most placid contemporary psychoanalytic waters. For some years when I lived in Toronto I ran at my home a supper-group on the history of psychoanalysis; on one occasion I invited a Jungian, recently trained in Zurich, to present a paper. He came with a clinical presentation, and explained how he approached one young man's distressing dream (of self-fellation) with an interpretation drawn from ancient Greek mythology. Although it seemed to me a perfectly plausible way of holding the alarmed patient in treatment, a particularly mild-manned Freudian had come prepared in advance to denounce the Jungian's whole way of proceeding; right in front of our eyes this analyst had temporarily transformed himself, on the occasion of an unpaid guest being nice enough to present something about his way of going about things, into an impassioned monster of ideological intolerance. I suppose there might have been trade-union rivalries (Jung has had more appeal in Canada than the States) that had been aroused, but to intellectual historians it was a shocking spectacle of old-fashioned dogmatism. I regret to say that it is precisely such passions that are capable of inspiring adherents in the first place, and that many different schools of thought have precisely the same potential for argumentativeness.

The Trauma of Freud: Controversies in Psychoanalysis is not designed to reopen old wounds unnecessarily, but to try and make it less likely that we will take for granted essential points of view that we are better off becoming aware of. Enduring differences do exist in how analysts of various persuasions go about their work, and it can serve no useful purpose to pretend that there are fewer alternatives available than what history has left us with. I think that Freud's whole approach can be taken to rest on the ancient Socratic conviction that the unexamined life is not worth living, and it is in that spirit that I am proceeding here. The richness of the tradition of depth psychology started by Freud lies in the variety of viewpoints that it has given rise to; as long as we do not allow any of these systems of thought to become tinged with the worst emotions connected with religiosity, looking at them all with as much dispassion as possible can become an adventure all its own.

Today's clinicians are unlikely to be aware of the ins and outs of some of these classic controversies, and I want to repeat for the sake of newcomers that my bringing these issues up now is not for the sake of rattling any skeletons in the family closet. Although we live in an era when what might seem to count are only questions of pragmatic technique, I can assure the reader that the spiritual bases for the long-standing attraction that psychoanalysis has had go far deeper than immediate clinical concerns. It can be worth being reminded of the idealistic purposes that have attracted people in the first place to this field.

It is my conviction not only that ideas in general matter, but also that Freud's whole enterprise rested on the significance of intellectual life for how we come to order our world. Donald W. Winnicott, who was in his own time an innovator who could be subject to sectarian abuse, told me that he had once mentioned Jung's name at a meeting of the British Psychoanalytic Society, and the silence his presentation aroused meant that he never tried to do so a second time. I believe that it is in keeping with Freud's central message to suppose that psychoanalysis will be best equipped to cope with the next century of its existence if it is unafraid to deal with its own past.

Freud succeeded in decisively transforming how we think about ourselves — this is the "trauma" to which my title refers. Freud shocked civilized readers, and reactions to his system of thought have seemed mandatory. It has recently been suggested that "one could say that the history of psychoanalysis consists of a continuous conversation with Fraud. . . . "[7] No matter how skeptically we come to evaluative specific parts of what he proposed, I think it should be a tribute to what he accomplished how later thinkers felt forced to come to terms with his work. The varieties of these responses make for a central part of the history of ideas of the last century. It remains to be seen what new twists and turns the future reaction to Freud's heritage has in store for us. But the vitality of these past controversies seem to me in itself a sign that we have by no means seen the last of the effects of Freud's momentous impact on the life of the mind.

These esays were all originally written for separate occasions, and I have done my best to try to smooth out the whole narrative so as to reduce possible redundancies. I fear that I may not have been completely succesful, but given the still rudimentary historiographical state of this subject that may not be an entirely unfortunate result and I have often highlighted key points that I think justify being reiterated. It is easy often to think that one has been knocking one's head against a stone wall, given all the existing pre-existing ideological prejudices. But in any event readers may doubtless read this book in selective order depending on what most critically concerns them first, and I attempted also to keep that in mind in presenting *The Trauma of Freud.*

Notes

1. "On the History of the Psychoanalytic Movement," *The Standard Edition of the Complete Psychological Works of Sigmund Freud*, ed. James Strachey (London, The Hogarth Press, 1953–1974), Vol. 14, pp. 7–66. Hereafter this edition of Freud's works will be referred to simply as *Standard Edition.*
2. Paul Roazen, *Freud and His Followers* (New York, Alfred A. Knopf, 1975, reprinted, New York, Da Capo, 1992), Parts V-VI.
3. Paul Roazen, *The Historiography of Psychoanalysis* (New Brunswick, N.J., Transaction Publishers, 2001).
4. Paul Roazen, "Charles Rycroft and the Theme of Ablation," *British Journal of Psychotherapy*, Vol. 18, No. 2 (2001), pp. 269–278.
5. Paul Roazen, *Political Theory and the Psychology of the Unconscious*, Part I (London, Open Gate Press, 2000).
6. See Roazen, *Freud and His Followers*, *op. cit.*, Part VII, Chs. 6 & 7, pp. 355–71; Clara Thompson, with the collaboration of Patrick Mullahy, *Psychoanalysis: Evolution and Development* (New York, Grove Press, 1950); Erich Fromm, *The Dogma of Christ*, "Psychoanalysis — Science or Party Line?," pp.131–44 (New York, Holt, Rinehart & Winston, 1963); Arnold Rachman, "Death By Silence (*Todschweigen*): The Traditional Method of Silencing the Dissident in Psychoanalysis," in *The Death of Psychoanalysis: Murder? Suicide? Or Rumor Greatly Exaggerated*?, ed. Robert M. Prince (Northvale, N. J., Aronson, 1999), pp. 153–64; Carlo Bonomi, "Flight Into Sanity: Jones's Allegation of Ferenczi's Mental Deterioration Reconsidered," *International Journal of Psychoanalysis*, 1999, pp. 507–42; Sandor Ferenczi, *Selected Writings*, ed. by Julia Borossa (London, Penguin Books, 1999).
7. Joseph Schwartz, *Cassandra's Daughter: A History of Psychoanalysis* (London, Penguin, 1999), p. 60.

1

The Problem of Seduction

The first controversy I would like to discuss is that connected with what has come to be known as the "seduction theory," even though Freud never advanced anything under that specific title. Curiously enough this is a dispute whose literature has only proliferated relatively recently. At the time it first took place, especially in the 1890s and the first decade of the twentieth century, Freud's views about seduction must have had a major impact on the standing his work had among his immediate contemporaries. But it is only in the last two decades that this subject, dating from the beginnings of psychoanalysis, has become of central historical concern.

Freud's 1897 abandonment of the theory he had first held in the mid–1890s, which attributed central significance in the origin of neuroses to the sexual seduction of children, is generally considered momentous enough that both his devoted friends and ardent foes consider that to be the time when psychoanalysis as a distinct entity arose. Thanks to the survival of Freud's correspondence then to his intimate friend Wilhelm Fliess we have an unusual contemporaneous record of the workings of Freud's professional thought processes. It is true that whether one reads Freud's letters as a young man, or those composed during the most painful years of old age, he continues to sound very much like he was during the phase which has come to be known as the Fliess period. Freud was perhaps emotionally freer in writing to Fliess than he was in his more guarded later years, but the overall continuities and consistencies stand out.

Freud's official biographer Ernest Jones thought that the fall of 1897, when Freud first wrote Fliess about the collapse of his own confidence in his seduction hypothesis, "was a turning point in his scientific career," and most students of the field would agree with Jones's assessment. Jones, however, took a propagandistic view when he maintained that the crisis connected with the abandonment of the seduction theory "tested his integrity, courage and psychological insight to the full. Now he had to prove whether his psychological method on which he had founded everything was trustworthy or not. It was at this moment that Freud rose to his full stature."[1]

Freud had characteristically abruptly changed his mind in such a way that he was able to minimize self-criticism, although others, including his patients, were not to escape blame. Freud, feeling more right than ever, plunged almost immediately into his theory of the Oedipus complex, and it may not be surprising that Fliess, usually stigmatized only as a wild thinker, decided initially to remain silent about Freud's version of the significance of the Oedipus story.

We can get something of the range of opinion about this incident in which Freud gave up his central emphasis on childhood seduction if we remember, first, that Jones felt that "1897 was the acme of Freud's life."[2] Ronald Clark, unlike Jones an outside biographer, called his chapter about this incident "Splendid Isolation: Disaster."[3] And Jeffrey M. Masson subtitled a whole book "Freud's Suppression of the Seduction Theory," as Masson alleged Freud's cowardice in the face of contemporary medical criticism.[4] There was weighty significance to Masson's notion that Freud had suppressed rather than abandoned his early concept, and the difference in words gives an idea of what a curious world psychoanalytic history can be. All objects of devotion, religions in both the best and least attractive senses, lead to others becoming embroiled in terminological disputes which are bound to seem incomprehensible to impartial observers.

No one can know the exact frequency of the dreadful occurrence of the sexual abuse of children, either in Freud's time or our own, yet to argue as Freud did, in writing to Fliess in April of 1896 and in a 1896 paper, that Freud had discovered the equivalent of the source of the Nile, now looks to many as off the wall. It is not surprising that Freud's 1896 professional audience, before whom he presented a memorable paper on the origins of hysteria, should have given him in his words "an icy reception," or that the famous psychiatrist-sexologist Richard von Krafft-Ebing should have reportedly observed of Freud's theory, "It sounds like a scientific fairy-tale." Freud wrote Fliess about what had happened, and said that such skeptics were "asses" who could "go to hell, euphemistically expressed."[5]

Yet Freud jumped headlong, after giving up his seduction theory, only a little more than a year after this, to a conviction about the Oedipus complex which he held tenaciously to the end of his life. It has taken almost a hundred years of psychoanalytic revisionists who have sought to alter Freud's own mature commitments to succeed in amending his version of oedipal emotions. In his last years he accepted the concept of the pre-Oedipus phase of childhood thinking, but I doubt that many reasonable outsiders would be likely to share our own respect, as historians of ideas, for the intricacies of those who have consciously or unconsciously labored to change Freud's ideas so as not to be excommunicated from the fold of the faithful.[6]

My own tack will be to try and approach this whole matter in the spirit of intellectual history; detachment seems to be relatively out of fashion these days, yet it remains, I think, a necessary scholarly ideal. It is always easy to make past figures look ridiculous in their thinking by the mere passage of time, but my objective is not to damage the reputations of any psychoanalytic pioneer, much less Freud himself. He initiated a revolution in ideas about human nature which continues to influence how we think about motives and feelings; studying his work, alongside that of his followers and rivals, is incumbent on anyone who wants to make sense of some of the most deeply contested controversies of the twentieth century. But I readily acknowledge, just as in reflecting on other historical or theological disputes, that it can take restraint not to smirk at some of the curious belief systems that were once entertained.

Freud's central publication on the sexual seduction of children was his 1896 "The Aetiology of Hysteria." But earlier that same year he had published an article "Further Remarks on the Neuro-psychoses of Defence," the first section of which was devoted to the problem of hysteria; Freud's introductory remarks should be enough to alert one to the dangers of any infallibilistic ways of reasoning. Psychoanalysis was, he held, a "laborious but completely reliable method," one which he had used in making "investigations" which also constituted "a therapeutic procedure."[7] Even after Freud repudiated the theories he once expressed about hysteria (and seduction supposedly had played a central part in obsessions and psychoses as well) Freud clung to the firmest conviction about the reliability of his methods. He waited until 1906 to acknowledge publicly, in qualified terms, that he had changed his mind, nine years after confiding with Fliess about it in private. It never seems to have dawned on orthodox Freudians that Freud's initial reasoning had provided realistic grounds for the iciness of the reaction to his 1896 ideas. And by waiting so long to express his new position, I believe that Freud had helped damage his own professional standing in Vienna. His early campaign in 1884 on behalf of the supposedly safe medical uses of cocaine (which may well be the first of the many controversies in Freud's career[8]) left him exceptionally exposed to further medical criticism.

It is, I think, greatly to Freud's credit that he was struggling to get beyond the therapeutic nihilism that can be associated with an exclusive concentration on hereditary factors. Many of the same problems about nature versus nurture continue to arise in today's contemporary clinical practice. Further, Freud was on a pathbreaking course in trying to penetrate, as a psychologist, behind patients' symptoms to their causes. In 1896 Freud was still, and this would last up to 1914, relying on the authority of his Viennese mentor Josef Breuer, even though their collaboration had come to an end by 1894. Freud, in fact, came to loathe Breuer in private, yet cited him approvingly long after their falling out. The whole relationship between Freud's personal thoughts as opposed to his public behavior is a complicated subject in itself; Henry James memorably understood the naïve American confusion and moralistic awe, a set of emotions that I happen to share, in the face of the complexities of European manners.[9]

Hysterical symptoms, Freud had maintained, cannot arise from reality alone, "*but . . . in every case the memory of earlier experiences awakened in association to it plays a part in causing their symptoms.*"[10] For years afterwards Freud continued to be, from today's perspective, too insistent on looking for a traumatic scene that might prove curative when recalled, but his overall concern with memories marked him from the outset as preeminently a psychologist.

Freud pulled no punches about the centrality of sex in his 1896 paper on hysteria: "*in the end we infallibly come to the field of sexual experience.*"[11] He cited eighteen cases to support his position. (Jones was such a blind proponent of Freud's that he did not seem to realize how he was endangering Freud's position by the claim that these were "fully analyzed cases,"[12] whatever that hyperbole might be taken to mean.)

Freud was unusually persuasive as a writer in part because he anticipated possible objections. And he raised the point that what might have happened is that he had forced "such scenes upon his docile patients, alleging that they are memories, or else that the patients tell the physician things which they have deliberately invented or have imagined and that he accepts those things as true. . . ." Freud took comfort from the fact that "only the strongest compulsion of the treatment can induce them to embark on a reproduction" of the childhood scenes. Nor did he shy away from saying, in his own behalf, that the patients had "no feeling of remembering" such childhood traumas. "Why should patients," he asked, "assure me so emphatically of their unbelief, if what they want to discredit is something which — from whatever motive — they themselves have invented?"[13]

Fliess knew Freud well enough, and understood enough about the impact of the psychoanalytic treatment setting as conducted by Freud, to propose later (in Freud's words) that "the reader of thoughts merely reads his own thoughts into other people," a proposition which Freud felt rendered all his "efforts valueless,"[14] and one of the central grounds for Freud breaking their friendship. One can imagine that Fliess could not jump through each new hoop as rapidly as Freud could hold them up, and it ought not to be surprising if Freud's reversal on the score of seduction tarnished the standing Freud's method could have for Fliess.

Still it is noteworthy that in Freud's 1896 paper he had proposed to cure hysteria "by transforming . . . unconscious memories of the infantile scenes into conscious ones." Such a procedure, once detached from the quest for the finite memories of specific experiences, comes close to what modern psychotherapy, with the aim of heightened awareness, would be interested in. Freud attributed to hysterics "a general abnormal sensitivity to stimuli," a "high degree of readiness to feel hurt on the slightest occasion," which he attributed in part to "a physiological basis." Freud concluded his paper by asking that his concrete conclusions be accorded less attention than the procedure he was introducing. That "new method of research," exploring "processes of thought which have remained unconscious," was recommended by Freud as a "new pathway to knowledge" that even psychiatry would benefit from.[15] (Freud's own training was in neurology, a field in Vienna which was distinct from psychiatry.)

In 1905 Freud began publicly, if guardedly, to retract his seduction theory, presumably in a way that his methodology could survive intact. I am not suggesting that Freud was proceeding with dishonest intent; rather, he was so committed to the neutral validity of his approach that I think he really believed that reversing himself on seduction need not cast doubt on the validity of his method for arriving at what he called his "findings." In the course of his *Three Essays on the Theory of Sexuality*, Freud brought up the sensitive issue of his 1896 proposal about the central role of seduction:

> I cannot admit that in my paper on "The Aetiology of Hysteria" I exaggerated the frequency or importance of that influence, though I did not then know that persons who remain normal may have had the same experiences in their childhood, and though I consequently overrated the importance of seduction in comparison with the factors of sexual constitution and development.

After having claimed what he could not "admit," it seems to me that Freud immediately went on to do just that. "Obviously," he concluded with the hindsight of his new conviction about the significance of infantile sexuality, "seduction is not required in order to arouse a child's sexual life; that can also come about spontaneously from internal causes."[16]

Then once again, in a 1905 paper that appeared in 1906, Freud was more explicit about his retraction. His theory, he claimed, had culminated in the thesis: "if the *vita sexualis* is normal, there can be no neurosis." (He was not only restating his 1896 argument, but now begging the question of what might be deemed "normal.") Although he did not concede that any of his assertions had been "incorrect," he felt "in a position, on the basis of deeper experience, to correct the insufficiencies, the displacements and the misunderstandings under which my theory then labored." His material had been "scanty," and "happened by chance to include a disproportionately large number of cases in which sexual seduction by an adult or by older children played the chief part in the history of the patient's childhood." In this way Freud explained how he had "over-estimated the frequency of such events," "though in other respects they were not open to doubt." Freud also had been, in his earlier work, "unable to distinguish with certainty between falsifications made by hysterics in their memories of childhood and traces of real events." (Freud seemed to be implying that later on he had been able to make such distinctions.) Fantasies of seduction could be a means of avoiding memories of infantile sexual activity such as masturbation. This alleged "clarification" supposedly "corrected" the "most important" of Freud's "early mistakes."[17]

At this point it is well to consider the exact terms of Freud's private 1897 explanation to Fliess about the rejection of his early theory of aetiology. He mentioned first his "continual disappointment" in his "efforts to bring a single analysis to a real conclusion. . . . " Further, the fact that "the *father*, not excluding" his own, "had to be accused of being perverse. . . . " (Freud's father died at the age of eighty in October 1896.) Thirdly, "the certain insight that there are no indications of reality in the unconscious, so that one cannot distinguish between truth and fiction that has been cathected with affect." Finally, "in the most deep-reaching psychosis the unconscious memory does not break through, so that the secret of childhood experiences is not disclosed even in the most confused delirium."[18] It seems to me remarkable that not one of these four 1897 points got included in Freud's later publications. But by then Freud was able to smooth over and rationalize harmoniously a serious disjunction in his thinking.

In his 1914 *On the History of the Psychoanalytic Movement* Freud wove the tale of the seduction theory into the story of the origins of the "cause" which had recently been, in his view, "deserted" by Adler, Jung, and their respective followers. He alluded to the significance of infantile sexuality, and "a mistaken idea" which "had to be overcome which might have been almost fatal to the young science." Freud maintained that he had been "influenced by Charcot's view of the traumatic origin of hysteria," which led Freud to be "readily inclined to accept as true and aetiologically significant the statements made by patients in which they ascribed their symptoms to passive sexual experiences in the first years of childhood — to put it bluntly, to seduction." (Notice that Freud no longer mentions the objections patients had had, overcome "only by the strongest compulsion of the treatment.") This aetiology of seduction had broken "down under the weight of its own improbability and contradiction in definitely ascertainable circumstances," a mysterious enough explanation. Freud had been ingenious in the way he was able to correct his own mistake, although today it may seem as if he were too confident about how he resolved the problem. By taking "psychical reality . . . into account alongside practical reality," Freud could give weight to the fantasy lives of patients. But he cited the 1896 meeting with Krafft-Ebing in the chair, as if Freud had made "ordinary contributions to science," and as if it were the simple case that "assertions on the part played by sexuality in the aetiology of the neuroses cannot count upon meeting with the same kind of treatment as other communications."[19]

In a 1922 paper, published in 1923, Freud referred to "the error of greatly overestimating the importance of *seduction* as a source of sexual manifestations in children and as a root for the formation of neurotic symptoms." It appears that by then Freud was willing to make an admission that he had denied in *Three Essays on the Theory of Sexuality*. Freud was now proposing that this "misapprehension" about seduction could be "corrected when it became possible to appreciate the extraordinarily large part played in the mental life of neurotics by the activities of *phantasy*, which clearly carried more weight in neurosis than did external reality."[20]

By 1924 Freud was even bolder about acknowledging what had happened in 1896. In a footnote added to his "Further Remarks on the Neuro-psychoses of Defence" he acknowledged, "This section is dominated by an error which I have since repeatedly acknowledged and corrected." He conceded that he had in the early days "not yet" been able "to distinguish between my patients' phantasies about their childhood years and their real recollections." But this line of argument was at odds with the proposition, communicated to Fliess, that it was, in principle, impossible to distinguish between reality and fantasy in the unconscious. He was admitting that he had attributed to seduction "a significance and universality that it does not possess." Overcoming this "error" meant that he could then see "the spontaneous manifestations of the sexuality of children." Nevertheless, Freud wanted to insist that "seduction retains a certain etiological importance," which meant that "some" of his 1896 "psychological comments" were "to the point." And that same year of 1924 Freud also added a footnote to his 1896 "The Aetiology of Hysteria"; when he had written about patients having had no feeling of remembering the scenes, Freud commented, "All this is true; but it must be remembered that at the time I wrote it I had not yet freed myself from my *overvaluation* of reality and my *low valuation* of phantasy."[21] Once again, one can wonder whether Freud had provided enough of an explanation to get himself out of his earlier misstep.

By 1924 Freud also had already come down with cancer of the jaw, and knew concretely that his lifespan was limited, and in his *Autobiographical Study* (1925) he sought to mythify further the past of psychoanalysis. In the course of describing how he had come upon "the fact of infantile sexuality," he brought up "the error" into which he had fallen "for a while and which might well have had fatal consequences for the whole of my work." He no longer blamed the impact of Charcot's teachings, but rather vaguely cited that he had been "under the influence of the technical procedure" which he then employed:

> Under the influence of the technical procedure which I used at that time, the majority of my patients reproduced from their childhood scenes in which they were sexually seduced by some grown-up person. With female patients the part of seducer was almost always assigned to their father . . . .My confidence was strengthened by a few cases in which relations of this kind with a father, uncle, or elder brother had continued up to an age at which memory was to be trusted.[22]

Freud never explained exactly which aspect of his "technical procedure" had been at fault, or how he had proceeded differently in later years. And his accusation about the role of fathers for his female patients was novel, although in two 1924 footnotes revising *Studies On Hysteria* he indicated that he had earlier disguised the guilt of the fathers in two of his case reports.[23]

Freud's *Autobiographical Study* expanded on the significance of his having had to reject the seduction theory:

> If the reader feels inclined to shake his head at my credulity, I cannot altogether blame him; though I may plead that this was at a time when I was intentionally keeping my critical faculty in abeyance so as to preserve an unprejudiced and receptive attitude towards the many novelties which were coming to my notice every day.

Jones later elaborated on the constructive uses of Freud's credulity, but neither he or Freud ever adequately explained, in contrast to Freud's detailed letter to Fliess, exactly why Freud had given up the seduction concept. (By the way, no one has ever successfully accounted for just why Freud had ever made dreams so important.) Freud preferred to skate over what happened during the crisis in his thinking in 1897:

> When, however, I was at last obliged to recognize that these scenes of seduction had never taken place, and that they were only phantasies which my patients had made up or which I myself had perhaps forced on them, I was for some time completely at a loss.[24]

In fact it took a while for Freud to propose that it was fantasies of the patients which were at fault, and he never sufficiently explored how he might have "forced" the idea on them. Nor can it be substantiated, thinking of his letters to Fliess, that he was "for some time completely at a loss."

Supposedly Freud's confidence in his "technique and in its results" was severely damaged:

> When I had pulled myself together, I was able to draw the right conclusions from my discovery; namely, that the neurotic symptoms were not related directly to

actual events but to wishful phantasies, and that as far as the neurosis was concerned psychical reality was of more importance than material reality.

This alleged sequence of events succeeded in becoming established in orthodox Freudian historiography. But whatever Freud might seem to have conceded, he was still insisting that he had not been responsible for arousing such fantasies in his patients: "I do not believe even now that I forced the seduction-phantasies on my patients, that I 'suggested' them." Freud claimed to have simply "stumbled for the first time upon the *Oedipus complex*. . . . " And "moreover, seduction during childhood retained a certain share, though a humbler one, in the aetiology of neuroses." Freud was taking away with one hand what the other had just given. In his retraction of the seduction theory he was reasserting a measure of its validity. At any rate, this is how I understand his claim: "But the seducers turned out as a rule to have been older children."[25]

Freud's repeated attempts to prop up the legitimacy of his early belief in the seduction theory also led him once to implicate phylogenetics, although this proposal has attracted little support from within orthodox psychoanalysis. The possibility of seduction was classed by Freud during World War I as one of the "primal phantasies" which are part of our "phylogenetic endowment." Supposedly "the individual reaches beyond his own experience into primaeval experience at points where his own experience has been too rudimentary." So that the seduction of children would have once been among the "real occurrences in the primaeval times of the human family, and . . . children in their phantasies are simply filling in the gaps in individual truth with prehistoric truth."[26] (It is perhaps telling that James Strachey, with his excellent editorial notes but a down-to-earth skeptical temperament, neglected to include the appeal to phylogenetics in his many references to the history of Freud's involvement with the seduction theory.)

I have not tried to exhaust all the references in Freud's writings to the issue of seduction. It might go without saying that the possibility of incest always remained a central part of Freud's thinking. Although Freud's 1897 letter to Fliess does represent a turning point in Freud's thinking, he never completely gave up his interest in seduction as a source of psychopathology, and he continued to accord it an aetiological role.

In the somewhat tortuous steps by which Freud arrived at the formulations he put forward in his autobiographical study, there are several conclusions that stand out. Freud had no way of knowing then that his letters to Fliess still survived, and would one day appear in print. So he did not have to worry that someday historians would be able to compare and contrast his own later accounts with a contemporaneous one. He was free to engage in mythmaking that was designed to enhance the story of his early struggles. No possibility existed of ignoring his 1896 papers, and so he made a virtue out of necessity, describing an early misstep as a tribute to his open-mindedness and a way station to his supposedly discovering the truth about the importance of infantile sexuality.

I do not believe that Freud was consciously being deceptive. He fully believed in the truths he thought he had uncovered, and only deceived himself about his own role in producing those so-called facts which made up what he thought of as his "findings." Like other men of action, Freud could be taken in by his own propaganda, and was ideologically blinded from acknowledging his own part in his early conjecturing. For him to have adequately accepted the power of suggestion implicit in his practice of psychoanalysis would have meant conceding too much about the built-in biases entailed by his therapeutic approach. (Before World War I Jung had declined to blame suggestion although he conceded that the sexual trauma had proved "to a large extent unreal":

> You may perhaps be inclined to share the suspicion of the critics that the results of Freud's analytical researches were therefore based on suggestion. There might be some justification for such an assumption if these assertions had been publicized by some charlatan or other unqualified person. But anyone who has read Freud's works of that period with attention, and has tried to penetrate into the psychology of his patients as Freud had done, will know how unjust it would be to attribute to an intellect like Freud's the crude mistakes of a beginner.[27])

In 1925 Jung gave lectures in which he stated that when he "met Freud, he said that about some of these cases, at least, he had been fooled . . . There is then a certain untrustworthiness about all these earlier cases."[28] (Although Jung may not have explicitly related Freud's defensive tendency to the problem of seduction, Jung noted how Freud was characteristically apt to escape from a current mental conflict — for example his own 1890s sex life — by placing it in the past. Similarly, the question was once suggestively raised by Otto Rank whether Freud's account of the dramatic effect his father's death had on him in 1896, and the past it stirred up, may not have been partly a self-deception, a regressive evasion of a present-day conflict — a denial of the importance of the separation that was then taking place between Breuer and him.[29])

As a matter of principle Freud could acknowledge the possibilities of the abuse of power in psychoanalytic therapy, but it was tempting for him (and others who followed) to think that despite everything he had come up with a neutral technique which anyone properly trained could employ. To have started to acknowledge his own full participation in the creation of psychoanalysis — and this perhaps helps to account for his curiously long-lasting public deference to Breuer — would have been to admit the full subjectivity of what he had accomplished. No one can be fully self-aware autobiographically, and it does not reduce Freud's stature that he too has to be considered subject to mankind's propensity for self-deception.

Yet one final text of Freud's leaves me baffled. In his *New Introductory Lectures on Psychoanalysis* (1933) Freud mentioned "an interesting episode in the history of analytic research" which "caused" him "many distressing hours":

> In the period in which the main sexual interest was directed to discovering infantile sexual traumas, almost all my women patients told me that they had been seduced by their father. I was driven to recognize in the end that these reports were untrue and so came to understand that hysterical symptoms were derived from phantasy and not real occurrences. It was only later that I was able to recognize in this phantasy of being seduced by the father the expression of the typical Oedipus complex in women.[30]

Note how he begins so distantly — "the period in which the main interest was directed to discovering infantile sexual traumas," as if he personally were detached from what happened then. Nowhere else had Freud ever maintained that "almost all" his female patients had "told" him they were seduced, and not by their fathers. What became of the effects of "the strongest compulsion of the treatment," and the absence of memories? Did patients reproduce such scenes, and Freud's reconstructions put them together, or did they tell him of seduction? The contradictions between Freud's 1933 account, and what he wrote in 1896, are bothersome, and a source of personal anguish to me; perhaps one should invoke the arbitrariness of Freud's extreme old age. (Others have earlier noted troubling discrepancies in Freud's published accounts.[31]) Freud in 1933 did not enlighten us about what drove him to see that "these reports were untrue," which helps explain why his 1897 letter to Fliess has been cited so often. He was mentioning the alleged culprit being the father at a time in the thirties when he was increasingly able to recognize the early developmental significance of the mother.

The earliest orthodox Freudian view of the Fliess period, as illustrated by Ernst Kris's Introduction to his edition of those letters, was that the abandonment of the seduction theory had been set off by Freud's self-analysis.[32] On the other hand I have long felt that Freud's self-examination was stimulated by how he had gone wrong about the seduction theory. He did not, however, succeed in getting as far in autobiographical knowledge as one might like. A close examination of the seduction theory, and how Freud dealt with his doing away with it, makes for a slippery-sounding story. One almost inevitably wonders how regularly Freud could have cooked his own books, hiding things even from himself. If, for instance, one were to look at exactly what

Freud meant by the concept of "*vita sexualis*," I would expect to find some intricately involved reasoning. To what extent were Freud's early critics correct in suspecting that he was being exploitive or sensationalist in his emphasis on sex?

I think we must conclude with another quandary. If Freud's 1896 account was accurate, then his 1933 version was misleading. Freud can be expected to have forgotten what he wrote to Fliess, but would not one suppose him to anticipate that future readers would look over what he had written in 1896? Another possibility exists: perhaps in 1896 he had over dramatized the resistances of his patients, in order to highlight the hypothesized underlying truth that he then wanted to propound. But if he was straightforwardly "told" about the seductions, why wait so long to unveil what happened?

The quotations that can be assembled are troubling in their inconsistencies. If, as some might perhaps think, Freud was a liar, he certainly was not doing a good job of it. Jones, remember, thought that the abandonment of the seduction theory was among other things a test of Freud's "integrity." I prefer to think that Freud was suffering from a form of emotional blocking rather than that he was lying; in any event it behooves us to be on our toes about each of Freud's other autobiographical memories.

Having reread the relevant passages in Freud for the first time in years, I am reminded again of how persuasive and charming his prose is capable of being. His mastery of rhetoric makes it easy to slip over the differences between Freud's claims at varying periods in his work. After repeatedly fudging matters, we are confronted with the starkly different 1933 claim, which would however be consistent with Jung's 1925 version. Like others with political objectives, it was easy for Freud to think that the end — the promotion of his "cause" — justified the means. To cite a recent political analogy, one need just think of the last days of France's President François Mitterand to realize how easy it can be not only to function in the face of public and private inconsistencies, but to manipulate them for the purpose of self-justification. And Franklin Roosevelt campaigned in 1940 on the pledge that American boys would not be sent into "foreign" wars; when asked at the time how he could make such a commitment, given the possibility that America might be attacked, FDR reasoned that then it would not be a "foreign" war.[33] Guile is a key aspect to worldly success. Probably each of us, with our convenient memories, shares in the kind of personal mythmaking that can be troubling when it shows up in great leaders.

Hopefully others will reexamine what Jones said was "the acme of Freud's life." Ernst Kris, whose editorial notes to the Fliess letters seem to me often superior to those in Masson's later unexpurgated edition, shared Jones's ideological blinders; for he argued that Freud's 1897 letter to Fliess about his mistake on the issue of seduction "tallies with that given in his published works."[34] Such wishful thinking can be attributed to the need for self-deception that Freud held was so central to the human condition.

Notes

1. Ernest Jones, *Sigmund Freud: Life and Work*, Vol. I, revised edition (London, The Hogarth Press, 1956), p. 292.
2. *Ibid.*, p. 294.
3. Ronald Clark, *Freud: The Man and the Cause* (New York, Random House, 1980).
4. Jeffrey M. Masson, *The Assault on Truth: Freud's Suppression of the Seduction Theory* (New York, Farrar, Straus & Giroux, 1984).
5. *The Complete Letters of Sigmund Freud to Wilhelm Fliess*, ed. & translated by Jeffrey M. Masson (Cambridge, Mass., Harvard University Press, 1985), p. 184.
6. Paul Roazen, *Freud and His Followers*, *op. cit.*, pp. 428, 430–31, 468, 472.
7. "Further Remarks on the Neuro-psychoses of Defence," *Standard Edition* , Vol. 3, p. 162.
8. Paul Roazen, *Encountering Freud* (New Brunswick, N.J., Transaction Publishers, 1990), pp. 7–11; Paul Roazen, *How Freud Worked: First-Hand Accounts of Patients* (Northvale, N. J., Aronson, 1995), pp. 4–9.
9. Paul Roazen, "Was Freud A Nice Guy?," *New Analysis*, Fall 1999 & *Society*, Sept./Oct. 2000 (and in Roazen, *The Historiography of Psychoanalysis*, *op. cit.*, pp. 23–36).
10. "The Aetiology of Hysteria," *Standard Edition*, Vol. 3, p. 197.
11. *Ibid.*, p. 199.
12. Jones, *op. cit.*, p. 290.
13. "The Aetiology of Hysteria," *op. cit.*, p. 204.
14. *The Complete Letters of Freud to Fliess*, *op. cit.*, p. 447.
15. "The Aetiology of Hysteria," *op. cit.*, pp. 211, 216, 217, 216, 220, 221.
16. "Three Essays on the Theory of Sexuality," *Standard Edition*, Vol. 7, pp. 190–91.
17. "My Views on the Part Played by Sexuality in the Aetiology of the Neuroses," *Standard Edition*, Vol. 7, p. 274.
18. *The Complete Letters of Freud to Fliess*, *op. cit.*, pp. 264–65.
19. "On the History of the Psychoanalytic Movement,"*op. cit.*, pp. 17–18, 21.
20. "Two Encyclopaedia Articles," *Standard Edition*, Vol. 18, p. 244.
21. "Further Remarks on the Neuro-psychoses of Defence," *op. cit.*, p. 268; "The Aetiology of Hysteria," *op. cit.*, p. 204.
22. "An Autobiographical Study," *Standard Edition*, Vol. 20, pp. 33–34.
23. Breuer and Freud, "Studies on Hysteria," *Standard Edition*, Vol. 2, pp. 134, 170.
24. "An Autobiographical Study," *op. cit.*, p. 34.
25. *Ibid.*, pp. 34–35.
26. "Introductory Lectures on Psychoanalysis," *Standard Edition*, Vol. 16, p. 371.
27. Carl G. Jung, "The Theory of Psychoanalysis," in R. F. C. Hull (translator), *The Collected Works of C. G. Jung*, Vol. 4 (Princeton, N. J., Princeton University Press, 1961), p. 95.
28. Carl G. Jung, *Analytical Psychology: Notes of the Seminar Given in 1925*, ed. William McGuire (Princeton, N. J., Princeton University Press, 1989), p. 16.
29. Roazen, *Freud and His Followers*, *op. cit.*, p. 78.
30. "New Introductory Lectures in Psychoanalysis," *Standard Edition*, Vol. 22, p. 120.

31. Frank Cioffi, "Was Freud A Liar?" BBC Talk, 1973; Han Israels and Morton Schatzman, "The Seduction Theory," *History of Psychiatry*, Vol. 4 (1993), pp. 23–59; J. G. Schimek, "Fact and Fantasy in the Seduction Theory: A Historical Review," *Journal of the American Psychoanalytic Association*, Vol. 35 (1987), pp. 937–65; Mikkel Borch-Jacobsen, "Neurotica: Freud and the Seduction Theory," *October 76* (1996), pp. 15–43; Mikkel Borch-Jacobsen, "How a Fabrication Differs from a Lie," *London Review of Books* (April 13, 2000), pp. 3–7; Rachel Blass and Bennett Simon, "Freud On His Own Mistake(s): The Role of Seduction in the Etiology of Neurosis," *Psychiatry and the Humanities*, Vol. 13 (Baltimore, Md., Johns Hopkins University Press, 1992), pp. 160–83; David H. Gleaves and Elsa Hernandez, "Recent Reformulations of Freud's Development and Abandonment of His Seduction Theory: Historical/Scientific Clarifications Or a Continued Assault on Truth," *History of Psychology*, Nov. 1999, pp. 324–54.
32. Ernst Kris, "Introduction," *The Origins of Psychoanalysis*, ed. Marie Bonaparte, Anna Freud, and Ernst Kris, translated by Eric Mosbacher and James Strachey (London, Imago, 1954), p. 216.
33. Robert E. Sherwood, *Roosevelt and Hopkins*, Vol. I (New York, Bantam, 1950), p. 235.
34. Kris, "Introduction," *op. cit.*, p. 29.

2

Carl Gustav Jung: The Zurich School

Rethinking the proper standing of Jung (1875–1961) may be the single hardest problem for Freudian loyalists today, which in itself, I think, justifies a general review of the most recent literature that concerns him. Jung was one of the earliest to realize the revolutionary implications of psychoanalytic psychology, and undoubtedly the most talented of all Freud's followers. Jung first wrote to Freud in 1906, and although rather less dedicated to the art of letter writing than Freud, their correspondence remained intense until their falling out in 1913.

For some years before their famous split, Jung labored to forward psychoanalysis. At that time psychoanalytic ideas had not yet won psychiatry's recognition, and as a leader of a famous Swiss psychiatric clinic (the Burghölzli) Jung represented to Freud a notable acquisition in a realm in which he hoped to extend the influence of his ideas. Freud was encouraging and supportive to his student, though in later years Jung might sometimes prefer to trace his indebtedness to Eugen Bleuler, the Swiss expert in schizophrenia; other candidates for having spiritually mentored Jung have been proposed, but nothing is harder in the life of the mind than to try and demonstrate the supposed "influence" that books themselves can have. At any rate, all the extensive letter writing between Freud and Jung leaves little doubt of Jung's extended discipleship to Freud. For a time Jung even wanted to exclude from attendance at the Swiss psychoanalytic society those who were inadequately stalwart as supporters of Freud's cause.

There were, however, long-standing sources of tension between Freud and Jung, which eventually culminated in their separation. Jung had hesitated to extend the concept of sexuality as broadly as Freud wanted to. And Jung came to interpret much so-called infantile clinical phenomena as of secondary rather than primary causal importance; current conflicts could, he held, reactivate past ones, and as we have seen this point is relevant to understanding the genesis of Freud's seduction hypothesis. Although half a century later many therapists would agree with Jung that the past could be used defensively to evade the present, at the time Freud merely saw Jung as retreating from the boldness of psychoanalysis's conclusions. Curiously enough, as a man Jung led a far less restricted sexual life than Freud, and being relatively more satisfied in that area Jung perhaps needed to make less of sex in his theories.

When Freud had first named Jung his heir in psychoanalysis it offended many of his leading Viennese followers, like Adler and Wilhelm Stekel, who were upset at Freud's making Jung president of the International Psychoanalytic Association (IPA). Most of the early analysts were, like Freud, Jewish; Jung, as a Gentile, was a valuable ally in Freud's attempt to save psychoanalysis from being dismissed as a psychology appropriate only for Jewry. Although in 1914 Freud in print accused Jung of anti-Semitism, no hint of such prejudice appears in their correspondence that finally appeared in print in 1974. I think that the publication of the correspondence between Freud and Jung may be the single most important piece of documentation about the history of psychoanalysis to have appeared in the last thirty years. When these letters were brought out, they sent shock waves through the intellectual community. It was the first time that Freud as a correspondent had been allowed to be seen in an untendentiously edited way.[1] Although the Jung family insisted on making cuts in Jung's words (about Bleuler, for example), the Freud family had at last wisely decided to let Freud speak for himself.

Even some sophisticated observers were startled at how outspokenly unlike his orthodox stereotype Freud could be. The vested interests of organizational life keep wanting to use Freud to defend the status quo, but the real Freud is far more interesting than his true believers would make him appear. I think Freud usually stands out as subversive of received wisdom and conventional understanding. For example, his defense of the Earl of Oxford as the true author of Shakespeare's works was not just an isolated eccentricity but part and parcel of how Freud could go (even if in this instance wrongheadedly) against the grain of received wisdom.

Ernest Jones thought this set of letters with Jung was the best of all the Freud correspondences, even as Jones remained unremittingly hostile to Jung. From the point of view of intellectual historians, this correspondence between Freud and Jung makes for an indispensable part of this past century's life of the mind. Freud and Jung started out from different backgrounds and perspectives, and it is a tribute to them both that their intimacy lasted as long as it did. Jung's wife, Emma, sent Freud some particularly poignant letters as she tried to stave off the breach that was starting to grow up between the two men.

Perhaps the most striking new information these letters supply bears on the final break in their relationship. Jung had urged that all future analysts be analyzed, a suggestion Freud was grateful for and one that has for many years now been standard practice. But it seems that Jung's proposal arose from his perception of some of the human failings of Freud, who had himself never been analyzed.

As Jung had grown in stature, he felt Freud's organizational demands increasingly onerous. Less rationalistic and suspicious of the unconscious than Freud, Jung began to formulate his own views on the important compensatory function of symptoms, which led Freud to suspect that Jung's innovations meant he harbored death wishes toward himself. Freud's inner conflicts led him to faint twice in Jung's presence, and although Jung declined to interpret these incidents in letters to Freud, Freud picked up a slip of Jung's pen in order to prove Freud's suspicion of heresy. Jung replied with an insolent letter, admitting his own ambivalences but pointing out Freud's need to use symptomatic interpretations for the sake of maintaining his own power, enabling Freud to remain blind to his own weak spots. Freud never forgave Jung for this letter, although it took over a year for Freud to excommunicate Jung from psychoanalysis. Freud's composition of his *Totem and Taboo* was part of an effort to drive a public wedge between himself and Jung.[2]

It is one of the ironies of our time that Freud, a neurologist with almost no psychiatric training, was to have so much more of an impact on North American psychiatry than Jung himself, even though Jung came professionally from the best traditions of Swiss psychiatry. The Central European distinction between neurology and psychiatry, which was so important in Freud's own day, bears reiterating since it is apt to elude many general readers today.

Freud's success with his creation of psychoanalysis is in part a tribute to his superior command of language as well as to the devotion of his followers, who did so much to put his discipline in good shape for historical scholarship. By editing his works carefully the disciples of Freud made sure that his ideas got the best possible hearing. Jung, on the other hand, who from our own perspective looks so prescient about some of the central inadequacies in Freud's way of thinking, still has not received anything like his due. Jung did not write as clearly as he might have, and the general biographical understanding of him, his psychology, and his movement are still in its early stages.

Reading the letters between them is profoundly challenging because both Freud and Jung anticipated most of the problems that have come up in psychotherapy since then. *The Freud-Jung Letters* were magnificently edited by William McGuire, who fulfilled the task of keeping the reader expertly informed without engaging in any partisanship. The 1988 paperback edition had a new preface by McGuire, which I found informative in that it contains material on Sabina Spielrein that has appeared since the publication of Aldo Carotenuto's important book, *A Secret Symmetry*.[3]

Although almost ninety years have elapsed since the historic falling out between Freud and Jung, the mythology of their relationship has been extraordinarily tenacious. Jung himself did later comment about his difficulties with Freud, and wrote a bit about what had happened, still by and large Jung's version of things has received attention only from his immediate circle of followers. Consequently most intellectual historians, even though they have not always acknowledged their own partisan allegiances, have adopted one variant or another of the position that Freud first set forth in 1914.

Recently there have been promising signs that Jung is at last getting serious attention beyond the bounds of his disciples. Linda Donn's *Freud and Jung: Years of Friendship, Years of Loss* is not a scholar's book, but it is open minded and lively; it should do much to forward the cause of a dispassionate reexamination of the issues between Freud and Jung.[4] Donn has a splendid eye for colorful details, and general readers will appreciate the way she constructs an absorbing narrative; further, specialists will be grateful for her putting aside the old myths in favor of examining the available historical evidence.

Donn has, however, allowed some notable omissions in her account. She entirely fails to mention not only the date but the idea that Freud had first in 1902 when starting to assemble the psychoanalytic group around him in Vienna. And then she omits to discuss how, once Freud had chosen Jung to be his successor as leader of the IPA, as a concession to his Viennese following Freud proceeded to elevate Adler to the presidency of the affiliated Vienna Society. Surely Freud's full difficulties with Adler, and the trial-like investigation of Adler's views that Freud conducted, should have given Donn a precedent for the later heresy hunting Freud engaged in over Jung's so-called defection. She even leaves out Freud's composition of his *On the History of the Psychoanalytic Movement*, although that text was a critical weapon in his war against Jung. If I may make one further complaint, the reader would have had a better idea of the contrast between Freud and Jung had Donn chosen to quote from William James's memorable 1909 letters comparing the two men.

Despite these shortcomings, Donn deserves to be congratulated for the amount of investigative digging that she engaged in. The book relies on manuscript materials that she consulted at the Library of Congress in Washington, D.C. Although the Freud Archives in New York City continues to impose absurd restrictions on what can be seen at the Library of Congress, with the passage of time more and more documents are becoming available. (But the Freud Copyrights in England have complicated things by its policy of refusing to allow scholars to xerox any Library of Congress Freud material.) Donn was given permission to quote then unpublished Freud letters to both Sandor Ferenczi and Ernest Jones, and even the most knowledgeable readers have things to learn from Donn's careful research. (I particularly admired a paragraph of Donn's about the special receptivity of turn-of-the-century New Englanders to fresh schools of psychotherapeutic thought.)

The current state of Jung scholarship continues to leave a great deal to be desired. The Jung family allowed his hundreth birthday in 1975 to pass without authorizing an official biography of him. The Jungs evidently are proper Swiss and have had trouble dealing with his extramarital affairs — for years he was involved with a former patient, Toni Wolff, and in addition it is now generally thought that he had an affair with Sabina Spielrein. (The Spielrein liaison is the more scandalous because it started while she was still in treatment with him; but then the Jungs have also balked about the Toni Wolff matter since that relationship extended over decades.) For some time the Jung family has been reported to be in search of a biographer, and, if so, we might someday have access to family documents that will make Jung more humanly comprehensible.

The difficulties those of us raised within Freud's school have had in gaining access to Jung's special terminology has not been helped by the obscurities of his prose style or by the passion of some of his disciples. Nonetheless he did make, I believe, some signal contributions to modern psychology. It was he, to repeat, who first proposed that all future analysts be themselves analyzed; and he therefore deserves credit (and perhaps blame) for inventing the idea of a training analysis. Jung was also aware, even though it took orthodox Freudians over half a century to agree with the point (within their own terminology), that infantile material could be used defensively during a clinical encounter; much that Freud thought was etiologically significant was instead seen by Jung as a smokescreen thrown up by the patient to evade current life-problems. Jung was dubious about the value of transference reactions, and he took a wholly different view of both dreams and symptoms than Freud. Understanding dreaming was for Jung not so much a question of overcoming self-deception but rather listening to truthful inner urgings. And symptomatology was for Jung a reliable guide to what we need to harken to positively (a point which R. D. Laing later did much to popularize). Jung's whole conception of the unconscious was more constructive and hopeful than Freud's. Donn's book should do more than just promote a much-needed reevaluation of the difficulties between Freud and Jung; it should also help to ensure that Jung will, at last, be accorded the place he deserves in the full history of modern psychotherapy.

The Ability to Mourn: Disillusionment and the Social Origins of Psychoanalysis by Peter Homans is an impressive, challenging book, written without the ideological blinkers that have interfered with so much of the scholarship in this area.[5] The author had written an earlier 1979 book, *Jung in Context,* and ranks as a leading figure in the new generation of Freud scholars who hold out hope for the future of psychoanalysis as a scholarly discipline. Those of us who have been around in this field for a while now can take some reassurance that independent scholarship has a secure place in today's academic life. *The Ability to Mourn* is, however, a difficult book, and the author pursues his theses with a relentlessness that sometimes is excessive; the book, though it cannot hope to have a popular success, makes for a rewarding read, and has a number of important and interesting insights to offer.

Part I of the book, which deals with "disillusionment and the ability to mourn as a central psychological theme in Freud's life, thought and social circumstances, 1906–14," seems to me a relatively weak part of the book; maybe this is because I read it earlier when it appeared in volume 2 of Paul Stepansky's (ed.) *Freud: Appraisals and Reappraisals.*[6] My impression is that Homans has successfully emancipated himself from some of the worst orthodoxies of an earlier generation, and he is certainly much taken with some of the central ideas of Heinz Kohut. Homans rightly wants to take his stand on behalf of the middle ground "on the continuum between slavish loyalty (the followers) and rebellious defiance (the dissenters)." But it remains for me too much of a single-track exercise to reduce the origins of psychoanalysis down to being "the result of a long historical mourning process. . . . " Despite the fact that I find it too simplistic to see psychoanalysis as "a creative response to . . . loss," Homans's book nonetheless teems with valid individual insights.[7]

The central conceptualization, which focuses on mourning, disillusionment, and de-idealization, is explicitly intended to introduce "revisionist perspectives" into our understanding of the beginnings of psychoanalysis. I do not understand why Homans is convinced that this new set of theories, although no doubt more refreshing than an old-fashioned invocation of Oedipal conflicts, is capable of exhausting the problem he has set out to understand. But his practice is better than his doctrine; so that although it is too much to see the concept of individuation as "the fruit of mourning," at least Homans is aware that the development of the self should be a critical aspect of modern psychological theory. Homans's "major intellectual commitments," he tells us, are "revisionist psychoanalysis and a social (rather than a purely psychological) theory of culture."[8] And so Kohut and Donald W. Winnicott, two excellent modern analytic thinkers, are key figures in Homans's argument.

Although Homans uses the framework of the most recent theorists of narcissism, at more than one point I was reminded of some of the old ideas of Erich Fromm, which are too often nowadays neglected.[9] For example, Fromm pointed out, more notably than anyone I can think of, the way one can detect what Homans calls "the persistence of maternal motifs in his [Freud's] dealings with other men." Fromm is evidently now out of fashion, but he had his own theoretical reasons for pointing out in Freud's life what Homans calls in Freud an "entirely split-off current of rage toward his mother based on an unconscious senses of loss, separation, and rejection."[10]

Thinking over the entire literature on the history of psychoanalysis, it seems to me also bothersome that Homans can overestimate the contributions of recent analysts like John Gedo and Masud Khan.[11] Each of these analysts, both in different ways, have been wedded to largely polemical versions of the history of Freud's ideas; I cannot begin here to try to demonstrate how these analysts have been guilty of a seriously biased use of sources, but I would not want any outsider to conclude that their amateur work can at all rank as a serious contribution to the historiography of psychoanalysis.

Homans himself seems to me entirely right to emphasize the key significance of Jung in Freud's life, and in particular to stress how Jung has to be understood in terms of his relationship to the values of Christian culture. Freud both sought to be accepted by the Gentile world and also aimed to overturn its ethics, and so Freud was both attracted by Jung as well as partially repelled by his thinking. Incidentally, I think it was Fritz Wittels, in the first biography of Freud ever published (a book which is still in print, but does not get cited by Homans), who was the earliest to suggest that Freud's struggle with Jung and others was an attempt to master elements of Freud's own soul — a point which Homans restates in terms of Kohut's self-psychological terminology.[12]

On a number of occasions Homans takes Freud's texts and interprets them in the light of fresh and interesting hypotheses. I found myself agreeing with Homans, and yet more often than not I thought Homans's approach a bit too narrow to encompass the full complexities of what he set out to explain. It would be bootless to pursue the particular examples in *The Ability to Mourn*, except to say that I think readers will find Homans's argument instructive, enlightened, and not motivated by unfair ideological purposes. I often found Homans shrewd and perceptive, and in tackling the significance of Jung in Freud's life it seems to me that Homans is absolutely on the right path. It is, I think, importantly true that "Jung was attached to bourgeois European society in a way that Freud was not, and he identified with the regnant ideals of European Christian humanism in a way that Freud could not." Furthermore, Homans is correct to say that for Freud "Jung was not simply a young, promising, enthusiastic — and unknown — psychiatrist; he also represented to Freud very strong attachments to European culture and to its Christian, humanistic heritage."[13] The details of Jung's unsavory collaboration with the Nazis, however, about which I will say more later in this chapter, serve to complicate the whole story.

It does strike me as unfortunate that Homans, with his interest in the issue of "disenchantment," thinks he has found "a master theme in Freud's life and thought." It is possible to put aside that hobbyhorse of the author's and thoroughly appreciate the individual points that Homans has to make. Homans does successfully understand the sectarian character of the psychoanalytic movement, even if he underestimates how long that religiosity has stayed within psychoanalytic thinking. Although the secret Committee Freud formed before World War I to protect psychoanalysis may have formally dissolved by 1927, it is not true, as Homans seems to think, that afterwards "the movement, understood as a highly personal group, disbanded." Psychoanalysts with a concern for the politics of "the cause" are apt today to talk about pluralism within the field, but I am afraid that such ideological tolerance is far more true of socialism in Eastern Europe at the time the Berlin Wall came down than within today's psychoanalytic orthodoxy. Although even someone as broad-minded as Homans does not appear to know, when he writes that "all the early analysts were alienated from their religious traditions and were consequently searching for new forms of cultural experience to heal their alienation," he is echoing a point Fromm made long ago in his *Sigmund Freud's Mission.*[14]

As astute as Homans is in seeing Jung as the first self-psychologist, it would be well to try also to come to terms with the neglected contributions in this direction that a thinker like Paul Federn made.[15] Federn, however, was a member of Freud's Vienna Psychoanalytic Society, and even after Freud's death Federn struggled to keep his ideas from too directly clashing with Freud's own. It is strikingly true of the whole history of analysis that whether a thinker succeeds in attracting disciples is a key to his or her later influence. And so right now Kohut's work has been successful in reorienting people about the significance of the self, largely because Kohut inspired followers who have dedicated themselves to forwarding his ideas. Someone like Erik H. Erikson, who remained fearful of being excommunicated and therefore like Federn fudged some of his key concepts, has had his work slighted recently.[16] Erikson never trained any followers, and it would seem that his ideas are going needlessly therefore to lose some of the impact that they deserve to have. Although Homans is generous-spirited, he can be more narrowly read than I might like. Nevertheless, *The Ability to Mourn* is a most interesting book and a welcome sign about the future of this whole field.

I think we have to take it as a given that Jung remains a relatively neglected figure, both for intellectual historians and among practicing clinicians. For all those who have identified with Freud's side in the multiple controversies with which his name has been associated, no figure is as odious as Jung. This rancor can only partly be explained by the fact that Freud chose early on to put his special version of events into the history books. Jung, who like Adler had also been attacked by Freud, did not reply at the time, and, as we have mentioned, the relative silence of both men about what had gone wrong with Freud left the battlefield to a foe who was a superb controversialist.

There is plenty of evidence about how Freud in 1913 had mourned the loss of Jung and even indications that Freud later understood how he himself partly shared the responsibility for what happened. But Jung's politics in the 1930s, especially during the early days of Hitler's regime in Germany, seemed to alienate permanently those within psychoanalysis who might otherwise have been expected to resonate to his writings. Erik H. Erikson was exceptional in crediting Jung's pioneering within depth psychology. But to acknowledge Jung's standing was to risk being associated with the most notorious heresy in the history of psychoanalysis, and even someone like Kohut, who was himself to be stigmatized by Anna Freud as "antipsychoanalytic,"[17] steered clear of acknowledging the extent to which Jung's ideas had been a precursor to his own.[18] An early self psychologist, such as Federn, whose phenomenological ego approach is liable to be neglected today, would have been even less likely than Kohut to credit Jung's accomplishments. For an analyst within Freud's school to associate with Jung's work is still to run the risk of not being taken seriously professionally.

A good part of the explanation for how Jung has been slighted can also be attributed to Jung's own circular-seeming writings, for as I have already implied they lack Freud's unique clarity. Although sometimes Jung can be strikingly original and even poetic, there are too many dull patches in his works (and reliance on foreign terms) that are hard to untangle. If he was, as I believe, the best critic Freud ever had, that alone would make him required reading; but, in addition, he had contributions of his own to modern psychology that remain singularly important. For instance, Jung thought unlike Freud that "the lack of transference was actually a positive factor in the analytic relationship."[19] Also, Jung showed how "one's own emotional interest can even seem to influence supposedly scientific data in a way that supports one's own unconscious expectations."[20]

Unfortunately Jung's disciples lacked the thoroughness of Freud's pupils. For all the criticism that James Strachey has drawn for his superb edition of Freud's works,[21] Jung's writings have appeared with appallingly little in the way of any editorial apparatus.

So in this context Robert H. Hopcke's *A Guided Tour of the Collected Works of C. G. Jung*[22] is a real step forward. Too much of the secondary literature about Jung is expressed in his own technical jargon so that it is hard for an outsider to use it to secure entrance into Jung's thought. The part of *A Guided Tour* that I appreciated most concerned Jung's interest in alchemy. Years ago, in a memorable bit of psychoanalytic warfare, Edward Glover made fun of Jung's involvement in alchemy.[23] Such an eminent historian, however, as Hugh Trevor-Roper[24] has (without any interest in Jung) written fascinating accounts of Paracelsus and Paracelsianism, providing documentation to support the existence of links between the alchemical interest in spiritual transformation and what Hopcke calls "a continuing stream of unorthodox, underground culture within Western civilization."[25]

A Guided Tour has be one of the best single introductions to Jung that I have seen; it does not, for course, purport to substitute for reading Jung, but the book can make it easier for the uninitiated to make their way through Jung's writings. *A Guided Tour* covers much more than the concepts of archetypes and the collective unconscious, which are dealt with in the opening chapter. Thirty-nine other short chapters include a thorough examination of all facets of Jung's works, with copious suggestions for further reading.

Sensitive subjects, like Jung's love life, are left out of Hopcke's book. Furthermore, Jung and Freud shared many more ideas in common than their respective followings ever have acknowledged. Therefore we find Hopcke rather naively, like an early Freudian, proposing that Jung's central concepts rest on a so-called empirical rather than a philosophic or moral basis, and Hopcke uncritically believes that Jung held, like Freud, that "the individual human being recapitulates in his or her individual psychological development the stages that the species has gone through. . . . "[26] Yet since Jung played a central, and yet largely unacknowledged, role in the history of modern psychotherapy, Hopcke's book might go far to secure Jung's rightful place in the fascinating story of the growth of depth psychology.

One of the special problems with Jung studies is that while there are stunning passages containing important clinical wisdom strewn throughout Jung's work, few of his books carry readers as effortlessly along as Freud's succeeded in doing. Even for those already predisposed to be interested in this subject, it takes a special imaginative leap to overcome the Freudian atmosphere in which most of us have been reared.

Although no comprehensive biography has yet been commissioned by the Jung family, Barbara Hannah's 1976 *Jung* is about the best I have come across, and yet it has an amateurish flavor.[27] The reluctance of the Jung family to authorize a proper biography, relying on all the documents in their possession, tells us something about the standards of privacy and propriety that still influence Swiss life. The problem has been compounded by the relative sloppiness of Jungian scholarship that I have already alluded to. Whatever criticisms have been made about Strachey's edition of Freud, it is testimony to his care that Strachey's notes to the texts have been translated wholesale into new German editions of Freud. Unfortunately, huge editions of Jung have been allowed to come out with hardly any editorial apparatus at all.

I am not being novel in raising the problem of ideological blinders, although regrettably tunnel vision will also pertain to evaluating Anthony Stevens's *On Jung.*[28] It should go almost without saying that sectarianism has almost crippled our knowledge of the whole history of depth psychology. Jungians are capable of being as fanatical toward themselves as well as the outside world as Freudians, Adlerians, Kleinians, or Lacanians, although the struggles within each different school do tend to have characteristically special features to them.

One of the central consequences of our ignorance of the intellectual history of psychoanalysis is that repeatedly new wine has been poured into old bottles. Without trying to take away anything from the contributions of Kohut, and it is hardly my intention to tarnish him by making this point, Jung was writing about Kohut-like problems of selfhood starting at least as early as the 1920s. One of the few defects to Stevens's *On Jung* is that he does not specifically challenge Freud's uncharitable view of Jung in Freud's *On the History of the Psychoanalytic Movement*, nor does Stevens weigh the exact points Jung had been trying to establish before the final falling out between himself and Jung. It is too easy to fall into the ahistorical tendency to read back into the past ideas that Jung developed only later.

If one starts from the premise that genuine scholarship in this area is in short supply, then Stevens's book is an excellent one. I found it thoroughly readable, balanced, and full of information. While some of the secondary literature about Jung is apt to assume too much on the reader's part, in that Jungian concepts are still hard for many of us to absorb, *On Jung* is straightforward without being patronizing or hermetic. Stevens goes a long way in linking Jung up to recent ethological writers, as well as psychoanalytic theorists like Donald W. Winnicott and Erik H. Erikson, so that at no point did I feel in any danger of falling off the sled of Stevens's argument. It is a tribute to the clarity and concreteness of Stevens's examples that despite how many previous books about Jung I have read, only with *On Jung* did I think myself fully comfortable with the specialized terminology.

While the old canard, promulgated by Freud, was that Jung had repudiated the concept of the unconscious, Stevens makes it evident that fundamentally Jung had simply taken a different view toward it:

> Whereas Freud assumed that most of our mental equipment is acquired individually in the course of growing up, Jung asserted that all the essential characteristics that distinguish us as human beings are with us from birth and encoded in the collective unconscious. While Freud insisted on an exclusively sexual interpretation of human motivation, Jung saw this as dogmatic reductionism — he referred to it as "nothing but" psychology . . . Whereas Freud espoused the principle of causality and proposed an almost mechanistic form of determinism, Jung insisted on the freedom of the will . . . Where Freud confined his attention to the problems of libidinal development in childhood and their malign consequences for later adult life, Jung conceived of the life cycle as a whole of which childhood was but a

> highly significant part . . . Where Freud's approach was clinical and focused on pathology, Jung stressed that the healthy functioning of the psyche was of primary concern . . . Where Freud was interested primarily in signs and symptoms, Jung was interested in meanings and symbols . . . Finally, where Freud considered religion as an expression of infantile longings for parental protection and an obsessional means of expiating guilt, Jung saw religious practices as representing a fundamental archetypal need.[29]

It would be misleading for me to suggest that *On Jung* is primarily concerned with comparing and contrasting Jung with Freud, but long before modern psychoanalytic ego psychology Jung proposed that the psyche was self-healing. Jung "had learned to see that the greatest and most important problems of life are all fundamentally insoluble. They must be so, because they express the necessary polarity inherent in every self-regulating system. They can never be solved, but only outgrown."[30] Stevens's book succeeds in presenting us with Jung's unique world-view; and he does it through interweaving Jung's concepts with his biography. So what we get is no dry-as-dust conceptual outline but a full account of Jung's original point of view.

I missed some key points, however, and although I admire what Stevens has accomplished, we are far enough along in scholarship for us to be able to demand that certain issues be addressed. For example, I am convinced that one of the key points at issue between Freud and Jung was a clinical one: to what extent is so-called infantile behavior in analysis a direct response to the apparently neutral laboratory structure of the "classical" psychoanalytic situation, and to what degree is such regressive conduct a genuine sign of the specific human propensity to become childish? Jung charged Freud with being authoritarian, and promoting Oedipal reactions both in his pupils and patients. Jung therefore came to consider it dangerous for an analyst to mobilize transferences, and this led Jung to technical recommendations entirely different from Freud's own.

Unlike Freud, who held that analysis was automatically the same as synthesis, Jung insisted that it was impossible to separate moral and philosophic concerns from clinical ones. I would have been happier had Stevens been more up front on how far Freud deceived himself about the so-called scientific standing of his alleged findings. Stevens does tell us that Jung's clinical advice was designed "to prevent infantile regressions and dependencies. . . . "[31] All the same, I was appalled to find Stevens arguing that Freud, supposedly unlike Jung, had "no interest"[32] in the matter of occultism, when, in fact, Freud was both attracted and repulsed by the issue of the occult.

Stevens' *On Jung* is so successful an addition to the history of ideas that one almost does not notice a terrible and glaring oversight: there is no discussion whatever in *On Jung* of Jung's notorious collaboration with the Nazis in Germany. There is much to be said on this matter, and I will return to this problem later in this chapter. It is also necessary, I think, to explore the character of Jung's anti-Semitism, and his lack of respect for Western democratic procedures. (We will discuss Freud's own relationship with Mussolini in chapter 6.) Jung's unfortunate politics have to be considered a serious matter; Jung chose to go to Germany in the first months of Hitler's regime for the sake of distinguishing between Freud's "Jewish" psychology and Jung's so-called Aryan convictions. The bitterness on Jung's part toward Freud, who Jung thought had helped ruin his practice for years after the breakup of their friendship, was such that after Hitler was in power Jung wrote to an associate in Germany saying now was the appropriate time to close down the Freudians there.

Stevens's narrative does provide at least some basis within Jung's psychology for the dreadful politics he endorsed. "Jung's psychology," Stevens tells us, "has been attacked as self-centered (i.e., ego-centered) and anti-social."[33] In contrast to Freud, who left the aims of psychoanalytic therapy vague and was loath to discuss what might be meant by normality, Jung boldly announced a program involving "the fullest possible realization of the self,"[34] or what he termed individuation. Jung's conceptualization sanctioned in my view too much selfishness and self-centeredness. (Freud probably erred in the same direction.) The section of Stevens's book where he deals with Jung's extramarital affairs accepts at face value Jung's own fancy footwork for his misdeeds; it is not hard to think that Jung had devised an original set of rationalizations for sexual infidelity.

I would like to record one telling anecdote about Jung told to me some thirty-five years ago by Jolande Jacobi, a disciple of Jung's. She had initially gone to him for help because when the Nazis had marched into Austria she found herself cut off from her family and her whole previous life. While Jacobi said she was in acute distress because of a real life crisis, it seemed to her that Jung was bored and nodding off to sleep, so she switched her tack, and instead brought up a dream she had recently had, and Jung appeared to snap to attention. Patients can consciously as well as otherwise find out what is of fundamental interest to their therapist.

The narrative in *On Jung* is consistent with Jacobi's view of Jung, and the general literature we already have. Stevens rightly points out how powerfully Jung succeeded in handling the problem of projection; according to Jung we not only project our "shadow," or lower selves, but also find in the outside world, by means of the constructive use of projection, a means of support for our aspirations. Unlike Freud, who took such a negative view of religion, Jung thought that, especially in the last half of the life cycle, people need to find from religion the meaning that gives order and significance to their conflicts.

Freud never forgave Jung for his supposed "defection," and after Jung wrote his bulky book on psychological types, Freud responded with his little article on libidinal types.[35] If character typology mattered, Freud implied, then he would show how it was possible to account for it within libido theory, without going into Jung's distinction between extroverts and introverts, much less the four different functional categories Jung proposed — feeling, intuition, sensation, and thinking.

The clash between Freud and Jung was not a minor one hinging on their respective personalities, but rather their psychological systems were the outcome of the characteristic differences between the two men. Studying the problems between Jung and Freud raises one of the central issues in this past century's intellectual life. And it is an accomplishment of Stevens's *On Jung* that he genuinely helps us better to understand the position Jung took, which until now has been undervalued by most intellectual historians and the so-called mainstream within psychoanalysis.

So even today Jung remains a difficult figure to assess. As I have already mentioned, a good part of the problem in appreciating his work comes from the sectarian way in which so many of us have been educated in the history of depth psychology. At least in the early stages of one's interest in Freud and psychoanalysis, it has been common to find Jung dismissed as a rejected, if not despised, rival. Even among the most ideologically emancipated contemporary psychoanalysts, relatively few are familiar with Jung's clinical contributions.

The difficulties in understanding Jung do not stem simply from the narrowness of the reading lists at most training centers, although that surely is a good part of the problem. Jung was, as we have already said, not so great a literary stylist as Freud. And professional Jung studies have been late in starting; independent historians are bound to feel frustrated about the state of appreciating Jung's work. Even the editing of Jung's texts has been, as I have indicated, decidedly on the perfunctory side.

It is perhaps a lot to expect busy clinicians to exert the effort necessary to explicate Jung's contributions. And so we have had a whole series of books that attempt to orient the beginner to what Jung had to say. J. J. Clarke's *In Search of Jung: Historical and Philosophical Enquiries*[36] is admirable in that he approaches his task from the standpoint of an intellectual historian. The book is primarily an attempt "to locate Jung's thought within the history of ideas,"[37] and Clarke's work is, I think, largely successful.

The first chapter is entitled "Freud and Jung," which seems to me superior to thinking of these writers as in some sense alternatives to one another. Although Jung became such a trenchant critic of Freud's, Clarke does not explore too extensively the differences between them. He rightly argues that "it is Freud who has found favor with the intellectual establishment"[38] and on those grounds rather skips over the various problems that arose between the two men. Clarke underestimates the extent to which Freud and Jung, despite their conflicts, continued to share certain presuppositions; Clarke sees as his main task the explication of Jung's body of work as a whole.

Clarke finds Jung a pioneer of "the symbolic/hermeneutical view of the psyche"[39] and shows how Jung became centrally concerned with the issue of meanings and purposes, as opposed to Freud's quest for causes and origins. (Here again Jung preceded by decades what has only become fashionable recently within Freud's school.) Clarke seems to be implying that most psychoanalysts since Freud's death have in fact been pursuing lines of thought that were prefigured much earlier in Jung's own writings. Jung was not, as many orthodox psychoanalysts have assumed, rejecting the concept of the unconscious but instead was proposing a different and more positive outlook on unconscious motivation than that espoused by Freud himself.

Clarke does an especially good job of locating Jung within Western philosophy and in particular in relating Jung to his predecessors within German thought. Unlike Freud, who often tried to separate his own ideas from philosophical speculation, Jung was explicit in acknowledging his links to Nietzsche, to take just one example of an earlier thinker with whom he sought to associate himself.[40] Many of Freud's outspoken critics have been unwilling to see how much of their own work bears similarities to that of Jung; Erich Fromm, for instance, shared Jung's respectful orientation toward religious belief. (The defenders of psychoanalytic orthodoxy for the most part still feel entitled to dismiss Jungianism as a wholly different undertaking.)

Jung's politics have doubtless helped repel, at least within the political Left, those who might otherwise be receptive to his point of view. Clarke does devote about a page on "some injudicious remarks"[41] Jung made in contrasting so-called Aryan and Jewish psychology at a time when the Nazis had recently come to power in Germany. But Clarke does not do much more, in connection with Jung's anti-democratic flirtation, than say that "the accusation of collaboration [between Jung and the Nazis] is more complex."[42] *In Search of Jung* is not a long book, and doubtless a further exploration of the subject would have thrown off the balance of the text as a whole. But if we are to appreciate why Jung is still such an underrated figure in the history of ideas, surely the political position he took in the 1930s partly accounts for this state of affairs.

A large body of literature has emerged from the school of thought that Jung ended up founding, and Jungians are apt to be far more familiar with Freudian concepts than the other way round.[43] Jung experimented with the idea of interruptions in therapy long before Franz Alexander did, and Jung's concern with selfhood and processes of individuation came well before thinkers like Erikson or Kohut pursued similar themes. Although Erikson, late in his career, acknowledged that Jung had been one of the founders of the tradition of depth psychology, I doubt that Kohut, given his own ideological problems in remaining within the so-called mainstream of psychoanalysis, ever would have admitted that there might be merit to Jung's early formulations. Winnicott too, as I mentioned earlier, knew the partisan dangers of linking his ideas to those of Jung.

Clarke's book would have been strengthened, however, if he had paid more attention to how Jung had "sometimes been accused, along with psychotherapists in general, of encouraging an unhealthy degree of narcissistic self-regard."[44] It remains an open question of how one evaluates the challenge that Jung, and Freud too, laid down to traditional Judeo-Christian ethics; and the extent to which selfishness was sanctioned by the whole revolution in thought which psychoanalysis began has yet to be adequately explored. (Although the literature on Adler is even poorer than that on Jung, Adler was prescient on this point.) Jung's concern with inwardness and self-awareness may sound virtuous, compared with the more materialistic-sounding metaphors found within Freud's ideas. But self-transformation can never take place in a social vacuum, which is perhaps why the problem of Jung's politics during the 1930s has continued to damage his reputation.

Like many other post-Freudian theorists, Jung saw "the fundamental need of the human psyche for growth, integration, and wholeness."[45] And, in keeping with many revisionists, Jung appreciated the constructive "role of the primitive and the infantile, of fantasy and dream."[46] Jung's special techniques, such as active imagination and art therapy, followed from his general theoretical orientation. Even his notion of collective archetypes has been followed up by what ethologists understand as innate releasing mechanisms. And, as Clarke puts it in evaluating Jung, "it is not so much that he neglected childhood but that he saw it as only one phase in the whole cycle of life. . . . "[47] The perspective Jung offers is a complicated one, and it behooves us to investigate its complexities further. The time should come when Jung receives adequate recognition, as writers like Clarke would like, within the whole story of the growth of the tradition of depth psychology.

As we have seen, literature about Jung has taken a longish time to get off the ground. Although books written by those whom he succeeded in inspiring now sell better than ever, we still wait for a professional biography of him. There are many trots to understanding Jung's ideas, and a number of fascinating although narrow glimpses in print about what he was like. Since Jung is a more opaque writer than Freud, one feels an acute need for more work about him.

Aside from the way Jungian works have been recently making it to the *New York Times* best-seller lists, he deserves to rank high among those who created psychotherapy as we now understand it. Compared to what we have learned about the early Freudians, too little is currently known about Jung's immediate disciples,[48] but his work has borne important fruit. For example, recent theories about dream life advanced by those knowledgeable about the biochemistry of the brain seem to fit Jung's approach better than Freud's. Even if Jung is rarely credited with how he secured a legitimate place for short-term psychotherapy, he played an important part in evolving an approach at odds with Freud's objectives in his pre-World War I papers on technique.

Richard Noll, a clinical psychologist studying the history of science, has written a surprising book, for his *The Jung Cult*[49] seems bent on assaulting Jung's reputation even before Jung has made it securely to the pantheon of those remembered as part of the history of ideas. Jung's unfortunate politics during the 1930s, at a time when the Nazis were destroying psychotherapy in Germany, have long appeared to be opportunistic if not outright anti-Semitic; from his home in Switzerland Jung traveled to Hitler's Germany, making anti-democratic comments and differentiating between Freud's psychology and "Aryan" truth.

Noll's book is devoted to dissecting the origins of Jung's ideas in the Nietzschean pagan stream of thought. And there is no doubt that Noll has performed a valuable service in placing Jung's work within an occult context that few of us have been aware of. One wonders, though, whether the thesis that Jung created a charismatic movement could not be extended to all the creators of psychotherapy. Those who refrained from promoting a cultish following have largely been ignored by intellectual historians, but key features of Noll's argument could be easily extended to Adler, Melanie Klein, Wilhelm Reich, Jacques Lacan, and others, including Freud himself.

Noll focuses on the side of Jung that led him to find a substantial congruence between his own approach and the ideology of Nazism. But Noll neglects to tell us — and this has to be distinctly odd — about the clinical bases to Jung's work, not to mention the current scientific standing that Jung's ideas now deserve. There were plenty of murky sources for Jung's point of view, but then Freud and others also shared in at least some of this unattractive ideology. Noll proceeds without any discussion of why the creator of psychoanalysis chose Jung as his crown prince to inherit the empire of the psychoanalytic domain.

The difficulties that arose between Freud and Jung were partly personal, but theoretical as well. And here Noll has not done enough to explain the sources for the falling out between the two men. As a matter of fact, although Noll has come up with much new material to locate Jung's ideas in the turn-of-the-century context of Central European mysticism, we do not find out about the values and beliefs that that included, as opposed, for example, to those of Freud himself. The extensive correspondence between Freud and Jung is almost never mentioned in *The Jung Cult.*

Noll may well argue that what he has neglected to explore has been covered elsewhere in the literature. But then he has failed to point the reader in the direction scholars need to look, and the result is a treatise bound to seem unbalanced and stacked against Jung. Loading the dice in such a way will only succeed in convincing non-partisan outsiders that this field is full of passionate advocates of one perspective or another. Students in the field will find abundant valuable spadework in *The Jung Cult*, but the book makes for a hard read that will mainly interest specialists.

The confrontation between Freud and Jung remains an enduring intellectual issue, but for a variety of reasons it is only within recent years that the literature about Jung has begun to flourish. The Jung family, as we have mentioned, has valued its privacy over the importance of establishing Jung within the history books, and it remains to be seen how much primary source material will be turned over to the only professional biographer, Deirdre Bair, who has undertaken to write a balanced life of Jung. Then too, Jung's politics — the extent to which he curried favor with the Nazis in the 1930s — has turned away many from giving Jung any kind of second chance. To reiterate: sectarianism has been a major hindrance to the growth of Jung studies; while orthodox Freudians have followed the master's lead in dismissing Jung as a "mystic," Jungians themselves have concentrated mainly on the difficult task of making Jung's works accessible to outsiders. In spite of the lateness with which serious work on Jung began, his popularity among general readers seems now to be greater than ever, and one frequently encounters young people who say they prefer Jung to Freud.

Robert C. Smith's recent book *The Wounded Jung* makes an excellent read.[50] Smith was in direct contact with Jung and wrote his Ph.D. thesis on Jung and Martin Buber.[51] I wonder, though, how influential *The Wounded Jung* will succeed in being, since traditional Freudians will probably pay no attention to it and many Jungians will no doubt be put off by the extent to which Smith explores the psychopathology underlying Jung's creativity. Incidentally, despite Smith's daring in exploring the psychological bases of Jung's achievements and all the tortured conflicts in Jung's life that can be hypothesized, the subject of Jung's regrettable politics of the 1930s again fails to come up. Anti-Semitism is not something that many observers can easily forgive, and it will do the cause of proclaiming the significance of Jung's contribution to the history of ideas a disservice unless writers about Jung get used to coming to terms with this issue. (In philosophy Martin Heidegger's Nazi affiliations, and how it relates to his philosophical convictions, have become a standard subject for discussion.[52])

Smith's approach to Jung's childhood and the relationships with his mother and father seems to me original and well worth considering. Smith's book, a short exercise of interconnected essays, moves immediately to the conflict between Jung and Freud, and nobody is blamed for what appears to have been an inevitable clash between differing temperaments and philosophic outlooks. Jung had a bad time of it emotionally after the break between himself and Freud, and Smith tries to understand how this period can be understood as a "creative illness" on Jung's part. (Henri Ellenberger had pioneered on this point in his 1970 *The Discovery of the Unconscious.*[53]) We now know a good deal about Jung's need for multiple women in his life, and Smith discusses what can be understood about the roles that Sabina Spielrein and Toni Wolff played in Jung's writings.

As we have already mentioned, Jung had a strikingly different outlook on religion and mythology from that of Freud, and the second half of *The Wounded Jung* tries to show the strengths of Jung's point of view. Much of the psychoanalytic work since Freud's death has, unknown to the theorists themselves, echoed ideas that Jung long ago advanced. Although the differences between Freud and Jung reflect contrasting backgrounds and ideological outlooks, Smith is correct, I think, that there is room for reconciliation between their theories in our post-Freudian and post-Jungian climate of opinion.

Busy clinicians, both in the Freudian and Jungian world, cannot be expected to keep up with the scholarly literature, but some time ago Sonu Shamdasani in London came upon the discovery that the Jung family had suppressed a second volume of Jung's autobiography, which still remains unpublished today. Smith does not seem to know about the existence of this text, which surely bears on his attempt at biographical reconstruction. Further, the Italian who first unveiled the story of Jung and Spielrein, Professor Aldo Carotenuto, reports that Jung correspondence, which was initially censored and does not appear in the English or American volumes that he edited, has in fact been published in Germany. If, having visited the house outside Zurich in which Jung lived with his family, I may add a little addendum of my own, it is such a splendid structure, beautifully located on a large lake, that it contrasts sharply with Freud's own relatively Spartan living conditions in Vienna and provides one more reason why Freud chose Jung as his "crown prince."[54] Swiss divorce laws might also be relevant to Smith's tale; as I understand it, a husband in those days was entitled to a wife's wealth. (Emma Jung was a rich woman.) Despite a few shortcomings, *The Wounded Jung* makes an admirable addition to a literature that is bound to grow over the years.

Like most professions, psychiatry has its conformisms. So despite all the brouhaha over the years between rival schools of psychotherapeutic thought, a large but usually unspoken area of agreement exists. Survey evidence indicates that the top leaders of various ideological factions in the field tend to behave more like each other than anybody else.

Anthony Storr, a British psychiatrist, is unusual. Although he comes from a broadly Jungian background, he is not attached to the dogmas of any particular school of thought. He moves effortlessly within all the modern scientific literature in psychiatry, and is familiar with a wide range of different contributions. He has partaken of none of the partisanship that has afflicted so many in the field. An examination of only one of his many books shows how different an outlook from a stereotypical Freudian one a humane Jungian can have.

Storr, a cultured man who has been particularly interested in the problem of creativity, argues in *Solitude: A Return to the Self* that current conventional wisdom has exaggerated the degree to which interpersonal relationships of the most intimate kind are the main source of happiness.[55] Storr insists that by looking at the lives of the most creative individuals we discover that this common assumption does not stand up to scrutiny. A remarkable number of the greatest thinkers in Western history have not raised families or established close personal ties — Descartes, Newton, Locke, Pascal, Spinoza, Kant, Leibniz, Schopenhauer, Nietzsche, Kierkegaard, and Wittgenstein never married, and most of them lived alone.

Storr does not find that creative people are especially disturbed; he also believes that not all who are solitary are unhappy. The modern-day insistence that true happiness can only be found in personal commitments, especially in sexual fulfillment, would exclude so many remarkable people as to lead Storr to question the basic premise.

Not only people of genius find their chief satisfaction in impersonal pursuits. Storr argues that generally "interests, whether in writing history, breeding carrier pigeons, speculating in stocks and shares, designing aircraft, playing the piano or gardening, play a greater part in the economy of human happiness than modern psychoanalysts and their followers allow."[56] Interests, in addition to relationships, help define individual identities and give meanings to lives. We need sources of fulfillment beyond our intimate lives.

Storr believes that we have freighted interpersonal relationships with too much of a burden of value so that expectations about personal fulfillment get exaggerated. By romantically idealizing the personal, we have paradoxically undermined the stability of marriages. "If we did not look to marriage as the principal source of happiness," writes Storr, "fewer marriages would end in tears."[57]

Storr objects to those psychotherapeutic theorists who would ignore our validity as isolated individuals. To establish his thesis, Storr relies on examples of exceptionally creative people who have left behind accounts of their thoughts and feelings on the grounds that "they exemplify, in striking fashion, aspects of human striving which are common to us all but which, in ordinary people, escape notice."

Storr shows that the current emphasis on intimate relationships as the touchstone of health is a relatively recent phenomenon. He considers it unfortunate that love has been over-emphasized to the disadvantage of work as a path to salvation. And what goes on in our minds when we are alone is central in those who are capable of achieving creativity. The capacity to be alone is taken to be a reflection of a basic inner security.

Solitude: A Return to the Self ranges among historical examples of creative individuals, but Storr keeps the reader's mind on a memorable quotation from Edward Gibbon, which helped make up the title to the English edition of this book. "Conversation enriches the understanding," Gibbon wrote, "but solitude is the school of genius; and the uniformity of a work denotes the hand of a single artist."[58]

Storr is aware of more than just historical and clinical findings; he cites the most recent experimental evidence on dream and sleep research, as well as studies on sensory deprivation. Nor does he ignore the significance of inherited temperament. In keeping with Storr's Jungian background he stresses the mind's need for unity, wholeness and integration, in contrast to alternative approaches which emphasize the regressive elements in human experience. Storr rejects the old-fashioned psychoanalytic view first advanced by Freud — that fantasy is escapist or defensive — in favor of the doctrine that imagination is preliminary to altering and enriching reality in a newly desired direction.

Solitude is the work of an unusually enlightened psychiatrist. It is full of fascinating vignettes drawn from the lives of creative artists, because Storr thinks they are especially apt to choose relationships which will forward their work. Creativity, he holds, is more than a substitute for losses. Clinically Storr thinks that the capacity to be alone becomes increasingly important with the aging process; sex can only be one among a variety of ways of achieving unity.

Storr represents the finest in humane psychiatric thinking. Sexual fulfillment is no kind of test for so-called normality; it can at best alleviate a limited number of human problems, and should not be burdened with more than it can safely sustain. He has written a lucid and well-organized book, and gently drives his central point home with balance and sophistication.

Having seen the best side of the Jungian influence, it is high time that we turn to the vexing issue of Jung and anti-Semitism. This is a subject that I do not approach with any eagerness. Since I am myself a Jew, although an inadequately practicing one, I am bound to have a special concern with the fate of the Jewish people. On the other hand, I am also a student of the history of psychoanalysis, and I am convinced that Jung's stature in the story of the development of depth psychology has been badly misunderstood. Perhaps one anecdote can serve to illustrate the historiographical problem I believe we face. Once, during the course of a few luncheon discussions I had a few years ago with Paul Ricoeur in Toronto, we got onto the subject of his book *Freud and Philosophy*.[59] Since Ricoeur was both modest and self-critical about how he thought he had failed to achieve his objective in this book, I raised the subject of Jung. It seemed to me, and I told Ricoeur, that if he wanted to accomplish the philosophic purposes he had in mind, he would have been better advised to pick Jung as a central thinker instead of Freud. For Jung's view of the unconscious, rather than Freud's, seemed to me much closer to Ricoeur's thinking. The mention of Jung's name, however, posed a special perplexity for Ricoeur. For one could not in Paris, according to Ricoeur, read Jung; he was "on the Index" of forbidden books among French intellectuals.

Ricoeur is himself a Protestant, and one of his sons is a practicing psychoanalyst in France. I found Ricoeur enlightened about the struggles within French psychoanalysis, where so much is being published these days in connection with Freud, and yet Ricoeur seemed wholly unfamiliar with Jung's writings. And there was I, who had written on Freud, suggesting to Ricoeur the overlooked significance of Jung.

And yet as an intellectual historian I think it is impossible to divorce Jung's psychology from his politics. When I used to teach at my universities the writings of Dostoevsky and Nietzsche, a standard question I asked was whether, and to what degree, their psychologies must need lead to their politics. Just as Freud himself admired Dostoevsky,[60] without at all going along with his particular set of political beliefs, so it is possible, I think, to say of Jung that he made a great and lasting contribution to psychology, without ignoring the nature of his collaboration with the Nazis. (In the 1930s Freud's politics could be acutely disappointing too.[61])

I should spell out more concretely why I consider Jung to be so important in the history of ideas. It is often said that Freud himself saw some of his own worst failings, and there is a good deal of truth in that proposition; yet Freud usually managed to handle all the possible objections to his own system of thought so masterfully that readers have been inclined to go along with his dismissal of the possible flaws in his psychology.

Jung, however, was to my knowledge the first to insist that authoritarianism was implicit in Freud's therapeutic technique. (The central issue of power also continues to go undiscussed within today's biological psychiatry.) Jung was, doubtless in part because of his personal contact with Freud, the earliest to suggest, as we have seen, that all analysts in the future be obliged to undergo training analyses. I should say that I am not by any means sure that this was such a good idea; the concept of a training analysis has had some unfortunate side consequences, in infantilizing candidates for example, and ensuring their indoctrination into a particular teacher's way of doing things. It is of course for others than myself, since I have never been a clinician, to weigh the pros and cons of the institution of a training analysis in connection with the problem of authoritarianism.

I do believe, however, based on my own historical research, that not enough attention has been given to the whole vexed question of psychoanalytic education. Supervised psychoanalyses were invented precisely as a device to check the power that a senior training analyst is bound to have. But one finds so much sectarianism in psychoanalysis, right up until today, that it does not seem to me that previous devices have succeeded in being as effective as they should be. The literature keeps repeating itself; one finds people from different schools of thought unaware of what others have been up to.

Two examples can illustrate what I have in mind. Once, during my interview with Jolande Jacobi in 1966, I raised the concept, then fashionable in orthodox psychoanalysis, of "regression in the service of the ego." Although Dr. Jacobi had known Ernst Kris personally in Vienna, and immediately understood the purport of what I described as his notion, she had not been familiar with it; she agreed with me that it bore striking similarities to Jung's own approach. To give another instance, I recall Anthony Storr telling me after he had stayed in Chicago once that the Freudian analysts there seemed to have picked up some of Jung's ideas about how to proceed with short-term psychotherapy. The Chicago Psychoanalytic Institute was founded by Franz Alexander, and although I am confident that Dr. Alexander was not directly influenced by Jung, he had worked out his ideas on his own in the 1940s that bore many analogies to those Jung had had a generation earlier. Ideological enemies of Alexander, like the orthodox Kurt R. Eissler, would have been no doubt delighted to hear of Jungian parallels in Alexander's work, but I am raising the analogy in connection with intellectual history rather than as an aspect of the partisan politics of sectarian squabbling.

Different schools of psychoanalysts are like ships passing in the night. Although it might seem that the two examples I have just given are instances of people who have grown up within Jung's framework not being aware enough of Freudian contributions, I am certain that the general neglect is much more the other way around. In my experience those who have been trained as Freudians are far less likely ever to have read Jung than Jungians are apt to be familiar with Freud.

Perhaps the most striking instance of this in my own research came in the course of an interview I once conducted with René Spitz in Switzerland during 1966. "You won't believe," he told me, what Jung once "claimed": Jung had told Dr. Spitz that he had invented the idea of a training analysis. Spitz considered this preposterous, and as far as I know most Freudians today still agree with him. Yet some years ago I came across a passage in Freud's writings where he specifically credits "the Zurich school," meaning Jung, with that suggestion; Freud was doing so in the course of writing a paper which every analytic candidate is required to study, yet that striking reference to "the Zurich school" continues to go unnoticed.[62]

Since I have indicated some of my reservations because of the drawbacks that I think have been associated with training analyses, I should immediately list some of the more unquestionably positive contributions that I think Jung was able to make. He understood, fifty years before it occurred to orthodox analysts, that clinically infantile material could be used as a dodge. The idea that a preoccupation with the childhood past could become an evasion was only much later dubbed by Max Schur as "resistance from below."[63] Jung also knew that dreams are not just expressions of wishes and that they had to do with the dreamer's own self, not only past loved ones. As we have mentioned, Jung looked on the unconscious more favorably, and with less suspicion, than Freud did, and therefore Jung was likely, at least according to his theory, to take a more tolerant attitude toward the presence of symptoms.

In reality, of course, despite the difference in age between the two men (nineteen years), Jung and Freud shared much in common. If one reads some of Jung's social philosophy, it sounds strikingly like that of Freud himself, even though both men wrote their own social works long after their association was over. And in Freud's *Moses and Monotheism*, for example, he commits himself to many views on the nature of symbols that sound to me very like Jung's. Although I do not have the space to document this point here, I am pretty sure that in their concrete clinical practices both Jung and Freud, despite their falling out, continued to share more things in common than one might expect.

But I am afraid that in the course of indicating my respect for Jung's stature within intellectual history, I have drifted too far from the subject at hand: anti-Semitism. It is obviously a good sign that Jungians were able publicly to face up enough to this problem as to propose a series of New York City 1989 conferences on the same theme. Yet I myself was put in a great deal of inner conflict in having to address this topic before guests who had invited me to appear before them.

Anti-Semitism is a vast subject, extending throughout Western thought, and the variety of prejudices about Jews constitutes a matter on which I cannot hope to be expert. With Jung, however, we are dealing with a specific problem that arises uniquely in connection with mid-twentieth century intellectuals. Henry Adams, for example, died too early for anyone to get terribly exercised about the specifics of what he thought about Jews. It would be ahistorical to consider his views in the light of later events. Anti-Semitism is a deeply rooted part of Western culture and has touched many otherwise admirable thinkers. Hannah Arendt once wrote that the rise of the Nazis had finally put an end to comments about Jews that once were considered culturally allowable, for as soon as it became possible to see that anti-Semitism could lead to gas chambers, then no respectable person could permit cracks about Jews that once might have been thought acceptably run-of-the-mill.

Other eminent figures in the middle of this past century, besides Jung, have been caught in the same bind of having expressed morally compromising points about Jews that have a special status because of their timing. I take it mainly as a matter of authority that Heidegger was a great philosopher; he is perhaps the most extreme example of the betrayal of an intellectual's ethics that comes to mind, since he actually joined the Nazi party; although he might not have generalized about Jews, he allowed himself at least one negative reference to an individual academic as a Jew that struck other Nazis as so poisonous that it backfired. Ezra Pound's poetry is, I am told, a great work of world literature, yet Pound gave hundreds of perfectly dreadful broadcasts on behalf of Mussolini's regime, programs that sometimes were rebroadcast from Berlin. To cite another illustration: T. S. Eliot's poetic references to Jews have subsequently been strenuously held against him. And then again, it has recently been discovered how Paul de Man, the eminent literary critic, wrote anti-Semitic newspaper articles in his youth during the German occupation of Belgium in World War II.

Of all these men, Jung is the only one about whom I feel expert enough to defend, in terms of the great contribution he made to psychology. If, however, I were French, and my family had endured World War II, I might well be in Ricoeur's position of not ever having read Jung. (The French intelligentsia somehow has not held Heidegger's Nazism fatally against him.) The closer one is to the Holocaust, the harder it becomes to take some distance toward the political views that Jung was associated with. I am, however, among the lucky ones, born on this continent; but the accident of geography and history does not spare me the obligation of thinking about the ethical implications that Jung's political commitments entail.

I should be more explicit. It is not correct to compartmentalize psychology and politics. At the same time we should not go to the other extreme and weigh everything on the scale of political judgment; it is the totalitarian regimes that have made all of reality subservient to politics. And yet, without overdoing the implications of what Jung wrote and did in the 1930s, it has to be relevant to an overall appreciation of his standing.

The details of the controversy about Jung and anti-Semitism are already well known. Nevertheless, though I admire Robertson Davies's novels, I once read a book review of his in the Sunday *New York Times* in which he blankly repudiated the idea that Jung was an anti-Semite. Curiously enough, to me at least, it was Freud himself who first leveled this charge against Jung, though I detected no signs of such prejudice on Jung's part coming up in their exchanges. But I have no doubt that on Freud's side his enthusiasm about Jung as a disciple stemmed in part from Freud's own special kind of anti-Semitism, his concern that psychoanalysis not become exclusively a Jewish affair and that the movement be led by a Gentile. The bitterness of Freud's disappointment in Jung, and Freud's disillusionment with himself as a leader, can be found in the themes that were preoccupying Freud in *Moses and Monotheism.*

It is not easy for me to cite chapter and verse of what Jung wrote about Jews. In 1934 he argued:

> The Jew, who is something of a nomad, has never yet created a cultural form of his own and as far as we can see never will, since all his instincts and talents require a more or less civilized nation to act as host for their development . . . .The "Aryan"* unconscious has a higher potential than the Jewish; that is both the advantage and the disadvantage of a youthfulness not yet fully weaned from barbarism. In my opinion it has been a grave error in medical psychology up to now to apply Jewish categories — which are not even binding on all Jews — indiscriminatingly to German and Slavic Christendom. Because of this the most precious secret of the Germanic peoples — their creative and intuitive depth of soul — has been explained as a mass of banal infantilism, while my own warning voice has for decades been suspected of anti-Semitism. This suspicion emanated from Freud. He did not understand the Germanic psyche any more than did his German followers. Has the formidable phenomenon of National Socialism, on which the whole world gazes with astonished eyes, taught them better? That is why I say that the Germanic unconscious contains tensions and potentialities which medical psychology must consider in its evaluation of the unconscious.[64]

I have no doubt that much of what Jung had to say has some validity to it; I think that the truth of the matter is that Freud's psychology is characteristically a Jewish one, and that this accounts for some of its strengths as well as for the defects in it that are in need of correction.[65] But the point is, and here I am speaking as a political scientist, the worst of what Jung wrote came in the early days of the rise to power of the Nazis in Germany. Further, Jung took the trouble to go there to deliver his message; he undertook to make political choices, for which he must historically be held responsible. It was a time when, it will be recalled, Jewish psychotherapists were being forced to flee abroad or were suffering in Germany, and when Jewish patients could increasingly not been seen by Gentile therapists.

Jung seems to have been politically naïve, even stupid, but I must say that what often looks like stupidity can mask prejudice and conviction. In Jung's case it is not as if others in the field did not try to point out to him at the time where he was going wrong. Wilhelm Reich was among those who denounced Jung, as did Gustav Bally of Zurich, eliciting Jung's 1934 "Rejoinder to Dr. Bally." It was Erich Fromm, a man of the Left, who advised me to consult with Dr. Bally about Jung's politics. (Unfortunately Bally died too soon for me to have been able to see him.)

* I am told that no quotation marks around the word Aryan appear in the original publication of Jung's article.

Jung always claimed that he had undertaken to accept the leadership of the German Medical Society for Psychotherapy in June 1933 in order to protect the profession, and the Jews who practiced it, from needlessly being penalized during the ravages of the Nazi regime. (Jones and orthodox Freudians made their own unsavory organizational compromises with Hitler's regime.[66]) I have no doubt that Jung helped many Jewish refugees from Germany to reestablish themselves abroad. But when, in 1935, the Dutch members of Jung's reconstituted international society refused on political grounds to act as hosts for a congress, Jung wrote to them that they were compromising the neutrality of science.

It is simply not the case, however, that when one is talking about the Nazis it is possible to sustain such an appeal to neutral science. The Dutch were, I think, morally right in refusing to collaborate with Jung's call. Those of us intellectuals who during the Vietnam conflict felt passionately that the war was immoral found ourselves experiencing utter frustration for years; it is not easy to point to more than a few mild acts of protest on our part, and I do not claim to be myself some kind of political hero. But it is unnecessary to gloss over what Jung did, or avoid calling a spade a spade.

After World War II it might have been possible for Jung to have better made amends for what had happened. According to the Index of the papers of the British Foreign Office, in 1946 a "booklet" existed that bore the title "The Case of Dr. Carl G. Jung — Pseudo-Scientist Nazi Auxiliary" by Maurice Leon, which outlined "Dr. Jung's connection with Nazis and Nazi Plans." Evidently there were Foreign Office minutes on a "proposed trial as war criminal." I have not succeeded in obtaining this documentation, which as I recall was still covered by a rule restricting access to state papers. Even if this particular file turns out to be wholly innocuous, still it is striking to me that as far as I know Jung never adequately acknowledged the full impropriety of his conduct. It might have been logically possible for him to have owned up much more to his having made an error in judgment.

Politically we are not talking about any minor matter. It is not as if we were evaluating why a particular political leader failed to resign, for example, from a government doing business with Hitler; appeasement does differ from being a fellow traveler. We are not even discussing the question of going along with a government that pursues a course that we disapprove of, or even would prefer to dissociate ourselves from.

In my opinion the rise of the Nazis is the most significant political event of the twentieth century. It is appalling to find Jung in 1933 remarking approvingly, "as Hitler said recently. . . . " In the same interview on Radio Berlin he referred to "the aimless conversation of parliamentary deliberations" that "drone on. . . . "[67] And, as Edward Glover long ago pointed out, in 1936 Jung said: "The SS men are being transformed into a caste of knights ruling sixty million natives."[68] I have not attempted, nor could I bear to do so, a comprehensive review of all of Jung's political commentary. (It is though noteworthy how Hitler also duped former British Prime Minister David Lloyd George, who as late as 1936 was convinced that Hitler was a "great man.")

Hitler did not seize power by force, but was duly elected to office; and the regime he displaced was a democratic one. So that for me one of the most distressing aspects of the whole matter is that a people willingly chose Hitler, knowing his program beforehand. Those of us who like to believe in democratic processes, and the enlightenment we associate with higher education, have to face up to the fact that Nazism came in such a highly cultured community. No one could have appreciated ahead of time the full horrors of the Nazis. But intellectual historians do rightly wonder about what elements in Western culture may have fed the long-term sources of Hitlerism. Can it be that an emphasis on the legitimacy of the irrational in psychology does also, when introduced to the world of politics, encourage Nazi-like movements? It would not be too speculative, I think, to suppose that some of Jung's ideas had enough echo in what he heard from Germany's Nazis for him to think that his work might successfully fit in there. But to the extent that his actions were opportunistically motivated, he is not going to come off well on this particular score.

Many will already know the story of the children at an international school in Paris who were once asked to write essays on the elephant. The English boy wrote about hunting elephants in Africa, the German boy composed "The Sorrows of a Young Elephant," and the French child presented "On the Love Habits of the Elephant." The Jewish boy called his contribution: "The Elephant and the Jewish Question."

The issue of anti-Semitism, however, does go beyond the parochial, and seems to me especially pertinent to Jung's thought as a whole. I know I could have chosen to address myself more evasively to the subject of the New York City conference called "Lingering Shadows," but I originally accepted without qualification the invitation to speak on the issue of Jung and anti-Semitism. It took me ages before I could sit down and write what little I had to say; I pondered the matter for months, each time putting the matter to the back of my mind, and more than once I cried out in anguish to myself: "What am I going to say!" I do not believe in pussyfooting, and yet I hope it is clear that I have not approached the topic in an embattled mood. I trust that what I have said will not, under the circumstances, seem offensive. But I have tried my best to address myself to the designated problem.

Each of us makes choices, and these decisions become deeds. We in North America know little of the tormenting moral problems that have wracked less fortunate societies. Hitlerism is the worst form of evil I can think of, although I believe Stalinism (and perhaps Maoism) would be solid competitors for that same level of wickedness; because of Jung's politics and their links to the Nazis, his genuinely great contributions to psychology can only be fully appreciated and evaluated once they are understood in terms of their association with his social views, and yet somehow ultimately detached from the actions of Hitler's regime. Just as it is possible, I think, to divorce Dostoevsky's psychology from his politics, so I hope Jung's psychology will endure in spite of his brand of anti-Semitism.

Notes

1. *The Freud/Jung Letters: The Correspondence Between Sigmund Freud and C. G. Jung*, edited by William McGuire, translated by Ralph Manheim and R. F. C. Hull (Princeton, N. J., Princeton University Press, 1974).
2. "Totem and Taboo," *Standard Edition*, Vol. 13, pp. xiii–161.
3. *The Freud/Jung Letters: The Correspondence Between Sigmund Freud and C. G. Jung*, edited by William McGuire, translated by Ralph Manheim and R. F. C. Hull (Cambridge, Mass., Harvard University Press, 1988). Aldo Carotenuto, *A Secret Symmetry: Sabina Spielrein Between Jung and Freud,* translated by Arno Pomerans, John Shepley, Krishna Winston (New York, Pantheon Books, 1982).
4. Linda Donn, *Freud and Jung: Years of Friendship, Years of Loss* (New York, Charles Scribner's Sons, 1989).
5. Peter Homans, *The Ability to Mourn: Disillusionment and the Social Origins of Psychoanalysis* (Chicago, University of Chicago Press, 1989).
6. See Roazen, *The Historiography of Psychoanalysis, op. cit.*, pp. 60–61.
7. Peter Homans, *The Ability to Mourn: Disillusionment and the Social Origins of Psychoanalysis, op. cit.*, xii, 4.
8. *Ibid.*, pp. 7, 9, 11.
9. See Paul Roazen, *Political Theory and the Psychology of the Unconscious, op. cit.*, Part III, Ch. 1, pp. 99–123.
10. Homans, *op. cit.*, pp. 17, 22.
11. Paul Roazen, *Encountering Freud: The Politics and Histories of Psychoanalysis, op. cit.*, pp. 219–23; Roazen, *The Historiography of Psychoanalysis, op. cit.*, pp. 297–99.
12. Fritz Wittels, *Sigmund Freud* (New York, Dodd, Mead & Co., 1924), p. 233.
13. Homans, *op. cit.*, pp. 59, 73.
14. Homans, *Ibid.*, pp. 4, 198, 79; Erich Fromm, *Sigmund Freud's Mission: An Analysis of His Personality and Influence* (New York, Harper & Brothers, 1959).
15. Roazen, *Freud and His Followers, op. cit.*, pp. 304–10.
16. Paul Roazen, *Erik H. Erikson: The Power and Limits of a Vision* (New York, The Free Press, 1975, reprinted Northvale, N. J., Aronson, 1997); Roazen, *Political Theory and the Psychology of the Unconscious, op. cit.*, Part III, Ch. 3, pp. 152–171; and Roazen, *The Historiography of Psychoanalysis, op. cit.*, pp. 291–94.
17. Elisabeth Young-Bruehl, *Anna Freud: A Biography* (New York, Summit Books, 1988), p. 440.
18. Jeffrey Santinover, "Jung's Lost Contribution to the Dilemma of Narcissism," *Journal of the American Psychoanalytic Association*, Vol. 34 (1986), pp. 401–38.
19. Robert H. Hopcke, *A Guided Tour of the Collected Works of C. G. Jung* (Boston, Shambhala, 1989), p. 59.

20. *Ibid.*, p. 73.
21. Roazen, *The Historiography of Psychoanalysis, op. cit.*, pp. 409–10.
22. Hopcke, *A Guided Tour of the Collected Works of C. G. Jung, op. cit.*
23. Edward Glover, *Freud Or Jung?* (New York, Meridian Books, 1957; reprinted, with a Foreword by James William Anderson, Evanston, Illinois, Northwestern University Press, 1991).
24. Hugh Trevor-Roper, *The European Witch-Craze of the Sixteenth and Seventeenth Centuries and Other Essays* (New York, Harper Torchbooks, 1967).
25. Hopcke, *op. cit.*, p. 165.
26. *Ibid.*, p. 141.
27. Barbara Hannah, *Jung, His Life and Work: A Biographical Memoir* (New York, G. P. Putnam's Sons, 1976).
28. Anthony Stevens, *On Jung* (London, Routledge, 1990).
29. *Ibid.*, pp. 262–63.
30. *Ibid.*, p. 51.
31. *Ibid.*, p. 270.
32. *Ibid.*, p. 16. See Roazen, *Freud and His Followers, op. cit.*, p. 232–41.
33. *Ibid.*, p. 267.
34. *Ibid.*, p. 57.
35. "Libidinal Types," *Standard Edition*, Vol. 21, pp. 217–20.
36. J. J. Clarke, *In Search of Jung: Historical and Philosophical Enquiries* (London, Routledge, 1992).
37. *Ibid.*, p. 57.
38. *Ibid.*, p. 3.
39. *Ibid.*, p. 8.
40. Roazen, *Political Theory and the Psychology of the Unconscious, op. cit.*, Part I, Ch. 2, pp. 28–48.
41. Clarke, *op. cit.*, p. 135.
42. *Ibid.*, p. 136.
43. Andrew Samuels, *Jung and the Post-Jungians* (London, Tavistock/Routledge, 1985).
44. Clarke, *op. cit.*, p. 165.
45. *Ibid.*, p. 92.
46. *Ibid.*, p. 110.
47. *Ibid.*, p. 131.
48. But see William McGuire, *Bolligen: An Adventure in Collecting the Past* (Princeton, N.J., Princeton University Press, 1989) and Thomas Kirsch, *The Jungians: A Comparative and Historical Perspective* (London, Routledge, 2000).
49. Richard Noll, *The Jung Cult: Origins of a Charismatic Movement* (Princeton, N.J., Princeton University Press, 1994). Also Richard Noll, *The Aryan Christ: The Secret Life of Carl Jung* (New York, Random House, 1997), and Sonu Shamdasani, *Cult Fictions: C. G. Jung and the Founding of Analytical Psychology* (London, Routledge, 1998). Further, see Anthony Stevens, "Critical Notice," *Journal of Analytical Psychology*, Vol. 42 (1997), pp. 671–689, as well as Richard Noll, "*The Jung Cult* and *The Aryan Christ*: A Response to Past and Future Critics," posted on the web: March 1, 1998.
50. Robert C. Smith, *The Wounded Jung: Effects of Jung's Relationships on His Life and Work* (Evanston, Ill., Northwestern University Press, 1996).
51. See also Paul Roazen, "Introduction," *Martin Buber on Psychology and Psychotherapy: Essays, Letters, and Dialogue*, edited by Judith Buber Agassi (Syracuse,

N.Y., Syracuse University Press, 1999).

52. See, for example, Hans Sluga, *Heidegger's Crisis: Philosophy and Politics in Nazi Germany* (Cambridge, Mass., Harvard University Press, 1993) and Victor Farias, *Heidegger and Nazism*, edited by Joseph Margolis and Tom Rockmore (Philadelphia, Temple University Press, 1989).
53. Henri E. Ellenberger, *The Discovery of the Unconscious: The History and Evolution of Dynamic Psychiatry* (New York, Basic Books, 1970), Ch. 9.
54. Roazen, *The Historiography of Psychoanalysis*, *op. cit.*, pp. 183–90.
55. Anthony Storr, *Solitude: A Return to the Self* (New York, Collier Macmillan, 1988). My citations will be to the English edition of this book, entitled *The School of Genius* (London, Andre Deutsch, 1988).
56. *Ibid.*, p. xii.
57. *Ibid.*, p. xiii.
58. *Ibid.*, p. ix.
59. Paul Ricoeur, *Freud and Philosophy: An Essay On Interpretation*, translated by Denis Savage (New Haven, Conn.,Yale University Press, 1970).
60. Roazen, *Political Theory and the Psychology of the Unconscious*, *op. cit.*, Part I, Ch. 3, pp. 49–71.
61. Paul Roazen, "The Exclusion of Erich Fromm from the IPA," *Contemporary Psychoanalysis*, Vol. 37, No. 1 (2001), pp. 5–42.
62. "Recommendations to Physicians Practising Psycho-analysis," *Standard Edition*, Vol. 12, p. 116. See Paul Roazen, "The Problem of Silence: Training Analyses," *International Forum of Psychoanalysis*, in press.
63. Paul Roazen, *Encountering Freud*, *op. cit.*, p. 216.
64. Quoted in Roazen, *Freud and His Followers*, *op. cit.*, pp. 291–92.
65. See *Ibid.*, especially pp. 22ff.
66. Roazen, "The Exclusion of Erich Fromm from the IPA," *op. cit.*
67. *C. G. Jung Speaking: Interviews and Encounters*, edited by William McGuire and R. F. C. Hull (London, Picador, 1980), pp. 77–78.
68. *Ibid.*, p. 103.

3

Sandor Ferenczi: The Budapest School

Andre Haynal, a Hungarian who has been a professor of psychiatry in Geneva and also regularly comes to teach at Stanford Medical School, California, has written an excellent overview of the story of the Budapest school of psychoanalysis.[1] Although the literature about the early followers of Freud may seem immense, in fact there remains a substantial gap between what is generally acknowledged within clinical circles and what has succeeded in reaching the broad reading public. So that while Sandor Ferenczi's path-breaking innovations are now widely appreciated among practicing analysts, Freud's own private judgment that Ferenczi's late technical recommendations meant that Ferenczi (1873–1933) had become psychotic got widely circulated in Jones's popular authorized biography of Freud. Yet the full extent to which Ferenczi's contributions anticipated later liberal trends in psychoanalytic thinking deserves the emphasis Haynal gives it; otherwise the substance of Ferenczi's clinical thought may get reproduced without adequately acknowledging the credit Ferenczi deserves for those achievements.

For new material Haynal relies on Ferenczi's 1932 *Clinical Diary*, which first appeared in French in 1985 and in English in 1988.[2] Haynal also had early access to the full three-volume Freud-Ferenczi correspondence, which was prepared for publication in Paris and has been a key recent addition to our understanding of early psychoanalysis. Furthermore, Haynal has worked with the Balint Archives in Geneva; Michael Balint was Ferenczi's main student, the most noteworthy follower to develop the insights that Ferenczi first made.

Ferenczi became primarily interested in being a healer. As Freud complained in his otherwise flattering obituary,

> we learnt that one single problem had monopolized his interest. The need to cure and to help had become paramount in him. He had probably set himself aims

> which, with our therapeutic means, are altogether out of reach today. From unexhausted springs of emotion the conviction was borne in upon him that one could effect far more with one's patients if one gave them enough of the love which they had longed for as children. He wanted to discover how this could be carried out within the framework of the psychoanalytic situation.

Despite the distance that had grown up between himself and Ferenczi, Freud still singled out Ferenczi's "lovable and affectionate personality."[3] Ferenczi's desire to cure meant that he advised abandoning what he regarded as the authoritarian attitudes in traditional psychoanalysis. Ferenczi wanted to shift away from aiming at the recall of so-called repressed memories, and he was not closed to the benign possibilities of regression in therapy. Above all, Ferenczi sought to understand the analyst's own role in the therapeutic process; he thought that the analysis of the patient entailed also the analysis of the analyst. (Ferenczi was going well beyond the formal requirement that all analysts be themselves analyzed.) Ferenczi was critical of the Berlin school of thinking, which followed Karl Abraham's over-concentration on abstract theory.

Haynal devotes considerable attention to the life and work of Michael Balint. Memories in the history of psychoanalysis are short; while in his lifetime Balint was a powerful force for open-minded thinking about psychoanalytic treatment, his death in 1970 has meant that he is now apt to be neglected. Balint shared the old Hungarian charm that so enriched the practices of the Budapest school[4]; during his years in London he helped lead the Middle Group, trying to steer an independent course between the disciples of Melanie Klein and Anna Freud. Yet the Middle Groupers did not have an easy time of it, and Balint himself would have been more outspoken if he had not been so acutely conscious of the consequences of Ferenczi's own independence having brought down on him the wrath of an aroused orthodoxy. Many others have seen that psychoanalysis cannot just be a technique but must amount much more to a relationship between two people. Perhaps only those who grew up with an ingrained fear of excommunication would have had to tread so cautiously in an obviously sound direction.

I think Haynal overdoes the extent to which Balint was personally willing to work against all dogmatisms and taboos; it seems to me that that generation of early analysts necessarily internalized a host of superfluous constraints on free thought. But Haynal does quote Balint as having been bold enough to maintain the following two key propositions: "First, not everything that happens in human development is repeated in the psychoanalytic situation; and second, what is repeated is profoundly distorted by the conditions prevailing there."[5]

Ferenczi had emphasized that analysis is "a social fact," and Balint took up this insight in making the interactions between transference and counter-transference "the cornerstone of his research." As so-called pluralism becomes more acceptable within today's psychoanalytic thinking, the issue of "loyalty" to a frozen conception of Freud should diminish. Haynal's clearly written book is intended to help legitimize "new research and openings towards new horizons."

Psychoanalysis is obviously in serious trouble within American medicine. The dead hand of orthodox Freudian teachings so restricted the thinking at major centers of psychoanalytic training that not only has the quantity of potential candidates dwindled but the prospective patient population has also become restricted. Once — in the early 1960s for instance — every major psychiatric department in a city like Boston was headed by an analyst, but today being an analyst would almost be a bar to anyone's rise within the psychiatric profession.

Biological psychiatry has been sweeping the field, and the discovery of new drugs has rendered outmoded many of the practices that were once highly touted by orthodox analysts. For some in the literary and philosophic communities, who are still justifiably enchanted with the power of Freud's mind and the capacities he had as a great writer, these developments in medicine may seem inconsequential. Perhaps, for psychoanalysis as a whole, this radical swing of the pendulum away from it may be a constructive one in that the people who are attracted to psychoanalysis now are likely to be more similar to the early Freudians themselves, outsiders with a serious commitment to the life of the mind. Conformism will be less likely to afflict psychoanalysis itself, and careerist getting ahead in the profession will be a problem for other, more successful schools of thought. In the meantime, there is no doubt in my mind that psychoanalysis, properly understood, has something uniquely valuable to contribute to the practice of modern psychotherapy.

Andre Haynal is like a fresh breeze in the field; his openness and tolerance are hopeful signs that there is still life in the profession. I am not as impressed by what he has to say philosophically in *Psychoanalysis and the Sciences*, although I find nothing to object to there, as I am by his sweeping aside so much of the historical mythology associated with Freudianism. Haynal quotes Wittgenstein as having explained, "I believe that my originality (if that is the right word) is an originality belonging to the soil rather than to the seed. (Perhaps I have no seed of my own.) Sow a seed in my soil and it will grow differently than it would in any other soil. Freud's originality too was like this, I think."[6] Haynal is using his philosophical background to slice through to the historical Freud.

Here is European culture at its best: Haynal uses a cosmopolitan ethical perspective to understand some of the central dilemmas of clinical practice. Psychoanalysis had its origins in nineteenth-century Europe, a world that has entirely vanished. Those of us who like to think that improvements have been made on Freud are apt to forget that he possessed a degree of human and social sophistication alien to our own less nuanced time. Yet there are a few rare exceptions — analysts like Haynal, who are aware of what needs correcting in old-fashioned psychoanalysis and still retain old-world cosmopolitanism.

It is all the more persuasive to me that Haynal relies on the Freud-Ferenczi story because that makes concrete what so often becomes abstract. What is the nature of a clinical indiscretion, and how does one understand it? In some sense, as Freud liked to quote another authority, morality has to be "self-evident." Without a central core it is senseless to engage in ethical discussion. At the same time, psychoanalytic thinking is a legitimate opening to the ancient question, raised in a contemporary context, of how one ought to live. The last sentence of Haynal's book is representative: "It is within the age-old tradition of questioning and challenging existent knowledge . . . that I wish to stand."[7]

Haynal does not always seem to realize how the historical tales he tells have an ethical dimension to them, but the examples he gives cry out, to me at least, for moral self-examination. Haynal has been one of the supervising editors of the full edition of the Freud-Ferenczi correspondence that first started coming out in 1993, and the most interesting parts of this book come from the rich kinds of primary material contained in those fascinating letters.

The most powerful section of the book, for me, was the one that concerned the contributions of Ferenczi. There are so many stereotypes about what sort of therapist Freud was that the bare bones of the tale of Freud, Ferenczi, and Ferenczi's stepdaughter Elma, to which we will return, is exemplary, at least as instructive as the story of Freud's having analyzed his daughter Anna. In terms of concepts, Haynal is able to demonstrate that "for Freud, the term 'love' means 'transference love'; for Ferenczi it means 'countertransference love.'" Ferenczi understood that counter-transference could not be just a therapeutic obstacle, but also a positive instrument, a point first made by Helene Deutsch in a 1926 article.[8]

Haynal's humanity infuses everything he writes about. He argues, consistent with Ferenczi's teachings, that "the moment we began to speak of a classical technique, we entered a stage of *illusion*, an illusion that there exists a technique that one need only learn and apply 'correctly' and on which 'textbooks' can be written." At the same time Haynal's generosity can lead him, in his historical narratives, to smooth over too much the discontinuities between the past and the present. If one wants to stretch things, for example, one can find similarities between the rationalistic approach advocated by James Strachey and that of Ferenczi's proposal of emotional reexperiencing, but the stark differences also should be pointed out. And it is altogether too revisionistic to conclude, as Haynal does, that the "systematizations" of psychoanalysis were somehow "not" Freud's "doing" when in reality the responsibility for what we inherited is in truth largely Freud's.

Haynal insists that psychoanalysis has had an unfortunate propensity to become an ideology. He is an analyst willing to state publicly that Freudians have had "their dogmas and fanaticisms." He wants to bring psychoanalysis into contact with the other sciences, human as well as natural, and he explicitly maintains that "in its wish to preserve its 'purity' it can only be deprived of the stimulation presented by such exchanges." The generous spirit Haynal infuses into his thinking can give hope to all those who cherish the strengths of a psychodynamic perspective.

The strongest argument in behalf of Ferenczi's outstanding leadership in modern psychotherapy can be found by immersing oneself in his *Clinical Diary*.[9] This one text can demonstrate why Ferenczi has now achieved central standing as a proponent of clinical practices in analysis that are an alternative to those of the orthodox approach. Certainly others have also notably challenged traditionalism; but Carl Jung's recommendations, for example, are so encased in such an alien vocabulary for those of us educated conventionally in Freud's school, that Jung's ideas on clinical matters have scarcely gained much currency within the so-called mainstream. In any event the name Jung is still so colored by the charge of analytic heresy that, combined with the fact of his political collaboration with the Nazis, it is hard for Freud's descendants to listen to reports of Jung's work without feeling that they have somehow betrayed their origins. The works of Karen Horney and Franz Alexander (oddly enough, one of Horney's critics), both of whom initiated important clinical departures from Freud's own stated recommendations, have also been too easy for many analysts to sidestep, since organizational difficulties tended to leave them both relatively isolated.

Although considerable controversy has been associated with Ferenczi's name, it is impossible for the history of psychoanalysis ever silently to skip by him because of the many years in which he was in such close and intimate contact with Freud. The full publication of the Freud-Ferenczi correspondence, under the overall guidance of Judith Dupont who is also responsible for the editing of the *Clinical Diary*, should establish the full intimacy between the two men, as well as help us understand the circumstances of their ultimate falling out.

Paradoxically, although Ferenczi during his last years in contact with Freud and for the period of the *Clinical Diary* devoted a great deal of attention to matters of technique, within the psychoanalytic movement as a whole he was not someone who attracted a notable batch of pupils for training from abroad. He did, it is true, analyze Ernest Jones, and Clara Thompson among others sought his help, but compared to Karl Abraham, for example, who even though he died early (1925) managed to train a host of young analysts, Ferenczi evidently did not have the same reputation for having had unusually sound clinical judgment. Part of the problem had to do with language, in that Abraham's German was more accessible than the Hungarian encountered in going to live in Budapest for the sake of being analyzed by Ferenczi, but still one does suspect that insiders may have known what they were doing when they sought out Abraham rather than Ferenczi. It is known that Freud admired Ferenczi's capacities for speculating along phylogenetic lines; but, in addition, everyone I ever met who spoke of having known Ferenczi emphasized his special personal warmth and empathy.

This diary covers almost ten months in 1932; by then his relations with Freud were badly strained. Ferenczi had been devoting himself to the problem of psychoanalysis as therapy; he had once been in love with a woman who ended up his stepdaughter, and had become preoccupied with the clinical significance of child abuse. In Freud's earliest practice he had been far more outgoing as a therapist than in his last, dying phase, but by the 1930s, Freud was in no mood to encourage Ferenczi's clinical innovations. At a time when Freud had been more committed than ever to the concepts of psychoanalysis as a pure science, Ferenczi became, as Judith Dupont says in her introduction, a haven for cases considered "unanalyzable" or hopeless. No one has ever written more bitingly than Ferenczi in his *Clinical Diary* about the drawbacks of what Dr. Dupont calls "the professional hypocrisy and technical rigidity of the analyst." Even though Ferenczi knew that in practice Freud as an analyst behaved quite unlike the model implied in the written rules he recommended in his papers for others to follow, still Ferenczi also felt that Freud had, in Dr. Dupont's words, "gradually developed an overly impersonal, pedagogic technique giving rise to a much too exclusively paternal transference."[10]

To be sure, aspects of Ferenczi's technical experimentation are bound today to sound pretty wild. He tried to undertake so-called mutual analysis, allowing patients to follow his own free associations; he was tempted to abandon all "technique." Part of what makes this *Clinical Diary* so humanly touching is that Ferenczi was willing to treat patients who sound pretty crazy if not diagnostically psychotic.

Whatever the limitations to what Ferenczi sought to achieve, his *Clinical Diary* is full of nuggets of wisdom. For example,

> Any kind of secrecy, whether positive or negative in character, makes the patient distrustful; he detects from little gestures (form of greeting, handshake, tone of voice, degree of animation, etc.) the presence of affects, but cannot gauge their quantity or importance; candid disclosure regarding them enables him to counteract them or to instigate countermeasures with greater certainty.[11]

Also, Ferenczi acknowledged "an exaggerated tendency in me to attach too much importance to the wishes, likes and dislikes of other people," but it is certainly welcome that this early analytic pioneer was willing to discuss the give-and-take of "mutuality" with his patients. Freud warned in this context, according to Ferenczi, that Ferenczi was "too much under the influence of . . . patients." Ferenczi persisted in looking for "the healing element in psychotherapy," which he concluded was "actually a kind of re-experiencing." Ferenczi was one of the most notable clinical critics of Freud's excessive rationalism which aimed at the reconstruction of early childhood.

Freud, seventeen years Ferenczi's senior, had himself analyzed Ferenczi. Ferenczi commented about Freud:

> My own analysis could not be pursued deeply enough because my analyst (by his own admission, of a narcissistic nature), with his strong determination to be healthy and his antipathy toward any weaknesses or abnormalities, could not follow me down into those depths, and introduced the "educational" stage too soon. Just as Freud's strength lies in firmness of education, so mine lies in the depth of the relaxation technique.[12]

Ferenczi remained deeply identified with Freud, for Ferenczi continued on to say about his own reliance on technical elasticity: "My patients are gradually persuading me to catch up on this part of the analysis as well. The time is perhaps not far when I shall no longer need this help from my own creations."[13] Freud too had thought of his own patients as his "creations," which is one reason why he had such difficulty tolerating their differing with him.

Ferenczi maintained that "real analysis can come about only when relaxation takes place in the child-parent relationship, that is to say, total trust and the surrender of all independence." From today's perspective it looks like Ferenczi should have been more concerned about the disadvantages of such a "surrender" on the patient's part. But Ferenczi worried about at least some of his motives: "Could it be that my entire relaxation therapy and the superkindness I demand from myself toward patients are only an exaggerated display of compassionate feelings that basically are totally lacking?"[14]
Ferenczi also questioned Freud's own motivation:

> Is Freud really convinced, or does he have a compulsion to cling too strongly to theory as a defense against self-analysis, that is, against his own doubts? It should not be forgotten that Freud is not the discoverer of analysis but that he took over something ready-made, from Breuer. Perhaps he followed Breuer in a logical, intellectual fashion, and not with any emotional conviction; consequently he only analyzes others, but not himself. Projection.[15]

Ferenczi quotes Freud, in contrast to Ferenczi's own humanitarianism, as having said in private, "Patients are a rabble!" In Freud's view "patients only serve to provide us with a livelihood and material to learn from. We certainly cannot help them." To Ferenczi "this is therapeutic nihilism, and yet by the concealment of these doubts and the raising of patients' hopes, patients do get caught." Ferenczi thought that "originally Freud really did believe in analysis," but that he had "returned to the love of his well-ordered and cultivated super-ego." Ferenczi cited Freud's antipathy toward and deprecating remarks about psychotics, perverts, and everything in general that was "too abnormal." From Ferenczi's perspective the impersonality of Freud's approach was responsible for artificially provoking what Freud later described as "transference."[16]

Plenty of evidence has long existed to support Ferenczi's complaint that Freud's pessimism about therapy was unacceptable, but Ferenczi was close enough to go further in interpreting Freud's character:

> The ease with which Freud sacrifices the interests of women in favor of male patients is striking. This is consistent with the unilaterally androphile orientation of his theory of sexuality . . . .The author may have a personal aversion to the spontaneous female-oriented sexuality in women: idealization of the mother. He recoils from the task of having a sexually demanding mother, and having to satisfy her. At some point his mother's passionate nature may have presented him with such a task. (The primal scene may have rendered him relatively impotent.)[17]

Even today most analysts have followed Freud in talking about himself and his father, ignoring Freud's mother. Psychoanalysis teaches us, however, that everyone suffers from self-deception. Ferenczi, like Jung before him, objected that Freud felt "he is the only one who does not have to be analyzed."[18]

Throughout his *Clinical Diary* Ferenczi was consistently bold in his criticism of the orthodox approach: "The analytic situation, but specifically its rigid technical rules, mostly produce in the patient an unalleviated suffering and in the analyst an unjustified sense of superiority accompanied by a certain contempt for the patient." Ferenczi was unremitting in exposing the sources of a classical analyst's grandiosity: "Analysis offers to persons otherwise somewhat incapacitated and whose self-confidence and potency are disturbed an opportunity to feel like a sultan, thus compensating him for his defective ability to love."[19] (Uncannily enough Freud would begin his obituary of Ferenczi with sayings clearly implying Freud's own identification with a sultan.) In Ferenczi's "catalogue of the sins of psychoanalysis" he included the way it "lures patients into 'transference,'" and how there can be "sadistic pleasure" in a patient's suffering and helplessness. For Ferenczi believed, within the context of psychoanalytic thinking, that "only sympathy heals." Furthermore, Ferenczi held that "the analytic technique creates transference, but then withdraws, wounding the patient without giving him a chance to protest or to go away; hence interminable fixation on the analysis while the conflict remains unconscious."[20] Whatever the limitations of Ferenczi's insights as recorded in his *Clinical Diary*, he was full of important ideas that have still not been adequately evaluated.

The final day's entry to Ferenczi's diary is particularly moving; he knew he was fatally ill with pernicious anemia, and that his difficulties with Freud were unlikely to be capable of being overcome. Like others earlier in the history of analysis, as for example Victor Tausk in his own struggle with Freud (and also Karl Abraham later on), Ferenczi seems to have felt that death was the only solution to his professional and personal dilemmas. Ferenczi asked himself, "Is the only possibility of my continued existence the renunciation of the largest part of one's own self, in order to carry out the will of that higher power to the end (as though it were my own)? Is the choice here one between dying and 'rearranging myself' — and this at the age of fifty-nine?"[21]

In his final entry Ferenczi said he felt abandoned by his colleagues "who are all too afraid of Freud to behave objectively or even sympathetically, in the case of a dispute between Freud and me." Ironically Ferenczi was touched to receive "a few personally friendly lines" from Ernest Jones, who in later years would do so much damage to Ferenczi's reputation by Jones's alleging, evidently on Freud's own say-so, that Ferenczi died suffering from a psychosis. The early analysts did too readily impute mental illness to those who disagreed with the master; and Ferenczi preferred to think that in dying he was choosing death to avoid psychosis: "A certain strength in my psychological makeup seems to persist, so that instead of falling ill psychically I can only destroy — or be destroyed — in my organic depths."[22] (Freud shared such magical beliefs, to the extent of writing Jones that Ferenczi's organic illness was the expression of psychological conflicts.[23]) Ferenczi, who died in May 1933, was in his diary adopting a romantic doctrine that imputed too much psychological intention to his own illness, but then Ferenczi was one of those touchingly lovable people who cannot accept the indifference of the reality of the outside world. His romanticism made him a giant in the history of modern psychotherapy, one who would never accept his era's conception of unanalyzability; and his desire to help, embodied in this diary as well as his life-work, should be a memorable example for future practitioners.

Over three decades ago, when I first got interested in the history of psychoanalysis, a number of analytic practitioners talked about being discontented with Freud's written rules recommending the analyst's neutrality, and skepticism was sometimes expressed about the desirability of offering patients a blank screen on which they were supposed to deposit their emotional transferences. For years there were prominent professionals who were rejecting the orthodox approach, but it still remained the dominant reigning paradigm.

Whatever the disputes about technique might have been, throughout the 1960s psychoanalysis was highly regarded as a therapeutic procedure.

Academic departments of psychology (then as now) had virtually nothing to do with the whole Freudian tradition, although philosophers, historians, and literary critics could be receptive to psychoanalytic thinking. Of course, there was a pervasive if often unspoken cultural impact of Freud's teachings. Relatively few books existed in those days on the story of the growth of Freud's school, or perhaps it would be more accurate to say that whatever had once appeared in print was bound to be at least temporarily overshadowed by the publication from 1953 to 1957 of the three-volume official biography of Freud written by Jones. Two prominent literary critics at Columbia University, Lionel Trilling and Steven Marcus, had helped popularize Jones by publishing in 1961 a one-volume edition of his Freud biography.

In the mid–1960s it seemed to me that personally meeting the surviving early analysts was a decisive way of cutting through to find out for the sake of the history of ideas what the beginnings of analysis had been all about. It was by chance that an analyst in London (Masud Khan), whom I subsequently discovered was known for being brilliant as well as arrogant and high-handed, mentioned in passing that he had, under his supervision at the British Psychoanalytic Society library, Jones's collection of papers.[24] Supposedly there was "nothing special" to be found there, but perhaps, I was told, I just might uncover something of interest. Everything was informal, I signed nothing before looking at Jones's material, but I was soon so excited by what I had come upon that it was rare that I told anybody about what I had stumbled upon.

One intriguing tale, which I intended back then to follow up on, bore on the career of Ferenczi, Freud's chief Hungarian disciple. Jones had been notably rough on Ferenczi, Jones's own analyst, although one of Freud's relatives, in the course of an interview with me, had typically referred to Ferenczi as "the milk of human kindness." Jones had characterized Ferenczi in his last days as having suffered from a psychosis; the point is so incredible that it bears repeating: this illness, Jones maintained, accounted for Ferenczi's final difficulties with Freud. And Jones was, by this sort of *ad hominem* attack on Ferenczi, able to argue that these personal difficulties of Ferenczi explained why he undertook such a different therapeutic approach than the so-called classical one, which found expression in Freud's published recommendations. (It was Ferenczi who invented the term classical psychoanalysis.[25]) The fact that Ferenczi had been suffering from pernicious anemia at his death, mentioned in Freud's obituary of Ferenczi, did not once come up in Jones's narrative account.

In our own time, when there are Ferenczi study groups and even an International Sandor Ferenczi Society, it may not be remembered just how low

Ferenczi's reputation had once sunk. Since almost at the outset of my interviewing I was in London, besides seeing others I also met Michael Balint, Ferenczi's literary executor.[26] When I first saw him he was wearing the ring that Freud had bestowed on Ferenczi as a member of the small Committee that had been set up after the loss of Jung from Freud's loyalist ranks; this group was supposed to defend the essence of psychoanalytic teachings.

Balint was an especially distinguished figure, although tactful enough so that Jones had allowed him at the time of the Nazis to immigrate to England. By the time I saw him Balint had published many books, and was known, among other things, for his interest in teaching general practitioners about psychotherapeutic issues. In going through Jones's files, I had come across correspondence between Jones and Balint, intended first as background material for Jones's biography, and then instigated because of Balint's protest at Jones's public account of Ferenczi's last days. While Jones was writing his third volume, his physical health was declining; he sent some prepublication galleys to Balint, who wrote back eloquently about how he saw things differently. But it was only after the appearance of Volume 3 that Balint decided that he really had to do something to correct the historical record.

Balint submitted a letter to Dr. Willi Hoffer as editor of *The International Journal of Psychoanalysis*. At the same time that Balint sent his draft to Hoffer, he also forwarded a copy to Jones. From Balint's point of view there were two central points of disagreement between himself and Jones; first, the value of Ferenczi's last writings, and second, exactly what sort of deterioration there had been in Ferenczi toward the end. Balint raised the point about the pernicious anemia, and how the damage to the spinal cord had meant that during Ferenczi's last months he had to stay in bed. Since at the time of Ferenczi's death (1933) Balint had been present in Ferenczi's Budapest, Balint was in a position to be able to refute Jones's version, which claimed that Ferenczi had been paranoiac. Balint had composed one sentence in his letter that Jones crossed out. Balint had written: "As both of us were — at some time — analyzed by Ferenczi, it is possible that both Dr. Jones's interpretation and mine are biased." Although Balint gave in to Jones's objections to this point, letters from both Balint and Jones did ultimately appear in print.[27] Erich Fromm, as early as 1958, had notably objected in public to what Jones had done to Ferenczi (and also to Otto Rank) in the biography, but Fromm's protest only made it into hardcover in a 1963 collection of essays.[28]

In looking through Jones's files, however, I found some fascinating exchanges between Jones and Balint, at least as revealing as what appeared by them both in publications. Jones had written to Balint on December 16, 1957 in an apparent attempt to mollify Ferenczi's defenders; Jones alluded to Ferenczi's two stepdaughters and the memory of their mother, Gizella: "Perhaps you might tell Elma and Magda that I was extremely careful to avoid dealing with Ferenczi's personal life, e.g., the way he treated Gisela [sic], his intimacy with her daughter, etc., but kept strictly to his relations with Freud." As if Jones had not tactlessly gone far enough, he added a further coal to the flame he had lit: "Freud himself was in no doubt at all that the change of views as well as his [Ferenczi's] personal estrangement were due to personal mental changes."

Balint fired back a letter to Jones on December 19 that challenged Jones's account of Ferenczi's last days, and Balint provided the evidence of others who knew Ferenczi then and agreed with Balint's version. Balint not surprisingly wanted to know the name of the so-called witness Jones claimed to be relying on. (Jones was not letting on about a telephone conversation of his own with Freud — or Freud's letter to him after Ferenczi's death.) But Balint sounded especially hot under the collar about what he might have taken to be the implied threat on Jones's part to be willing to go even further in invading Ferenczi's privacy. Balint insisted, "When I handed over the whole [sic] correspondence to you . . . I made the stipulation that as long as Elma and Magda are alive nothing from it may be disclosed to anybody concerning Ferenczi's private life, especially his relation to Gisela and Elma."

I had read these exchanges between Jones and Balint before I was able to succeed in seeing Balint, so I had some preparation about what I might want to be inquiring about. Balint said that he had only cooperated with Jones in supplying him with copies of the huge Freud-Ferenczi correspondence at the suggestion of Anna Freud, who had authorized Jones's biography of her father. Balint at one point said that he had withheld from Jones some letters of Ferenczi's that described Jones unflatteringly, and at another moment in our two interviews Balint expressed regret that he had helped Jones at all. Balint thought he knew who Jones's alleged witness of Ferenczi's supposed mental deterioration had been, and it turned out that Balint blamed Lajos Levy, Ferenczi's physician, as the only possible source. (Levy's widow, however, repudiated to me Jones's version of Ferenczi's death.[29] Balint evidently did not imagine that Jones could have cooked up the whole idea of a witness. In a 1933 letter to Jones, Freud had said that he thought that the pernicious anemia was a physical expression of underlying psychological forces, but that document was unavailable until recently.[30] It is possible that Jones felt licensed to publish what he did because he was implicitly relying on what was to him the highest possible authority.)

Since I had read Balint's December 19 letter to Jones, as well as Jones's stunning reference to Ferenczi's "intimacy" with Gizella's daughter, that was a subject in the back of my mind as I saw Balint. He had claimed that the reason he had not protested even more strongly about Jones's account of Ferenczi's death was that Balint knew that Jones was a dying man without much longer to live. Under the circumstances, though, it should not be surprising if I wondered to myself whether Balint had not also been intimidated by the possibility that Jones was capable of exposing still worse scandal in Ferenczi's life.

Balint was planning on publishing all the Freud-Ferenczi letters, but felt hampered because Anna Freud had not yet agreed to the project. Balint was free to publish just the Ferenczi side of the correspondence, but that would have made little sense. Balint somehow never mentioned the existence of Ferenczi's *Clinical Diary*, which he also had in his possession. (Balint also had in his files the Freud-Rank letters.) Balint was looking for help with the editing and translating chores; he sought grant money to help defray the expenses of his editorial work. When I went back to see Balint for a second interview, in the fall of 1966, I brought him a publishing proposal from an American university press, to help get the Freud-Ferenczi letters in print. (Balint had thought I could not proceed with any of my work on the history of psychoanalysis without those letters.) Balint was not quite satisfied by the terms of the offer, or perhaps also the prestige of the publishing house.

At my first interview with Balint, on the basis of what I had read in the Jones archives, I had asked Balint about the whereabouts of Ferenczi's "children." I suppose it was for fear of alienating Balint that I only brought the matter up at the end of my seeing him. Balint blankly stated that Ferenczi had not had any children. I then corrected my question, referring instead to "stepchildren," and Balint acknowledged that they did in fact still exist.

In my second interview with Balint I had virtually nothing to lose, and at some point brought up the allegation of "intimacy" between Ferenczi and Elma. Balint denied that there had been any sexual relationship but acknowledged that they had been very deeply in love. Balint told me that Elma had gone to Freud for an analysis before World War I, and that she had married a man named Laurvik shortly thereafter, but the marriage had not lasted. She was, Balint told me, now living in New York City, and I made a note to myself to try and go to see her. Balint thought that the relationship between Freud, Elma, and Ferenczi was all in the letters between Freud and Ferenczi, making a moving personal tale. Balint thought that there were so many alleged stories "worse than the truth" that it was better to have it all out in the open through the publication of the letters themselves.

It was only in the spring of 1967 that I finally got to meet Elma at her New York apartment. She was living with her younger sister Magda, who had married one of Ferenczi's siblings, and it had to be striking how the name Ferenczi was next to the doorbell on the building. (It was a modest place, not on the scale of some of the Park and Fifth Avenue apartments where Freud's orthodox followers had settled.) I remember Elma as an unusually sensitive and humanly distinguished person, an old lady of eighty, and it was impossible for me under the circumstances to do more than talk around the unspoken issue of the "intimacy" that Jones had raised privately with Balint.

She told me how she had married an American in 1915 and that only afterward had her mother gone through with marrying Ferenczi. Elma's husband had been a freelance journalist and she somewhat ruefully added that he had been "freelance" about everything in life. He had originally come to Budapest to write up a conference. While Elma was with him in California, as the world war was taking place, she had decided to marry him.

Most of my interviewing time was spent on Elma's memories of Freud, although I asked as much as I could about Ferenczi too. Her father's family had come from the same small Hungarian town as that of the Ferenczis; after getting married her mother had lived there, and so had Elma with her sister. "Dr. Ferenczi" had been "very good with children," since he took everything they did "naturally." He had loved children and animals (such as dogs), and it was from him that Elma first heard of "Professor Freud." Earlier Ferenczi had talked with Elma's mother about Freud, but her father (Geza Palos) was not so interested. Ferenczi had been in love with her mother while Gizella was still a married woman, and he wrote poetry for her.

According to Elma, her mother would never have divorced her father while the girls were not yet married. She described Geza as a "kind soft man" who had had "bad luck in everything." Early on he grew deaf and could not "communicate" with people; he was "sad." On the day of Gizella's wedding with Ferenczi, Elma's father had died of a heart attack. Elma denied that it was a suicide, a story that I had heard from Levy's widow; her husband would have been privy to all sorts of medical secrets, and it remains conceivable that Elma was not told the truth.

It was naturally easier for me to talk with Elma about Freud, and my general-interest in the history of psychoanalysis had been the basis for Elma's agreeing to see me. She reported that her analysis with Freud had taken place in Vienna and lasted three months; it has been made possible through "Dr. Ferenczi's influence," although it was Elma's parents who arranged it. She dated it in 1907 or perhaps 1908 (she was born in 1887), but added that it had taken place "at least" four or five years before her marriage. She recalled that at the time Freud had been "yet an unknown man in the world." He was "extremely nice," and although she was of course "very frightened in the beginning," he had been "very easy" to talk to.

Elma remembered how she had lain on the analytic couch while Freud had "nearly constantly" puffed on his cigars. He had been "low-voiced" and not "exaggerating" in his remarks. Elma thought that Freud had helped her "a lot," and that she had come back to Hungary "a different person." She remarked about herself having been an "unbalanced" girl in those days, someone whose "youth took hold" of her. Elma said she had not corresponded with Freud afterward, but she cited his parting words concerning what he had liked most about her, "As soon as you understood something you could make use of it." It seemed to me characteristic that Freud would enjoy working with someone normal enough to be able to benefit from the type of rational interpretive insight he could offer.

Elma said she had seen Freud only once afterward, in 1938, presumably after the German annexation of Austria. Her mother had asked her to visit him then, since she was an American citizen and could travel safely. (Elma left her husband after eight years, returning to Hungary, but was never divorced.) Elma took away an "unforgettable impression" of a man working without excitement or any "nervous" talk at all. He was like "a giant or god" as he was "peaceful and working to the last." Elma surmised that Freud must have "probably" known he would succeed in getting "safe conduct" out of Vienna. Freud did not seem to her "much changed" from when she had known him during the analysis.

Evidently Freud had told her mother at the outset of the treatment that he would not be able to see Elma for more than three months. He had been "sure" that he could help her in that time, and "really he did." Elma thought Freud had been "kind enough" to say that he had enjoyed the analysis too, and it had not just been Elma who had responded positively.

The analysis had been "very easy" for her, and "evidently" for Freud too. The treatment was not "a weight," although for "some people" it can be "an upheaval." The time she spent with him added up to "a pleasant thing"; he was so kind that it "soothed" her. Although Freud had "hardly talked about her problems," he reacted to anything that occurred to her and he had understood everything "in terms of her problems." Elma was "grateful" for the analysis in that it had "enlightened" her, so it made her life easier.

Her father had paid for the analysis, even though he was uninterested and disapproving of psychoanalysis. Elma specified that his having seen Ferenczi's "approach" to her mother shaped Geza's attitude. Geza was "very tender and passive," accepting of everything and without the "courage" to stand up to the romantic situation between Ferenczi and Gizella. Elma thought that Freud had been "very simply human," and she proposed that he was especially "fond" of Elma because of her physical resemblance to her mother.

I inquired about what Freud had so liked in Ferenczi. Elma singled out Ferenczi's "brilliance and enthusiasm." Whether two or twenty people were together, Ferenczi was the center of attention not because he wanted it so but he attracted others by talking in such "an interesting way." Elma knew that toward the end of Ferenczi's life there had been "a sort of break" with Freud, but she thought they continued to "love" one another, only they could not "agree" on certain things. Ferenczi was only fifty-nine when he died and was "very bitter." He had "weakened and weakened" until he could not move anymore. He felt his life "waning" and yet he wanted to live in the midst of his scientific work. Although he had had pernicious anemia, he had not been "confused" but could be "very silent." (Elma remembered his having been "jolly" with a young maid.) Levy was his physician, but he had not prepared "us" that Ferenczi would "surely die." Despite what Jones wrote, Ferenczi had not "been a bit crazy." Elma knew there were stories about Ferenczi's having failed to keep "quite the distance he should have with patients," but it was not anything she knew more about.

Elma understood that I had learned rather more about her relation to Ferenczi than we were discussing, but she thought that when the letters between Freud and Ferenczi appeared there would be time enough to have further information come out. The day after she saw me she wrote to correct some dates, "whether or not" I wanted to make use of the interview itself. Her sister had been certain that the wedding between her mother and "Dr. Ferenczi" had been March 1, 1919, "the same day our father died." Elma planned on asking the help of a cousin in Budapest in order to get clear the year of the analysis with Freud. Elma also asked whether Balint had known the reason for my visit with her, and she wanted me to tell her again the nature of my profession. I must have written to her, since in July she wrote me another note: "I trust you will keep your promise. Forget the 'Laurvik incident' altogether." Although I can no longer be certain, I presume Elma was concerned that I protect the privacy of the relationship between herself and Ferenczi, something we had not really touched on. But, to repeat, I suspected she was aware that I was more knowledgeable than anything I explicitly talked about.

In 1975 my *Freud and His Followers* had two chapters about Jones and Ferenczi, as I was trying to rescue Ferenczi from the reputation of having been mentally ill, and therefore someone whose ideas could be ignored.[31] I cited in passing the 1959 letters between Jones and Balint, and alluded to the triangle between Gizella, Ferenczi, and Elma. But I did not know much more than in the 1960s. Elma had died in 1970, and I never heard any protest over what I put into print about Ferenczi and her.

Only in early 1994 did the first volume of the Freud-Ferenczi letters appear in English, and it had to come as a shock to me.[32] It turned out the correct date for Elma's analysis was 1912 and that Ferenczi had treated her both before and after she had seen Freud. Ferenczi had also analyzed Gizella, who in turn was personally known to Freud. Although it had been widely understood that Ferenczi had been briefly in analysis with Freud in both 1914 and 1916, that only took on new meaning in the light of what else it was possible to know about Freud's involvement with Elma, Gizella, and Ferenczi.

I also learned of the behind-the-scenes correspondence between Gizella,

Balint, and Anna Freud about the Freud-Ferenczi letters; after Gizella's death in 1949 Elma had taken over her mother's part. By 1951 Elma sounds eager to see the correspondence in print, although aware that Anna Freud had been responsible for delaying the publication. Balint advised Elma that it would be necessary to wait a few years before the letters could succeed in getting printed.

When I had been to London in the summer of 1965, I had at least alluded with Balint to knowing about the emotional relationship between Elma and Ferenczi. By the spring of 1966 Balint had reached a tentative agreement with Anna Freud about the publication of parts of the Freud-Ferenczi correspondence. Balint was then proposing that he write a biography of Ferenczi, but he was concerned about Elma's reaction. As he wrote her:

> To write a biography of Sandor, particularly in the years that immediately preceded and followed the First World War, without mentioning the role that you played in his life, would be a falsification, or at least a *supressio veri* [suppression of truth]. Moreover, as you can well imagine, a certain number of people know (by hearsay) an approximate version of that history, and if the official biography were to remain silent on this point, it would give rise to fresh gossip and new rumors.

Balint was obviously trying to be as careful as possible with Elma: "I ask you to think about this very personal and delicate problem, and let me know your feelings in this matter."[33]

The letters reveal that Ferenczi had fallen in love with Elma while analyzing her, and that it was Ferenczi who had proposed that she go to Freud for an analysis, partly to find out if she shared his own feelings. (In later years, Ferenczi, who wanted children of his own, expressed his resentment at how Freud had thought he should still marry Gizella, although she was eight years older than himself.) Elma had written her memories[34] to Balint, and he replied in the spring of 1966:

> You asked me how many and what sorts of people know about that episode. This is a question that is of course impossible to answer. Let me say simply that when I began my analysis in Berlin in 1921, I heard all kinds of gossip on the subject; and having begun another analysis with Sandor, I found myself in great difficulties during the first few weeks of sessions, because I felt a strong resistance to saying what I believed I knew about the matter.[35]

By 1968 Balint was proposing to use a pseudonym for Elma. Balint then died in 1970, Anna Freud in 1982, and others became responsible for the appearance of the Freud-Ferenczi correspondence, which was in the end published in its entirety; volume I created such a literary sensation in Paris that 7,000 copies sold out within the first eight weeks.

Even before the Freud-Ferenczi letters started officially to come out, scholars were starting to study them in manuscript form. In 1990 we learned bits and pieces about Elma's depressed feelings before her analysis with Ferenczi, and that a boyfriend had committed suicide. When she had seen Ferenczi in treatment, as she wrote Balint in 1966, she felt she had been "immature, spiteful, vain, and love-starved."[36]

Nothing prepared me for the fact that throughout most of volume 1 of the Freud-Ferenczi correspondence Elma plays a central role: if only because of her relationship with Ferenczi she emerges as one of the more important female patients in Freud's career. The Elma Palos story may eventually seem like one of the more shocking stories connected with the early history of psychoanalysis, and I think now I understand better Anna Freud's impulse to allow only the partial publication of these letters. It is a mystery how she thought the truth might be shielded, without any such censorship calling even more attention to what had been suppressed. The full tale could be damaging to the pretensions some psychoanalysts have had that they have been working in behalf of a developed science.

Elma first comes up in the Freud-Ferenczi correspondence in January 1911, when her mother was taking her to Vienna to correct a scar that had resulted from a tooth problem Elma had had. Ferenczi and Gizella also had in mind asking Freud's advice about "a rather difficult matter (marriage and love affair . . .)" of Elma's. Freud did not get to see Gizella and Elma until the next month, but he alarmed Ferenczi by making a verbal diagnosis of "dementia praecox" about Elma. Ferenczi said he was both depressed as well as surprised by such a serious-sounding diagnosis, and Freud wrote back to explain himself:

> Frau G.'s visit was very nice; her conversation is particularly charming. Her daughter is made of coarser material, participated little, and for the most part had a blank expression on her face. Otherwise, of course, there was not the slightest abnormality noticeable in her.

Ferenczi at the time was centrally involved with Gizella, Elma being only her elder daughter, but still Freud had startled and worried his Hungarian pupil. Of course, Freud was, like Ferenczi, not a psychiatrist, but they both had trained as neurologists; that professional background underlies the looseness about invoking such a dire psychiatric category as dementia praecox (nowadays schizophrenia) with only that one meeting to go on. In defending himself, Freud explained that "the diagnosis says nothing about its practical significance."[37]

In July 1911 Ferenczi reported to Freud that Elma was now in treatment with him. Freud wrote back about his skepticism concerning how far Ferenczi could get therapeutically with her, but Ferenczi thought things were going well and he promised to report orally to Freud. In October there was a suicide "on her account" by one of the young men in whom she was interested. Within a month Ferenczi had reacted to Elma's distress by what he called "fantasies" of his marrying Elma. In no time at all (less than a month) after that letter Ferenczi was reporting that Elma had "won" his heart.[38]

Freud advised Ferenczi to break off the treatment of Elma, and Gizella turned to Freud for advice. Freud replied to her in a letter that he wrote as if it could possibly remain "completely" between them. Freud interpreted Ferenczi's marital preference for Elma as due to Ferenczi's craving for children, which Freud attributed to Ferenczi's so-called homosexual craving for offspring: "It is the case with him that his homosexuality imperiously demands a child and that he carries within him revenge against his mother from the strongest impressions of childhood."[39] Gizella's age, marriage, and children meant to Freud that she could be seen as a mother figure for Ferenczi.

Ferenczi kept writing about the possibility of his marrying Elma, although her father was unwilling to bless the proposed union. Once Elma hesitated to proceed maritally with Ferenczi, he thought she needed treatment for an "illness," and Ferenczi decided that he could not continue her analysis. Elma agreed to go to Freud instead, which Ferenczi saw as his turning her over to him. Freud referred to Elma now as a "charming young woman," one who was also "noble," but Freud said he was doubtful whether the complexities of the situation would be favorable for analytic success. Ferenczi reported that Elma had wanted to continue to be treated by Ferenczi, without her suspecting that Freud had been "opposed to their marriage."[40]

Freud wrote in detail to Ferenczi about the course of the analysis of Elma. She had, for example, started off "quite inhibited, obviously wants to be the good child, to please, to be treated with tenderness; fears loss of love if she admits something." In the meantime, Geza Palos got into the psychoanalytic act: Elma's father, Ferenczi told Freud, was supposedly "a very eccentric, self-centered person," and he "was somewhat upset by the details of the analysis, which Elma, incomprehensibly, shared with him and which he doesn't have a clue about, wants to write you a letter."[41] So there were missives going back and forth between Freud and Ferenczi, Freud and Gizella, and Elma was writing to both her parents as well as Ferenczi.

Ferenczi was still stung by Freud's original diagnosis of dementia praecox and was putting the best face on it by interpreting it in the light of her supposed inability to love. Ferenczi sent quotations to Freud that were extracted from Elma's letters to himself and to her mother. Ferenczi tried to resume his relationship with Gizella, but said that his "attempt at intimacy ended with sadness and depression on both sides."[42]

By February, Freud had changed his diagnosis to a far more benign one, and he wrote Ferenczi that "the only legitimate diagnosis" would be "infantilism,"[43] a characteristic that according to Freud's theories afflicted all neurotic mankind. It was a significant retraction on Freud's part from an outlook which, based on my own one meeting with Elma, struck me as incomprehensible. Freud could not have been then toying with a diagnosis of psychosis in order to discourage Ferenczi's infatuation with Elma, since at the time Freud first invoked the dire-sounding diagnosis Ferenczi had not yet lost his heart to her.

Ferenczi, in the same spirit as Freud had written to Gizella in confidence, wrote Freud likewise, as he continued to send portions of Elma's correspondence, at the same time that he could visit Vienna to discuss matters with Freud, although Elma was not to know of his trip. (When Ferenczi later complained against psychoanalytic secrecy he knew what he was talking about.) Ferenczi was on better terms with Gizella, although he had worries about Elma being "normal" and "healthy" as well as perhaps unable to love.[44]

Freud worked out some elaborate-sounding hypotheses about the nature of Elma's case, and a letter in March to Ferenczi includes a large diagram outlining Freud's schematization of Elma's history. Freud thought he had made "real progress"[45] with Elma, and he had decided to send her home for Easter despite her desire to stay on longer with him.

In April, Ferenczi suggested to Elma that they resume their own analytic relationship, and she "agreed rather easily" to once again become Ferenczi's patient. By August Ferenczi had "given up Elma's analysis and in so doing severed the last thread of the connection between us." Elma was "in despair," as Ferenczi accompanied her home "and handed her over to her mother."[46] At this point it is hard not to at least suspect that Elma was being victimized by the medical narcissism of both Freud and Ferenczi, and the whole human impropriety of the psychoanalytically inspired meddling in her life.

Part of the interest in the story of Elma stems from its fitting into a pattern that looks like overweening ambition in Freud's actual clinical practices. For example, when Jones was sent by Freud for an analysis with Ferenczi, Freud was analyzing a woman who had been living with Jones for some years. Freud and Ferenczi wrote back and forth about their respective cases, and Freud also sent letters to Jones about the treatment of his lady friend, just as Freud could be indiscreet about Jones with Freud's own patient, Jones's longstanding lover. (Freud's most famous papers on technique, advocating neutrality, were written in 1911–15, virtually at the same time as the height of the Elma-Ferenczi tale.)

It seems to me not enough to characterize such invasions of human privacy as analytic "indiscretions," since they seemed to be part and parcel of Freud's chosen way of proceeding, whatever he wrote recommending that others proceed with detachment as if analysis could be comparable to some sort of surgical procedure. At one time over thirty years ago I was startled by how Freud could send a senior analyst, Victor Tausk, into analysis with a newcomer (Helene Deutsch) who was then in analysis with Freud himself; Freud had been rejecting Tausk's entreaties to be analyzed by Freud, and a few months after Freud broke up Tausk's treatment with his analyst, Tausk — who had been subject to depressions — committed suicide.[47] In those days, when I first heard about the Tausk incident, long a guarded analytic secret, I also discovered that Freud had personally analyzed his youngest child, Anna[48]; that too had been a closely held secret, but in the light of the Freud-Ferenczi letters, and how they touch on Elma, such licenses on Freud's part seem like the tip of the iceberg, or what should have been expected.

The human consequences for Gizella, Elma, and Ferenczi were not ended by Ferenczi's terminating Elma's analysis. Gizella persisted in thinking that it might be best for Sandor and Elma to get married, even after Elma had gone off to America. And it took years of vacillation on Ferenczi's part before at last he went through with marrying Gizella. At Ferenczi's request it was Freud who made the final marriage proposal in a letter to Gizella.

It seems at best ironic that Freud allowed himself to get so intimately enmeshed in the lives of patients and followers; at the same time the central reproach that orthodox analysts, following Freud, have had against Ferenczi was that he went too far in proposing that analytic technique become less distant and more humane. Over time Ferenczi's name became a symbol for advising therapeutic flexibility, and the formal ideals of neutrality, abstinence, and lack of analytic activity seem more and more to have been artifacts constructed as ideals that were nonetheless at odds with Freud's own conduct.

Volume 2 of the Freud-Ferenczi correspondence is relatively undramatic, as Ferenczi has finally settled down to preparing to marry Gizella. But the book, which carries the relationship of Freud and Ferenczi up to 1919, contains one more human tangle, this time between Freud, the Hungarian Anton von Freund, Ferenczi, von Freund's second wife, von Freund's favorite sister, and von Freund's married mistress. Von Freund was afflicted with cancer as well as marital problems, and was immensely grateful for the help of psychoanalysis.

One can only wonder whether Elma ever adequately realized how her own private world had been intruded upon. She was in 1912 only an impressionable twenty-five years old, and Freud, following Ferenczi, had captured her spiritually. I am not suggesting that Elma's gratitude to Freud was lacking in subjectively felt genuineness. Detached outsiders could at least be entitled to shake their heads at all these curious goings on.

On the one hand, all education, and most forms of psychotherapy, have to involve the use of authority for the sake of promoting ultimate self-development. Jean-Jacques Rousseau once wrote about the need to "force" people to be "free." Yet it is also true that with the best of intentions do-gooders can become fanatics, threatening the very individuality they set out to promote. One can ask whether Freud was not encouraging people to go beyond the limits of intrusion which can be morally justified.

From today's perspective it looks at best as naïve for Freud and his followers to allow themselves to get involved with so many human dilemmas which are apt to look like so many cans of worms. In our own time physicians, using the most advanced psychopharmacological drugs, are fully capable of acting in a highly authoritarian fashion. Lord Acton's old liberal adage that power corrupts, and that absolute power tends to corrupt absolutely, is worth remembering in the context of all psychotherapy.

Freud inspired a messianic spirit so that common-sense cautions were often thrown to the winds. Freud wrote Ferenczi in 1913, "We are in possession of the truth; I am as convinced of that as I was fifteen years ago."[49] Critics of Freud had all along been making sound and respectful reservations about his approach.[50] But I do not think that Freud's worst enemies earlier in the past century could have imagined just went on between Freud, Elma, and Ferenczi. It is all the more striking that Freud thought of himself as primarily a scientist rather than a leader of a new political and religious cause.

It is possible to lean over backward in favor of Freud's courage in trying out new therapeutic possibilities. As Freud wrote in 1910 to Oskar Pfister,

> Discretion is incompatible with a satisfactory description of an analysis; to provide the latter one would have to be unscrupulous, give away, betray, behave like an artist who buys paints with his wife's house-keeping money or uses the furniture as fire-wood to warm the studio for his model. Without a trace of that kind of unscrupulousness the job cannot be done.[51]

If Freud erred in what he wrote or did, it was a result of his outgoingness, and it is possible to attribute to him the best of motives. But then even if it can be a relief to find out that Freud was by no means as cold and neutral as his formal recommendations to beginning analysts appear to suggest, he could drop people arbitrarily. In Ferenczi's case the final falling out between the men came over the issue of therapeutic technique. It might sound ironic now that Freud was capable of chastising Ferenczi in 1931 over new technical devices: "Either you relate this or you conceal it. The latter, as you may well think, is dishonorable. What one does in one's technique one has to defend openly. Besides, both ways soon come together. Even if you don't say so yourself it will soon get known, just as I knew it before you told me."[52] We now know that Ferenczi was able to retort,

> You will probably recall that it was I who declared it to be necessary also to communicate matters of technique, so long as one applies them methodically; you were more in favor of being sparing with communications about technique. Now *you* think it would be dishonorable to keep silent, and I must counter by saying that the *pace* of publication should be relegated to the tact and insight of the author.[53]

Although psychoanalysis is now over a hundred years old, and the continuing literature about its development and crises show no sign of slowing down, it may well seem time that we once again try to evaluate the contents of Freud's achievement. A sober assessment of what he accomplished may make less likely the kind of shallow polemical assaults on Freud that have become so fashionable lately. Freud can well have been wrong about many central issues, but the fact that it has taken this long to establish his errors should be a tribute to the vitality of his system of thought.

Whatever the merits of Freud's concepts turn out to be, there was I think an enduringly attractive feature to these people to the extent to which they found human meaning in their mutual devotion to the "cause" of psychoanalysis. Their shared militant commitment, amounting to a religious kind of devotion, meant an immense amount of self-scrutiny and soul searching. If despite everything Freud and his followers were still capable of being self-deceptive, especially in the name of science, that lends support to Freud's principle that we are all inevitably caught in the power of forces which necessarily remain unconscious.

Any lessons that can be drawn from Elma Palos's story should include a tolerant understanding of the hearts of the various people who were involved. It should be a Freudian truism that psychoanalysis will deserve to thrive the more honestly we are able to confront its past. Yet Kant long ago insisted on the ethical principle that people be used as ends, not means, a standard that psychotherapists might make more use of. I hope it will be understandable why it has been impossible for me now to follow Elma's 1967 injunction that I forget the "Laurvik incident," despite whatever promise I once made to her.

The whole story of the Budapest school, under what principles it arose and how it compared with the more standard approach advocated by Freud's orthodox followers, makes a fascinating tale. It becomes impossible, the more one knows, to detach abstract concepts from the fallible people who were involved; the conflict between Freud and Ferenczi is not quite like that of any of the other difficulties in the history of Freud's work. And yet this particular set of disagreements, which can be seen as a combination of great success as well as notable failure, has to enrich our understanding of what was at issue at the time. Following the intricacies of what happened then is bound to have lessons for us today, even if it should be unnecessary for us to rush to any premature moralistic judgments.

Notes

1. Andre Haynal, *Controversies in Psychoanalytic Method: Freud, Ferenczi, Balint*, translated by Elizabeth Holder, with a preface by Daniel N. Stern (London, Karnac, 1988).
2. *The Clinical Diary of Sandor Ferenczi*, edited by Judith Dupont, translated by Michael Balint and Nicola Zarday Johnson (Cambridge, Mass., Harvard University Press, 1988).
3. "Sandor Ferenczi," *Standard Edition*, Vol. 22, pp. 227–29.
4. Eva Brabant-Gerö, *Ferenczi et L'École Hongroise de Psychanalyse* (Paris, l'Harmattan, 1993); Michelle Moreau Ricaud, *Michael Balint: Le Renouveau de l'Ecole de Budapest* (Paris, Érès, 2000).
5. Haynal, *Controversies*, *op. cit.*, p. 85.
6. Andre Haynal, *Psychoanalysis and the Sciences: Epistemology-History*, translated by Elizabeth Holder (Berkeley, University of California Press, 1993), p. 125.
7. *Ibid.*, p. 250.
8. Helene Deutsch, *The Therapeutic Process, the Self, and Female Psychology: Collected Psychoanalytic Papers*, edited and with an Introduction, Paul Roazen (New Brunswick, N.J., Transaction, Publishers, 1992), Ch. 19, pp. 223–38.
9. *The Clinical Diary of Sandor Ferenczi, op cit.*.
10. *Ibid.*, pp. xviii-xix, xxiv.
11. *Ibid.*, p. 11.
12. *Ibid.*, p. 62.
13. *Ibid.*
14. *Ibid.*, p. 86.
15. *Ibid.*, p. 92.
16. *Ibid.*, p. 93
17. *Ibid.*, pp. 187–88.
18. *Ibid.*, p. 188.
19. *Ibid.*, p. 194.
20. *Ibid.*, p. 210.
21. *Ibid.*, p. 212.
22. *Ibid.*, p. 213.
23. *The Complete Correspondence of Sigmund Freud and Ernest Jones 1908–1939*, ed. R. Andrew Paskauskas (Cambridge, Mass., Harvard University Press, 1993), p. 721.
24. See Paul Roazen, *The Historiography of Psychoanalysis*, *op. cit.*, pp. 297–99.
25. I owe this idea to Dr. Ernst Falzeder.
26. See Roazen, *The Historiography of Psychoanalysis*, *op. cit.*, pp. 155–65.
27. *International Journal of Psychoanalysis*, Vol. 34 (1958), p. 68.
28. Erich Fromm, "Psychoanalysis — Science or Party Line?," *op. cit.*, pp. 131–44.
29. See Roazen, *How Freud Worked*, *op. cit.*, Ch. 6.
30. *The Complete Correspondence of Sigmund Freud and Ernest Jones*, *op.cit.*, p. 721.
31. See Paul Roazen, "The Freud-Jones Letters," in *Behind the Scenes: Freud in Correspondence*, ed. Patrick Mahony, Carlo Bonomi, & Jan Stensson (Oslo, Scandinavian University Press, 1997), pp. 273–287. See also Roazen, *The Historiography of Psychoanalysis*, *op. cit.*, pp. 113–23.
32. See Roazen, *The Historiography of Psychoanalysis*, *op. cit.*, pp. 125–31.
33. See Andre Haynal, "Introduction," in Eva Brabant, Ernst Falzeder, and Patrizia

Giampieri-Deutsch (editors), *The Correspondence of Sigmund Freud and Sandor Ferenczi*, Vol. I, *1908–1914*, translated by Peter T. Hoffer (Cambridge, Mass., Harvard University Press, 1994), p. xxxii.
34. Andre Haynal, "Brefs apercus sur l'histoire de la correspondance Freud-Ferenczi," *Revue Internationale Histoire de la Psychanalyse*, Vol. 2 (1989), pp. 248–329.
35. Haynal, "Introduction," *op. cit.*, p. xxxiii.
36. Martin Stanton, *Sandor Ferenczi: Reconsidering Active Intervention* (London, Free Association Books, 1990), p. 18.
37. *The Correspondence of Freud and Ferenczi*, Vol. I, *op. cit.*, pp. 248, 253, 254.
38. *Ibid.*, pp. 304, 312, 318.
39. *Ibid.*, pp. 319–20.
40. *Ibid.*, pp. 324–26.
41. *Ibid.*, pp. 326–27.
42. *Ibid.*, p. 336.
43. *Ibid.*, p. 340.
44. *Ibid.*, p. 347.
45. *Ibid.*, pp. 351, 356.
46. *Ibid.*, pp. 369, 402.
47. Paul Roazen, *Brother Animal: The Story of Freud and Tausk* (New York, Alfred A. Knopf, 1969; 2nd edition, with new Introduction, New Brunswick, N.J., Transaction Publishers, 1990).
48. Paul Roazen, "Freud's Analysis of Anna," in Robert Prince, ed., *The Death of Psychoanalysis: Murder? Suicide? Or Rumor Greatly Exaggerated?* (Northvale, N.J., Aronson, 1999), pp.141–51.
49. *The Correspondence of Freud and Ferenczi*, Vol. I, *op. cit.*, p. 483.
50. Roazen, *The Historiography of Psychoanalysis*, *op. cit.*, pp. 429–34.
51. Sigmund Freud, *Psychoanalysis and Faith: Dialogues with the Rev. Oskar Pfister*, ed. Heinrich Meng and Ernst L. Freud, translated by Erich Mosbacher (New York, Basic Books, 1963), p. 38.
52. Quoted in Ernest Jones, *The Life and Work of Sigmund Freud*, Vol. 3, *op. cit.*, pp. 163–64.
53. *The Correspondence of Sigmund Freud and Sandor Ferenczi*, Vol. 3, *1920–1933*, ed. Ernst Falzeder and Eva Brabant, with the collaboration of Patrizia Giampieri-Deutsch, translated by Peter T. Hoffer (Cambridge, Mass., Harvard University Press, 2000), p. 424.

4

Kleinianism: The English School

It sometimes seems as if the history of psychoanalysis consists only of a series of recurrent blow-ups, each of which plays a part in the general mythology about the story of the growth of Freud's following. I think that these well-publicized, if still little understood, difficulties repeatedly have arisen because of an inadequate degree of normal give-and-take within psychoanalytic communities. For if differences of opinion were more of a commonplace matter, and people were encouraged to disagree without its involving stakes of personal friendship, loyalty, and above all, transferences, then volcanic eruptions would be less likely to break out.

The Freud-Klein Controversies 1941–1945, edited by Pearl King and Riccardo Steiner,[1] is a scrupulously detailed account of the struggle within the British Psychoanalytic Society over the ideas and practices of Melanie Klein (1882–1960). I know of no comparable set of key documents apart from the *Minutes of the Vienna Psychoanalytic Society.*[2] Like the *Minutes*, *The Freud-Klein Controversies* were not edited by professional historians but by members of the psychoanalytic family, and therefore both texts suffer from a lack of academic distance ideally brought to bear on primary historical evidence. Although the *Minutes* at the time of their publication went largely unreviewed and not professionally discussed, I have already read two fine accounts of *The Freud-Klein Controversies*[3]. So there is reason to think that some advances have been made in the integration of psychoanalysis into the history of ideas as it should be studied at universities.

The editing of *The Freud-Klein Controversies* leaves, I think, something to be desired. Both King and Steiner are members of the British Psychoanalytic Society, and inevitably they are trying to tidy up the story of their group. For example, the book opens with a series of "biographical notes" on the main participants in the Freud-Klein controversies. There is much interesting material here, but one has to be on the alert to notice what is being left out or glossed over. The first name listed among the participants is that of Michael Balint; we are told that "Jones, who found him difficult to deal with, arranged for him to settle in Manchester."[4] Balint, as we have alluded to in the last chapter, was an independent and original thinker and a student of Ferenczi's to boot, so of course an autocrat like Jones would not want Balint in London, although Balint did end up living there. On the other hand, Balint was sufficiently politic for Jones not to have barred him from coming to settle in England at all.

To cite another example of the tact of the editors, they write that Anna Freud "worked with her father,"[5] although they neglect to mention that she was analyzed by him; that curious relationship between Freud and Anna has become widely known within the profession, and one wonders why the editors do not specify its occurrence. And Karin Stephen, a sister-in-law of Virginia Woolf's, is said to have never been "made a training analyst (perhaps because of her deafness)"[6]; I was authoritatively told that what kept her back was the emotional instability that eventually led to her suicide, which goes unmentioned in *The Freud-Klein Controversies*. Perhaps I am being too picky about these notes and about the editing of this volume in general; on the whole, it does succeed at a high level, and the editors deserve our congratulations and thanks. Surely every student of Kleinianism will find *The Freud-Klein Controversies* indispensable. The volume is a truly remarkable achievement.

Still, let me point out some of the larger problems with this text, which I think can lead us to what can be learned from it. At no point do the editors weigh and assess what we know about Freud's own attitude toward Klein's work. Some of this information has long existed in print.[7] But further evidence of Freud's attitude toward Klein exists. Freud was partly offended by Klein's criticisms of Anna Freud, which Freud thought an indirect way of Klein's challenging him. Freud deemed her a schismatic and a "deviant," and this harsh assessment, known to his intimates, licensed the quarrel that took place after his death and that is painstakingly recorded in *The Freud-Klein Controversies*.

Anna Freud and Melanie Klein had led rival branches of child analysis since the 1920s. Then when the Freuds, along with their Viennese supporters, moved to London in 1938, the fat was in the fire. London was chosen for Freud, not Anna, since it was from her point of view a trouble spot. Switzerland was deemed Jung's territory; otherwise Freud might have safely chosen to go there instead while fleeing from the Nazis. (Switzerland was close to Freud's Vienna doctors, but expensive to live in; the Netherlands was another option considered. Both countries could then be considered less safe from the Nazis than England.) As it happened, everything remained quiet in London as long as Freud lived; then Klein and some of her allies left for the countryside during the beginning of the war. As analysts returned to London in 1942, the worst of the ideological fight broke out. Anna Freud, like her father, regarded Klein as heretical and sought to do what she could to check Klein's influence.

The most important figure here is Edward Glover[8]. He has been savagely referred to in the Kleinian literature, and Steiner tells us that Glover's forecasts for the British Society were "apocalyptic and ferociously one-sided." Steiner also calls Glover "fanatical."[9] King is decent in her biographical notes, explaining that Glover "was a good administrator" and helped "Jones in his negotiations with the British Medical Association."[10] For years Glover was Jones's deputy, the second-in-command. By the outbreak of World War II, when Jones retired to the country, Glover was the effective president of the Society and slated formally to succeed Jones. The offices Glover simultaneously held were Chairman of the Training Committee, Scientific Secretary, Director of the Society's Clinic, and also Honorary Secretary of the International Psychoanalytic Association.

Glover had also been the analyst of Melanie Klein's daughter, Melitta Schmideberg. *Cherchez la femme* is no idle historical principle. Although it has widely been alleged in Kleinian circles that Glover behaved improperly about Melitta, I think, on the basis of my interviews in the 1960s with both of them, that she was, as her mother thought, mentally ill. I do not think that Glover handled the situation successfully, for he allowed himself to get sucked into a seductive set-up. Melitta had private scores of her own to settle against the woman she referred to with me as "Mrs. Klein." But Glover may well have come to the conclusion, with the backing of Anna Freud and her Viennese allies, that now was the propitious time to strike at Kleinianism. I do not have any idea of what can be meant by one particular biographical note: "Many of those present felt that Jones was unable to control Melitta."[11] What was Jones supposed to have done? Melitta was already qualified as a member of the British Society.

A central point that has so far escaped the literature is that Glover was an exceptionally kindly and gentle spirit. Some, like myself, thought he was a historical victim of what happened. I mention the positive aspects of his character because people nowadays feel appallingly free to write about him only disparagingly. For example, an exceptionally conscientious student of the history of psychoanalysis has called Glover "an abrasive and unpopular man,"[12] an overall judgment to which I take the strongest possible exception. It is true that Glover could be combative in print — he had attacked Otto Rank's work — and Glover would later be independent enough to go after Jung, Heinz Hartmann, and others.[13]

Glover, who lived until 1972, is the central figure, at least for me, in *The Freud-Klein Controversies*. His resignation from the Society, which took place early in 1944, put an end to the battling. Glover and Anna Freud had temporarily been allied, but it was Glover who led the fight; once he concluded that it was a lost cause, he quit. And Anna Freud withdrew then from the Training Committee. (Although it does not come up in *The Freud-Klein Controversies*, Anna accepted Jones's appointment to replace Glover as Honorary Secretary of the IPA.) Only later was the arrangement worked out so that her own people could be trained in a separate group without being "contaminated" by Kleinian ideas.

I interviewed many of the participants who appear in *The Freud-Klein Controversies*, and as I read the documents now they sound in my mind like the voices of people I once knew. Glover thought he was standing up for principles, and doing what Freud, and Anna, felt and wanted. I do not think that Glover was incapable of making his own independent assessment; on the contrary, I suspect that he and Anna Freud dealt with each other at arm's length. (His earlier receptivity to Klein might have left Anna Freud enduringly wary.) But he allowed himself to become captured by Melitta, who in my view — and that of Jones too — was a malicious but clever paranoiac.

The editorial apparatus to *The Freud-Klein Controversies* does tilt away from the Anna Freud side. She presented a paper on May 5, 1943 before the British Society, but we are not even told the title of her presentation. When Glover wrote a memorandum (replying to James Strachey) justifying Glover's resignation from the Training Committee, it gets assigned no date. The publication of *The Freud-Klein Controversies* is itself a form of triumph of the Kleinian point of view.

I should also add that, in my opinion, Kleinianism stood for some pretty extreme ideas. She, for example, was proposing to cure children of their "psychoses," although without any medical training herself, and she had the messianic idea that all children should be analyzed as a prophylactic measure. To compound how abstract psychoanalytic debates could be, throughout *The Freud-Klein Controversies*, which take up almost 1,000 pages, virtually no clinical material whatever appears. One rare clinical example has to do with a Kleinian mentioning a girl of sixteen months who played a favorite game with her parents: picking "small imaginary bits off a brown embossed leather screen in the dining-room, carrying these pretended bits of food across the room in her finger and thumb and putting them into the mouth of father and mother alternately." The analyst felt justified in treating this as the girl's feeding her parents "with symbolic faeces."[14]

There are plenty of extravagances in *The Freud-Klein Controversies*. I am not sure that the distinctions between the theoretical position of Glover and Anna Freud, as contrasted with that of the Kleinians, are always sound and down to earth enough. As a matter of fact, I think both sides in this dispute are almost equally theological. If I had to pick one over the other, and I would only do so with the greatest reluctance, I would steer clear of the

Kleinian position; her concepts were often in principle unverifiable, and she was throughout this contest engaged in a substantial power move. I know something of how fruitful Klein's concepts have proven to be in enlivening psychoanalytic thinking, but my reaction is colored by what I take to be the editorial stacking of the deck for Klein throughout *The Freud-Klein Controversies.*

For example, one of Klein's supporters in the debate was Paula Heimann. The history of psychoanalysis has been beset with problems associated with unresolved transferences and countertransferences, but it is striking that Paula Heimann was then in analysis with Klein. Later she had a second analysis with Klein that ended unhappily. At that time Mrs. Klein sent formal notes to the members of the British Society indicating that Paula Heimann no longer was a representative of the Klein group. Paula Heimann went on to serve on international committees, but I must say that when I met her she was hardly one of the most impressive people I had come across, certainly not compared with someone of Glover's stature.

One 1940 letter of James Strachey's to Glover is cited by the editors and deserves to be quoted here:

> I should rather like you to know (for your personal information) that — if it comes to a show-down — I'm very strongly in favour of a compromise at all costs. The trouble seems to me to be with extremism, on both sides. My own view is that Mrs. K. has made some highly important contributions to PA, but that it's absurd to make out (a) that they cover the whole subject or (b) that their validity is axiomatic. On the other hand I think it's equally ludicrous for Miss F. to maintain that PA is a Game Reserve belonging to the F. family and that Mrs. K.'s ideas are totally subversive.
>
> These attitudes on both sides are of course purely religious and the very antithesis of science. They are also (on both sides) infused by, I believe, a desire to dominate the situation and in particular the future — which is why both sides lay so much stress on the training of candidates; actually, of course, it's a megalomaniac mirage to suppose that you can control the opinions of people you analyse beyond a very limited point. But in any case it ought naturally to be the aim of a training analysis to put the trainee into a position to arrive at his own decisions upon moot points — not to stuff him with your own private dogmas.
>
> In fact I feel like Mercutio about it. Why should these wretched fascists and (bloody foreigners) communists invade our peaceful compromising island?[15]

The reader of *The Freud-Klein Controversies* will see how many angels can successfully dance on the head of a pin. All the more striking is the number of discussions that occur under the heading of "scientific" meetings.

Strachey's point of view has not yet succeeded in placing a plague on both houses. But I think that what he had to say about training analyses was right to the point. Nowadays in France some of the most far-seeing analysts are proposing to abolish the institution of a training analysis. As I have already mentioned, the idea was in the first place Jung's, and I believe that he came up with it out of dissatisfaction with Freud as an unanalyzed leader of the movement; the proposal was beaten back, with the help of Victor Tausk and Otto Rank, at the Budapest Congress in 1918, and went through at the international meetings only after Freud had already fallen ill with cancer. Yet it is now heralded as an implication of Lacan's admitted genius to question the requirement of training analyses, but no one seems to remember that Glover was calling attention to this issue some sixty years ago.

A central defect of *The Freud-Klein Controversies* is that, with the exception of Pearl King's reference to him as an administrator, no other view of Glover is presented other than the one adopted by the partisan Kleinians. I cannot believe that Anna Freud's papers do not show a different side of the story. For some reason, Steiner reports that he "regretted that only limited material from Anna Freud's archives have been available to the editors," and he maintains that "it has been impossible to consult . . . the papers of Anna Freud. . . . "[16] But those of us on this side of the Atlantic have been free to browse through all her fascinating files which are open at the Library of Congress. The papers that most need study would have been those of Glover, but in the absence of any other interest in them in London, they got destroyed on the instructions of his executor.

It may seem pedantic to some, but I want to point out one striking omission from the bibliography of *The Freud-Klein Controversies*. After the quarrel was over, Glover published critiques of the Kleinian system; one appeared as a separate pamphlet, and a shorter version came out in *The Psychoanalytic Study of the Child*.[17] Neither of these is cited in *The Freud-Klein Controversies*. Edward Bibring's 1947 hostile dissection of Kleinianism[18] goes unmentioned, while Hannah Segal, who became the prophet of the Kleinian sect, has her books explicating Klein cited. The text of *The Freud-Klein Controversies* includes an unnecessary number of references to minor articles by the editors. To round out what may seem a scholastic set of complaints, the index of names is sorely inaccurate. Psychoanalysis should be destined to be more than an aspect of the history of religion.

So many heated controversies have accompanied the story of psychoanalysis, there may be only one thing everyone agrees on: the commonplace notion that because Freud was a man, he could not do justice to the psychology of women. It turns out, however, that while Freud was alive, women psychoanalysts went straight to the top of his movement. No career in the twentieth century was more open to female talent, and Freud must take at least some credit for this phenomenon. While he was still practicing, there were more prominent women in psychoanalysis than would be the case within medical psychology today, more than sixty years after his death.

Janet Sayers's brilliant *Mothers of Psychoanalysis: Helene Deutsch, Karen Horney, Anna Freud, Melanie Klein*[19] demonstrates the key role that four notable women played in the early history of psychoanalysis. As a group, they shifted the center of gravity of Freud's work toward a mother-oriented psychology, which was in keeping with what someone like Ferenczi had also had in mind.

One of them, his youngest daughter Anna, followed most closely in Freud's footsteps, yet even she concentrated on working clinically with children and observing their problems. Freud's own distance from the world of child analysis meant that publicly he could claim neutrality between the rival efforts of Melanie Klein and Anna. The other prominent women, such as Helene Deutsch and Karen Horney, sometimes pursued social insights, and on other occasions followed more biological lines of thought, but they all were managing to develop in directions that disagreed at least somewhat with Freud's own original position. Sayers offers us biographical sketches and links these four women's ideas to their lives, producing sparkling essays in intellectual history.

Not long ago, any women like these early analysts who tried to emphasize some of the psychological differences between the sexes might have been accused of being traitors to the female sex. Now, however, we are in a later phase of the politics of the women's movement, so that that same attention to sexual differences is acceptable; such differences are taken to be grounds for women's special needs and entitlements. These early analysts, who once might have seemed old hat, are now taken to be valuable precursors.

While these four women had complicated personal relations with one another, and sometimes criticized each other's writings, Sayers ties all their contributions together as an aspect of the history of ideas. Sayers herself never adopts any ideological slant of her own and proceeds to describe each analyst's work in its best possible light. *Mothers of Psychoanalysis* is a triumph of dispassionate inquiry in a field notorious for being a minefield of intolerances. Historians are at their best when, like Sayers, they have no axes to grind.

The development of psychoanalysis in Great Britain has differed from its course in North America. Its British practitioners have included a higher proportion of so-called lay, nonmedical analysts; and psychiatry in Britain has held itself aloof from the influence of analysis. In terms of prestige, cultural impact, and money, British analysis has lagged far behind what Freud's followers achieved on the other side of the Atlantic. Yet, in its intellectual vitality, analysis has been as vigorous and challenging in Britain as anywhere.

Melanie Klein was chiefly responsible for the special ideological course that analysis took in London. From the time of her arrival from the Continent in 1926 she had the backing of Ernest Jones, whose wife and children she treated. Jones was at that time the powerholder in the British Psychoanalytic Society, and Klein had ideas and techniques that were to shape the distinctive contribution of British analysis.

Starting in the mid–1920s Klein proposed to treat children with an undiluted analytic approach. She thought that the use of play with children could substitute for the absence of free associations, and that children develop transferences which can be directly interpreted to them. Unlike Anna Freud, who at the time was the alternative figure with proposals about how children could be analyzed, Klein did not undertake to use a pedagogic approach or rely on parents as an aspect of the environment of the child. Klein was so missionary in her convictions that she thought all children could benefit from analysis as a prophylaxis.

Up until 1938, when Freud and the Viennese analysts immigrated to London, Klein was such a dominant force in British analysis that some thought the British might constitute a new heretical schism. Freud himself abhorred the direction of Klein's work, although in his published writing he tactfully acknowledged her ideas. Freud felt that Jones was using Klein to attack Freud's daughter Anna and in that way to counter some of Freud's own most cherished convictions.

During World War II, as we have seen, the British Psychoanalytic Society held its series of "controversial discussions" to determine whether Klein's views were a "deviation." In the end they worked out that compromise in which Anna Freud could have her own training facilities in the Society, where her students could be separate from Klein's concepts or disciples; the rest of the British analytic group felt able to withstand a heady dose of Klein's work.

Until her death in 1960 Klein continued to develop her ideas, and a good many of them were so outrageous as to be grotesque. Although Klein had no medical training she proposed to explain the origins of schizophrenia; to reiterate, she ambitiously thought that one of the main tasks of child analysis was the discovery and cure of psychosis in childhood. Klein tried to elaborate Freud's theory of the death instinct clinically, and she developed a theology-like system about the nature of infancy and early childhood. Because she felt that children have such evil impulses, many have seen in Klein's work a secular rendition of the doctrine of original sin. That Klein also emphasized the importance of the child's need for atonement is in keeping with the religious-sounding doctrine that inspired her disciples with their dogmatic certainties.

Phyllis Grosskurth's biography *Melanie Klein: Her World and Her Work*[20] is the first on Klein and was based on extensive interviewing as well as personal material that Klein's executors made available. We knew that Klein's supporters could treat patients as guinea pigs, since some of her followers thought that analyses should last ten years for the sake of research if not for therapy. Now it turns out that Klein herself treated her own children analytically and described them in disguised case reports. How she proceeded with her family was to become historically important once her daughter Melitta Schmideberg, an analyst herself, was to accuse Klein venomously during the fight over Klein's views in the British Society.

Grosskurth's biography of Klein is full of invaluable primary documents. There are extensive quotations, for example, from the World War II debates in the British Society. Yet, too often Grosskurth presents the arguments over theories in an unevaluated manner. Grosskurth succeeds superbly in interweaving biographical narrative and the development of Klein's ideas. In my opinion, though, Grosskurth fails to challenge Klein's approach enough. Kleinian contentions could be pretty weird, as the breast became almost a mystical entity. I think that Edward Glover, probably Klein's chief critic, was correct in seeing Jungian features in Klein's views, and Grosskurth could have made more of an effort to put Klein's work into the context of the broad history of analysis. Grosskurth's book is rich in its portrayal of intimate human struggles among early analysts, and it has become an essential source for a fascinating chapter in the history of psychoanalysis.

Psychoanalysis ranks as such a momentous part of the history of ideas that the subject deserves the best scholarly scrutiny. As we have already seen, there are some promising signs that writers have recently been able to emancipate themselves from the unfortunate cultism of the past, and the story of the growth of Freudian thought has increasingly become part of the study of intellectual history. Robert Caper's *Immaterial Facts: Freud's Discovery of Psychic Reality and Klein's Development of His Work*[21], however, is an unfortunate sign of the persistence of sectarian amateurism in this field.

Part I, entitled "Freud's Discovery of Psychic Reality," takes up almost exactly half of the book and contains not a single original idea. At the same time, Caper repeats many well-worn cliches that have long been exploded. It is late in the game, for example, to be citing lengthy extracts from Freud's case histories of "Dora" and "Little Hans" without any indication that a broad literature exists that approaches Freud's clinical work with the necessary detachment. Caper, though, proceeds as if there were in existence no bibliography on the so-called discovery of psychoanalysis; he includes only a few isolated references to Kleinian literature, and his exclusive concentration on Kleinian writings fails to support his contention that "psychoanalysis is not a philosophical school with a body of canonical texts, but, rather, an empirical approach to the mind. . . ."[22]

The only way to establish the proposition that Kleinianism represents an "unfolding" of something "implicit" in Freud would be by entertaining the hypothesis that before and after Freud's death other writers have sought to take psychoanalysis in alternative directions. Caper simply excludes any other psychoanalytic contributions from consideration and does not even try to come to terms with some of the critics of either Freud or Klein.

Instead, his book is a smoothly flowing bit of propaganda in behalf of the general importance of Klein's teachings. Freud himself hated the direction Klein took, a point that Caper understates, and in spite of Hanna Segal's "Foreword" which seeks to distinguish Klein's work from the "heresies" of Jung and Adler, Freud himself classed Klein's ideas with those earlier "deviations." Of course, even Freud's explicit excommunication of a thinker ought not to be the end of the matter, and he might have been wrong in any instance of seeking to separate his own point of view from that of others. But some argument on Caper's part would be necessary to establish his case in a way that would satisfy intellectual historians.

It is particularly striking that Caper makes no effort to utilize recently published biographical evidence about Klein or to link such material about the personal struggles in her own life with what she achieved in her work. Clinicians such as Caper ought not to be able to think that they can proceed to bat out books about psychoanalysis without being called to account by the normal standards of everyday university life.

By now it would be impossible to contest the notion that Melanie Klein represents a historically important extension of psychoanalytic thought. During her lifetime she established her own school in Great Britain, which has continued to be influential there and has subsequently had a notable impact on Latin America and elsewhere as well. When she first started developing her theories, Freud viewed her work as a challenge to himself that was assuming the form of an attack on the efforts in child analysis of his daughter Anna. As the years passed, Klein developed her ideas into what she considered a "system." She took a different approach, for example, to the psychology of women, she worked with play as a technique for treating children, and she sought to link normal development much more closely to psychotic problems than so-called classical psychoanalytic theory has ever accepted.

Following the fierce debate over Kleinianism that raged within the British Psychoanalytic Society toward the end of World War II, Klein and her supporters not only succeeded in not getting repudiated as "heretics," but, in the end, it was Anna Freud who felt obliged essentially to withdraw from the British Society in order to spend her efforts at her own child therapy clinic in Hampstead. (In a way she knew better how to protect her father than to promote herself.) Although the British Society remained formally united, two separate training streams were set up within it so that Anna Freud's students would not have to be involved with the concepts that Klein cherished. But Kleinianism as a whole succeeded in Britain unlike almost anywhere else.

Jean-Michel Petot's *Melanie Klein, Volume I: First Discoveries and First System 1919–1932*[23] is a curious book. Perhaps the single most notable point to comment on is that it first appeared in France in 1979, and then in English in 1990. Since this text covers Klein's work only in its first phase I am reluctant to generalize about all Petot has to say, but there is enough here to be disquieting, not just about the nature of Kleinianism but about the state of publishing in the United States on the history of psychoanalysis as well.

I cannot understand how the publisher could allow this 1979 book to appear in translation without any attempt to bring the material up to date. A lot of historical research has appeared over the years between the book's original appearance in France and then in English, and it seems irresponsible to allow an old text to come out without a new introduction, by the author or someone else, trying to incorporate recent research into the story as originally reconstructed in 1979.

Furthermore, Petot seems to have an inadequate amount of distance from Klein's theories. We are told, for instance, that the child patient in an early 1921 paper of Klein's was really her youngest son. I am troubled by the fact that Petot makes no effort to come to terms with the moral propriety of Klein's having treated her son. Furthermore, it is now evident, although Petot did not know it in 1979, that Klein may have analyzed her two other children as well and put them into her writings as disguised clinical cases.

Even more fundamentally, I would question the correctness of describing Klein's writings as in any sense "discoveries," as proclaimed in the subtitle to this book. As far as I am concerned, Freud himself contributed a critical new way of looking at things; to call his concepts, or those of any of his followers, "discoveries" has to imply a degree of scientific standing that is belied by the very nature of the kind of unreconstructed text that *Melanie Klein, Volume 1* constitutes.

Science entails change and fresh developments, as well as the possibility of confirmation. The fact that the publisher felt free to bring out a 1979 text without revising it in the light of new knowledge indicates something of the nature of the essentially religious side of what has happened to all too much of psychoanalytic literature.

Those outside of psychoanalysis have long bewailed the absence of genuine research in this field, and the publication of this book only confirms the worst of what critics have thought Freudians have been up to. Melanie Klein herself not only lacked medical training but never attained any kind of higher education; her ideas might of course be sound nevertheless, but it is striking that she proposed that the psychoanalyst's task was to "cure" all children of their so-called psychoses, an enterprise that I myself have to regard as a menacing kind of proposed undertaking.

General readers deserve help in trying to understand Klein's work, even if they cannot swallow the idea that she succeeded in creating a theoretical structure which deserves to be analyzed and interpreted as if it were a developing holy scripture. Petot's book is not reliable as history. If readers want to look at an interesting account of another early child analyst, I can highly recommend George Maclean's and Ulrich Rappen's *Hermine Hug-Hellmuth: Her Life and Work.*[24]

The preface to C. Fred Alford's *Melanie Klein and Critical Social Theory*[25] seems to me off-putting, for Alford begins by telling us, "My first reaction to Melanie Klein was that I could not imagine a psychoanalyst whose work is less relevant for social theory." The implausibility of using Klein's theories is then transformed, in the hands of this obviously clever academic, into "really the strength of her theory." So Alford has proceeded to give us what he considers "a Kleinian version of Herbert Marcuse's *Eros and Civilization.*" Just as Marcuse chose certain Freudian concepts for the sake of developing a radical version of psychoanalysis, uniting Freud and Marx in an idiosyncratic way, so Alford wants to do something similarly synthetic on behalf of socialist thought by making use of Klein's concepts.

Alford tells us that "the implications of a single question guide this book: What would be the consequences for social theory and philosophy if the psychoanalytic theory of Melanie Klein is correct?" One would have thought that an intelligent approach would assume something more cautious; most clinicians I know would think that even if some aspects of Kleinian theory are sound, others are not. Unfortunately the state of clinical research is such that almost no effort goes into testing different theories of psychopathology. Kleinianism poses exceptional problems in that much of what Klein postulated about infantile development is in principle incapable of being verified. Klein proposed a starker version of original sin than anything Freud ever thought of, and few outside her most devoutly faithful followers have ever suggested anything as black and white as the conceit that her theory might be "correct."

At one point Alford quotes a Kleinian as having maintained that her model of the mind was "theological." But he does not pursue the unsettling full possible implications of the imagery of this contention. Klein did, I think, have a far greater sensitivity to religious emotions than Freud. But some of her ideas were dotty. She thought at one point that all children needed to undergo analysis just as they require a school education. To repeat: Klein having had as her therapeutic objective the "curing" of the so-called psychoses of children has to sound presumptuous. I think that no one should talk even metaphorically about insanity without at least some attention to the biochemical side of things, and Klein's confident belief that patients, to become "well," need to reexperience their psychotic anxieties fails in my opinion to live up to the standard of being in any way "correct." Some Kleinians are so enthusiastic about their purposes as apparently to use patients for purposes of research; in effect they treat people in trouble as an experiment, without explicitly informing their patients beforehand.

Unfortunately, intellectuals like Marcuse are capable of using theoretical concepts like things. Marcuse was an admirable, charming man and a brilliant teacher, but he had not the slightest interest in the clinical side of psychoanalysis. Therefore, he felt free to use psychoanalytic concepts for his own purposes, which were defined largely by the state of the version of Marxist theory promoted by the Frankfurt school of critical sociology. Even some of his close ideological allies, like Theodor Adorno, could not go along with Marcuse's own peculiar reading of Freud.

I regret being tough on Marcuse, but it is about time someone spoke bluntly about the limitations of his knowledge of psychoanalysis. Academic life seems to reward ingenuity without enough regard for the merits and substance of an effort. Marcuse's curious union of Freud and Marx has attracted much more attention than it deserves, if only because of the arbitrary way he chose to pick up isolated concepts from the psychoanalytic literature.

Alford is himself aware of some of the central defects in Marcuse's approach to Freud, which is partly why he has turned to Klein as an alternative to the founder of psychoanalysis. But he would have done better to examine to what extent Kleinianism is sound, rather than to make a finger-exercise out of the assumption that one can treat her theories as if they were "correct."

Alford is sophisticated within the confines of the Kleinian literature, and he is also well educated about political theory. The book is a serious one, and within its own narrow terms can be highly recommended. It does make for a slow read, not so much because Klein's concepts are hard to understand as because one has repeatedly to suspend clinical disbelief about most of them.

I think that the Frankfurt school made an error in repudiating "neo-Freudian revisionism," and that Marcuse was terribly unfair in his assault on a thinker like Erich Fromm. (I leave it to nonpartisans to make what they can of Adorno's recommendation for correcting Fromm's critique of Freud: "I would strongly advise him," Adorno wrote Max Horkheimer about Fromm, "to read Lenin."[26]) On the other hand, Klein did have a school which attracted some fierce disciples, and those sorts of apostles do tend to have a greater impact on thought than more balanced alternative perspectives. Consequently, Kleinianism has indeed had a striking influence on a variety of social thinkers, and Alford's examination of some of their recent work, and the limitations of these social ideas, is better than I have ever seen discussed before.

Klein was exceptionally interested in the origins of morality, and Alford has done an excellent job of making plain for political theorists what her ideas add up to. He is particularly astute on Kleinian aesthetic theory. He does not, unfortunately, have the proper center of gravity about the whole field of psychoanalysis, and therefore treats concepts — negative therapeutic reaction, for instance — as if they were realistic objects instead of conjectures. Alford is a brilliant young thinker, and I only hope that in the future he will take a broader standpoint, weighing a variety of pros and cons, before putting his considerable talents to examining a theoretical problem.

A History of Child Psychoanalysis by Claudine Geissmann and Pierre Geissmann[27] is the first full-length book on the subject, and comes with a preface co-authored by Anna-Marie Sandler and Hanna Segal. So this text appears with the endorsements of key contemporary leaders of both the Anna Freudians and the Kleinians. Furthermore, *A History of Child Psychoanalysis* has a foreword by Serge Lebovici, a prominent Parisian student of Anna Freud's. This book not only is number 30 of the New Library of Psychoanalysis, as edited by Elizabeth Bott-Spillius, but was supported with the assistance of the Melanie Klein Trust, the Anna Freud Center, and the French Ministry of Culture. Despite all this establishmentarianism, *A History of Child Psychoanalysis* is an excellent work, and future studies in this area will have to rely on it as the pathbreaking innovator.

Lebovici gets the book off to an unfortunate bad start with the claim that Anna Freud's analysis by her father was "no secret,"[28] as were the analyses of the children of some other early analysts. But knowledgeable readers will already know of organizational efforts to cover up and prettify the beginnings of psychoanalysis.[29] The authors, both from France, are best on continental matters; despite occasional howlers like that by Lebovici, I plugged on and read every word, finding the experience a rewarding one.

There are even a few opening pages about Jung, although the Geissmanns give him what I think is short shrift. This seems to me especially regrettable since the one patient (Irmarita Putnam) of both Freud's and Jung's whom I interviewed was insistent that, compared with Jung's view around 1930, a child patient's mother was apt to be ignored in Anna Freud's circle in Vienna.[30]

Although the Geissmanns feel, for reasons beyond me, duty-bound to mention someone as insignificant as Hilde Abraham and how her father had analyzed her, *A History of Child Psychoanalysis* really gets going with the discussion of Hermine Hug-Hellmuth, whom the Geissmanns somehow call the "most obstinate of Freud's disciples."[31] The Geissmanns do not seem to realize that there was a quarrel over money between Hug-Hellmuth's nephew and her, and that that dispute played a role in the boy's becoming her murderer. The crime became an international sensation at the time.[32] Nor do the

Geissmanns seem to appreciate that the culprit, who tried to get analyzed as a victim of psychoanalysis after serving his sentence in prison, lived on until the 1990s. No one I know was intrepid enough to succeed in interviewing him. The Geissmanns are correct in pointing out how many of Hug-Hellmuth's ideas anticipated those of Anna Freud later on, but these authors are in error about the first impression Anna Freud made when she started out practicing in Vienna. Nobody then anticipated how Anna Freud's career would blossom. (People of the stature of Sandor Rado and Helene Deutsch were at first embarrassed by Anna Freud's presentations, and Freud himself could be defensive.) Hindsight can color any historian's viewpoint; and so the Geissmanns wrongly repeat the charge that it was ever proposed in the British Psychoanalytic Society that the Kleinian school be "excluded."[33]

The Geissmanns are not particularly astute about Anna Freud's early friendship with Eva Rosenfeld.[34] And for some reason the Geissmanns neglect to mention Alexander Etkind's fine *Eros of the Impossible: The History of Psychoanalysis in Russia*, first published in France and which has essential material on Vera Schmidt's work with children.[35] I have already questioned whether it is possible, at this late date, to still write about psychoanalytic "discoveries," an image which comes up repeatedly here in connection with Melanie Klein's contributions and also Donald Winnicott's. (At least twice Klein's critic Edward Glover is renamed as "Ernest.")

The chapters on Eugenia Sokolnicka and Sophie Morgenstern contain new material that is especially rewarding. (Helene Deutsch, however, did not grow up in the same Polish town as Sokolnicka, despite what the Geissmanns maintain.) Incidentally, the Geissmanns write in connection with Rank's first wife, "Roazen supposes that Tola [Rank] must have known about the beginnings of psychoanalysis in France, but there is no formal proof of this."[36] Would one not have expected the Geissmanns to try to contact me, when I could have easily provided the "formal proof" they yearn for?

The Geissmanns' review of the Freud-Klein controversy in London is not at the level of their understanding of other matters. But the Geissmanns are outstanding in their overview of how the ideas of Anna Freud and Melanie Klein spread elsewhere in the world. But if Klein did claim to have done analytic work with an "autistic child,"[37] then the Geissmanns should have been more critical of the early abuse of the concept of autism. They are curiously silent, by the way, about the full uproar that arose in connection with Bruno Bettelheim's work after his own dramatic suicide. Bettelheim had accused the Jews in concentration camps of having behaved like sheep going to the slaughter. When he killed himself, his half-dressed body was found in a hallway — he evidently had been struggling to get the plastic bag off his head. In his suicide note he wrote to only two of his children, excluding the third with whom he was at odds.[38] Bettelheim became such a totemic figure in French intellectual life that the Geissmanns appear strikingly negligent about the relevant literature.

In discussing Anna Freud's contribution to the concept of "psychological" parenthood and how that worked its way into North American law, the Geissmanns should have been more critical of what the implications of these ideas amount to. I wonder whether most would now agree that psychological "experts" (like Bettelheim) are entitled to displace the rights of so-called biological parents. It is not that the Geissmanns tilt toward either Anna Freud or Melanie Klein. Even though the Kleinian literature does not make much of it, I think that Klein's work on identification had to be historically dependent on Helene Deutsch's earlier concept of "as if" phenomena.[39] But I suggest the Geissmanns should have been more cautious whenever Kleinian theory proposed to enter the realm of psychosis, a medical subject on which Klein can have had no professional experience.

The Geissmanns are excellent on Donald Winnicott and his notion of "the ability to self-repair."[40] Here Winnicott was at one with Erik H. Erikson, an analyst with whom Winnicott maintained he was in much agreement.[41] The Geissmanns are wrong to suppose that Erikson was "one of the inner circle" in Vienna.[42] The Geissmanns approvingly quote Winnicott as having written: "I ask that paradox be accepted, tolerated and that it is admitted that it does not have to be resolved."[43] Still, I wonder if the current idealizations of Winnicott have not gone rather far and, without disrespect to his memory, whether it is not possible also to be critical of what he stood for. One has to remember the full extent of his training of Masud Khan.[44]

The strengths of the Geissmanns's work stem partly from their backgrounds in France, where a high level of intellectuality is taken for granted in analysis. But surely the Geissmanns should have known that Ernst Kris became a practicing analyst in America, and that Loewenstein, Jacques Lacan's analyst, had the first name of Rudolph not Kurt.[45] They state that "no doubt"[46] Margaret Mahler underwent an analysis in Vienna, when it is well established from her memoirs that one of her analysts there was Helene Deutsch.

The Geissmanns tell us, "American psychoanalysts seem to be struck with terror at the idea of notions such as . . . the 'death instinct.'"[47] In my opinion, Americans have been rightly dubious about that concept, which clinically helps account for the rise of ego psychology, much maligned on the continent. Throughout the Geissmanns' text one gets glimpses of an unfortunate remnant of dogmatic certitude. Thus we are told of Bettelheim (who may be a special problem of French psychoanalysis) in 1936, "after his own analysis was complete,"[48] as if Freud or anybody else emancipated from ideology ever proposed that there could be such completion short of death itself.

The Geissmanns rightly talk about the special role of Arminda Aberastury in Argentina, but though they are straightforward about continental suicides of analysts, they do not seem to have heard about this Latin American one. It is an intriguing incident historically because of its similarities to and differences from Victor Tausk's self-inflicted death. The Geissmanns provide interesting new material about François Dolto in Paris, and at least this reader wishes to learn more about a child analyst (and associate of Lacan's) who was capable of believing deeply in God.

I hope that my criticisms of *A History of Child Psychoanalysis* do not obscure the central point potential readers should know: the Geissmanns have produced a work of extraordinary thoroughness and dispassionate nonpartisanship, which should become a model for others in the future. Any demand for perfection is beyond the dreams of historical knowledge, which must content itself to be without the prerogatives of God-like omniscience. The Geissmanns have materially advanced our understanding of the controversies connected with Kleinianism, as well as those also that have been associated with Anna Freud.

Psychoanalytic Psychotherapy in the Kleinian tradition, edited by Stanley Ruszczynski and Sue Johnson[49] is a refreshing, and humane, survey of recent Kleinian thinking. After a short introduction, there are eight chapters by individual authors dealing with the issues of historical reconstruction, early loss, interrelationships between internal and external factors, denial, emotional knowledge, chronic depression, pedophilia, and terminations. I admit when I picked the book up I braced myself for the possibility of dogmatism; once upon a time Kleinianism could be almost messianic. But these papers all seem modestly concerned with the possibilities of psychotherapeutic improvement, and struck me as eclectic in spirit.

I found the attention to counter-transference reactions in therapists heartening. That phenomenon kept coming up in the writings of so many of these therapists that it must, I believe, represent a commitment to the interactive nature of therapeutic encounters which shows an admirable-sounding liberalism of spirit. Not once did I spot any lack of generosity toward patients, or grandiosity on the part of any of the therapists. The papers are all interesting and display no signs of the kinds of tunnel-vision that might have been present on the part of Kleinians several decades ago.

Some reservations did still come to mind. I realize that in a book dedicated to exploring the Kleinian tradition, bibliographical citations would have to be narrowed. But the authors do show less awareness of rival schools of thinking than is absolutely necessary. For example, when the defensive possibilities in historical reconstruction comes up, it would be nice if people were reminded that this was precisely a central point that Jung had tried to make to Freud before World War I. And Kleinians still seem to think that Paula Heimann's

1950 paper on counter-transference was somehow epochal, when in fact Helene Deutsch was writing on the positive uses of counter-transference feelings in her 1926 article on "Occult Processes." And if the here-and-now of therapeutic interactions are today considered central, then those pioneers like Ferenczi and Alexander who long ago tried to argue this point deserve to be remembered.

To continue on with a few reservations that came to mind, the subject of the use of medication only came up in one of the many clinical cases that got mentioned, and I would have liked to hear more on the topic; how do for example contemporary Kleinians proceed if, after a psychiatric consultation, drugs were to be tried? Also, the treatments described here seemed to be lengthy, and the frequency of sessions considerable; I wonder how today's Kleinians look on the value of regressions, and for what purposes they should be either encouraged or not. Most of the cases seemed to involve the use of the couch, but no discussion took place about the strengths and weaknesses of the alternative furniture in the therapeutic situation.

In the past I found that the Kleinian reliance on the significance of the phantasy life of the infant appeared off-putting and incapable of being tested. But these clinicians seemed to explicate and employ the classic Kleinian terms in an open-minded way. It was instructive to be introduced to a sampling of the recent literature, and in the future I will keep an eye out for further material exploring the implications of this British tradition which has become powerful, distinctive, and enriching.

Notes

1. *The Freud-Klein Controversies 1941–1945*, edited by Pearl King and Riccardo Steiner (London, Tavistock/Routledge, 1991).
2. *Minutes of the Vienna Psychoanalytic Society*, 4 volumes, edited by Herman Nunberg and Ernst Federn, translated by M. Nunberg (New York, International Universities Press, 1962–1975).
3. John Forrester, "Freudian Power Struggles," *Times Literary Supplement*, July 12, 1991, p. 10; Peter Rudnytsky, "Tough Morsels," *London Review of Books*, November 7, 1991, pp. 13–14.
4. *The Freud-Klein Controversies*, *op. cit.*, p. ix.
5. *Ibid.*, p. xi.
6. *Ibid.*, p. xxii.
7. Paul Roazen, *Freud and His Followers*, *op. cit.*, Part IX, Ch. 7.
8. See Paul Roazen, *Oedipus in Britain: Edward Glover and the Struggle Over Klein* (New York, Other Press, 2000).
9. *The Freud-Klein Controversies*, *op. cit.*, pp. 914, 618.
10. *Ibid.*, p. xiii.
11. *Ibid.*, p. xix.
12. Rudnytsky, "Tough Morsels," *op. cit.*, p. 13.
13. Edward Glover, *An Examination of the Klein System of Child Psychology* (Lon-

don, The Southern Post, 1945); "An Examination of the Klein System of Child Psychology,"in *The Psychoanalytic Study of the Child*, Vol. I, edited by Ruth Eissler (New York, International Universities Press, 1945); Edward Glover, "The Position of Psychoanalysis in Great Britain," in *On the Early Development of Mind: Selected Papers on Psychoanalysis* (London, Imago, 1956), pp. 352–363; Edward Glover, *Freud Or Jung?* (New York, Meridian Books, 1957; reprinted, with a Forward by James William Anderson, Evanston, Ill., Northwestern University Press, 1991); "Some Recent Trends in Psychoanalytic Theory," *Psychoanalytic Quarterly*, Vol. 30 (1961), pp. 86–107; Edward Glover, "Psychoanalysis in England," in Franz Alexander, Samuel Eisenstein and Martin Grotjahn, editors, *Psychoanalytic Pioneers* (New York, Basic Books, 1966), pp. 534–545. See also the interesting recent article by Joseph Aguayo, "Patronage in the Dispute over Child Analysis between Melanie Klein and Anna Freud: 1927–1932," *International Journal of Psychoanalysis*,Vol. 81 (2000), pp. 733–52.

14. *The Freud-Klein Controversies*, *op. cit.*, p. 690.
15. *Ibid.*, pp. 32–33.
16. *Ibid.*, pp. 227, 234.
17. Glover, "An Examination of the Klein System of Child Psychology," *op. cit.*
18. Edward Bibring, "The So-Called English School of Psychoanalysis," *Psychoanalytic Quarterly*, Vol. 16 (1947), pp. 69–93.
19. Janet Sayers, *Mothers of Psychoanalysis: Helene Deutsch, Karen Horney, Anna Freud, Melanie Klein* (New York, W.W. Norton, 1991).
20. Phyllis Grosskurth, *Melanie Klein: Her World and Her Work* (New York, Alfred A. Knopf, 1986).
21. Robert Caper, *Immaterial Facts: Freud's Discovery of Psychic Reality and Klein's Development of His Work* (Northvale, N.J., Aronson, 1988).
22. *Ibid.*, p.xiii.
23. Jean-Michel Petot, *Melanie Klein, Vol. I: First Discoveries and First System 1919–1932*, translated by Christine Trollope (Madison, Conn., International Universities Press, 1990).
24. George MacLean and Ulrich Rappen, *Hermine Hug-Hellmuth: Her Life and Work* (New York, Routledge, 1991).
25. C. Fred Alford, *Melanie Klein and Critical Social Theory: An Account of Politics, Art, and Reason Based on Her Psychoanalytic Theory* (New Haven, Conn., Yale University Press, 1989).
26. Quoted in Neil McLaughlin, "Origin Myths in the Social Sciences: Fromm, the Frankfurt School and the Emergence of Critical Theory," *Canadian Journal of Sociology*, June 1999, p. 118. See Roazen, *Political Theory and the Psychology of the Unconscious*, *op. cit.*, Part 3, Ch. 1, pp. 99–123.
27. Claudine Geissmann and Pierre Geissmann, *A History of Child Psychoanalysis* (London, Routledge, 1998).
28. *Ibid.*, p. xiii.
29. See Paul Roazen, *Meeting Freud's Family* (Amherst, University of Massachusetts Press, 1993), Ch. 7.
30. See Roazen, *How Freud Worked*, *op. cit.*, p. 179.
31. Geissmann and Geissmann, *A History of Child Psychoanalysis*, *op. cit.*, p. 40.
32. Roazen, *Freud and His Followers*, *op. cit.*, pp. 442–44.
33. Geissmann and Geissmann, *A History of Child Psychoanalysis*, *op. cit.*, p. 75
34. Peter Heller, *A Child Analysis with Anna Freud*, translated by Salomé Burckhardt and Mary Weigand (Madison, Conn., International Universities Press, 1990); Pe-

ter Heller, "Reflections on a Child Analysis with Anna Freud and an Adult Analysis with Ernst Kris," *Journal of the American Academy of Psychoanalysis*, Vol. 20 (1992), pp. 48–74; Peter Heller, ed., *Anna Freud's Letters to Eva Rosenfeld*, translated by Mary Weigand (Madison, Conn., International Universities Press, 1992). See Roazen, *The Historiography of Psychoanalysis*, *op. cit.*, pp.133–34.

35. Alexander Etkind, *Eros of the Impossible: The History of Psychoanalysis in Russia*, translated by N. &. M. Rubins (Boulder, Colo., Westview Press, 1997). See Roazen, *The Historiography of Psychoanalysis*, *op. cit.*, pp. 313–14.
36. Geissmann and Geissmann, *A History of Child Psychoanalysis*, *op. cit.*, p. 163.
37. *Ibid.*, p.204.
38. Richard Pollak, *The Creation of Dr. B.: A Biography of Bruno Bettelheim* (New York, Simon & Schuster, 1997); Roazen, *Political Theory and the Psychology of the Unconscious*, *op. cit.*, Part III, Ch. 2, pp.124–51; Roazen, *The Historiography of Psychoanalysis*, *op. cit.*, pp. 301–03; Nina Sutton, *Bettelheim: A Life and A Legacy* (New York, Basic Books, 1996).
39. Roazen, ed., Deutsch, *The Therapeutic Process, the Self, and Female Psychology*, *op. cit.*, Chs. 16 & 18.
40. Geissmann and Geissmann, *A History of Child Psychoanalysis*, *op. cit.*, p. 219.
41. Roazen, *The Historiography of Psychoanalysis*, *op. cit.*, pp. 295–96.
42. Geissmann and Geissmann, *A History of Child Psychoanalysis*, *op. cit.*, p. 254.
43. *Ibid.*, p. 222.
44. Linda Hopkins, "D. W. Winnicott's Analysis of Masud Khan: A Preliminary Study of Failures of Object Usage," *Contemporary Psychoanalysis*, Vol. 34 (1998), pp. 5–47.
45. Geissmann and Giessmann, *A History of Child Psychoanalysis*, *op. cit.*, pp. 254, 255.
46. *Ibid.*, p. 260.
47. *Ibid.*, p. 262.
48. *Ibid.*, p. 265.
49. Stanley Ruszczynski and Sue Johnson, eds., *Psychoanalytic Psychotherapy in the Kleinian Tradition* (London, Karnac, 1999).

5

Anna Freudianism

The kinds of normal scholarly debates that characterize intellectual history as a whole have never succeeded in being welcomed within the tale of the development of psychoanalysis. This is not just a simple-seeming matter associated with either sectarianism or trade-unionism, although both factors have for instance played their part in ensuring that as momentous a conflict in the history of ideas as that between Freud and Jung has still not been adequately surveyed. It has been as if the ideal of science led analytic practitioners to believe that by entertaining a variety of perspectives on the past of the discipline they would create a breach in the ranks of those who should be, supposedly, supporting the field by maintaining a monolithic conception of history.

Pluralism is more fashionable in theory than practice, and on their own part outsiders and literary critics can be doctrinaire in a way that clinicians, aware of the full complexities of their work, are not. It therefore may come as no surprise if historians of French psychoanalysis have been unaware of the many years in which a "dissident" like Otto Rank practiced in Paris.[1] And an influential biography of Freud completely ignored the name of Wilhelm Reich, and consequently his role in Viennese analysis, presumably because a discussion of such a controversial figure would be disagreeably painful to have to entertain.[2] Although in academic life in general careers should be able to be made by concentrating on neglected thinkers, the history of psychoanalysis is littered with instances of unconsciously suppressed conflicts.

Given the nature of the work that has failed to be done in this area, it follows that as I look back over all the possible changes that have taken place in the study of the history of analysis during the forty years this subject has interested me, the polarized nature of the controversies that have succeeded in coming up continues to stand out. Even during Freud's lifetime, as a matter of fact predating the outbreak of World War I, people tended to be either passionately favorable to his work or else adamantly antagonistic. Unfortunately both outsiders and insiders have been too easily made angry in this field, at the same time that it has continued to be rather simple to be original, since a little bit of tolerance goes a long way in making one open to the legitimacy of various rival points of view which have been contesting for public allegiance.

These preliminary considerations may help explain, or at least put in perspective, how Freud's analysis of his youngest child Anna (1895–1982) went publicly unmentioned for over four decades, yet that analysis constituted such a striking ethical transgression that I am even today left bewildered about its implications. This violation of his own stated rules for the practice of technique has to leave one questioning what he intended to accomplish with his written recommendations for future analysts. I am inclined to think that Freud's behavior here, and that of Anna too, stemmed from a kind of Nietzschean conviction that the chosen few were entitled to go beyond the normal bounds of conventional distinctions between good and evil.[3] Freud did think of analysis as a source of new moral teachings, and out of this treatment setting he hoped to be able to evolve fresh ethical standards. If the superior few had special entitlements, then lesser beings were to be controlled by a different set of restraints.

Freud felt proud of his ability to think and utter certain shocking thoughts, which takes us back to his identification with Nietzsche. There is no way of successfully shrinking Freud down to fit the practical needs of what we might prefer now the creator of psychoanalysis to have been like. He was a struggling innovator who defied preexisting categories, and it is only if we appreciate him in the round that we can begin to come to terms with some of the central aspects of the tradition he left us. Perhaps it is possible to look on Freud's analysis of Anna from a strictly political point of view, in terms of the wielding of power. How different was this one analysis from how other analysts have been trained? Here I am broadening the implications of Freud's treating Anna to question the possibilities of authoritarianism implicit in training analyses in general. Sectarianism has meant that too little debate about the institution of training analysis has been allowed to take place in public. Privately many analysts have reported being unable to tell anything like what they felt as the truth while in training, and that in hindsight it would have enriched their analyses to have been emancipated from the constraints of their formal education. The suppressions of feelings that take place in such a setting are of course all the more powerful for being unconscious at the time.

Although orthodox analysts have rarely understood the point, both Edward Glover in England and Jacques Lacan in France have long ago protested against the effects of training analyses. Outsiders warned all along that training analysis might be an act of spiritual violence. As I have already suggested earlier, my belief has been that Jung, when he first proposed before World War I that all analysts in the future be analyzed, was implicitly saying that Freud necessarily had not been able to overcome his personal neurosis. Much later Ferenczi was saying something similar in his *Clinical Diary*. When in 1918 it was initially proposed as a rule that analysts undergo analyses, and both Rank and Tausk opposed it, I doubt that they would have done so without the secure inkling that Freud himself was no enthusiast for the idea. In fact it only went into effect after Freud had become ill with cancer of the jaw in the 1920s, after which he could no longer hope to take such personal charge of the future of analysis. (Even analysts today with the greatest private reservations about continuing the institution of training analyses have little knowledge of this whole history.) It has to remain an open question whether Freud ever thought that Anna could take over as head of the psychoanalytic movement as we know she later did, or whether his analysis of her was part of any such planning on their side. And it is unclear to what extent one can suppose that she was trying to protect her father's creation by undergoing the analysis in the first place.

Someone like Robert Coles, who was trained as a pediatrician and child psychiatrist, has been notable for his idealistic commitment to studying children struggling spiritually in a variety of different social settings. Originally he did his field work as a civil rights advocate in the American South in the 1960s, but more recently his writings have taken on a far broader social range in a number of places, including French Canada. Coles's specialty has become studying children all over the world.

It turns out that relatively early on in his career, Coles derived considered inspiration from the personal example and teachings of Anna Freud, who was the only child of her father to carry on in the profession of psychoanalysis that he created. Her special interest was in adapting her father's technique and ideas to understanding and treating children. After she immigrated with her family to London in 1938, she helped found a clinic for children who had been separated from their parents during the Blitz.

In addition, Anna Freud was a considerable theoretician in her own right. She increasingly sought to understand the pattern of normal developmental lines that children go through. She wanted to be certain any diagnoses of pathology take into account the full living variety of childhood experience. As we have seen, Anna Freud also struggled against the school of child analysis in London led by her rival Melanie Klein, since Anna Freud knew how much her father disapproved of the millennial extremism implicit in Klein's approach then to treating children. Klein, who like Anna Freud had neither university nor medical training, sought to "cure" her child patients of their so-called psychoses, surely an extravagant enterprise.

Coles does not see Anna Freud primarily as a leader of her father's movement, or even mainly as a thinker. But he does record his own conversations with her when she was teaching at the Yale Law School in the late 1960s and 1970s. Coles's *Anna Freud: The Dream of Psychoanalysis*[4] is not a book about the same Anna Freud I met and saw in action, but I admire Coles's ability to bring forth a version of her that I never noticed. Even if I think his word-picture would be more appropriate for Mother Theresa than for the human being who was Anna Freud, we can be grateful for Coles's idealizing account of one of the notable women of this last century.

Elisabeth's Young-Bruehl's first biography, *Hannah Arendt: For Love of the World*[5] attracted a lot of attention. But as a biographer she lacked critical distance; hers was a serious study in which a superb essayist like Arendt got puffed up into a theorist whose own marginal notes in books were considered worth studying and quoting. Arendt's preferences, sympathies, and eccentricities were lovingly rolled together, accepted, and made to appear coherently justified.

Arendt was fiercely anti-Freudian, so one wonders how Young-Bruehl reconciles that biography with one of Anna Freud.[6] But consistency is not this biographer's objective; she does not even think of herself as writing history. "In a biography," we are instructed, "a life is held as it were in suspension, to be contemplated as a whole, with any records that might remain of the subject's self-understanding giving the only clues to what the life might have been like in the living, moment by moment." It is rubbish to say that "the only" such "clues" can be found in subjective knowledge. Young-Bruehl pursues this specious doctrine even though it is an unsound remnant of romanticism: "What Anna Freud discovered for herself and described for psychoanalytic theory in the years after the Second World War was the one way that human beings have to preserve a life, a life story, in a true dynamism." This biographer foists onto Anna Freud an exaggeration of the significance of identifying with others, historiographical nonsense which would exclude the possibilities of self-deception, hypocrisy, and lies, which themselves help provide "a true dynamism." Young Bruehl thinks she has found "the one way" of writing biography, even though she concedes that the method "of identification . . . is not a matter of history writing and it lacks the supposed objectivity of history. . . . "

The result is that Young-Bruehl has produced a partisan biography. In 1975 Anna Freud was unhappy about studies of her father, and proposed the creation of a "Defense League" like the secret Committee her father had brought together before World War I to preserve the "cause" of psychoanalysis. It looks like Anna may have succeeded in her objective, for this biography enlists Young-Bruehl in the ranks of those using their talents in behalf of an "orthodox" view of the history of analysis. Book sales indicate the continued popular rewards for taking the official line on things.

A key to the "orthodox" distortions of the past lies in the uses of silence. A general reader will be caught up in the narrative web of *Anna Freud* and its use of interestingly fresh documentary material. But how would someone necessarily know, for example, that between 1965 and 1967 Anna was particularly concerned about the impending publication of the book her father co-authored in the late 1920s with William C. Bullitt on President Woodrow Wilson? Not a word about Anna's negotiations with the publisher and her editorial efforts appears in *Anna Freud*. Perhaps it was left out because the Wilson study itself was disappointing.

In her lifetime Anna constituted an obstacle to research on the history of analysis. That which might or might not have offended her was enough to scare off independent thinking. But Young-Bruehl does not present a balanced account of Anna's pet hatreds. When she was disgusted by a now-famous paper of Erik H. Erikson's on her father, that reaction goes unmentioned. Bruno Bettelheim does not come up either, even in connection with Anna's little essay on concentration camp victims. Heinz Kohut's work was deemed by Anna to have become "antipsychoanalytic," and for this biographer no further comment is necessary. Wilhelm Reich's writings on character, and its influence on Anna's famous book *The Ego and Its Mechanisms of Defense*, are left out.

Although Anna played a part in the difficulties between Sandor Rado and her father, that episode does not appear here. Young-Bruehl discusses Anna's minor contribution to the subject of feminine psychology without once mentioning the name of Karen Horney. One way of dealing with schismatics is by consigning them to the outer darkness of nonpersons. Someone as unimportant as Berta Bornstein, whom Young-Bruehl concedes had "great difficulties in writing, if not in thinking," gets afforded a disproportionate amount of attention; but she was securely in Anna Freud's camp, so that one concludes that Young-Bruehl's book is the account of a religious sect.

At the same time Young-Bruehl does not seem to know about the best material on Anna's work, important essays written by her niece Sophie Freud Loewenstein. Although I think that Anna's most original writing consisted of her clinical descriptions of young children at her clinic in London during World War II, her official biographer leaves that aside and concentrates on a few papers of Anna's that Young-Bruehl considers autobiographically revealing. (The less said the better about the use of index cards for diagnosis under Anna's leadership at her Hampstead Clinic.)

I felt embarrassed for Anna's sake, with her hatred of publicity, at the attention Young-Bruehl pays to the issue of masturbation, and the "beating phantasies" which are supposed to have been Anna's efforts to ward off her incestuous desires. The theory Young-Bruehl relies on seems analytically antique, and it is crude to reduce Anna's problems — Freud told her she was "a little odd" — to autoeroticism.

The curious relationship between Anna and her intimate friend Dorothy Burlingham strikes me as humanly touching. (Dorothy was originally a Tiffany, got analyzed by Freud, and herself became a child analyst.) The two women worked out an original arrangement. Anna modeled herself on how her maiden Aunt Minna helped rear Anna and her five siblings, and Anna was able to do the same for Dorothy's four children.

Yet even when one of the Burlingham children killed herself in Anna's house in London, after years of analysis since early childhood, it would seem that Anna never allowed herself sufficient doubts about the efficacy of analysis as either therapy or prophylaxis. If Anna could not criticize herself, or was too involved in her father's whole way of thinking, at least her biographer should have asked some of the obvious questions. The ideal of historical truth exists to check the self-indulgence of those too apt to identify with their biographical subject.

This book is harsh toward anyone who crossed Anna's path without adequately scraping and bowing; it is no wonder that Melanie Klein and Anna went to war against each other over alternative approaches to child analysis, since they had such similarly autocratic personalities. But I read through *Anna Freud* with utmost fascination. It is amusing to find Anna complaining about Ernest Jones's supposedly "negative attitude" toward her father; to the rest of the world Jones rightly looks like a Freudian apologist. Freud hated having to write a public letter in honor of Jones's fiftieth birthday, since Freud thought Jones had made the contributions of a "schoolboy" and complained about his "dishonesty." Jones in turn wrote that Anna had "no pioneering originality." She did have an unusual simplicity and clarity of expression, especially speaking extemporaneously, but when put in front of graduate students at Harvard in 1952 she proved an embarrassment to her ideological allies.

Scholars will have to read this book even though it is littered with sloppy mistakes. Still, every new line by Freud that gets quoted from his correspondence is to me always interesting. There is a fine condolence letter from Freud to Dorothy Burlingham on the suicide of her husband. *Anna Freud* will inevitably do more to spur on the Freud industry, no matter how many books have already appeared. It is about time that someone pointed out how Freud, and Anna, too, were able to make politic use of old Viennese charm. Another way of describing that special tact and kindliness would be *schmaltz*, and an adequate degree of skepticism is needed about the habitual insincerities of cultivated people of that era.

Young-Bruehl does an inadequate job of trying to establish that Anna was a woman of imagination and fancy; a biographer has to be inventive to find "the ambitious adventurer lurking just below the cautious Miss Freud surface." The tragedy of Anna's life was that she was an unwanted child, but her biographer cannot come straight out and discuss the hatred Anna felt for her mother. It is preposterous to describe Martha Freud as dedicated "to elegant dresses, coiffures, and cosmetics." Freud's wife was more considerable a figure than his students ever wanted to acknowledge, and someday feminists may succeed in giving Martha her due. A couple of remarkable letters of hers are quoted here from her old age; in time the full correspondence from Freud's years of courtship will be published. (There are over a thousand letters between Jung and his wife that some day could get released.) When in 1923 Freud contracted his cancer of the jaw, Anna's mother had by then long since ceased to play a central role in Freud's professional life; it is not clear that Freud's wife even approved of the form of therapy that he practiced, although the skepticism on her part did not interfere with the couple's special kind of marital harmony in that distant era. Throughout Freud's illness, Anna was his secretary and guardian, increasingly the gatekeeper for those who sought access to him. Except for some interesting work during World War II, ignored by Young-Bruehl, on the way young children bond to mother-substitutes, Anna excluded mothers from her theories. As I have suggested, my own conviction is that Anna Freud's writings from those war years, and her concrete descriptions of the reactions of small children to the stress of separation, represent her finest contribution to modern psychology. One can only conjecture about how her own experience of maternal deprivation may have helped turn her toward her father's way of thinking, and also played a role in her special insights.

Freud himself had his ambivalences toward Anna. Young-Bruehl devotes many pages to Freud's lengthy analysis of Anna, without raising the obvious point that Freud was afraid what any other analyst might do to Anna. It has long been known that Freud referred to her as his Antigone and also Cordelia, but this is the first time we find him calling her "St. Anna." He was worried about how she would manage after his death; he was pretty sure she would never marry. She needed to earn a living, and he did everything he could to build up her position within analysis. But he did not send her to a university. Freud was addicted to her staying at home with him. Yet one would have thought that a biographer would discuss the specifics of Freud's last will, his leaving book royalties only to his grandchildren, and what role money played in interfering with Anna's relationships to her nephews in London and her American niece.

Young-Bruehl makes some attempts to drag in politics; we are told that though "not a socialist . . . her sympathies clearly went in the socialist direction, for scientific if not for political questions." I cannot make sense of such a contention, except that in contrast to Klein Anna talked about the "environment" of children. Anna's favorite English author was Rudyard Kipling, which one might have thought tellingly conservative. Young-Bruehl claims that "the analyst for whom Freud's social vision became a credo most deeply and most lastingly was his daughter." There were analysts who were not only socialists but also Marxists, and some became members of the Communist Party. Anna consistently voted for the Liberal Party in England. She was, Young-Bruehl says, "never one to expect anything of the political realm." During the 1934 civil war in Vienna that crushed the local Socialists, Anna like her father craved "peace and quietness." (Freud was by then a sick old man, but someone younger could afford idealism.)

Mythology about Anna has become an aspect of American intellectual history; her work has long been viewed with more skepticism in Great Britain and France. Once it becomes possible to put in perspective the veneration for her as a symbol of her father's genius, we will be better able to counteract the baleful impact of her collaboration in injecting questionable middle-class biases into legal doctrines affecting the welfare of children. On grounds of the need for continuity and the dangers of "confusing" children she was opposed to joint custody arrangements. She thought that the parent who got custody ought to have the right to control the visitation privileges of the non-custodial parent.

However reactionary Anna may sound, the early Freudians were like seventeenth century Puritans in their ascetic quest for theological introspection. Young-Bruehl cites some fascinating dreams (and associations) that Anna recorded and tried to understand, sometimes sending them on to friends like the Princess Marie Bonaparte in Paris. The circle around Anna, no matter how geographically scattered, was tied together by powerful allegiances; Young-Bruehl only tells us some of Anna's associates whom she analyzed, so we are still in the dark about the full role of the power of therapeutic transferences in her life.

Young-Bruehl has succeeded in recreating Anna Freud's hermetically sealed world, and it does hang together in a dreamlike way. Anna disliked her own first name, and dressed in an unusually plain and drab manner; entirely aside from the obvious triumphs in Anna's life, it is hard not to think of her with sadness since she remained so tied to unfulfilled longings. Anna chose to remain for the rest of her life in the house Freud died in; she once poignantly said she feared that if she left the house for one her father had not known, how would he be able to find her in her dreams? As far as *Anna Freud* goes, if one knows enough to ask elementary kinds of questions it collapses into a heap of isolated pieces of selectively chosen documents. There are other biographical tacks besides "the only clues" that Young-Bruehl relies on here.

Fortunately she is wrong about there being only "the one way" that biographers can preserve a life.

What clinicians do in practice has been notoriously hard to monitor. We know that Freud led the way in keeping a wide (if unacknowledged) gulf between his theories and his practices. Only naïve beginners should think that Freud's own written recommendations on technique can tell us much about how himself proceeded as a therapist. Even his famous published case histories are sometimes at odds with how we can reconstruct that he dealt with those patients clinically.

In this context Peter Heller's *A Child Analysis With Anna Freud*[7] is both fascinating and invaluable. For he was in analysis with Anna Freud in the years 1929 to 1932, from the ages of nine to twelve. The book consists of Anna Freud's extensive notes on the case, which she drew up for a clinical presentation and a vignette that she used in her *The Ego and the Mechanisms of Defense*. Heller was an unusually precocious child, and brought to his analysis not only drawings but also poems and stories as well. And he later took all this material and presented it to us with his retrospective associations and reconsiderations.

Heller was not just a patient of Anna Freud's, but in a sense became a member of the extended psychoanalytic family. His father had been in analysis in Vienna; he himself not only was treated by Anna Freud, but also attended the experimental school that she, along with her close friends Dorothy Burlingham and Eva Rosenfeld, oversaw. Peter Blos and Erik H. Erikson were among his teachers there. In addition, Heller fell in love at an early age with a school chum, Dorothy Burlingham's daughter Tinky, and they were married for some years. He therefore remained in touch with both Anna Freud and Dorothy Burlingham for the rest of their lives, and his life story becomes itself an aspect of the history of psychoanalysis.

The main reservation I have about Heller's account has to do with whether he ever fully realized just how extraordinary it is clinically that Anna Freud put him on the couch at such an early age. One gets the impression that she felt that any other therapeutic approach (including play) was somehow less moral and dignified. She took such a key part in Heller's early years that it is inevitable that he had trouble objectifying the experience. She not only was his therapist, and the analyst of his future wife (and the other Burlingham children), but she also enlightened him sexually. As a matter of fact I would think that the whole treatment procedure that she undertook with him amounted humanly to a massive seductive effort, and it is a tribute to Heller's resiliency and spirit that he was able to transcend the experience so successfully.

Heller states that he was "the case of a neurotic, privileged only child,"[8] but I am not sure that he was aware that clinically he did not come to analysis with any terribly severe problems. It is true that his parents had separated, and that his father had made it a condition of consenting to the separation that the boy remain with him. Both of his parents had their romantic involvements, but the boy was growing up in a cosmopolitan environment. Anna Freud starts off her notes with his night terrors, but however large that symptom might have loomed in her mythology it does not appear to me to have been anything particularly outstanding.

The detailed notes that she kept of the case are a kind of museum piece. She proceeded as if her father's theories were a scientific given, and whatever Heller brought she fed into the conceptualization that she had received. The child must have felt her conscientiousness and interest as a form of maternal affection. She, on her part, sounds reassured with his reality testing (and that of his family) when she remarks of his attitude toward Freud: "Considers my father somebody really great." On the other hand, she also noted that the boy "asks religion teacher about Freud, thus resistance."[9]

To a complete outsider Anna Freud's notes are likely to sound as far distant as the ruminations of a long ago divine. I do not just mean that she shared in the puritan asceticism of early psychoanalysis, but that she reified concepts into the status of being things. "Anal love"[10] gets invoked for an explanation entirely on a theoretical level; the so-called phases that she describes are really abstractions, the outcome of conceptual considerations.

In his associations to Anna Freud's clinical notes Heller is, in my view, urbane about his analytic experiences; he is also remarkably open about the remainder of his life history: "The impression of puritanical distance remains; as well as the suspicion that she who had insight into other people had little insight into their relationship to her, or was not quite capable of guiding such a relationship." With his maturity he observes that "therapy may play a dangerous game with passion even when it does no more than erode the possibility of passionate engagement and self-surrender." "Even in retrospect," he tells us, "I am annoyed at the solicitous dampening of the spirit of precocious intellectual superiority and uncommon talent. . . . "[11]

Heller was aware that "as a result of the migration, I now belong to an elusive segment of a lost generation."[12] So he remained naturally tied to his treatment by Anna Freud, and as critical of her as he sometimes could be he also absorbed more of her thinking that I believe in fact justified. Thus when he tells us of "a breakthrough to a deeper layer"[13] of self-understanding I found myself cringing at this cultured man's acceptance of a psychoanalytic cliché. Yet he was also fully capable of integrating the psychoanalysis he experienced with the social milieu in which he grew up. He pointed out the vexing "issue of the reduction to the sexual, or the preference of the sexual as the symbolic realm into which all problems could be translated. For the adults around me in . . . the late twenties and early thirties all seemed to share, in one sense or another, this tendency."[14]

Unfortunately Heller's powerfully argued "Afterward" which appeared in the original German edition of this book was entirely omitted in English, and only appeared later in a psychoanalytic journal, along with Heller's comments on a version of his second analysis with Ernst Kris.[15] Kris had also been analyzed by Anna Freud, and Heller was astonished — or rather, traumatized — to read how Kris in New York portrayed him by letters to Anna Freud in London. Heller was in the midst of a painful part of his marriage to Tinky Burlingham, and Anna Freud was of course in regular conduct with his mother-in-law. Anna Freud seemed to be repeating Freud's own sort of family over-involvement with Ferenczi and his fiancée's daughter Elma.

Anna Freud's reputation became legendary in North America. Although she pioneered in the area of child analysis, as a psychoanalytic thinker she was not initially considered in the front rank. Her most memorable book, *The Ego and the Mechanisms of Defense*, was written while she was working most closely with her father.[16] But although almost everything Freud himself ever wrote has at one time or another been subjected to the closest kind of critical scrutiny, I cannot recall ever seeing a reconsideration of Anna Freud's *The Ego and Mechanisms of Defense* which sought to be objective.

Once Freud died in 1939 Anna Freud became a living symbol of his heritage. And in the States that meant that despite how she shared her father's own bitterness for everything connected with things American, she was always able to come over to raise money for her clinic; she also not only had influence with publishers, but toward the end of her life she earned more honorary degrees in the United States than she cared to bother to pick up. While she could always count on the fact that in America everyone would be at her feet, in London, where she continued to live, the situation was quite different. As we have discussed, Melanie Klein had notably challenged Anna Freud's ideas about child analysis starting in the 1920s, and after the Freuds moved to England in 1938 there was a tense rivalry between the two women. The British knew Anna Freud as a person and treated her accordingly, while the Americans — slow to respond positively to Klein's ideas — never acknowledged how difficult Anna could be. In France, however, she provoked outright contempt; partly this was a consequence of her role in having ensured that Jacques Lacan could not self-respectingly stay in the International Psychoanalytic Association (he would have had to be demoted as a training analyst), but also I think it is a tribute to the unblinkered intellectuality of the French that they did not share in any myths about her but actually weighed and assessed her writings on their merits.

The Technique of Child Analysis,[17] which appeared two years before her death in 1982, consists of a text compiled by two of her London supporters and one of her American followers; it is obviously written imbued with the spirit of her own convictions, and the book contains not only a preface written by her, but also throughout each chapter direct quotations from her punctuate the pages. Although the book does not tell us exactly when these discussions took place, I would think that they did so at a time when she was in full command of her powers. From her students' point of view she had been relatively reluctant to publish. Therefore in *The Technique of Child Analysis* her "comments appear verbatim" while the "contributions from the other participants are blended into the text."[18]

The list of foundation that at various times supported Anna Freud's Hampstead Clinic appear in the "acknowledgement" to *The Technique of Child Analysis*, and it is enough to knock one's socks off; her success in raising money was an expression of the power she was able to wield, and it is noteworthy that virtually all the funds were American.

I regret to say that *The Technique of Child Analysis* seems to me to contain several striking conceptual flaws, although it may be the fault of her disciples that makes this text so vulnerable. For example: why should any child be treated? The book does not once question the advisability of putting a child into analysis. Surely every decent clinician will acknowledge that there are bound to be disadvantages of employing analysis as a therapeutic measure. But the unquestioned premise of *The Technique of Child Analysis* is that it is a good idea to utilize this form of therapy, presumably on all children. Because of the structure of the book, a narrative interspersed with quotations from Anna Freud, her observations are bound to appear oracular. It is therefore telling that at one point she observes of a particular patient: "Treatment was not really complete."[19] The implication that psychoanalytic treatment could in principle ever be "complete" seems to me nonsense.

Child analysis suffers from the occupational illusion of therapists that professionals can be trained to rear children in a way that is superior to the efforts of biological parents. Bruno Bettelheim tended to share that conviction. So it is not surprising to see Anna Freud referring in the first paragraph in her preface to "the unavoidable intrusion of parents" in the treatment she advocated.

What form of help the Hampstead Clinic (now renamed the Anna Freud Center) was offering needs to be highlighted:

> The Hampstead Clinic differs from the traditional child guidance clinic in that its orientation is wholly psychoanalytic. The bulk of the treatment provided takes the form of full psychoanalysis, in which each child is seen individually, five times a week, for sessions of fifty minutes, over an extended period of time.[20]

These children, whether they came from working-class backgrounds or anywhere else in the social hierarchy, were all supposed to be able to benefit from the effects of long-term treatment, lasting many years, which primarily relies on the effects of verbalized interpretations in producing insight and self-awareness. To me, one of the nightmares of the Hampstead procedure was that Anna Freud and her disciples developed the idea of indexing each case, and they evolved manuals for that purpose. It were as if they completely forgot the significance of the artistic and humanistic side of any therapeutic use of psychoanalysis, as they labored in the belief that they had a securely established science. One has to wonder to what extent the children involved in the Hampstead Clinic (about whom no independent follow-up study has ever been conducted) were being used as research objects. I found it appalling that in a book published as late as 1980 analysts could still allow themselves to ask whether a patient had "merely experienced an improvement in his symptoms or had in fact been analyzed."[21]

Instead of starting off the book with a discussion of the purposes of child analysis, the opening paragraph makes "the distinction between psychoanalysis and psychotherapy."[22] Anna Freud, herself analyzed by her own father, was determined that for other people the technique of analysis ought not to be watered down to "mere" psychotherapy. She maintains that for the sake of analysis "the most intensive contact feasible is needed. . . . ,"[23] and therefore five times a week was the desirable rule. Shorter forms of therapy would represent a "deviation," and *The Technique of Child Analysis* contains three separate pokes at Franz Alexander since he pioneered in alterations in the orthodox approach to the psychoanalytic therapy of adults. Curiously enough the name of Melanie Klein does not once appear in the book, although at several points in the argument her views are being directly contradicted.

For me *The Technique of Child Analysis* was a fascinating museum piece of orthodox psychoanalytic conviction. It is a sort of prayer book, and for those who are believers they will find in it lots of rules and regulations. To skeptics, however, it is wondrous how no one challenged more of this while Anna Freud was still alive. For example, although she was herself without any medical training whatsoever, she can comment about the effects of "interruptions" in treatment: "It is very much a question of the type of illness treated. With the severely ill child, either borderline or autistic," and so on.[24] Now the problem here is that she claims not only to be dealing with "illness," but even thinks that autism is a problem amenable to psychoanalytic influence. A whole generation of parents of autistic children suffered unnecessary guilt feelings since they were encouraged to think that it was somehow their fault (and not a matter of genes or biochemistry) that their children were so tragically different.

In the midst of all the recommended bits of technique (or hocus-pocus), we are eventually told in passing that "the aim of child analysis should be borne in mind": "to restore the child to the path of normal development."[25] But what on earth does normality consist in? One of Anna Freud's earlier books, *Normality and Pathology in Childhood*, had rightly highlighted how much harder it could be than with adults to determine what in a child can count as a so-called symptom.[26]

It seems to me bootless to go through all the passages in *The Technique of Child Analysis* that I found offensive. I do believe that in many ways Anna Freud was a remarkable woman, lucid in extemporaneous exposition and thoroughly devoted to her father's "cause." But long before I had any child of my own, when in 1965 I sat in on clinical case conferences at The Hampstead Clinic, I knew that I would never want any children of my own treated at that place. What remains troubling is that there has been so little challenge to the influence Anna Freud had, in the area of North American family law, for example. The literary critic George Steiner has recently raised what I consider the crux of the moral issues that bother me too:

> Deep ethical and social questions arise from the very idea of child-analysis, from the violations of privacy, from the stage-managing of incipient singularities and possibly fertile tensions which analysis inevitably comports. Imagine a Lewis Carroll, a Proust, a Nabokov being made naked and "more normally functional" by child analysis. But imagine also, the possible waste of the unknown in the unknown. One cries out: "by what right?" . . . .Where is the fresh air of doubt, where the salvation of irony? . . . .I find the psychoanalysis of very young children and the abuses of control to which it has led, notably in America, well-nigh indefensible. . . .[27]

Although it is true that increasingly intellectual historians have become interested in the history of psychoanalysis, it is not easy for neutral observers to get their bearings about psychoanalytic disagreements. Supposedly, according to the "orthodox" outlook, there is a so-called mainstream, fully loyal to Freud, which has continued to thrive despite the crises occasioned by alleged dissidents who have broken away from the organized movement. Too many continue to subscribe to the mythology put forth by the International Psychoanalytic Association (IPA), first founded by Freud in 1910, which claims to be the spokesperson for the adherents who truly deserve the credit for inheriting the techniques and theories propounded by Freud.

One problem, however, is that what constitutes orthodoxy in one decade is apt to be very different from what gets the seal of approval only a few years later. To cite one example, for years the work of Karen Horney would almost never get quoted in papers published under the auspices of the IPA, but in recent years, after the full-scale — and sometimes unfair — feminist critiques of Freud, Horney's name is now considered acceptable within orthodox psychoanalytic circles. Melanie Klein, who in London resisted being declared a heretic, had never been excluded from within the IPA, and one IPA President considered himself a committed Kleinian. The school of self-psychology, initiated by Heinz Kohut in Chicago, has succeeded in not being stigmatized as heresy, even though Anna Freud decided, as we have already mentioned, that Kohut himself had become "antipsychoanalytic." That dread designation has frightened many over the years, and the more timorous have tailored their thinking, often unconsciously, so as not to run the risk of being dismissed as "deviant."

In reality it has been the outsiders, those who could be considered trouble makers organizationally, who have had most of the fresh ideas. The "mainstream" itself has quietly assimilated the work of those who once were deemed schismatic. Psychoanalysis has been a Church, and its historians have their own partisan allegiances. But few seem to realize that when a favorite of Freud's like the late Heinz Hartmann introduced the concept of normality into psychoanalytic discourse, he was doing exactly what Freud himself, before World War I, had denounced Alfred Adler for attempting to accomplish. Despite the passage of time it is still impossible for most students in psychoanalytic training to get a fair-minded impression of the contributions of the most famous of the students of Freud who gave him the greatest trouble in his lifetime. So that the name Carl G. Jung remains an exceptionally odious one at orthodox training centers, and this is entirely aside from the issue of Jung's politics in the 1930s. To repeat: when Donald W. Winnicott, for example, once mentioned the name Jung at a meeting of the British Psychoanalytic Society, he found there was such a hush that he dared not repeat the exercise. Once Jacques Lacan was essentially driven out of the IPA in the early 1950s, with the endorsement of Anna Freud, it became difficult, at least in North American psychoanalytic journals, to cite works by Lacan without running the risk of having the articles rejected. Erich Fromm remains on the official enemies list, although he has been widely influential within the social sciences, and in Mexico where he lived for some time; once he was dead at least his books were allowed to be advertised in orthodox psychoanalytic publications, which was not necessarily the case while he was still alive and capable of writing upsetting thoughts.

One could go on about the ways in which psychoanalysis, as a modern-day religious equivalent, has failed to fulfill the ideals of scientific inquiry. One difficulty has been that the offshoots of the IPA, the psychoanalytic Left, so to speak, has been singularly unable to hang together. Those who were brave enough to risk the perils of going it alone were also unlikely to make stable alliances with one another. So a thinker like Erik H. Erikson, who warily struck out on his own and only belatedly credited Jung as a predecessor, steered clear of ever being associated with the work of Fromm, although from the point of view of intellectual history Erikson and Fromm had a good deal in common. Politically they were at opposite ends of the ideological spectrum, since Fromm was on the Left and Erikson was substantially conservative, but within psychoanalytic quarrels they both tried to introduce the social environment into Freudian thinking. In the meantime the membership of the IPA is now approaching ten thousand, although few of them have had the time to decipher the genuine history of their own discipline.

In all this maze of theoretical quarrelling, perhaps the most secure way of understanding what actually happened is to rely on first-hand accounts. And here is where Esther Menaker's *Misplaced Loyalties*[28] makes such a remarkable contribution. She tells what it was like as Americans for her and her husband to go to Vienna in the early 1930s; Esther was analyzed by Anna Freud, and her husband by Helene Deutsch. (Esther felt that when, in the course of free-associating in her analysis, she said that she was bothered by all the splinter movements — led by Adler, Jung, and Rank — Menaker thought that she had "put her foot in her mouth" as far as Anna was concerned. Anna's reply bears repeating: "Nothing is as important to us as the psychoanalytic movement.") The Menakers found the Europeans condescending to them as barbarian representatives of the New World. Although the Menakers had some positive experiences as well, and certain members of the Vienna Psychoanalytic Society proved to be exceptions, on the whole the Menakers felts disillusioned and belittled. In later years Esther Menaker became an outstanding exponent of the ideas of Otto Rank, a Viennese who ran afoul of the IPA and whose work, although often quietly incorporated within today's orthodoxy, has never succeeded in getting the genuine recognition it deserves.

If intellectual historians rely on such first-hand testimony, they will be less likely to accept the myths surrounding the development of the discipline. Psychoanalytic practitioners can themselves not be counted-upon to keep straight their own history. It is a risky venture for clinicians to disagree with their colleagues, since unconscious self-interest, connected with the possibility of continuing to get referrals, is bound to shape how therapists think. That trade-union aspect to psychoanalysis makes it all the more necessary for those in academic life to tell the tale of how these controversies took place. Actually it is a rich source of research, since so many of the issues that caused trouble were connected with rival conceptions of ethics, and how life ought to be lived. But one ought never to underestimate the continuing power of transferences; allegiances that arise in a therapeutic context are precisely why there is such an interest in who analyzed which analyst, and this has played a role that it is easy for those in university life to underestimate.

We know about the influence of Ph.D. supervisors on those they train, but the impact of individual analysts on their patients can be far more enduringly momentous. Now that psychoanalysis is more than one hundred years old, the story of its evolution is becoming more obviously acceptable within intellectual history as a whole. Esther Menaker's *Misplaced Loyalties* should be a classic for those who cannot accept the organizational legends about the field. The time may come before too long when partisanship, at least about the oldest quarrels, will not long count for much in academic life. The problem may instead be for the young ever to understand why such struggles needed to take place at all. One of the most attractive features to psychoanalysts has been their quest for self-understanding; but soul-searching also can be linked to sectarianism. As long as the Freudian heritage remains linked to ultimate concerns about the ends of human existence, it is unlikely that the disputatiousness that is so notable a feature among analysts is likely to evaporate.

The saddest aspect to this chapter about Anna Freud may be how she so failed to pay attention to the p's and q's of organizational politics that by the end of the twentieth century her heritage had been virtually wiped out within the British Psychoanalytic Society. The dominant family romance there today excludes her. Was she misled about the local situation by the extensiveness of her American position? A key early mistake may well have been her failure to follow more of Glover's advice, and cement a tie with her most powerful British ally. Instead she allowed herself to be co-opted by Jones into IPA office-holding, as she preferred to defer to Freud's promise to Jones when he came to England that she would not disrupt the Society. Did she altruistically surrender her life to her father? Being taken in—like Kurt Eissler—by Jeffrey Masson, which we will come back to in chapter 12, because of his Freudian fundamentalism was only part of her unworldliness and human naivete. Even her old consulting rooms, now in the Freud Museum on Maresfield Gardens, got wiped out in a bureaucratic shuffle, and were recreated in a distorted way on a lower floor. Although alive she could become a terror to me in my own historical work, I may be among the first as an independent scholar to insist how important it is fairly to evaluate her proper standing. Dissecting closely the writing of any psychoanalytic pioneer, including as we shall see in chapter 8 the currently triumphant Jacques Lacan, inevitably reveals flaws. Without blinding our critical faculties, the spirit of generosity and even-handedness should infuse the future's take on all the key figures in the whole of the history of psychoanalysis.

Notes

1. Roazen, *The Historiography of Psychoanalysis*, *op. cit.*, pp. 333–37.
2. *Ibid.*, Part VI, pp. 246–47.
3. Roazen, *Political Theory and the Psychology of the Unconscious*, *op. cit.*, Part I, Ch. 2.
4. Robert Coles, *Anna Freud: The Dream of Psychoanalysis* (Reading, Mass., Addison-Wesley, 1992).

5. Elisabeth Young-Bruehl, *Hannah Arendt: For Love of the World* (New Haven, Conn., Yale University Press, 1982). See Roazen, *Encountering Freud, op. cit.*, pp. 290–91.
6. Elisabeth Young-Bruehl, *Anna Freud: A Biography* (New York, Summit Books, 1988).
7. Peter Heller, *A Child Analysis with Anna Freud, op. cit.*
8. *Ibid.*, p. xlix.
9. *Ibid.*, pp. 19, 47
10. *Ibid.*, p. 18.
11. *Ibid.*, pp. 300–301
12. *Ibid.*, p. 341.
13. *Ibid.*, p. 351.
14. *Ibid.*, pp. 367–368.
15. Peter Heller, "Reflections on a Child Analysis with Anna Freud and an Adult Analysis with Ernst Kris," *op. cit.*
16. Anna Freud, *The Ego and the Mechanisms of Defense, op. cit.*
17. Joseph Sandler, Hansi Kennedy, and Robert L. Tyson, *The Technique of Child Analysis: Discussions with Anna Freud* (Cambridge, Mass., Harvard University Press, 1986.)
18. *Ibid.*, pp. 3–4.
19. *Ibid.*, p. 246.
20. *Ibid.*, p. 2.
21. *Ibid.*, p. 54.
22. *Ibid.*, p. 7.
23. *Ibid.*
24. *Ibid.*, p. 21.
25. *Ibid.*, p. 33.
26. Anna Freud, *Normality and Pathology in Childhood* (New York, International Universities Press, 1965).
27. George Steiner, "Review of Young-Bruehl's *Anna Freud*," *London Sunday Times Books*, June 11, 1989, pp. 1–2.
28. Esther Menaker, *Misplaced Loyalties* (New Brunswick, N.J., Transaction Publishers, 1995).

6

Ethics and Privacy

Myths about Freud have continued to be perpetuated by the unnecessary secrecy surrounding documents connected to the early history of psychoanalysis. If, for example, one has any special interest in the reception of Freud's work in Italy, an apparent obstacle is that the interviews with Edoardo Weiss, the effective founder of Italian psychoanalysis, conducted by Kurt R. Eissler on behalf of the Freud Archives in New York City, are restricted at the Freud Collection at the Library of Congress in Washington, D.C. until the year 2057. Like some other curious attempts by the Freud Archives to seal documents, the donors' true wishes have undermined efforts to maintain psychoanalytic pieties; so Weiss not only showed his copies of the Eissler interviews to me, but also left them in his own papers at the Library of Congress where they are now freely available to all scholars.

Publicity has already been given to the superfluous restrictions which have afflicted researchers in the history of psychoanalysis. The current head of the Freud Archives, Dr. Harold P. Blum, first announced a change in approach with a letter to the *New York Review of Books* in 1986.[1] He then maintained that a "new" policy had been inaugurated, so that everything which is being published, or has already appeared in print, will be "open to all scholars on the basis of equal access." At the time I felt it hard to believe that any researcher could feel indebted for that kind of help from the Archives, even on the exalted basis of "equal access," for material which was soon to be stale.[2] According to a 1986 letter to me from the Chief of the Manuscript Division of the Library of Congress, that supposed new policy of Dr. Blum's amounted solely to Dr. Blum's making unrestricted Freud's adolescent letters to Eduard Silberstein. These letters formed the basis for a 1971 article, and were extensively perused by at least one historian who discusssed them at length in a 1986 book.[3] They have by now been out in German and in English since 1990.

The Library of Congress has remained subject to the whims of its principal official donor connected to psychoanalysis, the Freud Archives. Whatever the wishes of those who gave or sold material to the Archives, the Archives' own position has been that the bulk of the significant documents will only start to be available after the year 2000. It was, I think, redundant for Dr. Blum, as Executive Director of the Archives, to have told "interested persons" to apply to the Library of Congress "for permission to view the material in the Sigmund Freud Collection, subject to the usual rules and regulations of the Library of Congress governing such scholarly use," when in fact the Library of Congress seems helpless in the face of arbitrary restrictions of the Archives. (I think it bears repeating how the Freud Copyrights in England even maintains control over whether one is permitted to xerox any Freud material at the Library of Congress.)

A laughable system of classification, first invented by Kurt Eissler but still in effect today, means that one of Freud's letters to his deceased eldest son is restricted until the year 2013, and another until 2032. A letter of Josef Breuer's was sealed until 2102.

Dr. Blum's 1986 announcement contained a promise about the future : "It is the intention of the Archives to release all letters and documents from restriction, as soon as possible, consistent with legal and ethical standards and obligations." At the time I worried what this worthy intent might amount to, since it would be the Archives which would be implementing this supposed new policy, and constructing its own rules. I publicly doubted whether there ever would be any change in the longstanding policy of the Archives in allowing certain ideologically acceptable individuals to use documentation which is in the meantime being barred to scholars at large.

Despite Dr. Eissler's ceasing (ever since the fiasco connected with Jeffrey Masson to be discussed in chapter 12) to be head of the Freud Archives, Eissler did still linger on "as Anna Freud's representative," in charge of allowing researchers to inspect the restricted Series A of the Sigmund Freud Collection at the Library of Congress, until Eissler's 1999 death.

In a 1990 English edition of the *Journal* of the International Association for the History of Psychoanalysis,[4] we were told by Dr. Blum some further apparent news about the Freud Collection at the Library of Congress: "All of Series D in the Library of Congress catalogue of the Sigmund Freud Collection has now been de-restricted." Within weeks of reading that news I went myself to the Library of Congress to find out the true story. In the past it was the case that fascinating material was contained in Series D, and I was dubious that much had in fact changed. It turned out that all that has been altered is that Series D is now no longer of much interest, and has for some time been reduced to being a minor part of the larger Collection. What has taken place over the years, although perhaps Dr. Blum remains unaware of the history of this change, is that what once was included within the now unrestricted Series D has become a part of the restricted Series Z. A cynic might well think of the model of a shell game.

Once again, in 1990, Dr. Blum restated his good intentions about the future of unnecessary restrictions: "The thorniest problem remains the condition under which restrictions were established and the current legal status of the original restrictions." Yet when Helene Deutsch, for example, while I was writing her authorized biography starting in 1978, tried to get back copies of Freud letters that she herself had donated to the Archives, it proved impossible for us successfully to retrieve them. (Now that they are finally derestricted, I cannot gain permission to have them xeroxed.)

Dr. Blum was correct in 1986 to raise the issue of "ethical standards and obligations," but I think it affects many more aspects of the history of psychoanalysis than just the traditionalist defense of the secrecy that continues to afflict the Freud Collection at the Library of Congress in Washington. For one of the most surprising aspects of the whole story is that these restraints do not pertain specifically to clinical issues, or the privacy of former patients. One has long suspected that what is at issue here is not a matter of appropriate discretion, but rather idealizations of Freud in need of being preserved.

Let us now explore one issue, which seems to be an important one ethically: revealing the names of former analytic patients. Ernest Jones, Freud's official biographer, was the first to disclose that Breuer's early patient "Anna O.," about whom Freud established an early legend, was in fact Bertha Pappenheim, the leader of the Jewish women's movement in Germany. Her "surviving relatives and friends were deeply offended. . . . " at Jones's revelation and her executor wrote in protest.[5] To cite another instance of an indiscretion, oddly enough it was Kurt Eissler himself, shortly after Freud's early patient the "Wolf-Man" died, who announced his real name.[6] On behalf of ethical standards I want to ask if this was a correct procedure for psychoanalysis to follow.

This matter of psychoanalytic morals is relevant to what I want now to explore, since two analysts[7], one a past President of the Italian Psychoanalytic Society, have revealed the last name of a female patient of Edoardo Weiss's; her father, Giovacchino Forzano, had been an old friend of Mussolini's and an important Cabinet member in Mussolini's government, and therefore a link between Freud and Benito Mussolini. I interviewed Weiss because he met Freud first in 1908, and stayed in contact with him until Freud's death. I can remember Weiss's saying to me, as we went through his files, to "forget" the name of his Forzano patient (whom he wrote about to Freud, and took for a consultation to Freud), and I never put it into print. I recall once coming across the Forzano name in a biography of Mussolini, but my inquisitiveness was inhibited by Weiss's injunction to me.

Perhaps because there was so much about the woman Weiss called in print "Ethel" (her name turned out to have been Concetta) contained in the correspondence of Weiss with Freud, Weiss was adamantly against revealing the Forzano name. Weiss also had two sisters in treatment with Freud; their names came up too in my interviews with Weiss, and doubtless he was trying to protect them as well. I feel certain that Weiss would have felt morally shocked at the name Forzano now being publicly revealed, and by psychoanalysts at that. Are we in academic life to be subjected to restrictions that somehow do not ethically restrain practicing clinicians?

Weiss told me specifically how he had given Jones photostats of Weiss's letters from Freud; Weiss had only asked that Jones get specific permission before using them. Jones, however, did not bother to contact Weiss again and just published whatever he wanted, turning the letters over to Freud's son Ernst. Weiss thereby felt he had lost control over the content of these letters; he told me he was concerned that there was a lot of material there on patients, including names, that he would not want published. (In defense of Jones it should be noted that he was ill as he was completing the last volume of his Freud biography, where he used so many of the Weiss letters, and Jones's ill health might mitigate his high-handed way of treating Weiss.)

It does seem to me that for an analyst to disclose the name of any analytic patient is a questionable procedure. I must admit that on this point I would propose a historiographical double standard; for I rather think that historians ought to have more latitude than psychoanalysts. (The Freud Archives has been functioning with a reverse double standard, allowing documents to analysts which are not shown to historians; such an approach does imply the existence of ethical restraints on what analysts reveal.)

In my 1969 *Brother Animal: The Story of Freud and Tausk* I mentioned the name of an American politician, Herbert Lehman, whom Paul Federn had crossed the Atlantic to try to help before World War I.[8] Perhaps it was wrong of me, as an American political scientist, to have raised the Lehman name, and the symptom of stuttering. I did not come across this information in a document but rather was told it verbally. It seemed to me extraordinary for a Viennese analyst to have come to the States just to treat one patient. (The Lehmans later helped Federn after he immigrated to New York City at the beginning of World War II.) Anna Freud, despite a seven-page letter to Eissler detailing her objections to *Brother Animal*, did not once raise the matter of Lehman. Eissler himself denounced me to my publisher for what I had done, although it was long after Lehman had died, it did no harm, and betrayed no professional standards on my part. What different morality licensed Eissler, immediately after the Wolf-Man's death, to announce that man's name?

I think that our tradition of depth psychology has in general not paid enough attention to the whole problem of moral values. Psychoanalysis is in fact far more enmeshed in ethics and philosophy than Freud liked to imagine. We are told by one of the Italian analysts who has used the Forzano family name that "Freud rarely voiced political opinions. And when he did so he always expressed himself with moderation, good sense, and measured skepticism."[9]

As a political scientist I know that this sort of idealizing of Freud is garbage. In reality Freud could like the rest of us be remarkably credulous politically. When warned of the danger to him of the possibility of Adolf Hitler's coming to power, Freud is supposed to have remarked, "A nation that produced Goethe could not possibly go to the bad."[10] And after Hitler was established in office, Freud is reported to have believed a host of stories about the dictator's supposed sexual perversions; some of these legends, supported by Freud himself, found their way into a psychoanalytic study of Hitler undertaken during World War II but only published many years later.[11] The Freud-Bullitt collaboration on Woodrow Wilson further illustrates my general point; their book was based on their mutual hatred of the American president, hardly supporting the idea that Freud's political opinions "always" were expressed "with moderation, good sense, and measured skepticism."[12]

This important matter can be tested by examining Freud's relationship with Mussolini. My own claim to competence in this area rests not on any special knowledge I have about Italian politics, or Central European history in general. I can add something to his subject only because I conducted so many interviews with Weiss in Chicago in the mid–1960s; we talked at length then about Weiss's handling of his patient who was a daughter of a Mussolini cabinet minister, and how this gave Weiss an indirect tie to Mussolini which then got, Weiss maintained, exaggerated out of all proportion in Jones's biography of Freud.

The 1970 Freud-Weiss correspondence, which incidentally Freud's daughter Anna did her best to block from coming out in England, formed part of the oral history that I accumulated, since Weiss and I together went through all his letters from Freud.[13] (A letter from Freud to Weiss about Freud's analysis of Anna still remains the firmest evidence we have about the reality of Freud's having himself treated Anna. When I first raised the matter in my *Brother Animal*, Anna Freud — even in private letters — did not try to contest the issue.) I am not suggesting that oral history can substitute for all other types of research; Weiss never told me about ever having been received, even on business, by Galeazzo Ciano, Mussolini's son-in-law, who at the time was Undersecretary of the Ministry of Press and Propaganda, nor did Weiss disclose that one of his students in Rome had one of the "Duce's" relatives in analysis.[14]

Weiss, who originally was from Trieste, had moved to Rome in 1931. In those days being an analyst in Italy, unlike now, meant a special sort of isolation, and Weiss was tempted to leave Italy because of all the disappointments he encountered in Rome. According to one of Weiss's sons a specific letter of Freud's was so unsympathetic to Weiss's plight that somehow it disappeared from the currently available collection; presumably, despite Weiss's awe for Freud, Weiss destroyed that one letter. (A. A. Brill's son reported how his father had done away with a Freud letter on the grounds that it might prove politically embarrassing to Franklin Roosevelt's administration, and he also destroyed part of a letter in which Freud had criticized Brill. Further, Sandor Rado destroyed at least two Freud letters to him.) So although oral history has its limits, we must also remain skeptical about how the documents that remain may have been culled.

According to Weiss the spread of psychoanalysis in Italy was seriously hampered by Freud's credulousness toward people who wrote to him; Freud, from Weiss's point of view, created problems by allowing himself to be taken in by a series of unreliable types. For example, Freud saw some newspaper people who afterwards wrote pieces which were disillusioning. In general, the Italian psychiatrists were hostile to all things that appeared to be German, and the old Austrian influence (which had once prevailed over large parts of Italy) was still resented; anti-Semitism could also be an obstacle. Of course the Church's opposition to Freud remained a difficulty too; it eventually closed down the psychoanalytic journal Weiss started in Italy.

Weiss was especially resentful of one point in Jones's biography of Freud which bore on the history of analysis in Italy, and which has acquired a permanent-seeming place in the history books. Weiss had had in Rome with him that daughter of a high official in Mussolini's government. Forzano was a playwright and movie producer; he and Mussolini had once co-authored three plays together. When in 1933 Weiss was having some special difficulties in treating Forzano's daughter, he took her with him for a consultation with Freud in Vienna. Forzano went along as well.

At the interview Forzano asked Freud for a signed photograph, and for an inscribed book for Mussolini, his friend. Freud, not without irony, picked a little volume of his consisting of a public exchange of letters with Albert Einstein entitled *Why War*? Weiss was very embarrassed at the time because he thought that Freud was obliged for Weiss's sake and on behalf of the Italian Psychoanalytic Society to consent to Forzano's request. For Freud to have refused a requested dedication would have hurt Weiss's position in Italy. Freud had chosen to write something gracious about what Mussolini had done for excavating and reconstructing archeological sites in Italy: "Benito Mussolini with the humble greetings of an old man who recognizes in the ruler the cultural hero."[15] (An alternative translation reads: "To Benito

Mussolini, with the humble greetings of an old man who recognizes in the man of power the champion of culture."[16]) As one analyst, wholly sympathetic to Freud, has put it, "The phrasing of Freud's inscription to Mussolini is unequivocal, and Weiss's attempt to play down its significance and importance is quite ineffectual."[17] Two months later Mussolini was hardly won over; he then wrote his only public reference to Freud: "Life is more and more difficult, and Communism more and more complicated. To follow it one needs to be competent in the new science or imposture called psychoanalysis, whose Pontifex Maximus is the Viennese professor Freud."[18]

Weiss, for all the independence of his later position in the States, was worried when I knew him about what others had made of Freud's willingness to write such a dedication to Mussolini. Alfred Adler, who was a dedicated socialist, did have a follower who picked up on Freud's collaborative-sounding deed.[19] Jones himself embellished (Weiss said "lied") about the significant fact of this particular patient of Weiss's, because Jones claimed that after the Nazis entered Austria in 1938 Weiss was in a position to be "in near contact with the Duce." Subsequently another orthodox analyst, following Jones's lead, wrote that Weiss "knew" Mussolini.[20] According to Jones, Weiss told him "that Mussolini . . . made a *demarché*, either directly to Hitler or to his Ambassador in Vienna. Probably he remembered the compliment Freud had paid him four years before."[21]

But Weiss insisted to me that Jones had invented the "near contact" between himself and Mussolini, and that Weiss had had a strict record of anti-Fascism. (That past president of the Italian Psychoanalytic Society says of Weiss that he was "perhaps a bit pedantic academically but spotlessly honest. . . . "[22]) It is true that "Ethel's" father had gotten the ban on Weiss's journal temporarily lifted, but then a powerful Franciscan at the University of Milan had again forced the withdrawal of Weiss's publication. Weiss said that he was never in any direct way in touch with Mussolini, and not Jones's source for such an idea. "Ethel" did say to Weiss that Mussolini had in 1938 sent a message to Vienna on Freud's behalf, but Weiss himself had no evidence as to the truth of such an intervention; her father also told Weiss that Mussolini had written Hitler about Freud, but Weiss thought it could not have been so and for all he knew Mussolini had done nothing whatever.

I think that Jones, who was in general overly impressed by powerful leaders, was probably taken in by some fantasies of Freud's own that Mussolini was particularly concerned to protect him in Vienna. (I was told by a famous American psychologist, Henry A. Murray, that Jones, a fiery little man, had set up his study in such a way that he had plenty of space to size someone up before they reached his desk — "just like Mussolini.") It always pleased Freud to think that a supporter of his had high political influence, and at that time Freud did not take an especially dim view of Mussolini.

As the sociopolitical upheavals grew worse, and psychoanalysis was threatened in Italy and in Vienna itself, Freud wrote that he was relying on the influence that he alleged that Weiss had. Freud was like many others throughout the 1920s and 1930s when Mussolini attracted a lot of support and admiration from abroad. In *Civilization and Its Discontents* (1930), before Freud inscribed *Why War*? for Mussolini, Freud had complained that America had failed to produce super-ego "leader-type" men.[23]

Although most observers abroad who had been inclined to be sympathetic to Mussolini were repelled by the Italian dictator's invasion of Abyssinia, Freud could still write in his *Moses and Monotheism* (1938) that "with similar violence" to what the Soviets were then using in Russia, "the Italian people are being trained up to orderliness and a sense of duty."[24] According to Weiss, Freud, although he admired Italian art and sculpture, did not think much of the Italian national character; it was typical for the Viennese of Freud's generation to look down on Italians.

By 1938 Freud had some special reasons for wanting to think well of Mussolini. Only in the summer of 1938, after Freud had left Vienna for London, had Mussolini adopted within Italy Hitler's policies against the Jews. The anti-Semitic campaign officially began in July, and the next month "the sudden announcement of Italy's anti-Semitic laws made the state of Mussolini's mental health not a matter of 'hints' but of serious speculation" among American newspaper correspondents.[25] Furthermore, right up until the German takeover of Austria it had been common for Viennese Jews to rely on Italy to protect Austrian independence.

Freud had special reasons of his own not to want to face up to the realities of Mussolini. Freud, I believe, knew that once he left his doctors in Vienna his medical condition would likely deteriorate. The London physicians, who did not know his case, were intimidated by him and hesitated to operate in time. I think that it was partly for the sake of staying in Vienna that Freud had, over the opposition of some of his favorite pupils, expressed support for an authoritarian regime in Austria, even after it had repressed — in a bloody civil war — a socialist uprising. Freud was extremely old, but it is noteworthy that it was in London that he finally put in press *Moses and Monotheism*, containing the relatively favorable mention of Mussolini.

Freud, towards the end of his stay in Vienna, maintained several significant life-lines abroad. Freud's Parisian analysand the Princess George (Marie Bonaparte) could be relied on by him, since she had royal connections and abundant money. In London, Ernest Jones knew which strings to pull politically on Freud's behalf. The American Ambassador to France then, William C. Bullitt, was a former patient of Freud's; independent of Bullitt, when the Nazis marched into Vienna we know that the American Under-Secretary of

State, Sumner Welles, cabled on behalf of Roosevelt's administration to the American consul in Vienna about Freud's safety. And Ruth Mack Brunswick, still another former patient of Freud's, was well-connected in high New Deal circles through her jurist father.

Throughout Freud's last years in Vienna he had, like others in defiance of Austrian currency regulations, kept money abroad. When the Nazis took Anna Freud for a day in Vienna it was almost certainly to inquire about the state of Freud's finances, which were being managed also by Freud's son Martin. Despite how much, as Freud wrote, the Nazis had "bled" him, his finances had been handled shrewdly enough so that he did not die poor in London.[26]

Mythmaking about Freud has been abetted by the credulity of his followers, which in turn has been promoted by the unnecessary secrecy about documents. We do know, thanks to the research of one Italian analyst, that Forzano, "Ethel's" father, did in fact write to Mussolini on Freud's behalf. In the Duce's private correspondence there is a letter from Forzano dated March 14, 1938: "I recommend to Your Excellency a glorious old man of eighty-two who greatly admires Your Excellency: Freud, a Jew." (The Nazi occupation of Austria took place on March 11.) It seems to me noteworthy that this one Italian analyst believes that "considering Mussolini's habits and the situation of the time, it is likely that Mussolini did in fact intervene."[27]

Weiss, however, took no direct part in contacting Mussolini, although "Ethel" remained in analysis with him until close to his departure for the States in early 1939. Jones was so eager to place Freud among the mighty, perhaps following Freud's so far unpublished version of his protectors abroad, that it was not evident to Jones that it did not add to Freud's reputation to have him relying on Mussolini at such a late date. But romanticizations of Freud are still so common that those for example influenced by Herbert Marcuse, and other Marxist readings of Freud which have flowed from the Frankfurt school of critical sociology, do not even acknowledge the existence of this ethical question.

Nothing in the Freud-Mussolini story can equal the appalling details of Jung's notorious collaboration with the Nazis. Yet by World War II a debate would rage about what the sources were within Western culture for the rise of Fascism. The philosopher Nietzsche would take some of the blame for what had happened, in that his program for going "beyond good and evil" had helped undermine Western standards of ethics. Freud shared many of Nietzsche's views.[28] Alfred Adler remained sufficiently disaffected from Freud that in private he could blame Freud for the rise of the Nazis.

It is possible, and I believe necessary, to weigh the significance of the political implications of psychoanalysis. I have, for example, long thought it was telling about Freud's conservative inclinations that in *The Interpretation of Dreams* he so readily identified with the victims of the French Revolution's Reign of Terror. His eagerness to think well of Mussolini, and the interest Jones had in helping to publicize the story of Mussolini's supposedly helping Freud, should tell us something about the nature of the ethical commitments of that first generation of analysts. For example, Wilhelm Reich, who had boldly denounced Jung at the outset of his collaboration with the Nazis, was informed by Jones in London that Reich had to choose between politics and psychoanalysis. (Reich was also objecting to IPA analysts agreeing to Nazi anti-Semitic regulations for their group.) Jones, like others at the time, had found it appropriate to work with Hermann Göring's cousin, the psychiatrist Dr. Matthias Göring, even after Freud's teachings were officially banned in Nazi Germany.[29] Alleged analytic neutrality often masks a commitment to an authoritarian status quo.

As a historian, I am grateful for learning the added details Italian analysts have provided; now we know that Forzano did in fact do something on Freud's behalf, although that still does not amount to Weiss having known Mussolini, nor been "in near contact" with him; and Weiss stoutly maintained to me that he had never told Jones anything about Mussolini having intervened for Freud.

Mythmaking about Freud can go on unchecked as long as idealizations about him are uncorrected. Few of us now would approve of his having flattered Mussolini in any way. Freud was politically on the naïve side, although not as foolish as Jung proved to be. Both of them were capable of acting opportunistically. In a situation like we find ourselves in, without adequate access to the appropriate documents, mythologizing can all too often flourish. It is precisely this sort of context that promotes indiscretion, since inevitably we are naturally eager to find out what actually happened. So as intellectual historians we are bound to be grateful for violations of psychoanalytic propriety. The superiority of one piece of historical research over another is often established by the most successful truth-teller.

But psychoanalysts must remember that they get paid for being discreet, and betraying the confidentiality of patient's names is bound to be a questionable procedure. When I wrote *Brother Animal*, and mentioned Herbert Lehman's name, I was doing so as a young intellectual historian, not an analyst. My *Helene Deutsch: A Psychoanalyst's Life* was written many years later, and with her authorization.[30] I found then that I implicitly identified with what she would have wanted me to remain silent about, and out of loyalty to her, for example, I failed to interview some former private analytic patients of hers (not in training analyses), even some she put into published case histories, because I felt that she would not have wanted me to transgress the norms which are opposed to the violation of a patient's privacy. (Melanie Klein's biographer pursued an opposite course.) I hope I retained my objectivity toward Helene Deutsch; but I feel just as deferential toward the memory of Edoardo Weiss as to her, and what they each would have approved, which is why I am now raising the vexing question of psychoanalysis and ethics in connection with the historical linkages among Weiss, Freud, and Mussolini.

Diane Wood Middlebrook's *Anne Sexton: A Biography*[31] raised the question of ethics and privacy in a different way from what we have discussed so far. Middlebrook wrote a powerful account of how Anne Sexton transformed herself from a suburban American housewife into one of the most popular contemporary poets, and Middlebrook's book makes for mesmerizing reading.

What made Anne Sexton famous as a poet was in part the way she used her work as a form of confession. She saw herself as an explorer of the unconscious, delving into forbidden areas of experience. Her suicide in 1974 has added to her stature as a poet who transformed spiritual anguish into artistic achievement. However good a poet she was, there are passages in her letters, cited in this biography, that are remarkable in their directness and command of colloquial English.

Although it did not interfere with her winning a Pulitzer Prize, Anne Sexton's madness had been apparent since the time she became the mother of two daughters. She was unable to cope when her husband was away from home, and her repeated suicide attempts and hospitalizations speak for themselves. Sexton's and many other writers' use of sincerity as a technique of capturing attention is a not so attractive side-product of the Freudian revolution in the history of ideas. But Anne Sexton was hardly alone in seeing poetry as a vehicle for describing therapeutic experiences.

Middlebrook's biography, authorized by Sexton's elder daughter Linda, who became her literary executor, makes clear that in her life Sexton violated almost every taboo. Not only was she an alcoholic who was addicted to a variety of drugs, she was even sexually abusive of her daughter Linda. The biography is made compelling by virtue of Linda's authorizing Dr. Martin Orne, a psychiatrist who treated Anne Sexton for eight years, to release audiotapes he made during hundreds of therapy sessions. She had been unable to remember anything of significance from one session to the next, and he used the tapes to maintain continuity in their working relationship.

Orne broke the rule of confidentiality. He also wrote a foreword to the biography, and subsequently defended himself against the charge of indiscretion in part by revealing a subsequent psychiatrist's sexual relation with Sexton while she was in treatment with him. All he says about this psychiatrist in the foreword is: "Although Anne initially did extremely well with another therapist, the therapeutic contract became untenable because of a change in their relationship. Unfortunately, this change also undermined her crucial relationship with her husband, thereby depriving Anne of what had been a vital interpersonal support." While Sexton was alive, Orne did not report this so-called "change" to the authorities who monitor the conduct of physicians. Still another therapist encouraged her to divorce her long-suffering husband, even though this took away a pillar of her stability; a year later she was dead.

Middlebrook's biography is so engrossing partly because it is a tale of transgression. Sexton not only lived life "to the hilt," as she put it, but her psychiatrists lost their foothold in attempting to treat her. Orne may have been correct in his belief that she "had a condition that was traditionally called hysteria," but this seems now a disingenuous way of characterizing her. Most physicians today would probably diagnose her as a "borderline" or psychotic. Even if she ever thought of authorizing the release of these tapes, the question remains whether she had the mental competence to do so. It has to be disturbing that someone as sick as she could at the same time manage to speak for the experiences of so many others in our time.

Middlebrook cannot be blamed for using whatever material she could get her hands on. A biographer's central responsibility is to the truth, and we have no way of knowing what she omitted on behalf of human discretion. In my own biographical work, I have often felt constrained to leave things out for a number of reasons. For example, when I published letters Helene Deutsch wrote about candidates in training with her, I successfully disguised the individuals' identities. Freud has often been criticized for his statement agreeing to the idea that morality was "self-evident." Yet there is no way of legislating the ethics of biography-writing; either one has a reliable set of moral standards or one does not.

How physicians should behave is another story. For my biography of Helene Deutsch, I sought to interview the internist who had taken care of her and her late husband for almost fifty years. He made it plain that he would not talk to me about her without her written approval, and that of her son. (Deutsch was in her mid-nineties, and although her doctor considered her mentally fit, he still wanted her son's approval as well.) When the physician's request was met, he went through her records with me, enhancing my understanding of the subject.

Some years earlier, I worked with Helene Deutsch on a study of the suicide of Victor Tausk, an early disciple in psychoanalysis who killed himself in 1919 after a frustrating struggle with Freud. Deutsch had been Tausk's analyst for three months, while she herself was being analyzed by Freud. The documents at my disposal about Tausk's difficulties, including his suicide note to Freud, came from the Tausk family. One of Tausk's sons came from Europe with the express purpose of seeing Helene Deutsch, and we talked about her version of the events during one long evening at her house. He subsequently went to see Anna Freud in London to make sure he had left no stone unturned in his search for uncovering the mystery surrounding his father's death. Helene Deutsch knew first hand of the conflict between Tausk and Freud. She told what she knew partly out of guilt over her former patient, but also to relieve the anguish of Tausk's son. At the time she joked about how I was a "spy," and I have often thought about Henry James's short story *The Aspern Papers*, a tale in which an old woman manages to evade the biographical sleuth.

Good features have been attributed to Martin Orne, including a dedication to research. But his avoiding an up-to-date diagnosis by invoking the old concept of hysteria seems to me suspect. In all likelihood Anne Sexton was highly seductive, and it is not surprising then that she should have succeeded in ensnaring her other psychiatrist. Perhaps this is the reason why Orne chose not to ruin this physician's career at the time. But surely if Anne Sexton had trances, or fugue states, which interfered with her memory to the degree that she could not follow from one session to the next, it can be considered questionable just how much she knew what she was doing when she left those tapes with Orne "to help others."

Let us assume that her close friends are correct in thinking she would not have objected to public use of the tapes. Still, she did not explicitly authorize her daughter Linda to do so. She made no mention of the tapes whatever in her will. Erica Jong's contribution to this whole debate is as outrageous as anything that has been argued about this whole story. In an op ed piece for the *New York Times*, she displayed what I consider an incoherent line of reasoning, beginning with a fictional set of instructions which Anne Sexton might have left her literary executor, authorizing disclosure of the tapes. Jong then went onto claim unique status for Anne Sexton as a poet.

In the past, defenders of Ezra Pound's special psychiatric privileges have cited — as does Jong for Anne Sexton — his special standing as a poet.[32] Aside from the issues of privacy and confidentiality, and the damage that may be done to the psychiatric profession, Jong added a new spurious issue: supposedly the controversy arose because of Anne Sexton's gender. Robert Lowell's psychiatric records, says Jong, would be considered more valuable.

Jong defies the principle of democratic equality by singling out poets as exceptions, and in keeping with this undemocratic elitism, she compounds the bias by adding Anne Sexton's gender as a factor. If Jong consulted the historical literature about Pound, she would find that there was as much concern with the abuse of psychiatric power then as it looks like there will have to be in the case of Anne Sexton, once the facts are clearer.

At this writing, we do not know all we might need. For example, the position of Linda Sexton may be the most troubling of all. She has been quoted in *The New York Times* as saying: "I sometimes wonder if Mother is angry with me" in connection with all the disclosures she has sanctioned. In an article in the Sunday *New York Times* book review section, Linda also wrote, "Sometimes I was able to obey the instructions left me, other times I had to override them." It would not be the first time that literary executors have violated the trust reposed in them.

Others of the extended Sexton family have objected to certain aspects of the biography, and this is where the proper recourse lies. As readers we can comment on the book's tastefulness, and perhaps speculate on Linda Sexton's motives. That she was sexually abused by her mother appears of obvious relevance, though it may be unfair to charge her, as some in the media have done, with seeking posthumous vengeance.

The possibility of ill effects of this story on psychotherapeutic patients in the future is not of great concern to me. On the whole I think people are far too credulous and trusting about the confidences patients place in their psychiatrists. Therapy works better if patients do not believe they have put themselves in the hands of a magician. Psychiatrists are put under enormous emotional pressure, especially in dealing with patients as acutely disturbed as Anne Sexton. There is no way practitioners can function without unloading some of their problems on their spouses and professional colleagues, so confidentiality is, in any event, a relative phenomenon. There is also the problem of malicious gossip, which psychiatrists indulge in like other human beings. Maybe it were better for all concerned if patients had greater savvy, and were therefore more careful and guarded in dealing with their therapists.

In the case of Anne Sexton, the sensationalism that has become connected with her biography is troubling. Why did Orne write a foreword to the book? He appeared to be unaware of the degree to which she wanted to please him by becoming a poet, desperately eager to hang on to his good graces. He did not seem sufficiently aware of the part he played in her symptoms, nor how the psychiatric help she sought ultimately facilitated her destruction. The grandiose tone of the conclusion of his foreword is disturbing: "Sadly, if in therapy Anne had been encouraged to hold on to the vital supports that had helped her build the innovative career that meant so much to her and others, it is my view that Anne Sexton would be alive today."

For me, two of her nieces show more common sense: "We don't know what made Anne the way she was, and never will. Was it a chemical imbalance? A misfitted chromosome? An accident of birth? A genetic misfortune? All the speculation in the world, including the wild speculation and completely unwarranted conclusions in Diane Wood Middlebrook's book, won't answer the question."

If Orne had chosen to write a case history of this patient, use of the tapes would have been justifiable and in keeping with Anne Sexton's wish to see them used for the sake of others. He would then have been obliged to disguise his material for professional presentation. The reality of case histories, Freud's or anybody else's, also illustrates one of the limits on psychotherapeutic confidentiality. But Orne agreed to meet with Middlebrook, then turned over the tapes, and in addition wrote what appears as a self-serving foreword. Once the controversy, concerning the biography and his part in it, was in the open, he added new information, like his view of the conduct of Sexton's subsequent psychiatrist, which he had not disclosed until then.

Of the three people involved, Middlebrook, Linda Sexton, and Orne, it is the therapist who I think was the most blameworthy. He had an obligation to his profession, no matter what Linda Sexton wanted. Based on this incident, one would not want to put oneself in his hands or see someone one cares about seek his help, even though, from the passages on the tapes Middlebrook quotes, he seemed in unusually close touch with his patient.

My research has been concerned with events and persons in the more distant past, and the passage of time does have some relevance to the stickiness of the moral dilemmas. For example, writing about Helene Deutsch's treatment of Tausk, I did not hesitate to point out where I thought she had gone wrong in conducting the therapy, and how she, like Freud and Tausk himself, had missed some vital aspects of the situation. In other words I was investigating the working therapeutic relationship between the key people. Middlebrook apparently did not interpret the contents of the tapes adequately. When she wrote to the *New York Times* that while listening to the tapes she felt as if Anne Sexton were talking to her directly, Middlebrook neglected to take into account the crucial elements of transference and counter-transference in the therapeutic relationship. Psychiatric consultations are not laboratory reactions. What transpires in a therapy session depends to a large extent on the interaction between patient and psychiatrist. Imagining, as she says she did, that Anne Sexton was talking to anybody but Orne, Middlebrook appears to fail to understand this critical point.

One would think that Martin Orne should have had more constraints on his actions. For example, if the FBI were to come to a psychiatrist for information about a patient, should the therapist feel obliged in the interest of national security to reveal therapeutic confidences? Or should the therapist take the principled stand of a physician-confessor? In the past, when clergymen often performed the functions now taken over by psychiatrists, some momentous struggles ensued between church and state over issues of conflicting allegiances. The doctrine that Anne Sexton was an exception, like the notion that her status as a poet and a woman justified special treatment, opens the door to excusing too many other possible abuses.

Whatever one might think of either Orne's or Linda Sexton's conduct,

Middlebrook's biography, *Anne Sexton*, is a good book. This is not to imply that the end justifies the means, but all the public issues connected to this tale should not obscure Middlebrook's literary accomplishment. The perplexities associated with the ethics of privacy get deepened with each occasion for such a controversy. Although the examples we discussed earlier connected with the identification of the names of psychoanalytic patients may be rather different from the specifics of the story connected with Anne Sexton, they all add up enough to demonstrate just how important and unresolved are some of the intricacies involved in ethical questions that arise as part of a contemporary effort to maintain the key value of privacy.

Notes

1. Harold P. Blum, "Letter to the Editor," *New York Review of Books*, July 17, 1986, p. 52.
2. Paul Roazen, "Letter to the Editor," *New York Review of Books*, Nov. 20, 1986, p. 59. See below, Ch. 15, pp.
3. Roazen, *Encountering Freud, op. cit.*, pp. 1–3.
4. *Journal*, International Association for the History of Psychoanalysis, No. 9 (Spring 1990): pp. 13–14.
5. Albrecht Hirschmüller, *The Life and Work of Josef Breuer: Physiology and Psychoanalysis* (New York, New York University Press, 1989), pp. 95, 365.
6. *International Journal of Psychoanalysis*, Vol. 61, Part I (1980), p. 105.
7. See A. M. Accerboni, "Psychoanalysis and Fascism, Two Incompatible Approaches: The Difficult Role of Edoardo Weiss," *Review of the International History of Psychoanalysis*, Vol. 1 (1988). pp. 225–240; Glauco Carloni, "Freud and Mussolini: A Minor Drama in Two Acts, One Interlude, and Five Characters," *L'Italia nella Psicoanalisis* (1989), pp. 51–60. See also A. M. Accerboni Pavanello, "Sigmund Freud as Remembered by Edoardo Weiss, the Italian Pioneer of Psychoanalysis," *International Review of Psychoanalysis*, Vol. 18 (1990), pp. 351–59.
8. Roazen, *Brother Animal, op. cit.*, p. 152.
9. Carloni, "Freud and Mussolini," *op. cit.*, p. 53.
10. Ernest Jones, *The Life and Work of Sigmund Freud*, Vol. 3 (New York, Basic Books, 1957), p. 151.
11. Roazen, *Freud and His Followers, op. cit.*, p. 533.
12. Paul Roazen, *Freud: Political and Social Thought*, third edition with new Introduction (New York, Alfred A. Knopf, 1968, New Brunswick, N. J., Transaction Publishers, 1999), Epilogue.
13. Edoardo Weiss, *Sigmund Freud as a Consultant: Recollections of a Pioneer in Psychoanalysis*, with new Introduction by Paul Roazen (New Brunswick, N.J., Transaction Publishers, 1991). Young-Bruehl, *Anna Freud, op. cit.*, pp. 434–35.
14. Accerboni, "Psychoanalysis and Fascism," *op. cit.*
15. Weiss, *Sigmund Freud As A Consultant, op. cit.*, p. 20.
16. Carloni, "Freud and Mussolini," *op. cit.*, p. 52.
17. *Ibid.*, p. 53.
18. *Ibid.*, p. 54.

19. Alfred Adler, *Superiority and Social Interest*, edited by Heinz L. Ansbacher and Rowena R. Ansbacher, third edition (New York, W. W. Norton, 1979), p. 320.
20. Max Schur, *Freud: Living and Dying* (New York, International Universities Press, 1972), p. 498.
21. Jones, *The Life and Work of Sigmund Freud*, *op. cit.*, pp. 220–221.
22. Carloni, "Freud and Mussolini," *op. cit.*,p. 51.
23. John P. Diggins, *Mussolini and Fascism: The View From America* (Princeton, N.J., Princeton University Press, 1972), p. 72.
24. "Moses and Monotheism," *Standard Edition*, Vol. 23, p. 54.
25. Diggins, *Mussolini and Fascism*, *op. cit.*, pp. 318–19.
26. Roazen, *The Historiography of Psychoanalysis*, *op. cit*, pp. 447–52.
27. Carloni, "Freud and Mussolini," *op. cit.*, p. 58.
28. Roazen, *Political Theory and the Psychology of the Unconscious*, *op. cit.*, Part I, Ch. 2, pp. 28–48.
29. Roazen, *Encountering Freud*, *op. cit.*, pp. 34–37. See also Roazen, "The Exclusion of Erich Fromm from the IPA," *op. cit.*
30. Paul Roazen, *Helene Deutsch: A Psychoanalyst's Life* (New York, Doubleday, 1985; with New Introduction New Brunswick, N.J., Transaction Publishers, 1992).
31. Diane Wood Middlebrook, *Anne Sexton: A Biography* (Boston, Houghton Mifflin, 1991).
32. Roazen, *Encountering Freud*, *op. cit.*, pp. 89–92.

7

The Power of Orthodoxy

It would be, I think, short-sighted to see Kurt Eissler as only an eccentric personal representative of Anna Freud, for that would be to personalize Eissler's special brand of fanaticism. It is true that his own repeated efforts at psychoanalytic housecleaning were designed to help drive out of the loyal movement people that he, and others like him, had long had their ideological suspicions about. It can be hard to pin down the sorts of clichéd thinking that once surrounded the centers of the most established psychoanalytic power. I have found it frequently the case that bystanders such as literary critics, philosophers, and even publishers are apt to be more doctrinaire and partisan than even some of the most well-known analysts. For them to reconsider ideological convictions might threaten the way they have managed to integrate their souls. One sign of the enduring strength of these sorts of monolithic thought processes can be found in the lasting invitation for mavericks to break ranks in order to express their own individual views; we will be returning to this issue of such "Public Scandals" in chapter 12 and also "Sandor Rado" in chapter 13.

Before getting to Peter Gay's influential Freud biography, a powerful representative of recent orthodoxy, I would like to discuss an earlier attempt at popularization, Irving Stone's 1971 biographical novel about Freud, *The Passions of the Mind.*[1] It appeared on the tenth anniversary of the publication of his best-selling book about Michelangelo, *The Agony and the Ecstasy.* Although Stone's bibliography for *The Passions of the Mind* was quite good, his attempt at popularizing Freud for the American audience resulted in as poor a job as Freud could ever have anticipated. (Freud had disdain and contempt for American life, even though in his last years Americans were his most lucrative patients. "America," he joked, "is a mistake; a gigantic mistake, but a mistake." He denied "hating" America; he merely "regretted" it. Freud justified his feelings about America with such a shifting variety of reasons that one can be sure only of the existence of his antipathy. Like Karl Marx in his distaste for Russia, Freud detested the country which chose him as its prophet. For psychoanalysis triumphed in America, during most of the twentieth century, on a scale greater than that in any other country.)

It is not that Stone failed to transpose accurately published comments into spoken ones. Nor did Stone neglect to fill his huge book with some lively and graphic details. It is almost mechanical how every time a new person enters the narrative we are given a detailed physical description of him, as if that could be part of either life or art.

Such apparent conscientiousness was I think designed to flatter the American public's hopes that in reading Stone it could be getting something of an education. Freud gets presented here in a boring way, a model husband, father, son, at least by the standards of the early 1970s. For instance, Freud is described as checking an infant daughter's diaper in the middle of the night to see if it is wet; in Stone's never-never land the diaper turns out dry (as if anyone would risk waking a sleeping infant), but it is worth remarking that the real Freud had nothing whatever to do with his children's diapers, whatever the duties of a contemporary American husband. (A son of Freud's has reported that one could not go walking with him until toilet training was completed.) In order to make Freud more sympathetic — that is, more like us — Stone claims in the face of all known evidence that Freud's wife shared fully in his work.

Peculiarly, Stone's tome skips Freud's childhood almost entirely, in spite of what Freud believed about the special importance of the early years of life. But then, since no theory and no version that Freud ever offered about himself is in the slightest way examined critically but accepted here at face value, any extension of Stone's book into childhood could not have led very far.

Stone concentrates, properly enough, on the years of Freud's greatest originality, but then fails to appreciate the inevitable isolation and loneliness of a genius. Along with being a great writer and psychologist, Freud was a revolutionary in the history of ideas, which means he was also hard and a fighter. Freud sought to affront the pieties of his times, and sometimes even consciously identified with the devil in Western history. Since all Freud's fierce and complicated rivalries cannot square with Stone's uplifty version of the great man, such competitiveness is simply left out.

As of two weeks before publication date, *The Passions of the Mind* had already sold 150,000 copies. Its success, unfortunately, must be some testimony to the accurate reading by Stone of the state of American culture then. One would have thought that to come to grips with a man like Freud inevitably meant an exciting intellectual adventure. (A limited, autographed edition of 500 copies was available for $35.)

Peter Gay has told us that although his *Freud: A Life For Our Time* was "in the making for a long time," it took him "two and a half short and intense years . . . to write it."[2] Since the book is such a long one, most researchers might question what could result from such a relatively brief writing stint. In fact, the book is smoothly written, and Gay evidently had his eye on the most general reading audience. Doubtless many people will pick up this book as a good one-volume introduction, as they once turned to Ronald Clark's excellent *Freud: The Man and the Cause*.[3] Clark made no pretensions to scholarly originality; he simply sought to make accessible the latest findings about Freud. In my view Clark's aims were remarkably well fulfilled. But Peter Gay had far greater ambitions, as evidenced by his lengthy Bibliographical Essay (to which I will return later) at the end of his book.

Gay's kind of work seems to me an effort to lead a counter-reformation within the history of psychoanalysis, to turn back the tide of revisionist Freud studies that have come out within the last couple of generations of scholarship.

Gay tells us that he "relied on my historian's professional distance to preserve me from the idealization that Freud thought the biographer's inescapable fate."[4] Already we must be wary of Gay's line of thought, since he has seriously misunderstood the complexity of motivation that Freud thought underlay the biographical enterprise. Freud repeatedly ascribed to biographers ambivalent motives, those which denigrate as well as idealize, so it does seem surprising for Gay to isolate only one side of things. He is in fact right to be worried about his own idealizations of Freud, since Gay's book constitutes an extended brief on Freud's behalf. Ronald Clark could not fall back on any credentials as a professional historian, but I think his one-volume attempt was in the end more fair-minded than Gay's.

It is striking that Gay should put so much weight on his own profession as a historian; for a proper historical outlook is precisely what Gay's book regrettably lacks. The subtitle to his book does seem to me a giveaway; for in writing this biography as "A Life For Our Time," Gay has betrayed the central achievement of modern historiography. One of the accomplishments of Renaissance humanism was the development of a sense of perspective on the past, the awareness of historical differences. People in the Middle Ages had had no understanding of the reality of historical time, so in medieval paintings figures from the classical Greek and Roman past would be dressed the way those in medieval times wore their clothes. "This tradition had a powerful hold on men's minds and indeed in many ways was not completely shaken off until the triumph of historicism in the nineteenth century."[5] Oddly enough, Gay has himself written much about nineteenth-century matters, and yet his *Freud* suffers from the anachronisms that follow from his attempt to make the creator of psychoanalysis our contemporary. Irving Stone's novel about

Freud, *The Passions of the Mind*, suffered from the identical sin of presentism that damages Gay's undertaking.

Let me take as one example of this presentism a sentence of Gay's: "By 1905, in his *Three Essays on the Theory of Sexuality*, he had reached the point where he could criticize his fellow psychiatrists for assigning far too much importance to heredity."[6] Now, the general reader does not know that Freud was a neurologist and an outsider to psychiatry; even those who nominate books for awards cannot be expected to understand that Freud's alienation from psychiatry is a key to his professional life in Vienna, as well as to why he later so much wanted the support of someone like Carl G. Jung, who was a psychiatrist. (Gay mixes things up more by erroneously referring to Julius Wagner von Jauregg, who was a psychiatrist, as "the great neurologist."[7])

A historian not bent on writing "a life for our time" would feel no need to flatten out and assimilate the historical Freud into our practices today. And therefore students of history are required to help us understand what Freud originally meant by the concept of neurosis and what kind of patients he first thought he could account for by his original notion of "narcissistic neurosis"; and then it would also be important to describe the grounds on which Freud, later in the 1920s, first began to draw a distinction between neurosis and psychosis. Those who are most familiar with Freud's clinical practices have no doubt that his lack of psychiatric training was a handicap to his diagnostic abilities; at the same time it also freed Freud from the traditionalistic restraint about how all patients were to be approached. Despite Gay's smooth writing he has, however, given us a perspectiveless, chronicle-like account of Freud; the creator of psychoanalysis is not placed in proper perspective in both time and space, an omission that has to be misleading to serious readers who might want to rely on his book.

The starting point of Gay's trouble appears to be his effort to remain a part of the powers-that-be in certain psychoanalytic circles. Although at many points Gay does acknowledge the existence of independent research done since Ernest Jones's authorized biography of Freud first appeared in the 1950s, the whole tenor of Gay's approach is to dust Freud off and protect him from those scholars who have been supposedly intent on blackening his name. (Many people are now aware of Jones's central biases; in any case, he was a participant in early psychoanalytic struggles and therefore in a sense humanly entitled to his prejudices.)

Like many other true believers, Gay cannot acknowledge the existence of a genuinely demonic side to Freud lest such a perception interfere with the presentation of Freud for today's public. On several occasions, which Gay does not mention, Freud identified himself with the figure of Satan; neither is

Freud's interest in Nietzsche adequately explored here, nor do we hear of Freud's biting dissection of the maxim "love thy neighbor as thyself." What Gay has come up with — and this is one central reason why I think the book has so little to teach — is pretty much what today's average practicing clinician might like to find in Freud. The founder of psychoanalysis is supposed to have been much as we are, so that we can be reassured that everything we do today is satisfactory. Gay cites a passage in which Freud writes that he had "never really been a doctor in the proper sense," but Gay omits the startling Nietzschean passage in which Freud says, "I have no knowledge of having had any craving in my early childhood to help suffering humanity. My innate sadistic disposition was not a very strong one, so I had no need to develop this one of its derivatives."[8] (Gay quotes only the second, but not the first, of these two sentences.)

In fact a wholly different outlook on the past would have attempted to reconstruct Freud in his own time, not ours; and such a Freud might have turned out to be disturbingly different from what many today might otherwise have expected. His clinical practices would be surprising, his ideas challenging. Such a Freud would be more alive, I believe, and also more enduring for the future, than this false image melted down to match our own preconceptions.

As a consequence Gay does not add much to our knowledge of Freud. Gay has, for example, a section on Freud's dream theory, and other of his ideas from the 1890s, but Gay writes as if no one has ever made a substantial challenge to Freud's approach to dreaming. I am not thinking of just the important criticisms of Jung, who early on insisted that it was possible to interpret dreams not only on an object level but on a subject one (or ego level, as we now might put it) as well. Gay, even in the enterprise of supposedly writing "a life for our time," barely discusses the work of people like Professor Allan Hobson or Sir Francis Crick, not to mention those who earlier performed experiments with people's dreaming. (Crick and a handful of others are touched on in passing in the Bibliographical Essay.) Gay has undertaken to try to put the best possible face on all Freud's original theories, even if it meant leaving out efforts to challenge the scientific standing of Freud's ideas from today's perspective. When Gay undertook this book, he started out with ideological blinkers on what he would discuss.

This narrowness of perspective extends to the people who played an important role in Freud's following. How is it possible that Gay has written such a huge book without a single reference to Wilhelm Reich, a point I have already alluded to? That Reich became a troublemaker is incontestable, but it is also indisputable that what Freud was doing in writing his *Civilization and Its Discontents* is never going to be credible unless one realizes that Freud had in mind answering some of Reich's chief Marxist points. I am not so much appalled by Gay's failure to credit Reich with certain key additions to psychoanalysis as we know it now as I am disturbed that in Gay's view Reich has literally become an Orwellian nonperson.

Franz Alexander and Sandor Rado also play too little a role in Gay's version of Freud's school, as does Ruth Mack Brunswick; it is impossible for me to argue the case here without going on at too great length. But what Gay has done is fashion his history to fit the needs of today's organizational myths. So while people who were key figures in Freud's lifetime are reduced to mere passing reference, someone like Anna Freud, because of the later role she played in psychoanalysis after her father's death, is blown up out of all proportion. Freud was worried about how she would fare after his death, and he was specifically concerned about her being able to earn an independent living; so he did all he could to build up her stature. She doubtlessly succeeded in magnifying some of Freud's own likes and dislikes, as she admitted at least some of her jealousies about Freud's favorites; but just as Gay's book lacks historical balance because of those he either leaves out or diminishes in stature, he exaggerates the position of others even though the impartial evidence does not sustain his position. The idea of Gay's that a photograph of Eduard Hitschmann be made as prominent as one of C. G. Jung in *Freud* is laughable; Hitschmann was almost completely lacking in originality, and there is reason to think that Freud came to despise him for it.

The main value of Gay's book will come from the few references he makes to primary documentary material he was permitted to see but that has not until now been made available for scholarly inspection; whether others in the future will be able to use the same documents that were shown Gay remains to be seen. (In the past, for example, I was not able even to get permission to use photographs from the Freud Copyrights unless I first submitted a copy of my completed manuscript.) There are many intriguing details in Gay's text, but he does not often follow them up interpretively. I have wondered, for example, how a few weeks after Victor Tausk's suicide in 1919 Anna Freud "dreamt that Dr. Tausk's bride had rented an apartment at Berggasse 20, across the street from the Freuds, in order to shoot her father dead with a pistol."[9] Tausk had had a fiancée whom he failed to marry before his death; did Anna really dream of her as a bride, as Gay says, and if so, why? And exactly why would Anna's dream-thoughts, which were characteristically simple, anticipate such an assassination? One can wonder if Anna was reflecting any of her father's own fears or wishes.

As long as I am on the topic of Tausk, whom Gay somehow calls a "pathetic errant disciple,"[10] I would like to point out some of the flaws in Gay's reporting "for our time" the circumstances of Tausk's death. Gay leaves out entirely what happened after Freud sent Tausk for an analysis with Helene

Deutsch, who was already in analysis with Freud; Gay cannot bring himself to mention the key fact that the analysis of Tausk with Deutsch was broken up at Freud's initiative. Perhaps Gay is identifying here with Freud himself, since in the passage from a Freud letter to Abraham, which Gay quotes here for the first time, Freud does not discuss the implications of the aborted analysis terminated at his own direction. The existence of a suicide note from Tausk to Freud also goes unmentioned, but, then again, Freud may not have discussed it with Abraham; in any event Gay feels no need to include it in his narrative. (Earlier in his text Gay had told us that since Freud "never commented on his reasons for shortening his first name, all conjectures about its significance for him must remain purely speculative."[11] Did psychoanalysis not teach Gay that all of us, even Freud, lack perfect self-understanding?) It is not correct of Gay, however, to summarize Freud's letter to Lou Andreas-Salomé about Tausk's end by saying that it merely repeated "almost word for word what he had told Abraham,"[12] since in reality Freud had also told Lou, who had once been intimate with Tausk, that he was a menace to the future of psychoanalysis.

Gay's whole book reads stylistically as though he had immersed himself in the subject without preconceptions or indebtedness. But facts never speak for themselves. Just as it is tendentious to suppose that Freud, as Gay would have it, worked with patients without preconceived ideas and empirically deduced his findings in the course of clinical encounters, so it is misleading of Gay to make it seem as though his own work derives simply from an examination of the available Freud manuscript material. Gay's book does have the authenticity that comes from citing primary sources themselves rather than the secondary words that usually bring evidence to our attention. But even here the result is to minimize the contributions of those who have already been working in this field.

Gay appended to his book "an extensive and argumentative bibliographical essay"[13] that he obviously thinks is going to help scholars in the future. In my judgment this will not be the case. Gay spends his time pontificating about other people's work, and since Gay's point of view is so partisan, his words grading others will not be given much weight. Gay's scholarship can be sloppy. For example, he claims that

> the most vigorous translations into English, capturing Freud's virile and witty German speech better than any other, can be found in vols. I-IV of Collected Papers (1924–25), mainly tr. by the brilliant Joan Riviere. Vol. 5, ed. James Strachey, appeared in 1950. No wonder this edition, which contains virtually all of Freud's shorter papers and his case histories, remains the favorite of older American psychoanalysts.[14]

No passage can better illustrate Gay's identification with authority, as well as his haste. For in that edition, Volume I has only 72 pages translated by Mrs. Riviere, whereas 272 pages were translated by others; Volume II has 157 out of 402 pages translated by her; Volume III, some 600 pages, was translated entirely by Strachey; and in Volume IV, Riviere translated a mere 70 out of 472 pages. But all of Volume V was not translated by Strachey, 94 pages having been translated by Riviere. It is incomprehensible to me how Gay could contrast Volumes I-IV and Volume V on the grounds of who was "mainly" the translator or why he should so grossly overstate Mrs. Riviere's translating role in the *Collected Papers*. (Such a maneuver would however rescue the *Collected Papers* from the criticism that has been directed at Strachey's twenty-four-volume *Standard Edition*.) And Gay's reference to what supposedly was "the favorite of older American psychoanalysts" implies that they knew what they were doing.

If Gay had worked more slowly, the book would doubtless have been improved. But he also would need to be more humble and less tendentious toward the work of others. He tells us elsewhere that he was first attracted to psychoanalysis by the writings of Erich Fromm,[15] and it does seem to me a pity that Gay has swung so far in an orthodox direction. But before anyone sits down to compile "a life for our time," he should think through the historiographical implications of such an undertaking; a catchy way of selling a book may fatally flaw the historical respectability of the whole undertaking. Gay has missed the chance to hold up the example of the real Freud who was inevitably a man of his time, and thereby a living challenge to us now. Unfortunately Gay has neglected to present a vision of how life might be lived differently from our own conventions.

Peter Gay has succeeded in becoming one of our culture's most successful popularizers of complex ideas. On the subject of the Enlightenment and, more recently, about Freud, he has become a high-class modern version of Will Durant. In addition, with *Reading Freud: Explorations and Entertainments,*[16] he presented to an untutored reader a most pleasant book of eight essays.

Reading Freud lacks thematic unity, but the isolated parts are still rewarding. For example, Gay examines Freud's odd belief that William Shakespeare's works were written by the Earl of Oxford. Instead of simply dismissing out of hand one of Freud's more dotty convictions, shared in fact by some others, Gay tracks down the details of Freud's curious notion.

There is also an essay on how Freud chose the names for his six children, and a piece here on the implications of psychoanalysis for a theory of freedom, as well as an attentive account of a minor 1907 letter Freud wrote about some good (but not great) books that he then chose to recommend. Gay also makes an attempt, even if it is not too successful, to come to terms with the critical issue of Freud's sense of humor, as well as of the vexing problem of whether Freud could ever have had a sexual affair with his wife's sister Minna.

Throughout the book it is not hard to detect that Gay is a defender of old-fashioned psychoanalytic orthodoxy. He even naively claims that "Freud's consulting room was his laboratory," despite all the evidence showing how Freud's way of clinically proceeding was tilted and biased. (One would think that more than one essay could be written on the unspoken impact which Freud's collection of antiquities had on his patients and students.) And Carl Jung, for example, gets contemptuously dismissed as "too unreliable a witness" on the issue of Freud and Minna, even though a batch of letters between them seems to be mysteriously missing.

The fascinating centerpiece of this book by Gay is a reprint of a 1981 article that was originally published in *Harper's* magazine. The piece purported to be a discovery that Gay had made of a hitherto unknown 1900 book review of Freud's *The Interpretation of Dreams*. The scholarly world did not find out the truth until Dec. 21, 1988, when a letter written by Gay was widely circulated among authorities on early psychoanalysis. In that letter, Gay wrote, "I must confess . . . although there is nothing to confess, that the whole thing is a hoax."

Gay had invented the review and even the journal name as part of his propaganda to prettify Freud for today. The 1988 letter of Gay's created an international furor which made it to newspapers. Now, in *Reading Freud*, Gay has chosen a different tack, abandoning the term "hoax" and including the same *Harper's* piece under the heading of one of his "Entertainments."

The reception of all Freud's early work is an important historiographical matter. A controversy revolves around whether Freud was as neglected and criticized as he himself chose to think. The review that Gay presented to *Harper's* magazine seemed almost too good to be true to the inner circles of contemporary psychoanalytic orthodoxy. No apologist for Freud could have constructed a document that presented Freud's theories in a better, more balanced light.

Gay, who was then a professor of history at Yale, should not be allowed to place himself above the scholarly law; universities should be a sacred refuge of honesty. The editor of *Harper's* subsequently claimed that he knew about the hoax beforehand, although Gay's article appeared in an otherwise sober series called "Revisions," in which authors (such as I. F. Stone on Socrates) reconsidered classics.

It took seven years for Gay's fabrication to become evident. The only people I know who have laughed over the incident are those who think that everyone who writes on this subject do not appreciate the significance of scholarly life, or must be crackers to begin with.

In 1981, when Gay published his piece in *Harper's*, he was a neophyte in the field of Freudian studies and setting out to lead a campaign against revisionist views of the creator of psychoanalysis. A handful of insiders knew at the time that Gay's 1981 review was a hoax. The partisanship of his subsequent books on Freud has been evident to independent observers. But Gay did not need that 1981 article to establish his credentials as a scholar, which is what makes the story so bizarre.

Every busy scholar is bound to make honest mistakes that later torture the soul. But Gay's publication of that 1981 *Harper's* article, and his arrogant and misleading defense of it in *Reading Freud*, display, I think, a shocking contempt for the normal standards of academic life, and the truthfulness that makes a civilized academic community possible.

An appreciation of the contrasting status of psychoanalysis in England and America is essential for understanding the appearance of a book like Richard Wollheim's *Sigmund Freud* in Frank Kermode's Modern Masters series.[17] Initially, Freud's disciples, both in England and America, saw their task as that of rounding off what he had introduced in only a fragmentary way. A successful movement, however, has a way of absorbing into itself some of the best ideas of the opposition, and by now there has been so much silent incorporation within psychoanalysis of ideas taken from Adler, Jung, and Rank that it is all too easy to read back into past "orthodox" doctrine what is accepted only today. While Freud's power lay in his capacities as a writer and clinician, for many years, at least in the States, psychoanalysis rested on an institutional base which was for most of the century bound up with the official psychiatry Freud had scorned.

In Great Britain, however, twentieth-century psychiatry developed along a different course from that which it followed in America. While Freudian concepts have long pervaded American culture, more old-fashioned attitudes have prevailed — at least until recently — in England. (A celebrity like Princess Diana was widely known to have gone to an analytic therapist there, as did Marilyn Monroe and Jacqueline Kennedy Onassis in the States.) Until recently Freud has been looked on with rather a higher degree of suspicion there, and medicine as a whole has been accorded nowhere near as high a status as in the United States. Leading British analysts have tended not to be English: Ernest Jones was Welsh, Edward Glover a Scot, and Melanie Klein as well as Anna Freud emigrated from the Continent. (Winnicott would be the exception proving the rule I have proposed.)

As happened in the early days of psychoanalysis, the very lack of popular acclaim has meant that in England psychotherapy as a career has attracted highly talented practitioners, able to resist the pressure to conform. British analysts who write are far ahead of any American rivals in clarity and scope.

In any case, although it was numerically much smaller than its American counterpart, at the end of World War II the British Psychoanalytic Society was wracked by the ideological quarrel, as we have discussed, over whether Klein's ideas were "deviationist." Now, paradoxically, the level of controversy in psychoanalytic circles is normally quite low. In the light of all the attention given to the splits in the history of psychoanalysis, this claim of mine may seem surprising; but having discouraged controversy and promoted conformity to the group's will (if not Freud's own), psychoanalysis has benefited less than might be expected by the ventilation of different varieties of opinion. When the occasional blow up has occurred, it has generally been disproportionately violent. Admittedly, as Freud himself once pointed out, the nature of the evidence in psychoanalysis is such that one cannot hope for the same degree of certainty as in other disciplines that aspire to scientific status. Observers do not share all the same evidence — and excommunication becomes more likely as a method of settling a dispute. But while in retrospect the wrangling over Melanie Klein may look like too much washing of dirty linen in public, the continuing presence of rival orthodoxies in Britain has stimulated the growth of new ideas. In contrast, the broad endorsement of Freudian ideas in America — at least until recently — has led to a less lively atmosphere.

Books on Freud will continue to be a minor industry; new editions of his letters, some to replace earlier texts which were once heavily edited and often lacked proper marks of omission, will continue to come out, more memoirs may be published, and undoubtedly further popularizations will appear. Few in the United States can expect to benefit from Wollheim's sort of book, but Wollheim, living at the time in England where the intelligentsia has traditionally been dubious about psychoanalysis, felt the need to present psychoanalytic ideas in a version that will render suitable homage to Freud. Wollheim explains that he felt the "need to retrieve what Freud actually said from the many interpretations and partial readings to which his words have been subjected." He "preferred exposition to interpretation or evaluation." The result is essentially a trot. It is hard to believe, on the basis of his account, that anyone could be interested in Freud as an analyst of the human soul. A comment that Freud is said to have made about the Viennese logical positivists is apposite here: "Those critics who limit their studies to methodological investigations remind me of people who are always polishing their glasses instead of putting them on and seeing with them."

It is remarkable that a writer as well educated as Wollheim should be so uncritical in this book. For example, even though there is by now a good deal of evidence concerning Freud's early use of cocaine, Wollheim ignores it to accept a version more congenial to Freud's view of himself; without giving any evidence whatsoever, Wollheim declares that "but for an unlucky accident, he [Freud] would have made himself famous as the discoverer of cocaine in its clinical use." Again, like other British philosophers, Wollheim has been heavily influenced by Melanie Klein. (Stuart Hampshire once quipped that the very improbability of her views had insured the interest of his colleagues.) Her analyst was Karl Abraham, and she continued to work with his ideas long after his death. I don't know how else can one comprehend, save by the power of analytic suggestion, Wollheim's statement that Abraham was "the most brilliant" of Freud's disciples. More brilliant than Carl Jung? Or than Sandor Ferenczi? Or than Otto Rank? For what it is worth, Freud would not have thought so.

A central inadequacy of Freud's training was his lack of rounded psychiatric experience, for his practice tended to exclude cases of grave mental illness. At the outset Freud thought that psychosis might be a form of neurosis, but he later saw psychosis and neurosis as alternative ways of resolving problems. Few clinicians today would classify or treat Freud's early patients as only neurotics. Freud himself came to be suspicious of what might be neurotic façades masking more serious disturbances. A neurosis is not the worst thing that one can suffer from, and indeed it may represent a high level of character development. In his last years Freud once identified the turning point in the recovery of a schizophrenic as the restoration of Oedipal feelings; the concept of the Oedipus complex is, as has often been observed, a highly rationalistic construct suitable for understanding only a limited range of mental problems.

Wollheim's own credulity about psychoanalysis, in what he claims is a non-evaluative study, is so great as to prevent his appreciating later developments in psychoanalytic thinking. For example, Freud assumed the absence of transference in psychoses, and even though contemporary analysts would repudiate this notion Wollheim presents Freud's view uncritically. He even restates Freud's position that the so-called narcissistic neuroses differ from the psychoses "not in kind but in degree and severity," without informing the reader that by the end of his life Freud had abandoned this early concept.

Wollheim believes that "psychoanalysis originated in therapy," and therefore he feels justified in ignoring the role of Freud's supposed self-analysis in the development of his theories. Wollheim observes that "there are commentators on Freud who would regard his commitment to dualism as an expression of his personality or as a character trait," but evidently the calling of an expositor is more exacting than that of a commentator: "any such interpretation can only be conjectural." Wollheim quotes Freud's early assertion that "the patient's symptoms constitute his sexual activity" without any critical distance whatsoever. Nor does Wollheim ask which emotions Freud might have neglected or failed to understand. Instead, we are told that "Freud was never a lover of humanity, but he did as much for it as any other human being who has lived."

Perhaps Wollheim's book can serve a useful purpose for an English audience, but from a North American vantage point his book largely serves to shore up a profession increasingly unable to count on writers within its own ranks for explanations of past controversies or recent changes in thinking. Ernest Jones was commissioned by the Freud family to write an authorized biography, and it has taken some time for us to realize how partisan an account accompanied all the new material he presented. For an author endowed with Wollheim's critical intelligence to present such an inhumanly elevated account of Freud is to promote an erroneous, bourgeois conception of normality, and an impoverished vision of human possibilities.

The history of psychoanalysis remains a peculiar subject. Although I know of no courses taught on it at any universities, the literature about it continues to multiply. Originally Freud himself, as we have discussed, set the contours of the field. In 1914 he published his lengthy article called "On the History of the Psychoanalytic Movement"; its composition was occasioned by his painful difficulties with Jung, and Freud took the occasion to draw a hard and fast line between his own form of psychology and that advocated by "dissidents" in analysis like Jung and Adler. Although by now over three-quarters of a century have passed, it is still the case that Freud has succeeded in imposing his own view of events on most people's understanding of what had happened between himself and his erstwhile followers. As I have suggested, since neither Jung nor Adler ever chose publicly to provide much information about their sides of the respective fallings-out with Freud, therefore Freud's own version of things prevailed partly by default.

Within the last generation or so there have been signs that the historiographic glacier of orthodox psychoanalysis has begun to break up. Throughout the twentieth century there were clear-eyed critics of some of the central defects in Freud's viewpoint, but his psychology has become the most powerful single influence on how we think about human motivation, and his own historiographic efforts have also held sway. Recently, however, intellectual historians have begun successfully to chip away at the mythology around Freud, and it now looks as if the subject matter of psychoanalysis might become a secure part of academic life. It will probably always be the case that practitioners of analysis will continue with amateur (and self-serving) efforts at understanding their past; but professional students of the history of ideas, with no axes to grind and without trade union advantages to defend, now seem able to make a significant dent in the field.

Edith Kurzweil has set herself an ambitious task in *The Freudians: A Comparative Perspective*: to understand the reception of Freud's ideas in a comparative national perspective.[18] It has long been known, as we have just seen, that the stories of analysis in England and America are very different even though Freud's works were made available in English by translators at approximately the same time in both countries. Similarly, the tale of how Freud's ideas fared in different countries on the continent can be linked to unique national factors. Kurzweil is a sociologist and therefore in a position to take an adequately professional view of the fascinating subject she has undertaken to explore: comparing the different courses taken by practicing analysts within various Western cultures.[19]

Unfortunately, the weakest part of the book comes at the beginning in Part One, "Psychoanalysis before 1945." Here Kurzweil rehearses some stale accounts of the early days of psychoanalysis, without having anything special to contribute of her own; and she does not take seriously enough the increasing body of literature which has come to challenge Freud's own view of things. She refers at one point, for example, to Jung's "mysticism," and does not go any further in exploring his special contribution; when she does pause to itemize Jung's supposed "central concepts," she presents — in half a sentence — a hodge-podge of notions that no reader can be expected to follow, and which leads one to suspect that she does not understand them either. Adler's work is also summarily dismissed, although as in the case of Jung's writings it is impossible to understand Freud's ideas apart from the different psychologies that his "heretics" tried to forward. While Kurzweil treats anything that Jung or Adler might have thought about with the greatest distance, a bizarre hypothesis of Freud's like the death instinct, for example, gets talked about like a fully serious proposal. Freud had some pretty wild ideas, and it does not add to our knowledge to treat everything he proposed with the same straight face.

Devoted as Kurzweil is to her subject, she is capable of committing howlers that no decent university press should have allowed into print. She tells us, for example, that the early patient "Anna O." was "relieved of her symptoms," and "embraced" Freud. In fact we have known for years now that Anna O. was a psychotherapeutic failure; for a time she became addicted to drugs. Her later recovery is shrouded in mystery and unconnected to any therapy we know about. But even more disturbing, Kurzweil does not know that Anna O. was never a patient of Freud's. Kurzweil invents the idea that Anna O. was turned over to Freud by his mentor Josef Breuer; in reality, Freud never saw her (she was an acquaintance of Freud's wife Martha), but only heard about the case from Breuer. Freud never "listened to her story" directly; therefore she could never have "embraced" Freud. The story of Anna O. is so central a part of the legend that Freud chose to weave about the origins of his work that the particular mistakes Kurzweil makes here should have been unthinkable. Although Kurzweil is on guard against what she, like others, calls Freud's "detractors," if I had not been assigned to review this book I would have read no further than her appalling misconceptions about Anna O.

The case of Anna O., which Freud later described as a success while knowing in fact that it was a failure, ought to alert us to the central problem of whether the treatment methods he recommended have been therapeutically successful. While Kurzweil simply assumes that "psychoanalysts are actually healing patients and gaining new clinical insights," Freud himself came to think that analysis was more for scientific understanding than for therapy. I know of no evidence to support Kurzweil's idea that during World War I analysts "cured a number of neurotic soldiers" or "had helped to rehabilitate thousands of neurotic solders." Kurzweil is even capable of perpetuating the myth that people can be "fully analyzed."

The Freudians cannot be relied upon for details. It is not enough to describe the quarrel with Adler as due to the fact that he "broke away," when it was also true that Freud sought to banish him. Kurzweil described Ernest Jones, who was Welsh, as "an Englishman." Although Kurzweil rightly spends time on the organization of the Berlin Psychoanalytic Institute, she somehow chooses to skip over the creation of the Vienna Psychoanalytic Institute. August Aichhorn appears once as "Alfred." The dates Kurzweil imposes on events are also often jumbled.

We are told that Freud was a physician who aimed to "improve the lot of society," even though there is abundant evidence of Freud's increasingly corrosive pessimism about the human fate. In the face of all Freud's reactionary predilections, Kurzweil stoutly maintains that "Freud and the early followers supported radical, sometimes Marxist, goals." It is true that Freud was in favor of sexual reform, and he had some classically liberal convictions, but that is as far as such an argument should go; even in *The Interpretation of Dreams*, as already noted, one can find his telling sympathies for the victims of the French Revolution's reign of terror. Despite abundant material to the contrary Kurzweil (like Young-Bruehl on Anna Freud) accepts the suggestion that Freud was some kind of socialist. One would have thought that Freud's repudiation of the Austrian socialists during the 1934 civil war in Vienna would be significant enough; but Kurzweil ought certainly to mention Freud's favorable attitude towards Mussolini, even after the war in Abyssinia.

Having said what I think needs to be critically reported about *The Freudians*, I should also add that Kurzweil's later chapters, when she is writing about what she has observed herself rather than accepted on faith, are excellent. She writes about analysis since 1945 with knowledgeability; I know I learned from her accounts of postwar analysis in Germany and France. It would seem that following 1967 the German mental health insurance scheme was almost as generous to analysts as the unprecedented largesse of the

Ontario Health Insurance Plan in Canada. (OHIP's generosity continues even after Germany has radically cut back its support for psychoanalysis.) Some of the same issues arose in Germany as in Canada connected with both "money-grubbing" among analysts and the problem of protecting privacy under circumstances of so-called third-party payment. Unique ethical and legal problems arose in Toronto, however, since many leading analysts have felt themselves entitled to charge patients — despite a ban on extra-billing — for allegedly uninsured services.

Edith Kurzweil holds, besides her university position, that of executive editor of the famed *Partisan Review*. Her belief system is a sign of the continued credulity about Freud among the American intelligentsia. In her conclusion to *The Freudians* she writes, "Thousands of studies have filled in and confirmed Freud's observations. These are the data allowing for predictions." Yet she immediately adds, "True, such predictions are not scientifically verifiable." In what sense, then, can Freud's so-called observations (she does not call them theories) be said to have been "confirmed" by the "thousands of studies" she thinks exist? "Data" which supposedly allow for "predictions" which are at the same time "not scientifically verifiable" would seem to be a clear contradiction in terms. Kurzweil had a worthy objective in proposing a comparative cultural perspective on the reception of Freud's ideas, and she provides much interesting material; but to succeed in such an undertaking requires a less blinkered view of the founder of psychoanalysis.

Psychoanalysis: The Major Concepts, edited by Burness E. Moore and Bernard D. Fine,[20] is a huge compendium of articles which has been designed as a companion text to *Psychoanalytic Terms and Concepts* also edited by Drs. Moore and Fine under the auspices of the American Psychoanalytic Association. The papers here are all written within the "mainstream" of orthodox American psychoanalytic thinking.

The first section deals with Clinical Psychoanalysis, which covers (1) therapeutic implications; (2) technical issues; and (3) other clinical phenomena. The second part of the book focuses on Theoretical Concepts, which include (1) factors affecting normality and pathology; (2) instinct theory, sexuality, and affects; (3) development, self, objects, and identification; (4) conflict, defense, structural theory, and metapsychology; and (5) psychoanalytic education and research. The range of subjects is encyclopedic, and it appears that every possible topic has been examined from a modern-day point of view. Although the starting point is always that of Freud's own writings, the authors of each piece make a genuine effort to survey the historical literature in order to bring the reader up to date.

Any such volume is certain to have flaws, and those of this book logically follow from the organizational auspices under which the project was undertaken. For example, I do not understand how it can be possible to have a chapter on narcissism that ignores what Jung wrote, especially since Freud's own 1914 paper on the subject was directly aimed at distinguishing his ideas from those of his former "crown prince." Intellectual historians teach that to understand any writer one has to follow in what ways enemies were being attacked, but *Psychoanalysis: The Major Concepts* proceeds as if these ideas arose without any challenges or bitter controversies.

As is generally characteristic of so-called classical psychoanalysis today, various innovative British theorists are sometimes cited along with the more standard references. On the whole, though, *Psychoanalysis: The Major Concepts* will not interest general readers or historians of ideas, although it may satisfy the needs of candidates in training at institutes recognized by the American Psychoanalytic Association. Otto Fenichel's *The Psychoanalytic Theory of Neurosis*[21] still stands as a monument to orthodox theorizing at about the time of Freud's death, while *Psychoanalysis: The Major Concepts* cites material from the more than fifty years since Fenichel's book appeared.

Paul Stepansky's *Freud, Surgery, and the Surgeons*[22] is one of the more peculiar recent additions to the history of psychoanalysis. He starts off with a couple of opening chapters devoted to Freud's now famous pre-World War I metaphor of the psychoanalyst as surgeon. Although Freud never repudiated the analogy he had made between psychoanalysis and surgery, Stepansky does point out that "in our own time, the surgical metaphor has surely been invoked more to be repudiated than affirmed or even qualified." Detachment, neutrality, and the "emotional coldness" Freud had recommended became an essential part of so-called "classical" psychoanalytic technique. Lately, however, a wide variety of different recent schools of psychoanalytic thinking have explicitly challenged the viability or desirability of the surgical metaphor. But not once in his book does Stepansky raise the point about how the image of surgery might encourage passivity in patients rather than the analytic ideal of self-reliance.

Having opened the book with two chapters about the surgical analogy, Stepansky offers a chapter about the rise of surgery as a branch of knowledge, and then a chapter about Freud's own contact with surgery during his medical training. One chapter goes over the well-worn territory of the Emma Eckstein episode and Wilhelm Fliess's botched operation on her nose. And a short chapter deals with Freud's Irma dream. (It is unfortunate that Stepansky woodenly maintains that "Irma" was Anna Hammerschlag rather than Emma Eckstein, as if these were the only alternative possibilities; one would have thought that psychoanalysis taught that dreams usually have multiple sources.)

Next Stepansky deals with World War I surgical experiences that Freud and a few members of his so-called "secret" Committee had. The chief sources Stepansky relies on are the Freud correspondences with Jones, Ferenczi, and

Abraham. In keeping with the recent tendency in the literature to rehabilitate the once-maligned Ferenczi, Stepansky studiously points out how Ferenczi used the analogy of the analyst as an obstetrician. Personally I found it appalling that Ferenczi's rich and thought-provoking 1932 *Diary* could get reduced down to Stepansky's tunnel-vision quest for traces of Freud's surgical metaphor.

The second half of Stepansky's book is devoted to "the metaphor in retreat," how after World War I Freud shifted toward an approach that sounds less surgically oriented. But it should have struck Stepansky that even as late as "Analysis Terminable and Interminable" (1937) Freud falls back on the scientistic image of how analysts working with repressed material might have been damaged the way early pioneers dealing with X-rays were harmed. Oddly enough a paradox that Stepansky does not raise is that in the very years during which Freud had given up the metaphor of surgery he became relatively less interested in therapeutic improvements than he had been at the outset of his analytic career. The Index volume to Strachey's *Standard Edition* has no entries under the word "surgery," so readers interested in the subject will find a fairly comprehensive coverage in Stepansky's book.

A chapter is devoted to aspects of the World War I literature about war neuroses, although Victor Tausk's own contributions are not politically correct enough in the conventional literature to get mentioned. The death of Jones's first wife (about which rumor has long had it that much more was to be unearthed) gets a whole little chapter of its own, once again potted history. In two chapters Stepansky runs through the most established literature associated with Freud's first operations for cancer of the jaw. One chapter deals with Abraham's death, unfortunately excluding Sandor Rado's own interpretation of what happened. The debate over lay analysis put a new face to the use of surgical analogies, and Stepansky highlights how it came up in the arguments of the various contestants.

Different analysts were to comment on the significance of psychoanalysis for the practice of surgery, but Stepansky overlooks Helene Deutsch's original 1942 paper. One longish chapter toward the end of the book is devoted to the horrendous practices of psychosurgery, and how weakly the psychoanalysts spoke out against them. An exception that Stepansky brings up is D. W. Winnicott, someone who has been much in style these last years. But Stepansky fails to mention that Winnicott also pooh-poohed the basis in hereditary or in biochemistry of psychosis, instead seeing it as a product of "environmental failure." (I am reminded how Edward Glover could dismiss Winnicott as "moonshiny.")

I said at the outset that this was a rather peculiar book, and that is because I am not sure why Stepansky chose to write it. On earlier occasions he has shown himself capable of valuable independent-minded work. He has his own publishing house, and a disproportionate percentage of the citations here are to works that he has brought out. (Although it is luckily not known abroad, one of American psychoanalysis's unique contributions has been that journals publish partially ghost-written works with artificially concocted bibliographies.) The final sentence to Stepansky's book reads: "Almost a century after Freud introduced his surgical metaphor, the question that remains is not whether doctors of the mind are surgeons, but rather what type of surgeon they choose to be." If that was the conviction motivating Stepansky to undertake this book, then I think it a mistake to have done so. Fair-minded people can debate the relevant weights to attach to art as opposed to science in the practice of psychoanalysis, but the metaphor of surgery has led in too many bad directions to defend it even as Stepansky does. The book jacket quotes two flattering pre-publication appraisals by reputable authorities, but I am afraid that I found *Freud, Surgery, and the Surgeons* an unfortunate enterprise which taught me a minimal amount.

Notes

1. Irving Stone, *The Passions of the Mind: A Biographical Novel of Sigmund Freud* (New York, Doubleday, 1971).
2. Peter Gay, *Freud: A Life For Our Time* (New York, W.W. Norton, 198), p. 781.
3. Ronald W. Clark, *Freud: The Man and the Cause* (New York, Random House,1980).
4. Gay, *Freud*, op. cit., p. 781.
5. Myron P. Gilmore, *The World of Humanism, 1453–1517* (New York, Harper, 1952), p. 201.
6. Gay, *Freud, op. cit.*, p. 123.
7. Ibid., p. 138. See Roazen, *The Historiography of Psychoanalysis, op. cit.*, pp. 241–43.
8. "The Question of Lay Analysis," *Standard Edition*, 20, p. 253.
9. Gay, Freud, *op. cit.*, p. 439.
10. *Ibid.*, p. 391.
11. *Ibid.*, p. 5.
12. *Ibid.*, p. 391.
13. *Ibid.*, p. xx.
14. *Ibid.*, pp. 741–42.
15. Peter Gay, *Freud For Historians* (New York, Oxford University Press, 1975), p. xii. See Roazen, *Encountering Freud*, op. cit., pp. 263–64.
16. Peter Gay, *Reading Freud: Explorations and Entertainments* (New Haven, Conn., Yale University Press, 1990).
17. Richard Wollheim, *Sigmund Freud* (New York, The Viking Press, 1973).
18. Edith Kurzweil, *The Freudians: A Comparative Perspective* (New Haven, Conn., Yale University Press, 1989).
19. Roazen, *The Historiography of Psychoanalysis, op. cit.*, Part 7, pp. 309–52.
20. *Psychoanalysis: The Major Concepts,* edited by Burness E. Moore and Bernard D. Fine (New Haven, Conn., Yale University Press, 1995).

21. Otto Fenichel, *The Psychoanalytic Theory of Neurosis* (New York, W. W. Norton, 1945).
22. Paul Stepansky, *Freud, Surgery, and the Surgeons* (Hillsdale, N.J., The Analytic Press, 1999).

8

Lacanianism

Psychoanalysis in France has attained a unique status today. It is not just a matter of the large number of different psychoanalytic organizations, or the quantity of practitioners in the profession. But one group alone, out of more than a dozen, does form the largest unit in the International Psychoanalytic Association first set up by Freud in 1910. Although Jacques Lacan was effectively driven out of the IPA in the early 1950s, it is a sign of the special impact he has had that despite all the heated splits associated with his name he remains the central figure in the history of French psychoanalysis. The liveliness and vitality of psychoanalysis in contemporary France owes an immense debt to the inspiration that Lacan succeeded in providing.

There are no bookstores in the world as filled with fresh texts on psychoanalysis as now can be found in Paris. The fact that the long-awaited multivolume Freud-Ferenczi correspondence first started to appear in French, before either German or English, is a sign of the special interest psychoanalysis evokes in France. Nowhere else has psychoanalysis been able to become so secure a part of university life as there, although something not too dissimilar has been taking place in Argentina. Additionally, French analysts are culturally sophisticated in an unusual way. Lacan liked to think that he had accomplished a "return" to Freud, and in my own experience of meeting many surviving early analysts who knew Freud personally I can say that I have never met as interesting a group of analysts, apart from the ones who were once around Freud, as can be found in Paris today.

Understanding Lacan's writings, his theories as well as his reported practices, is not an easy matter. And so when I heard that Lacan had a brother still alive, a Benedictine monk who was an intellectual in whom Lacan confided, it seemed to me one way to get a handle on Lacan's contribution was by trying to meet this brother. On September 24, 1992, while in Paris on a short lecture trip, I went to interview Marc-François Lacan. I had heard earlier that he was living in a monastery near Paris, but it turned out that he had recently moved to Notre Dame de Ganagobie in Peryuis, near Marseilles.

My motives in trying to see Marc-François were unclouded by any partisanship. I had been in Paris in 1991 and earlier in 1992, both times briefly. As a student of the history of ideas, with a special interest in psychoanalysis, I knew how important the work of Jacques Lacan had become to the life of the mind. The influence of Lacan's teachings had long since extended far beyond France, but only while I was in Paris did I begin to feel that I had begun to know enough to start asking some intelligent questions.

Once, on the very day, it turned out, that Lacan's analytic couch, among other items, was being auctioned off in Paris, I had had a most congenial meeting with Judith Miller, Lacan's favorite daughter from his second marriage. I was expected to see her at 5 rue de Lille, where he had practiced for so many years. On that day I walked from where I was staying on the Ile St. Louis to Lacan's old apartment, but I was so ignorant then of where I was headed as actually not to know, when instructed to turn toward the Left Bank, which bank of the Seine was the left. As I habitually do with my interviews, especially when I do not know where I am going, I arrived early. I found the street easily enough, and looked at the plaque on the apartment-house wall commemorating the fact that Lacan had once practiced there. The only other psychoanalyst I know to have been so honored is Freud himself. I went to a small café nearby, reading a book while having a late breakfast, until the time for my appointment arrived.

At the appropriate occasion I headed for rue de Lille, but only then at the front gate of No. 5 did I realize that I had not been given the code to get in. After gaining entrance by chance, I went to the concierge, who telephoned Judith Miller. She told me that there had been family problems that day, but if I waited she would come by shortly. She brought with her Luke, a son, and also Gloria, who had worked with Lacan for years as a private secretary. They opened up the apartment for me, showing me something of how elegant it had once looked. I did not know then why some of the pieces of furniture and paintings were missing. I felt I had stumbled rather badly when I inquired whether the apartment would be turned into a museum, thinking of Freud's house on Maresfield Gardens in London; such an approach was plainly far too static to match the fluidity of Lacan's thinking.

Luke's job was to help translate both the French and the English. I do recall the shy amusement we three felt, as Judith showed me one painting, when I understood directly from her French, after a few seconds of uncertain looking, that the picture was intended to be of a male orgasm. The most striking single aspect of what I learned that day came from Luke. He picked up a ping-pong ball, which had marks drawn all around it, and with love and affection in his voice described how his grandfather had liked to relax that way. It was a telling spontaneous gesture on Luke's part, and I felt as if I were beginning to understand how Lacan's system differed from the more linear Freudianism I was used to. Afterwards Judith took us to a splendid lunch, and Luke walked me around the corner for my lecture.

So it was that when on a subsequent trip to Paris I was planning to see Lacan's brother, I felt as if I already knew something of the family setting I was inquiring about. No matter how much I respect the legitimacy of abstractions, it is my firm conviction that concepts come from the minds and souls of real people. It is not reductionistic, or disrespectful toward the standing of ideas, to seek to appreciate the human context in which systems of thought arise. And in my experience of psychoanalysts especially, it is hard not to think that all psychologists necessarily rely on their own history and intuitions, much as they try to hold in check the subjective bias.

Getting to Peyruis was easier than finding an appropriate translator to take along, although a Parisian friend came up with someone excellently qualified for the task. My timetable in Paris was so tight that there was no question, as Marc-François had suggested in his letter, of renting a car to drive south. Instead the arrangement was that, starting at seven in the morning, we would take the TGV and then set about renting a car to drive from the train station near Aix to the Abbey itself. The Vaucluse, in southeastern France, at that time of year seemed unusually beautiful, and the tourist season was over. The road from the highway to the monastery turned into an extremely winding one, and I was to find that the Abbey had a magnificent view high over the valley below.

Notre Dame de Ganagobie dates from the tenth century, with parts of it built in the eleventh and twelfth centuries. The Benedictines are an extremely old order. Their monasteries were not intended as great centers of learning, but rather to exemplify piety and hard work. The Benedictine rule was, according to one historian, to be "wholly lacking in eccentricity,"[1] something which stood in stark contrast to Lacan's personality as I knew it. Portions of Notre Dame de Ganagobie had been constructed in the eighteenth century, and then renovations had been made in the 1980s and 1990s; they were done in keeping with the old style, so that what one felt everywhere were the imposing presence of ancient walls and the prospect of high-ceilinged rooms. I gathered that this was a strict community which made medical tools for orthopedic purposes.

I was instructed to leave the car just where one might have thought it should not have been put. An entrepreneur, who had business to transact, was helpful in telling me where to park. He said that we had to lock the car door, since "not only altar boys" might be here, though a Walkman had been left on the businessman's front seat. The mixture of the old and the new was, throughout my visit to Marc-François, striking, if not disconcerting. I was met at the front door, having rung the bell, by the Abbot, all in black, wearing a strikingly large cross. He was, I later learned, appointed from the outside in order to lead the priory.

It was characteristic of the monastery that we waited for Marc-François in a recently built hall whose construction was not quite finished. Looking around I could see a computer as well as a copying machine; the answering device at the abbey was only part of its up-to-date technology. I had time to see a multi-volume Catholic dictionary on the relatively bare bookshelves. (My translator-companion did not understand why I felt the need to take as many notes as I did; as a writer I believe that the devil lies in the details, but I mean to speak, in the context of interviewing Marc-François, only colloquially about the devil.)

Marc-François turned out to be a bent old man of eighty-four, who died not long after, in 1994. He was apparently scoliotic, and walked with a cane. A young monk accompanied him, helpfully bringing along some back cushions. Marc-François quipped that he was "very lucid" despite the existence of his back problem. He was a Father, which meant that he could conduct a mass; the monk who left and then came back with more cushions was a Brother who lacked such standing.

Marc-François came to the interview prepared with elaborate notes, but I do not recall, after the first few minutes, that he needed to rely on them for anything. Everything he had to say to me was in his head. Lacan, who had died in 1981, was seven years older than Marc-François. Lacan's death came on "the day" of the fiftieth anniversary of Marc-François's presence in a monastery. He had left Paris for an abbey, Hautecombe, outside the city, and then from June 1992 had lived where I was interviewing him.

Marc-François said he had been a philosopher from the age of eighteen. He did his philosophical studies at the Institut Catholique and simultaneously undertook to be a student of the law. Of all those he studied, St. Thomas Aquinas was for Marc-François the most outstanding. By the time he first entered a monastery in 1926, his brother was already a doctor, "going in the way of psychiatry and psychoanalysis." But when Marc-François was fourteen and Jacques twenty-one, they had both "decided" that "the aim of their life was to be the search for the truth."

This was an opening to ask about the relationship between Lacan and the Catholic religion. Marc-François could, he thought, only refer to "stray things." Lacan had "a very deep personal Christian culture," but when he started upon his medical studies it took him "out of the way of religious practices." He no longer went to mass. He "believed" in God, "of course," but he was very committed to his medical work. I inquired whether Lacan had always been a believer. "No one" could say that, and it was impossible "to resolve that question." Marc-François had his own personal view, and he understood his brother's outlook, but they were "very different" in these points about religion.

The issue of religion was one where I think there must have been a split between at least part of Lacan's family and some of his psychoanalytic followers. Elisabeth Roudinesco, for example, refers straightforwardly to Lacan's "atheism." And she says that he reproached himself for not having prevented Marc-François from having chosen "the path of perpetual confinement."[2] Yet a monastic life certainly seemed to suit Marc-François. Roudinesco tells us too that after Lacan's death Marc-François came to Paris to celebrate a mass in memory of his dead brother; the children of Jacques's first wife attended, while those of his second stayed away. He had been married at his first wedding in a church (the abbot of Hautecombe gave the blessing), and had had his children baptized. It does not seem to me surprising that he could have dreamt once of having had, according to Roudinesco, "an elaborate Catholic funeral."[3] If it had seemed inappropriate to Marc-François, or the children of his first wife, Marc-François would not have conducted that mass in his honor.

It seemed to me natural, both psychoanalytically and historically, to inquire about the immediate family of Marc-François and Jacques Lacan. The father had been "a salesman" in Paris; there was one sister of Marc-François's who was five years older, and still alive. Marc-François was therefore the youngest of the siblings. He asserted that the three of them had been extremely "close."

I specifically asked about the mother. Marc-François immediately responded by saying that, in understanding Lacan's life, she was "very important." Somehow in this connection Marc-François told me how when in 1932 Lacan did "a test," by which Marc-François meant Lacan's doctoral thesis on paranoia, he "dedicated" it to Marc-François. (He failed to inform me that the first dedication, before that one, was to his mistress.) The exact wording of Lacan's dedication to his brother struck a later commentator, Michel de Certeau, as "strange": "To the Reverend Father Marc-François Lacan, Benedictine of the Congregation of France, my brother in religion."[4] Supposedly, according to Marc-François, "everybody" had been "surprised" by the dedication, and the surrealists (among the first to respond to Freud in France) in particular were "astonished." If free associations mean anything, and by this point in the interview Marc-François was pretty relaxed with me, I would presume that he thought the dedication was something that his mother might have appreciated. (That dissertation would turn out to be the sole book Lacan ever wrote; it was only with reluctance that Lacan allowed it to be reprinted in France, and it has still not been translated into English.)

The mother herself had gone through a high level of intellectual studies, and was "very clever." Marc-François emphasized how deeply Christian she was. She had "a great faith." She had been able to follow Lacan's work "completely" until he went on to become a psychoanalyst, at which point she could not go further in understanding what he was doing. The profession and the doctrine were "so new for everybody" that she could not fathom what was going on. She had not gone to a university, but her education was sometime before 1900, at which point she attended a fine "high school." She was not then particularly interested in philosophy but rather in "general literature." She worked a lot with her husband's business, and the effort involved meant that for the sake of the work her husband did it was necessary for her to renounce any kind of reading of novels and poems.

Her husband, unlike herself, was "not an intellectual at all." He sold oil in Bordeaux, soaps in Nice, and was involved with a vineyard in Orleans. I asked if Marc-François's father had been successful: "Not very, but successful." In the world of business in which he lived "everyone liked him," and he knew his job very well. He was not too involved with religion, but the rest of the family was very "close" because of their religious faith.

Marc-François had himself gone to a well-known boys' school, the Collège Stanislas. It turned out that he had not only read his brother's first publication, the text on paranoia, but "everything" else he had written. For years there was a distance of some five hundred kilometers between them, but that did not interfere with their being intimately acquainted with one another's work. Marc-François had written his own articles on theology, and Lacan read them. Marc-François had produced some 60,000 pages from 1950 on about the Old and New Testaments and he had helped to translate an ecumenical version of the Bible. A book of his called *The Bible Vocabulary*, dealing with biblical themes, was not only translated into English but came out in some twenty different languages.

Freud talked about religion, and Lacan wrote about it "because" of Freud. Marc-François thought it was critical to know that Lacan knew German "very well." Lacan held that the first thing he wanted to do was to translate Freud's writings correctly into French. The "basis of all" Lacan's work was to "find the real meaning of Freud's texts." But Lacan understood that what St. Thomas would have said now would be very different from the thirteenth century. Lacan undertook an approach to Freud in that broad spirit. As far as Marc-François understood, Freud himself had changed "a lot" during the course of his own career as a thinker. Freud was considered an "agnostic," but Marc-François thought that was only the "bad" side to him, and that metaphorically speaking he had had the "Bible on his desk." (I shared Marc-François's belief that, despite Freud's occasional protestations to the contrary, he was a stern moralist; but his ideas also served to undercut Judeo-Christian morality in a way which I did not explore with Marc-François.) In

Marc-François's view Freud was "correct" in holding that his notion of obsessional neurosis could "in some cases" explain people's attitude toward God. Freud's own *Moses and Monotheism* was "a remarkable book."

I cannot reconstruct how we jumped to talking about Anna Freud at this point, perhaps in connection with what I thought was her own relationship to Judaism, which I think contrasted with that of her father, but Marc-François maintained that she had been "completely opposite" to Lacan. He had fought throughout his life for his freedom, and Marc-François thought he had achieved the truth that he aimed for. All his theories, the core of his "doctrine," were "completely" at odds with those of the IPA. (Like Lacan's followers, Marc-François's references to the IPA were made with obvious distaste.) By 1992 Lacan's "school" was important throughout the world, as far away as South America for example.

Among those who followed Lacan, Marc-François singled out Denis Vasse, a Jesuit who had written a book called *Time of Desire* that Marc-François thought I must read. He also singled out the work of Father Biernaert; but Vasse was "the best follower" of Lacan, in that he did not just repeat what Lacan thought, but had succeeded in developing his ideas. I mentioned François Roustang, who I understood had also once been a Jesuit; but Marc-François dismissed him for having "quit everything" to do with Lacanianism and as perhaps "a bit crazy." Even though Marc-François was not a psychoanalyst, he had picked up Freud's tactic, and perhaps Lacan's as well, of stigmatizing former students as emotionally disturbed.

Although we had already embarked on talking about the surrogate family Lacan had built up, and about the disciples who had turned out well in addition to those who had gone sour, Marc-François went back to discussing the family in which he had grown up. They had had a servant who was really one of them; it was this maid, Pauline, who had "raised up" the children. There is a picture album about Lacan that Judith Lacan Miller had put together which has a photograph of Pauline. It was very common at that time to have such a nanny, although Marc-François thought that that kind of maid "did not exist any more."

He held that Freud, with his "discovery" of the unconscious, represented a Copernican revolution in human self-understanding. Marc-François had not read everything of Freud's; Marc-François was not a reader of German, and did not like the official translations. I tried to discover how much Marc-François knew about old Vienna, since to me Freud was so intimately connected with the last days of the Austro-Hungarian Empire. But Marc-François said he was "not familiar" with Viennese culture.

I also asked about Carl G. Jung, who is commonly ranked Freud's greatest heretic. For Marc-François as well as Lacan, Jung "did everything except psychoanalysis." It was certainly a backhanded way of Marc-François's in discussing Jung to say that he and Lacan agreed that Jung was "interesting in all areas" except the one that mattered most to Jung. Marc-François went further, maintaining that Jung, who made much of the positive possibilities in religious thought, was "a complete stranger to the real Christian tradition." In fact, Marc-François insisted that Jung was so far from Christianity as to represent "a dangerous deviation" from it.

It was impossible for me not to think here of the thunderous way heretics have always been drummed out of the Church, as well as how Freud had acted in expelling Jung as well as others from within psychoanalysis. According to one of Freud's loyal Swiss disciples, Ludwig Binswanger, Freud had "often referred to his scientific Calvary." When Binswanger questioned Freud as to how it had happened that it was "precisely his oldest and perhaps most talented disciples, Jung and Adler, to give examples, who had broken away from him," Freud had replied: "Precisely because they too wanted to be Popes. . . . "[5] Freud was capable of irony about himself, and knew that in some sense he had tried to set up a new church.

Freud's loyal disciple Hanns Sachs had once described how "didactic" analyses were designed to train future analysts: "Religions have always demanded a trial period, a novitiate, of those among their devotees who desired to give their entire life into the service of the supermundane and the supernatural, those, in other words, who were to become monks or priests . . . .It can be seen that analysis needs something corresponding to the novitiate of the Church."[6] Freud himself once compared the psychoanalytic situation with confession, except that he expected more of analysands: "In confession the sinner tells what he knows; in analysis the neurotic has to tell more."[7] Lacan himself thought of the psychoanalyst as being "like that solitary being [a monk] who in past times ventured into the desert."[8] It is one thing to try to imagine what it might have meant for a Jew like Freud to have founded a church; it is an altogether different and more complex matter to follow what it might have meant for a Catholic like Lacan to break with a Jewish church.

Jung was the one disciple of Freud's most interested in salvaging something psychologically meaningful from Christianity. Yet Jung was, to Marc-François, "completely different from Freud." I already knew, since I had spoken to a nice Jungian group in Paris, how tiny an influence they had had on French intellectual life, although this was by no means the case elsewhere. Marc-François was inadvertently echoing Freud, or rather doing so out of identification with Lacan, in condemning Jung for having written "stupid, crazy things"; supposedly Jung had been guilty of confusing issues. Jung's concept of the collective unconscious was an "interesting idea," but not a "very clear notion." If I had ever thought of daring to raise the issue of Jung when I interviewed Anna Freud in the mid–1960s, I would have expected her to say something identical; so the heretic Lacan, whom she had helped to drive out of the IPA by trying to restrict his training activities, was on this one point about Jung completely in agreement with what she and her father had thought. Somehow, in connection with our discussion of Jung as a deviant within psychoanalysis, Marc-François brought up what he thought was one of his brother's "first discoveries": the significance of the mirror in early childhood, a developmental "step."

I had not set the agenda for what topics came up, but Marc-François moved to talking about how Lacan had left Paris to live in the Midi during World War II. (I do not know what the link was between discussing the mirror stage and those painful war years, except that Lacan had first proposed the idea about mirroring in 1936, and a revision of that early paper, under the title "The Mirror Stage as Formative of the Function of the I As Revealed in Psychoanalytic Experience," which he delivered in 1949, became his most famous single concept.) Marc-François raised the matter of Lacan's second wife having been Jewish, and said the police had compiled a "dossier" on her. (Earlier she had been married to the writer Georges Bataille.) According to Marc-François, at some point Lacan "took" the file and "destroyed" it. Lacan and his second wife remained in the south of France "from the beginning to the end" of the Nazi occupation; and he did have "some patients" while he was there. (I assume that Marc-François meant that Lacan had had analytic cases of some sort, or perhaps psychiatric ones, since he had long since become a specialist in that area.)

During the war Marc-François himself was in "the Italian zone," which I understood to mean that he lived in a monastery in an area under the control of Italian troops. He told how they had had a Polish bishop "hidden in their monastery," and that the Gestapo had come to get him. Unfortunately the Germans "succeeded" in ferreting out the Pole they were looking for, although Marc-François did not provide any further details.

At this point in talking with me he paused to indicate that he did not like journalists. I do not think there could have been any doubt in his mind that I was myself not in that category, since I had written ahead as a university professor, and I think I mentioned some of the books I had written. Marc-François qualified his distaste for journalism as a field by saying that he accepted the members of the profession when they were specialists and knew what they were doing.

He immediately went on to discuss the École Freudienne de Paris, which Lacan had dominated from 1964 to 1980, when he dissolved it, shortly before his death. This act of Lacan's was a subject of great bitterness among his pupils, many of whom felt betrayed and some of whom took Lacan to court. Subsequently Lacan had founded, with the assistance of his son-in-law Jacques-

Alain Miller, the organization known as the Champ Freudian, which until today has been the largest single exponent of Lacanian teachings, with affiliated organizations around the world.

Throughout the interview Marc-François referred to Lacan as "my brother"; this may seem a trivial point to bring up, but it was a part of what I found to be Marc-François's loyalty to Lacan. Melanie Klein's daughter, in contrast, when I interviewed her in 1965, was so disaffected and alienated from her late mother as still to refer to her as "Mrs. Klein."[9] Klein's daughter had become a bitter public enemy of her mother's. But from Marc-François's point of view, Lacan had himself been a genuine disciple of Freud. Lacan had been able to develop Freud's thought; he did not remain "just a follower."

For some reason, presumably because Marc-François felt that he had left important points undiscussed, he switched back to talking about the circumstances of his early childhood. Within the family he and his brother were "not treated the same." For Jacques Lacan there was "a very deep love." "No competition" between the brothers existed; Marc-François was the "little one," and Jacques remained the first-born. It seemed in keeping to ask if the mother suffered because of Lacan's attitude toward religion; she "did," but not because Lacan failed to become a monk, but because he "forgot" about religion. She was "very naïve," and saw everything "in a nice way." The father did "not really realize" what Lacan was doing, although the father knew he was an intellectual.

Marc-François likened Lacan to Balzac's Rastignac; at the age of twenty-one Lacan was living in Montmartre and took for himself the challenge to conquer Paris: "I will be your master, I will dominate you!" Marc-François had himself read all of Balzac, and thought that Lacan had indeed come to succeed in overwhelming Parisian life. As an analyst he was "in his métier." He was "very warm with people," and could be "close" to his patients in listening to them. Lacan taught Marc-François "a lot," and "I understood him." In support of this, Marc-François gave me the name of a woman who had been successfully analyzed by Lacan.

According to Marc-François, and here he sounded like a faithful disciple of Lacan's, the problem with American psychoanalysis is that they did not go further than the IPA (he readily used the shorthand "IPA" in talking to me, as Judith Miller also had.) Marc-François ridiculed the idea that "to have a big ego" could be the objective of someone concerned with psychoanalysis.

It would have been hopeless, and an interference, to try to set Marc-François straight about what I thought was the genuine significance of ego psychology in correcting the negativism about therapy, bordering on nihilism, which can be found in some of Freud's writings. It is a deeply ingrained prejudice within French intellectual life that ego psychology and America should be seen as identical, and both would have been written off on the grounds of advocating conformism if I had tried to correct Marc-François. In reality Freud himself had set ego psychology going; and that particular strand in his thought, which it is true was especially congenial to the needs of America, did much to correct earlier pessimistic imbalances within psychoanalytic thinking. Lacan did have a genuinely tragic view of the human condition, close to Freud's own central standpoint, which can perhaps be considered a secular version of the doctrine of original sin; but such a viewpoint could never be popular in the States.

According to the French mythology about the history of psychoanalysis, Lacan had bravely refused to go along with the conformist thinking of Anglo-American psychoanalysts. Lacan did manage to make the term ego psychology, which has especially flourished in America, stand for an incontestably bad concept in Paris. Yet the evidence does show how much effort Lacan put into winning recognition from the IPA; if he was a failure in preventing his excommunication, which was supported by Freud's daughter Anna, it was not for want of Lacan's trying. It is possible to provide fancy rationalizations for Lacan's relentless search for recognition by the IPA, such as that he sought to avoid becoming a master with his own school. But when one fully realizes the relative nonentities he was struggling against in the organization, it does seem a poor show for him to have accused others of unnecessarily bowing to the weight of authority.

Marc-François was seemingly up to date on the literature about Lacan's work. He mentioned in particular one small book written as early as 1969. He emphasized the role which linguistics came to play in Lacan's thinking; this had been true since 1953, and Marc-François thought that Lacan's 1953 essay on "The Function of Language in Psychoanalysis" was "the start" of Lacan's distinctive train of thought. There was a "unity" in Lacan's approach, in that he saw "man as a speaking creature." (Although I did not know it at the time I saw Marc-François, in one of his seminars Lacan said that "speaking brings God"[10]; he also expressed uncertainty about Nietzsche's claim that God is dead.) On the subject of speech I interjected a question, since I had heard that when Lacan's parents came to dinner, there was silence at the table. But according to Marc-François his parents "never" went to have dinner there.

His mother died in 1948; his father, in 1960. In those last years Lacan's father was "very lonely." He lived in "a nice suburb" near the Bois de Boulogne. Fortunately he was able to continue with his work right up until the very end of his life, and he had a nephew who was able to help him professionally.

Marc-François and I went back and forth between his brother's family life and his professional work. Since the Freud who came through in Lacan's writings, which seemed to be Marc-François's own Freud as well, appeared to me so at odds with the distinctively Jewish and Viennese figure that I knew, I raised the question of whether it was possible to detach Freud from his historical context. Too much of French psychoanalysis seemed to me to have a scholastic air. But it was Marc-François's explicit conviction that it was "only" possible to study philosophy if one knows history. He mentioned how this was true of medieval thought too, and that Etienne Gilson had undertaken to study St. Augustine and Descartes within their cultural context. Marc-François mentioned that Gilson had been in Toronto (where I was then living) during World War II.

As we were reflecting back on the history of ideas, Marc François noted how, when Lacan was "put out of the IPA," he had compared himself to Spinoza being excommunicated as a Jewish dissident. (At that time Lacan had stated: "I am not telling you — but it would not be impossible — that the psychoanalytic community is a Church. And yet, incontestably, the question arises of what within it offers a kind of echo of religious practice."[11]) In my dealings with Marc-François, it was clear that he was a keen student of intellectual history. For example, he emphasized the fact that St. Thomas had known Aristotle but not Plato, and he reminded me that in Aristotle the Platonic dialogue disappears.

Reflecting on his brother's work, Marc-François said he thought it certain that it had changed "a lot" during the course of his life. For example, there is the concept of the "real," that which it is impossible to know, not just unknown; the notion of the "symbolic" referred to the area of language and speaking. As for Lacan's idea about the "imaginary," there he completely changed his mind. (As in the case of Freud's notions of the id, ego, and superego, sometimes so attractive to beginning students, I think these terms can partly be understood as a shorthand way of packaging what pioneering analysts have to contribute.)

Putting aside for the moment Lacan as a formal thinker, Marc-François chose to exclaim about how "impeccable" was the way Lacan dressed. Marc-François, when I interviewed him, was not wearing a clerical habit but some sort of pajama-like clothing. Yet he admired the way Lacan had become "one of the most elegant men in Paris"; "he was a guy!" Marc-François thought he had taken "a risk" in agreeing to see me, but he did not "regret" it.

Marc-François chose to explore what he thought of as a "philosophical principle" connected to the "discovery" of the unconscious. The word "relation" meant something special to Marc-François; "one becomes who one is in relation to others." He proposed the "image of God" as "the couple," not any "one human being." In this connection he suggested how the doctrine of the trinity could be properly understood; no one can be a father without a son. What makes people "real" is the communication between them, the relationships that develop; the connection between the "I" and the "you" goes to make a human being. For Marc-François the loss of traditional families produces a lot of clinical problems, like addictions for example; ours is an "individualistic time," and he regretted that. Marc-François was himself of course living in the community of the abbey; the whole group had moved to Peyruis in order to get away from the "tourists" who congregated around Paris. The previous abbey he had lived in, for twenty-one years, was in the Alps.

Marc-François continued to move freely between family matters and theological issues. On the one hand he thought that Judith Miller's choice of Jacques-Alain had meant that because he became the son-in-law he had turned into an important follower of Lacan's. At the same time Marc-François was in his own way a disciple of Lacan's, except that Marc-François was drawing out the Catholic side of Lacan's thinking. The existence of a Christian God, the father of Jesus Christ, cannot be explained "mathematically." It is God who is the one we are in relation to; and this is necessarily so without our intellectual or emotional understanding. Marc-François had in mind a conception of God which was contrary to one "who tells you what to do." Instead, God was "a father that sets you free. One gets life, and must in turn give it; once one accepts becoming the son of God, one becomes a brother." Otherwise, in Marc-François's thinking, one cannot love God.

Jacques Lacan had tried to read Hebrew. But studying the Talmud would have been "too big"; it is full of "very interesting things" and can be subject to "multiple interpretations," supposedly unlike the New Testament. (Marc-François made no mention of the traditional Christian conception of the Talmud as the origin of Jewish erring.) But he did hold that each century reads the New Testament freshly; it was "wonderful" that it was impossible just to "repeat" it. "Freedom is the most important thing." And you are "free when you are responsible for other people."

I had come a long way to learn some elementary-seeming aspects to Lacan's thinking, at least as espoused by Marc-François. The whole conception of the significance of the mirror means that otherness is a key, early on, to character development. Many commentators have pointed out that Freud, in contrast to later psychoanalytic thinking, took an egoistic point of view. And this included more than his notorious indictment of Christian ethics, for example when he tried to show how the maxim "love thy neighbor" is both unrealistic and undesirable as a moral principle. Freud took for granted the nurturing functions of the mother, while the tie that Freud repeatedly wrote about was that of the child to his father. In a case history published as late as 1918, Freud talked about a male patient's father as "his first and most primitive object choice, which, in conformity with a small child's narcissism, had taken place along the path of identification."[12] Freud at that time thought that a small boy's "first and most primitive" human bond was to his father, not his mother. Freud was not excluding the mother's part in the psychopathology of his patients; but he understood the mother mainly as either a seductress in an Oedipal situation or the source of adult homosexual conflicts. Before World War I, Jung had challenged Freud on the role of mothers, and others in the movement (such as Sandor Ferenczi) later were to take a different orientation from Freud himself.

Erik Erikson, for example,, made an effort to spell out the positive significance of mothers. And Erikson, whose work remains relatively unknown in France, even though he was the first male child analyst, also tried his best to bring Christian ethics into psychoanalytic teachings. D. W. Winnicott, widely known in Paris, told me in London that the only analyst whose books that he, Winnicott, envied not having written himself were those by Erikson.

Lacan had, with his proposal of a mirror stage, in his own way attempted to make personality development what in North America would be called "interpersonal." I had written about Erikson as well as Freud, in the conviction that to the extent that Freud's disciples were able to come to different conclusions than the master himself they had in a way paid tribute to Freud's capacities as the creator of a field. Marc-François had a similar outlook as a follower of his brother. Erikson had, unknown to Marc-François, become a believing Christian, and to my way of thinking the ultimate other that Lacan had in mind had to be God. Built into my interviewing Marc-François in the first place was an operative belief that it would not be possible to understand Lacan in isolation, but that he and his younger brother might be appreciated in relation to one another.

The abbey Marc-François lived in when I saw him had been, like the other monasteries in France, closed after the French Revolution. Until relatively recently Notre Dame de Ganagobie had had no running water or toilets; perhaps one or two monks were living there before it was reopened. Now it had thirty-three members along with the Prior himself. Although the monasteries in France had been shut down at the end of the eighteenth century, which was also true in Austria and Bavaria, where the Jesuits were outlawed altogether, by 1833 the first monks had begun to come back in France. By 1905 the restoration of Notre Dame de Ganagobie was undertaken. These details were provided not by Marc-François himself, but by a Brother, wearing jeans and sandals, who had been the one to help Marc-François with the extra pillows and who wanted us to stay for supper.

Unfortunately we had to return to Paris that night, and could not remain to share a meal. But it was possible for us to walk around at least some parts of the abbey, which had twelfth-century mosaics. Since it was my first time in a monastery I could not hope to fathom all that was going on around me. We did hear vespers being sung. The whole atmosphere at the abbey was tranquil and friendly, a genuine island of peace. The Brother who showed us around explained that Marc-François's back problem arose from a bicycle accident he had had, and that the extent of his suffering went unexpressed.

Although Marc-François said he did not want to blame Jacques-Alain Miller for anything, it was clear he disapproved of his nephew. It was painful to think that Marc-François had not even got to know Judith Miller's nice son Luke, who was as much an admirer of Lacan as anybody. As we left the monastery with its red-tiled roof, it was hard not to be impressed by Marc-François's extraordinary attachment to his older brother.

One has to wonder why Marc-François had not been interviewed countless times before, given how important he was in Lacan's life. I asked straightforwardly whether he had ever spoken to anyone else, and there Marc-François grew slightly evasive; as far as I know, the only person I am sure he cooperated with was Roudinesco who at that time had already published two volumes about the history of psychoanalysis in France in which Lacan obviously plays a central role. Her best-selling biography of Lacan had not yet appeared in print. If nobody else from the outside had come to interview Marc-François, it was a sign of the extent of the emotional taboos concerned with Lacan's person. I thought that although it would obviously have been more desirable if I had been less ignorant about Lacan's thought when I saw Marc-François, the distance I brought to this material was in a sense an asset.

At the time I set out to interview Marc-François, Parisian analysts were not too hopeful about what I could come up with. But then I knew that in the past, as when I interviewed Freud's middle son Oliver in 1965, there was no telling exactly what one could learn from such a family member. (I got two chapters out of that one encounter for my *Meeting Freud's Family*.[13]) I was agreeably surprised to find out just how knowledgeable Marc-François turned out to be.

From a rationalistic Parisian point of view, Marc-François could be considered, as Roudinesco put it, to have undertaken a form of imprisonment in his monastery life. And from a straightforward Freudian point of view, it was odd indeed for such a young man as the one who showed us around the abbey to have given up a "normal" life for one with such restrictions. Yet the concept of normality is at least as complicated as the notion of atheism. I am reminded of two stories about Voltaire's last moments, neither of which I can verify but both of which sound right. He is supposed to have been asked if he believed in God, replying: "Now is no time for making enemies." And he was told that God would forgive him, about which Voltaire commented, "That's his métier." To describe Lacan as an atheist can too easily imply a jaunty view of God; atheism in a Catholic country should be an invitation to inquiry, rather than to close off Lacan's relation to ultimate concerns. I found a schoolmarmish Sunday-school atmosphere at Anna Freud's Hampstead clinic in the mid–1960s, in contrast to the intellectual excitement Lacan had bequeathed to Paris.

It should be obvious that I was deeply touched by the whole experience of being at Marc-François's abbey. Before then I had only heard Gregorian chants on recordings. Now I thought I knew more about why Lacan wore such a special shirt-collar, almost clerical-looking; it had been specially designed for him by Yves St. Laurent. Reflecting on what Marc-François had had to say, and the kind of movement Lacan succeeded in founding, I concluded it was hard not to think of him in quasi-theological categories. One person who had helped me to get to Marc-François had specifically asked not to be publicly thanked; there was that kind of fear of possible retribution, and of damage to a Parisian clinical practice, from within the more orthodox wing of Lacan's disciples.

In histories of psychoanalysis there has long been a controversy about how significant it is that Freud came from a Jewish background. It has seemed to some that to talk about the religious context in which his ideas arose would somehow be to diminish them. I think that the Catholic background to Lacan's work, as spelled out in Marc-François's special way, gives one an invaluable insight into the nature of Lacan's teachings. Yet thinking about how alienated Marc-François felt from Judith Miller's family, not to mention the long court battle between Lacan's two sets of children over his estate, it was hard not to conclude that such family struggles are tragic.

The link between Lacan and Marc-François, however, seemed to me a human triumph. Michel de Certeau had found the 1932 dedication introducing Lacan's thesis "strange." In Certeau's interpretation, "religion" meant the "religious congregation," and "brother in religion" pointed to what Certeau called "a brotherhood based not on blood but on a common sharing in the Order." Certeau thought that this statement of Lacan's was like the purloined letter of Edgar Allan Poe, "placed in the most obvious place and for this very reason obscured from view," but highlighting Benedictine characteristics which Certeau had not before observed.[14] In the 1975 edition of the thesis the dedication was simplified: "To my brother, the Reverend Father Marc-François Lacan, Benedictine of the Congregation of France." Certeau found many parallels between the Benedictine order and the Lacanian schools in Paris; I cannot pretend to that kind of knowledgeability, but I think it worth offering my brief contact with Marc-François for what it teaches about his brother's heritage.

Almost from the outset of my acquaintance with Freud I was fascinated by the comparative cultural reception of psychoanalysis, and I wrote a graduate seminar paper in the early 1960s about Freud in Britain as opposed to America. By now the range of my knowledge has expanded, so I know at least something about what happened in France, Italy, Germany, Argentina, Russia, Israel, Mexico, Ireland, and even China as well as India. Yet Freud's position in France remains unique. When Rudolf Nureyev was dying of AIDS in Paris, he was reported to have wondered whether he should seek a psychoanalysis. Freud's influence there has reached by now almost unprecedented heights; it should seem, I believe, no disrespect either to Freud or religion to remark that while once a priest might be summoned before death, now analysts have come to play a comparable role.

When in 1992 I first gave a talk with the provocative title "What is Wrong with French Psychoanalysis?" for the International College of Philosophy and the International Society for the History of Psychiatry and Psychoanalysis in Paris, the place was mobbed. It was not so much the provocative title of my lecture that attracted these people, but the distinguished panel of four analysts who were supposed to be discussing my remarks. Unfortunately it proved, from my point of view, impossible to make much of a coherent statement, since the responding analysts necessarily fragmented the discussion with their own individual observations. But I was told at the time that my proposed talk had, unexpectedly for me, touched on a raw nerve. For in the years since Lacan's death a vacuum has left many with an uncertain hold on which direction they should be moving in.

In 1992 I went armed only with a copy of Lacan's First Seminar in my hands, and I would like now largely to confine my remarks to that one text.[15] On ordinary grounds of scholarship I picked that book to try and talk about. Intellectual historians like myself prefer to start at the beginning, and hence that seminar seems a logical place to proceed from. I realize that there exist different and legally unpublishable versions of Lacan's seminars, and in out-of-the-way cities like Rosario and Tucuman (in Argentina) I once saw whole stacks of unofficial accounts of Lacan's seminars. The vexing problem of transcription makes me feel like I might be standing on quicksand, and I am aware of the dangers of constructing a straw-man. But that first seminar did appear while Lacan was still alive, and I feel obliged to do the best I can with the material that is now available in print. I would also like to repeat my frustration that Lacan's medical dissertation on paranoid psychosis remains somehow untranslated into English, although it has appeared in Spanish. I would have thought that all students of Lacan's ideas would like to begin there, but perhaps that is too pedantic on my part. In Freud's case there exist between 20,000 and 40,000 of his letters, whose publication will sometime in the future dwarf in size the twenty-four volume *Standard Edition*. So a tentative spirit behooves anyone working in this field.

Perhaps I should make plain what my own objectives amount to: I am primarily concerned with the history of psychoanalysis as part of intellectual life. I will be contending that one learns little about that subject by examining

Lacan's first seminar. One response might be that I have missed-the-boat, and that one should instead study that seminar as part of understanding what is new and interesting in Lacan's approach. I would not dispute that Lacan's body of work represents one of the most interesting legacies from within psychoanalytic thinking. It bears emphasizing that I am approaching Lacan's first seminar by means of the standards of intellectual history.

Nietzsche once maintained that it would be to repay one's teachers poorly if one did not challenge them. Let me make some general observations on Lacan's first seminar, which was devoted to Freud's papers on technique. These are essays by Freud which everybody interested in analysis knows almost by heart. They are taught to candidates in training all over the world. But I want to make some sweeping criticisms about Lacan's approach, and then back them up with some noteworthy examples. What I have to say can be extended to many other works emanating from within French analysis, and are not just relevant to this seminar of Lacan's. At the same time I am hoping that my respect for the immense vitality of analysis in France does not fail to get communicated.

First of all there is, I think, the general problem of what might be called psychoanalytic scholasticism, a static ahistorical way of proceeding. When I met with Lacan's brother we had talked, as I have just mentioned, about how the great medievalist Gerson had avoided this pitfall. (At the time when I first got interested in analysis, I would have thought this charge of scholasticism could best be levelled at the works of Heinz Hartmann, who devotedly tried to tidy up Freud without using any case history material. But he is decidedly out of fashion today, and not just because of Lacan's contempt for his approach.) In most institutes of analytic training there is little effort to put these papers on technique by Freud into any kind of proper historical context. I first made that point over twenty years ago, and as the time left to me shrinks I naturally feel more in a hurry. Freud was writing after his difficulties with Adler had come to a head, and while Freud was already aware of the conflicts brewing with Jung. In my opinion Freud's central purpose, as reluctant as he was publicly to talk about matters connected to technique, was to formulate the basis for the discipline of analysis in a way that distinguished it from any of his "deviating" disciples. That historical context to what Freud had to say remains almost always neglected in the way these papers of his on technique are understood.

But the issue of scholasticism is compounded by what I regard as the arbitrary secondary literature which comes up in the course of Lacan's seminar. And this touches on a general problem within the historiography of analysis which is perhaps more true in France than elsewhere. For there are continuities in the history of analysis which cannot be legitimately ignored. Freud's writings on technique have had a follow-up within the literature, but it requires a decent amount of attention to track down which papers bear importantly on what he originally wrote. At the same time it is necessary to be aware not only of the historical development of analytic technique, but also of the ruptures which have taken place. Not only the continuities, but also the discontinuities, require attention. Perhaps the best example of the violation of the occurrence of a discontinuity comes up in the course of Peter Gay's 1988 biography of Freud, generally well regarded in Paris; as I have already mentioned more than once earlier, Gay does not once even cite the name of Wilhelm Reich. As we know, Reich was one of the so-called trouble-makers in the history of analysis, yet he made in his time crucial contributions to the area of technique: for example, he insisted on the significance of searching for negative transferences, and the meaningfulness of nonverbal communications. It should be unthinkable to leave him out of any historical account. Gay's way of just ignoring Reich, avoiding him altogether, will not do, and yet it is all too characteristic of the way standard accounts of the history of analysis get constructed.

Let me train my guns on Lacan's seminar itself. (I will be referring to the English translation brought out in the States by Norton, but I have also tried to check that edition against the French.) Almost at the outset Lacan refers to the significance of Freud's article "Analysis Terminable and Interminable," which Lacan tells us "appeared around 1934."[16] I suppose when speaking off the top of his head Lacan could use a date like 1934, instead of the correct one which is 1937. For those of us who have devoted care and attention to Freud's last period, three years is no minor matter. Could not in the course of either the editing or the translating the exact year be inserted or provided in a footnote?

Shortly thereafter Lacan refers to Michael Balint having borrowed a term "from the late Rickman, one of the rare souls to have had a modicum of theoretical originality in analytic circles since Freud's death."[17] Now on what grounds can Lacan's reference to Rickman possibly be justified? Rickman was analyzed first by Freud, later by Sandor Ferenczi, and finally by Melanie Klein. I have it on the authority of Donald W. Winnicott that because of a specific early memory of Rickman's Freud had advised Rickman to get out of being an analyst. When Ernest Jones in 1932 wrote to Freud of Rickman that "the underlying psychosis must be regarded as incurable," I believe that Jones was echoing Freud's own opinion.[18] Of course Jones and Freud could both have been in error, but Lacan's singling Rickman out for such striking praise does seem to me to demand some justification, as opposed just to accepting Lacan's assessment. Winnicott, for example, remarked on how useless Rickman's "obsessional" collection of unpublished material proved to be after examining it following Rickman's death.

Early in his seminar Lacan announces that "History is not the past. History is the past in so far as it is historicized in the present. . . ."[19] Now Lacan's idea is a fine one, and widely influential, yet it needs qualifying. To take an example already discussed: whether or not Rickman was such a rare soul with "a modicum of theoretical originality" needs to be defended with some sort of scholarly inquiry — on our part of course, not Lacan's. We cannot simply accept what Lacan said as a matter of faith. Victor Tausk, for instance, had been virtually wiped out of the history books when I was writing my *Brother Animal*; the story of Freud and Tausk as I reconstructed it may even have damaged Tausk in history, in that because of the scandal that arose after the 1969 publication of the first edition of my book it is possible that certain orthodox analysts might have been less likely to cite Tausk than would have been the case before.

How history gets "historicized in the present" can be appallingly wayward. Gay's leaving out Reich (in a book subtitled "A Life For Our Time") was a form of presentism which is not acceptable; most of my writing career has been devoted to protecting the lost sheep in analysis, which means counteracting how history has so far been "historicized." (In the movie *Amisted* John Quincy Adams, in his speech before the United States Supreme Court, stoically welcomes the possibility of a civil war coming out of the differences over race; yet nobody in their right mind would willingly choose to accept the prospect of over 600,000 dead soldiers.) When Lacan refers to "*re-writing history*"[20] one has to be careful that Orwell's *1984*, in which truth-holes suck up the past, does not get fulfilled. Stalin relied on rewriting history for the sake of making the past disappear, and it should be the objective of intellectual historians to avoid the ideological partisanship of propaganda.

Lacan can suddenly bring up the name of Bergler, and in fact I think that Edmund Bergler is someone whose work has for some reason unduly fallen out of favor.[21] But I know of no special reason why Lacan should have chosen to single out Bergler in commenting on Freud's technical papers.

But to get to a more substantive point: Lacan refers to "the case of Lucy R:, which is so elegant," and was, Lacan claims, "entirely solved."[22] I do not even want to refer to Freud's text in his and Breuer's *Studies on Hysteria*, where he does not, as I recall, go so far. What can it mean to allege that a case were to be "entirely solved"? People are not, despite the image that Freud sometimes used, "puzzles" which can ever be solved, much less entirely solved. (Here I think Jung's clinical approach would have something special to teach.) Why does not Lacan, who announces so much indeterminancy in the writing of history, extend a similar kind of leeway, or give-and-take, to the cases that analysts confront? I have long felt that the literature is too bare about analyses conducted on a second, third, or fourth try; to a large extent analysts inevitably find what they are looking for, and different analysts could be expected to evoke contrasting clinical material from the same patient. (It is a pity that Lacan's seminars largely omit the dialectic of the questions and answers from the audience.)

Lacan does refer to the "reproach" levelled at Freud in connection with "his authoritarianism," but then it seems to me that Lacan does not do anything with that concept.[23] But he does go on to warn about the need for "a healthy suspicion of a number of translations of Freud."[24] Here I think there has been a mass of confusion. For instance, there are over a dozen translations into French of Freud's little 1925 paper "Negation."[25] It seems to me striking that this five-page paper should have attracted so much attention in France, as opposed to anywhere else in the world. But in general we know that all translations are necessarily interpretations; in English I think that the danger exists that the quest for new translations is bound to lead to making Freud's writings seem more sacred than ever, when in many cases human energy would be better spent acknowledging where he went wrong and trying to get on with thinking along new lines.

Lacan can refer to Richard Sterba's having in 1934 put something "in a most bizarre manner at the end of an atrocious, though entirely honest, article. . . . "[26] (Here Lacan sounds to me at his most breathtaking in his love of paradox, which Theodor Adorno shared in a different way; in psychoanalysis, Adorno once maintained, nothing is true but the exaggerations.) Sterba was himself a well-educated Viennese analyst, possessing a special interest in art and music, but Lacan's judgment about Sterba's piece seems to me striking. Doubtless Lacan was being playfully enigmatic, and I hope my own reaction does not make me sound an unimaginative pedant. I might have thought an "atrocious" article not worth mentioning, especially if a point had been made in "a most bizarre manner." To say that Sterba's piece had been "entirely honest" in this context was to damn it with faint praise, even though I see no reason in terms of intellectual history for singling out that paper. In 1934 Sterba was hardly a senior member of Freud's circle, and I would have thought that many other works would have been historically more central to be interested in.

Lacan begins chapter 5 by alluding to having subjected to exposition a so-called "central passage"[27] in Freud's paper "The Dynamics of Transference." In reality I do not believe that there is any such "central passage" to be found in the essay, anymore than it could be reliably said that a case were "entirely solved." Lacan can explicitly wax on about Freud's "Negation" piece: "This paper shows once more the fundamental value of all of Freud's writings. Every word is worthy of being measured for its precise angle, for its accent, its specific turn, is worthy of being subjected to the most rigorous of logical analyses."[28] Lacan's choice of this one paper, to repeat my earlier argument, seems to me idiosyncratic, historically unjustified, but by now a part of

French intellectual life. It also made little sense for Lacan to proceed to distinguish Freud in this one essay from his adherents: "It is in that way that it is distinguished from the same terms gathered together more or less hazily by his disciples, for whom the apprehension of the problems was at second hand. . . . "[29] It seems to me gratuitous for Lacan to take such a swipe at Freud's followers, who for all their deficiencies had a more balanced appreciation for the standing of Freud's essay on "Negation" than Lacan himself.

To continue my critique: Lacan says of the Wolf Man — "The patient is not at all psychotic."[30] What is going on here? And what could it mean to say of the Wolf Man that he was "not at all psychotic"? Lacan goes on to compound the difficulties: "He just has a hallucination. He might be psychotic later on, but he isn't at the moment when he has this absolutely limited, nodal experience, quite foreign to his childhood, completely disintegrated. At this point in his childhood, nothing entitles one to classify him as a schizophrenic, but it really is a psychotic phenomena we are dealing with."[31] Unpacking these sentences would require great patience. I just want to comment that childhood would seem to have acquired a theological status for Lacan. For what it is worth, in his own reminiscences the Wolf Man is reported to have complained that Freud had mis-diagnosed him, and that he was in reality schizophrenic.[32] (Despite what Freud wrote about psychoanalysis staying away from schizophrenia, at least once in the 1920s Freud personally treated at length a patient whom he characterized in a letter as schizophrenic, supposedly the same type as Jean-Jacques Rousseau.)

Lacan can at the same time refer to "one" of Ernst Kris's articles.[33] Would it really be too much to expect of the editorial apparatus that it tell us exactly which of Kris's papers is being referred to? Surely the Kris family would help, even if I have been informally told that Lacan was referring to Kris's 1952 contribution to an issue in the *International Journal of Psychoanalysis*. James Strachey has been taking a beating lately for his indispensable edition of Freud's work, but he never would have allowed himself the laziness of Lacan's editors.

Lacan is rough on Anna Freud, and she had not yet as of the date of this seminar helped put him out of the IPA. Lacan is obviously being ironic when he refers to "all the recent discussions which take the ego of the analysand to be the ally of the analyst in the Great Analytic Work. . . . " The capitalization is designed to show how disaffected Lacan was from any approach to the ego "as an autonomous function. . . . "[34] (Actually it was Hartmann, who briefly practiced in Paris, not Anna Freud, who proposed the theory of ego autonomy.) Lacan maintains that Anna Freud's approach "is intellectualist,"[35] as if that were at odds with Freud's, for example in *The Future of an Illusion*. Melanie Klein, as opposed to Anna Freud, is characterized as having had the merits of "her animal instinct."[36] (I already pointed out earlier for those interested in the vagaries of the history of psychoanalysis one should note how British analysts today are keen on denying how heretical Freud deemed Klein's work, for that judgment of his might tarnish the legitimacy of their lineage and psychoanalytic standing.)

Lacan has many interesting things to say about both Anna Freud and Melanie Klein. But then he maintains, "We must accept Melanie Klein's text for what it is, namely the write-up of an experiment."[37] Now I do not think that we "must" do anything of the sort. Melanie Klein may have been Anna Freud's enemy, and the principle of the enemy of my enemy is my friend is an old one, but otherwise there makes little sense in Lacan's approach to Klein's text. (Klein is widely influential in Paris, today, although as far as I know there are no Kleinian centers of analytic training there.) Klein did in fact succeed in making important contributions to the history of analysis, but what is gained by saying that we "must" accept her text for being "the write-up of an experiment"? What on earth is going on by proposing that any analyst's work can be treated simply as "an experiment"? Lacan would seem to be forgetting what he had earlier proposed by the concept of "historicizing" things in the present. Klein needs to be challenged at least as much as any other writer in the history of analysis, and calling any of her work "an experiment" only hides the inevitable subjectivity of her proposals. The curiously important standing that Klein's thinking has in France today can be partly explained by Lacan's influence.

In the course of a few pages Lacan can refer in passing to Otto Fenichel, Hanns Sachs, Sandor Rado, and Franz Alexander.[38] But I wonder how many within French psychoanalysis could distinguish between any of these four writers, showing their strengths as well as the weaknesses of their respective approaches; in the absence of decent scholarship name-dropping can become a source of mystification. (Julia Kristeva has unfortunately picked up the habit of tossing around the names of different analysts.) Lacan also pops in one paper of James Strachey's which Lacan calls a "fundamental article."[39] It is indeed a well-known paper, but should it not be subjected to criticism without *ex cathedra* calling it "fundamental"? Lacan cannot, in my opinion, get out of how he has presented analysis by his assertion: "There are a number of ways of introducing these ideas. Mine has its limits, like any dogmatic account."[40] (Freud in his *Outline of Psychoanalysis* used the analogy of dogma.) The problem is that readers in France, as well as elsewhere, are unlikely to take away from Lacan's seminar enough of a historical perspective on the different authors he chooses to cite.

Carl G. Jung is rarely mentioned in French psychoanalysis, and there is as yet an unwritten account of the reception of Jung in France. (I have already mentioned how Paul Ricoeur was unknowingly echoing Jung in his book

Freud and Philosophy.) Lacan brings in Jung by means of a discussion which can only obscure Jung's role in intellectual history. For example, Lacan mentions "the need to distinguish the psychoses from the neuroses." Now historically this is something that Jung, like Lacan a trained psychiatrist, was well aware of. Before World War I Jung was sensitive to this issue, one which Freud at the time was trying to bridge by the term "narcissistic neuroses" instead of the label of psychoses. (Alan Tyson, the official translator into English of Freud's famous essay on Narcissism, once challenged me to try and follow the intricacies of how Freud distinguished himself on narcissism from Jung, since Tyson could make little sense of Freud's subtle polemicizing.) When Lacan refers to "the Jungian dissolution" of the distinction between the psychoses and the neuroses one might never comprehend what had really happened.[42] It is wholly misleading about what was going on for Lacan to say:

> You are beginning to see, I hope, the difference between Freud's and Jung's appreciation of the place of the psychoses. For Jung, the two domains of the symbolic and the imaginary are there completely confused, whereas one of the preliminary articulations that Freud's article allows us to pinpoint is the clear distinction between the two.[43]

As I have pointed out, Anna Freud and Lacan together viewed Jung as a heretic. But in this passage Lacan is trying to foist off on Freud Lacan's own special distinction between the "symbolic" and the "imaginary." In reality it was not until the 1920s that Freud was even distinguishing between neurosis and psychosis. Lacan is, I regret to say, no more reliable here on Jung than about Klein.

Lacan can refer to a pioneering article of Sandor Ferenczi's as "very poor."[44] In truth it was, I think, one of the great papers in the history of analysis, but because of Lacan's immovable opposition to ego psychology he devalued Ferenczi's early attempt to deal with it. I try to keep reminding people of a story that Erik H. Erikson, a great innovator in ego psychology, used to like to tell: the son of an analyst gets asked what he wants to be when he grows up, and the boy replies "a patient." (Lacan showed no such signs of wanting to relativize the general significance of the analytic model of patienthood.)

While Ferenczi gets blasted, Lacan refers favorably to "our dear friend Michael Balint," even though Balint was one of Ferenczi's most loyal followers.[45] On the whole Balint's work, thanks partly to Lacan's influence, is better known in France than almost anywhere else. The whole relation of Ferenczi to Balint is one of those issues which it would be hard, if not impossible, for any reader of Lacan's seminar to make sense of.

Lacan devotes a special section to Ferenczi's disciple Balint, or it was the editors (presumably with Lacan's approval) who came up with the title "Michael Balint's Blind Alleys."[46] Once again Balint gets referred to as "our friend."[47] The reader will not find, I believe, much in Lacan's remarks that point toward what was most distinctive about Balint's contribution to the history of psychoanalytic thinking. But Lacan specified his unique purpose: he was trying to "render palpable . . . a certain contemporary deviation in relation to the fundamental analytic experience. . . . "[48] So Lacan, like Freud and the orthodox tradition in analytic thinking, was trying loyalistically to stick to the position that Freud had first staked out. (Great dissenters like Wilhelm Reich, Sandor Rado, as well as others like Klein tried to maintain that they had been more royal than the king.)

Lacan somehow comments that "up to 1930" Ferenczi "was to some extent considered . . . to be the *enfant terrible* of psychoanalysis."[49] The qualification "to some extent" pulls the rug from under Lacan himself. In fact Ferenczi, who died in 1933, was only in the last few years of his life considered by Freud or anybody else of questionable standing. Perhaps Balint retrospectively romanticized Ferenczi's role, given Balint's own difficulties with Jones as well as Anna Freud. But even as late as 1930 Ferenczi was considered one of Freud's most authoritative expositors. Since Lacan also refers to Balint as "our good friend," I would be willing to leave it to future intellectual historians to ferret out in Balint's papers what interchanges were taking place between he and Lacan. (The politics of IPA struggles played a role here, since Lacan was getting support from Balint; Balint in turn could see Ferenczi's near-term fate as a renegade in Lacan's own organizational troubles. Anna Freud had become more bitter about Ferenczi than Freud himself.)

Within the analytic literature Lacan refers in passing to a paper by Alexander, one by Herman Nunberg, and also one by Rudolph Loewenstein.[50] My problem here is that these three writers are in no sense on a historical par. It should be necessary to put in the context of his theoretical development what Alexander wrote. Also, one needs to understand just how morbidly loyalist the misanthropic Nunberg was. (According to legend Nunberg committed one of the great slips of the tongue in the history of analysis, when he maintained that a patient had been "successfully mistreated.") It would be easy, in my view, to establish the contrast between these two thinkers and Loewenstein. Only in France does Loewenstein, Lacan's own analyst, have any status to speak of. Elsewhere he has been consigned to the category of one of the least significant of analytic writers. In his aim to be "strictly orthodox" Lacan cannot duly credit an idea of Jung's,[51] even when Jung (as in his conception of archetypes, whatever one might think of it) has in reality been also invoked by Freud (in *Moses and Monotheism* for example). Lacan correctly recognized Edward Bibring's stature, cited Nunberg again, and then suddenly dropped down to a different level entirely when he mentioned a comparative nonentity like Willi Hoffer.[52] Lest it be thought that my judgment about Hoffer is eccentric, I would like to invoke the British Jungian Michael Fordham having agreed with my view of Hoffer.

At one point Lacan does perceptively interpret a dream of Freud's in terms of Freud's relationship with his wife.[53] Lacan not only was way ahead of others in perceiving an important aspect of Freud's feelings about his wife, but Lacan also was "aware of the brutality of his [Freud's] responses to those people who came to him with their hearts of gold, the idealists. . . . "[54] Lacan was outspoken, "fifteen years after Freud's death," in asserting that "we really should not fall to the level of hagiography."[55] It might not be amiss to summarize my approach by saying that at least unconsciously Lacan can be considered a Catholic, even if I do not like the idea of invading someone's privacy by invoking such a characterization. My central point is that the failings I have laboriously pointed out in Lacan's first seminar are representative of a general cavalier approach to Freud in France.

Let me cite some other examples, from writers I happen to admire. Jean Laplanche, with the belief in "the genius of the French language," has proposed to produce "a Freud in French that is . . . Freudian." It is awfully late in the game to think in terms of "the text, the whole text, and nothing but the text."[56] I hope it does not sound terribly immodest of me, but I could write a little book about what I think Freud was doing in those papers of his on technique, and come up with something wholly unlike Lacan's approach; yet I would be closer I believe to the ideal of the task of being an intellectual historian. Lacan's seminar almost certainly will be remembered long after what I might write would be recalled; I am not claiming originality as a theorist, just trying to stick to my calling in the study of the history of ideas.

Or I could take another example from the work of someone else I admire, Julia Kristeva. She happens to have written a long introduction to the French translation of Helene Deutsch's autobiography. Since I wrote Helene Deutsch's biography with her cooperation, I naturally followed up on Kristeva's introduction, if only because she has — along with Lacan and Simone de Beauvoir — helped keep Helene Deutsch's name alive in France. Kristeva, in writing about Helene's life, reports that she was analyzed by Victor Tausk. When I once mentioned this contention publicly in Paris, the audience broke out in laughter. The tale of *Brother Animal* is so well known in France that Kristeva's error needed no gloss from me. At the time *Brother Animal* first came out in Paris many thought it was about Lacan and a famous suicide in his circle. But that Kristeva could say that Tausk analyzed Helene Deutsch is one of those incomprehensible reversals that point to what I fear is a dubious use of psychoanalysis in French intellectual life. (Kristeva's great intelligence, beauty, and charm only highlight such a blunder.)

Louis Althusser's engrossing memoir *The Future Lasts Forever* is filled with the rarefied air of the Parisian intelligentsia.[57] Although a committed Marxist theoretician, he takes Freud almost woodenly for granted. Althusser's account of his own tragic life is almost impossible to put down, and the root of much of his trouble may have been that although he was in analysis for decades he did not seem to realize, even up to the time of his death, that he might have been medically mishandled. Althusser remained incredibly naïve about the efficacy of Freud's method. Although Althusser treats psychiatrists like a new priesthood, as a man of the Left it does not dawn on this otherwise sophisticated Parisian to question any of the key postulates to the Freudian framework he chooses to take as an ideological given. In the autobiographical memoir he appears appallingly uncritical of Freudian terminology and beliefs. Rayomnd Aron once accused Althusser of "an imaginary version of Marxism," which I think applies also to his Freudianism. Althusser makes one suspect that the more brilliant the French philosopher the less contact with common-sense existence. Freud once blamed common sense for most of human troubles, but I find it frightening that ideas are capable of being so addictive. (The visits of Foucault to the mentally hospitalized Althusser underline the significance of the extensive French misreadings of Freud.)

Although there is much more to be said about how difficult writing the history of psychoanalysis can be, I want just to touch on one French example: Otto Rank, once Freud's personal favorite, practiced analysis in Paris for over ten years, from the mid–1920s until the late 1930s, and he had a circle of writers, artists, and analysands around him. (His first wife helped me follow the story of early analysis in France.[58]) Yet in Elisabeth Roudinesco's *Jacques Lacan & Co.*, the second volume of her compendious history of analysis in France, Otto Rank's presence in Paris is simply ignored. Rank was, like so many of the other early analysts in Paris, not French, but he has evaporated in Roudinseco's book for different reasons than why Reich gets dropped from Gay's *Freud.*

Let me conclude on a bold note. Sometimes when I have been in France I have thought to myself: the French are, in the course of a few short years, committing all the mistakes in the history of psychoanalysis that occurred over the last hundred years. I never hear in France criticisms of the therapeutic use of the couch, or how analyses may be allowed to go on much too long with the same analyst. Someone like Jung, and Rank too, pointed out long ago the possible authoritarianism implicit in Freud's recommended therapeutic procedure, a point which Jean-Paul Sartre intuitively understood; for a variety of reasons, as I have indicated, Jung still remains with little influence in France. Voltaire's pungency was not Jung's style. Erich Fromm, rather than Erikson's more discursive approach, has appeal in France, even though it was Erikson who long ago pointed out how psychoanalysis can become an "exquisite" sensory deprivation, an insight which questions in a basic way the classical analytic situation.[59]

I should add that when I presented some of my thinking about what is wrong with French psychoanalysis back in 1992, the first time I cited what I considered a "howler" from Lacan the analyst nearest to me murmured "that is just a mistake," while across the face of another analyst on the panel I thought I could see the thought, "How dare you, a nobody from nowhere, come to criticize."

It is a pleasure in looking at Lacan's first seminar to find him conversant with St. Augustine as well as Sartre. (In an index[60] of all Lacan's seminars Aristotle's name is mentioned more than anyone, followed by Descartes, Hegel, and Socrates.) It has long seemed to me that both Sartre and de Beauvoir played a pivotal role in the reception of Freud in France, even if it generally goes unrecognized. When in Lacan's seminar he alludes to Sartre I doubt he also was recommending that his audience pay as much attention to Sartre's critique of Freud as I think it deserves. I suppose my notion of what is wrong with French psychoanalysis says too much about my own fairly pedestrian approach. But I do think that as intellectuals we ought not to let slide by the kinds of characteristic distortions that I have tried to point out in Lacan's first seminar.

It should go without saying that I would not have undertaken this inquiry into Lacan's first seminar unless I thought that Lacan were fully worth the effort of the most sustained sorts of inquiry. He made French psychoanalysis, translating a second-rate Society into one of the greatest contemporary sources of psychoanalytic originality. Jones did the same for the British Society, but he accomplished that objective as an organizer and via supporting Klein; Lacan succeeded by the fertility of his ideas, which have affected French intellectual life as a whole. Lacan brought psychoanalysis and philosophy back together, in a way which is reminiscent of the early Freudians. Just because of the beneficial effects of French psychoanalysis today, it behooves us to be aware of some of its possible shortcomings.

Analysis is by no means coming to an end at the turn of this new century. But the past gains power by the way in which we conceptualize it. Aspects of psychoanalysis, as in Freud's attack on Christianity, were revolutionary. But fragmentation has also occurred, so that bits of psychoanalytic history have broken off and become isolated. At the same time we need to be aware of the continuous stream of psychoanalytic thinking, without any authoritarian appeal to what might seem to be the "mainstream" of that tradition. What I have written here about French psychoanalysis may read like a scold, when in reality I am trying to communicate something of the excitement connected to studying the history of psychoanalysis. Future students will find plenty to work on during the coming years. I have never found a letter of Freud's which bored me, and intellectual historians can do worse than labor over the field which he created.

Elisabeth Roudinesco has performed an outstanding service in helping to introduce the rest of the world to French psychoanalysis. *Jacques Lacan & Co.*, the second half of a two-volume study (but the only part to have been published in English), is a fascinating introduction to a special reception of Freud's teachings.[61] Roudinesco's work is bound to expand the scope of those ideas outside France. For Lacan, who is today the dominant French psychoanalytic theorist, wrote in a difficult, hermetic style; with the help of the sweep of Roudinesco's tale the reader gets a foothold in a universe that is bound at first to seem topsy-turvy.

At the outset France, where Freud himself had gone to learn, was unresponsive to Freud's work, and for a long time French psychiatry and neurology thought it could do just fine without the addition of psychoanalytic teachings. Freud's work was stigmatized as an alien, Germanic-seeming influence, and even today there is still no standard edition of his work in French.

But starting in the 1930s Lacan was taking psychoanalysis in a novel direction within France. When he postulated an early mirror stage, in which the child both learns about its possibilities of autonomy and at the same time becomes enmeshed in a phantom-like existence, he started creating an idea that has attained wide currency. Even if Lacan has been misunderstood, thinkers like D. W. Winnicott have responded to his inspiration.

Lacan was determined to avoid the authoritarianism implicit in so many of the traditional psychoanalytic training centers, and he and his group got themselves expelled from the International Psychoanalytic Association in 1953. Willing to experiment with variations in time schedules for seeing patients, Lacan somehow tactically failed to mollify the Princess Marie Bonaparte. Anna Freud backed her old friend Marie, and Lacan was out.

For years Lacan struggled to get back into the good graces of the IPA, and even today members of his group in Paris, along with other French analysts, speak with great bitterness about the bureaucratic mentality of the IPA. Lacan became devoted to a kind of permanent revolution within psychoanalysis; and he later dissolved the first society he founded after leaving the IPA. His breaking up the group he had created took place over the objections of some of its key members; but Lacan was determined to maintain the creative flux that he thought so essential to psychoanalysis retaining its vitality.

Roudinesco knows with intimate familiarity the story she records — her mother belonged to what Roudinesco calls the third psychoanalytic generation in France. The author links psychoanalysis in France not only to certain distinctively French psychiatric traditions, but also to such movements of thought as surrealism, Marxism, and existentialism. Outside of the Princess Marie Bonaparte, Freud had no appointed disciple in France. Most of those he trained were, like Marie Bonaparte herself, relative outsiders in Paris, and not capable of bringing psychoanalytic doctrine into the center of French culture.

Events in the spring of 1968 were to mark a decisive shift in psychoanalysis's French fortunes; for afterwards Freud was taught in secondary schools as a necessary topic for those intending to go on to university; and at the reconstructed Sorbonne psychoanalysis attracted hundreds of students, who sought not necessarily to become therapists but to understand modern culture better. By 1990 there were, according to Roudinesco, some sixteen psychoanalytic societies in France.

Jacques Lacan & Co. is a work of great detail and diligence; on certain relatively minor points I found fault with Roudinesco's research. But to dwell on them would be to look at the individual trees while missing the forest at large.[62] For Roudinesco has successfully painted a sweeping canvas of the reception of psychoanalysis in France. I know no comparable work on another national culture responding to Freud, except for Nathan Hale's *Freud and the Americans*.[63] For readers who want to understand the French Freud, I know no better place for them to start than *Jacques Lacan & Co.*

Notes

1. Paul Johnson, *A History of Christianity* (London, Weidenfeld and Nicolson, 1976), p. 147.
2. Elisabeth Roudinesco, *Jacques Lacan & Co.: A History of Psychoanalysis in France, 1925–1985*, translated by Jeffrey Mehlman (Chicago, University of Chicago Press, 1990), pp. 104–05.
3. *Ibid.*, p. 679.
4. Michel de Certeau, *Heterologies: Discourse on the Other*, translated by Brian Massum (Minneapolis, University of Minnesota Press, 1986), p. 242.
5. Ludwig Binswanger, *Sigmund Freud: Reminiscences of a Friendship*, translated by Norbert Guterman (New York, Grune & Stratton, 1957), pp. 3, 9.
6. Roazen, *Freud and His Followers*, *op. cit.*, p. 323.
7. "The Question of Lay Analysis," *Standard Edition*, Vol. 20, p. 189.
8. De Certeau, *Heterologies*, *op. cit.*, p. 54.
9. Roazen, *Oedipus in England: Edward Glover and the Struggle Over Klein*, *op. cit.*, p. 55.
10. De Certeau, *Heterologies*, *op. cit.*, p. 59.
11. Roudinesco, *Jaques Lacan*, *op. cit.*, p. 362.
12. "From the History of an Infantile Neurosis," *Standard Edition*, Vol. 17, p. 27.
13. Paul Roazen, *Meeting Freud's Family*, *op. cit.*, Chs. 11–12.
14. De Certeau, *Heterologies*, *op. cit.*, p. 242.

15. *The Seminar of Jacques Lacan: Book I Freud's Papers on Technique 1953–54*, ed. Jacques-Alain Miller, translated with notes by John Forrester (New York, W. W. Norton, 1988).
16. *Ibid.*, p. 9.
17. *Ibid.*, p. 11.
18. *The Complete Correspondence of Sigmund Freud and Ernest Jones 1908–1939*, ed. R. Andrew Paskauskas (Cambridge, Mass., Harvard University Press, 1993), p. 697.
19. *The Seminar of Jacques Lacan: Book I, op. cit.*, p. 12.
20. *Ibid.*, p. 14.
21. *Ibid.*, p. 15.
22. *Ibid.*, p. 20.
23. *Ibid.*, p. 29.
24. *Ibid.*, p. 34.
25. "Negation," *Standard Edition*, Vol. 19, pp. 235–39.
26. *The Seminar of Jacques Lacan: Book I, op. cit.*, p. 49.
27. *Ibid.*, p. 52.
28. *Ibid.*, p. 55.
29. *Ibid.*
30. *Ibid.*, p. 59.
31. *Ibid.*
32. Roazen, *Encountering Freud, op. cit.*, pp. 185–86.
33. *The Seminar of Jacques Lacan: Book I, op. cit.*, p. 59.
34. *Ibid.*, p. 62.
35. *Ibid.*, p. 67.
36. *Ibid.*, p. 69.
37. *Ibid.*, p. 80.
38. *Ibid.*, pp. 110–12.
39. *Ibid.*, p. 111.
40. *Ibid.*, p. 113.
41. *Ibid.*, p. 115.
42. *Ibid.*
43. *Ibid.*, p. 117.
44. *Ibid.*, p. 127.
45. *Ibid.*, p. 139.
46. *Ibid.*, p. 201.
47. *Ibid.*, p. 203.
48. *Ibid.*
49. *Ibid.*, p. 208.
50. *Ibid.*, pp. 237, 240, 243.
51. *Ibid.*, pp. 244, 267.
52. *Ibid.*, pp. 284–85.
53. *Ibid.*, pp. 269–70.
54. *Ibid.*, p. 270.
55. *Ibid.*
56. Jean Laplanche, Pierre Cotet, and Andre Bourguignon, "Translating Freud," in *Translating Freud*, edited by Darius Gray Ornston (New Haven, Conn., Yale University Press, 1992), pp. 183, 148, 143.
57. Louis Althusser, *The Future Lasts Forever: A Memoir*, edited by Olivier Corpet and Yann Moulier Boutang, translated by Richard Veasey (New York. The New

Press, 1993). See Paul Roazen, "Wittgenstein and Althusser: Two Philosophers Analyzing Freud," *Queen's Quarterly* (Spring 1997), pp. 127–135.

58. See Roazen, *The Historiography of Psychoanalysis*, *op. cit.*, pp. 205–15.
59. See Roazen, *Erik H. Erikson*, *op. cit.*, pp. 70–72, 182, 191.
60. *Index Des Noms Propres et Titres D'Ouvrages* (Paris, E.P.E.L.)
61. Roudinesco, *Jacques Lacan*, *op. cit.*
62. For a more critical assessment of this same book, see Roazen, *The Historiography of Psychoanalysis*, *op. cit.*, pp.333–37.
63. Nathan Hale, *Freud and The Americans* (New York, Oxford University Press, 1971) and Nathan Hale, *The Rise and Crisis of Psychoanalysis in the United States* (New York, Oxford University Press, 1995). See Roazen, *The Historiography of Psychoanalysis*, *op. cit.*, pp. 317–19.

9

Erikson's Ego Psychology

Lacan made a full-scale campaign in Paris against what he thought was his main enemy within psychoanalytic thinking — ego psychology. It was partly a matter of Anna Freud's own role in helping to contribute to the development of ego psychology that drove Lacan in the direction he took; as his enemy within the International Psychoanalytic Association (IPA), Anna Freud's work, as we have discussed, was to be subjected to harsher criticism in Paris than anyplace else. But ego psychology became for Lacan an immense grab-bag encompassing everything he disliked, especially those ideas emanating from within America. Erik H. Erikson was in fact trained by Anna Freud, although he had a complicated and ambivalent set of feelings toward her. While he understood that it was not uncommon for former continental Europeans (like Robert Waelder) to dismiss his work as amounting to the "Americanization" of psychoanalysis, Erikson continued to fill out the implications of the directions his ideas had gone in.

By the mid–1970s, when he published his collection *Life History and the Historical Moment,*[1] Erikson was one of the world's most famous psychoanalysts; that text would turn out to be his last major publication. Although he had become renowned as an early advocate of "psycho-history," Erikson went out of his way to warn that he did not want to be associated with everything that came to be categorized under that term. His special interest was in making use of psychology to enrich the art of biography. Erikson observed how even anti-psychological biographers are apt to function with an implicit psychology, and therefore he tried to bridge the traditional gulf between the perspectives of the historian and the psychologist. He had in mind a reciprocal relationship between psychology and history in which the practitioners of the respective crafts would each have something to gain. Erikson insisted that historians recognize the fateful role that childhood plays in the structure of a society, and, at the same time, he welcomed the impact of history on psychoanalysis in the expectation that it would correct concepts that too easily appear universal rather than time-bound. Such interdisciplinary efforts can easily fall between stools, alienating people who each suspect different sorts of professional impurities.

In trying to evolve a common method for psychoanalysts and historians, Erikson highlighted the way a clinician necessarily interacts with and affects his evidence: the analyst influences what he observes, and therefore becomes a part of what he is studying. For Erikson "the first rule of a 'psycho-historical' study" is "that the author should be reasonably honest about his own relation to the bit of history he is studying and should indicate his motives without undue mushiness or apology." In his book on Gandhi, for example, Erikson wrote extensively about his personal interaction with the data he gathered. He cited Freud's concept of counter-transference to help explain his own experience of emotional involvement in historical research. Erikson's anthropological fieldwork gave him further insight into the ways an observer participates in the lives of his subjects and enabled him to formulate another rule of psycho-historical study: "that there be at least a rough indication of how the data were collected."[2]

Besides pursuing his biographical and methodological interests, Erikson tried in the course of studying great men to come to terms with the phenomenon of greatness itself. He aimed to study not only the origins but also the regularities in the growth of certain kinds of geniuses. On the surface, it is highly dubious to think that there was any common core of greatness at work in the scientists and politicians he studied. In reality, by greatness Erikson meant effective leadership and success, which might well exclude many writers or artists who failed to achieve immediate recognition or significant impact on their times. In terms of his background, however, Erikson can be understood as having been pulling away from negativistic aspects of the Freudian heritage. He proposed as an alternative to explore the crucial problem of creativity. He insisted that there was a difference between a clinical case history and a life history, and he viewed a focus on historical greatness as a way of exploring and emphasizing the concept of ego strength; this notion was designed in a clinical context to point to those human capacities which enable us to cope by reconciling "discontinuities and ambiguities."[3]

Historians have often wondered about the problem of verifying psychological hypotheses, and this collection of essays was unlikely to make psychohistory less controversial. It opened with an autobiographical essay which told us that Erikson "grew up in Karlsruhe in Southern Germany as the son of a pediatrician, Dr. Theodor Homburger, and his wife Karla, née Abrahamsen, a native of Copenhagen, Denmark. All through my earlier childhood, they kept secret from me the fact that my mother had been married previously; and that I was the son of a Dane who had abandoned her before my birth." When writing about Gandhi's autobiography, Erikson reported that "observers trained in clinical observation cannot accept an event reported in an autobiography. . . . " One problem with Erikson's account of his own origins is that at a conference in Geneva in 1955 he declared that his father had died around the time of his birth. Erikson's clinical papers were published under his stepfather's name of Homburger; then why, one had to wonder, when he decided to take a new name, did he not revert back to his natural father's name? Erikson was silent in his autobiographical essay on his choice of a last name. He did argue that "a stepson's negative identity is that of a bastard,"[4] which was one way of hinting that the issue of legitimacy played a key role in Erikson's life.

Erikson writes, again in connection with Gandhi, that "autobiographies are written at certain late stages of life for the purpose of re-creating oneself in the image of one's own method; and they are written to make that image convincing."[5] He had become a believing Christian; it would be impossible to understand his interest in Luther's theology and Gandhi's doctrine of non-violence or Erikson's contributions to clinical thinking, without appreciating the depth of his ethical commitment to Christianity. But what was he throughout childhood? Professor Marshall Berman, in a 1975 review, stated that Erikson's mother's maiden name sounded Jewish, and that Erikson therefore was guilty of disguising a Jewish past.[6] A one-sentence letter from Erikson to the editor would have stopped any damage to his reputation, but neither Erikson nor his associates could declare that his mother was not Jewish. Since his stepfather was Jewish too, and Erikson had had the customary bar mitzvah, it meant that his childhood was culturally thoroughly Jewish.

If one examines Erikson's autobiographical essay closely, the accusation of evasiveness about his Jewishness seems justified. We are told that his mother was a native of Copenhagen, and that his real father was a Dane. But Erikson said his stepfather came from "an intensely Jewish small bourgeois family." In the biography of Erikson by Robert Coles, Erikson's childhood begins with a wandering Danish woman bringing her son to live in a Jewish doctor's home in Karlsruhe. Why did Erikson describe his biological parents by their nationality, and the stepfather by his religion? Coles quoted Erikson as saying both his parents were Danish, but the stepfather got characterized as Jewish. (Here Erikson claimed that his parents were "separated" before he was born.) To complete this unfortunate tale, in his autobiographical reflections Erikson described himself as having come "from a racially mixed Scandinavian background."[7] What he meant was that there had been intermarriage with non-Jews on his mother's side of the family. Not even Erikson's mother may have known the real identity of the father of her first child.

Nowhere did Erikson describe his conversion to Christianity. He did not seem to realize that his method of disguising the facts of his origins damaged the nature of his commitment to Christian ethics. For it is bound to appear as if he was not only attracted by the merits of Christianity, but also repelled by the religion of his childhood.

Erikson did tell us of his search for a mythical father, and appropriately the second chapter of *Life History and the Historical Moment* discussed two posthumous publications by Freud, a surrogate father in Erikson's psychological life. One is a collection of Freud's letters to his friend Wilhelm Fliess, and the other is the study of Woodrow Wilson co-authored with William C. Bullitt. Erikson reviewed both books when they were published. Regrettably, Erikson was again guilty of evasiveness; for although at the outset of this book he stated that all his papers have been "re-edited for this volume," he introduced these two essays by declaring: "My original reviews of these two books follow here."[8]

In his account of the Fliess letters, first published in 1955, Erikson had made relatively few changes. He still refused to see that when Freud theorized about the sources of incomplete sexual discharge, and traced that problem to childhood seduction, he was engaging in a kind of autobiography. Instead of seeing the problem as his own limited potency or sexual difficulties with his wife, Freud characteristically escaped a current mental conflict by placing it in the past. (We have already encountered how Jung, and later Otto Rank, made this important point about Freud's general way of proceeding to use infantile material as a defense against current reality.) Erikson's need for a mythical father obscured his own historical vision. He again cited a 1900 letter of Freud's in which he spoke of having finished begetting children. At this point Erikson added an entirely new sentence: "The reference to his 'finished' procreative activities has suggested to some that, for Freud, who considered the then available contraceptives unbearable, this meant a cessation of marital relations altogether."[9] But what evidence there is in the Fliess correspondence for the sexual relations between Freud and his wife coming to an early end finds support not so much in that 1900 letter, but in an 1897 one, where Freud writes that "sexual excitation is of no more use to a person like me."

Other than touching on the issue of Freud's sex life, Erikson made relatively minor changes in his account of Freud and Fliess. Nonetheless, in connection with their falling out, it is worth noting that on the whole Fliess now got better treated. Whereas once Erikson thought it relevant to say that "after all, Fliess had not undergone an analytic process," he now stated: "After all, Fliess had not cultivated the correspondence for purposes of self-analysis . . . ." In 1906 Fliess had helped publish some letters of Freud's in relation to the Weininger-Swoboda incident.[10] In 1955 Erikson thought Fliess was displaying "a clearly paranoid public defense of his priorities"; but now Erikson softened down that judgment to "a more paranoid public defense of his priorities." Erikson also inserted a new parenthetical characterization of Freud's handwriting as "big and aggressively spiked."[11] Considering that the Freud-Fliess correspondence was bowdlerized, and Freud's subsequently published volumes of letters (up until those written to Jung) were also subjected to censorship, it would have been helpful to have the reader alerted to some of the new evidence.

The changes Erikson introduced in his account of the Freud-Bullitt collaboration were far more drastic. Since it was Erikson's prominently published review that, at the time, lent credence to the alleged inauthenticity of Freud's part in the manuscript (it subsequently became the official policy of the *Journal of the American Psychoanalytic Association* not to discuss this book), Erikson's second thoughts are worth highlighting. At several points Bullitt was now praised and patted on the back. New passages got inserted concerned Bullitt's modesty about helping Freud to escape from Vienna and Bullitt's "rare knowledge of international personalities and power struggles." Bullitt's resignation from Versailles was cited for showing "besides personal irritation . . . courage and foresight."[12] Two sentences were dropped entirely: (1) "Bullitt's preface obscures, even as it offers to clarify, the history of the manuscript," and (2) "For me and for others it is easy to see only that Freud could have 'written' almost nothing of what is now presented in print."

Erikson still thought the Freud-Bullitt book a bad one, but he was now willing to see more of Freud's hand in it. Rather than saying, as he did originally, that "One might even concede that some of the formulations are reasonable facsimiles of Freud's early theories," he now used "must" instead of "might." Erikson added a fresh sentence before quoting some particularly dreary parts of the book: "even as Bullitt's mechanization of psychic forces only caricatures a trend which does exist in the literature, so do the following excerpts only render more obviously absurd a kind of formulation not always absent from newer applications of psychoanalysis to history." Instead of working to rebut what to others "appears to be genuine Freud," Erikson now saw his opponent as what "appears as genuine Freudian history." Whereas once Erikson was so offended by the text that he doubted the veracity of the collaboration — "something like this seems to have been in Bullitt's mind when the 'collaboration' started" — now he was obviously changing grounds — "something like this seems to have been in Bullitt's mind when he convinced Freud of the desirability of collaboration."[13] (Who convinced whom remains an open question. A newly unearthed 1927 letter of Freud's to Bullitt indicates Freud's conviction that Bullitt appreciated Wilson more than Freud did.)

Most striking of all perhaps was Erikson's change in his more general assessment of the book. In 1968 he thought, "The only point to be made here is that the text now printed must be ascribed to Bullitt, because he either transcribed or wrote, translated or caused to be translated, every word of it." Now, however, Erikson wrote, "The main point to be made here is that Bullitt either transcribed or wrote, translated or caused to be translated, every word of the bulk of the book."[14] The ambiguities of the fresh wording — "every word of the bulk of the book" — revealed Erikson's own new hesitations.

While I agree with the general direction of the changes Erikson silently made in his view of Freud, the specific purposes he had in mind are worth noting. He wanted to perpetuate a myth about Freud's virtues, which Erikson's other writings also helped to propagandize; and at the same time, in keeping with Erikson's insistence on the psychological significance of continuities, he was trying to ensure that his own independent work did not land him in the camp of the so-called heretics in psychoanalysis. In his historical writing he concentrated on the role of discipleship in the lives of ideological innovators; and he commented on the resources creative people need to have "the courage of their own originality." Because, however, of what he considered his own "truly astounding adoption by the Freudian circle,"[15] Erikson became less than outspoken about the changes he introduced into prior psychoanalytic thinking.

Although Erikson said that the ideological conservatism of the Viennese psychoanalytic group made the idea of moving on an invigorating one, he acknowledged "little impetus either to find safety in orthodoxy or escape in heresy." Thinking himself "inept in theoretical discussion," Erikson succeeded in revitalizing the Freudian tradition through his striking case histories, anthropological studies, and biographies. Leaving behind his own early commitment to traumatology, Erikson's clinical writings focused on processes of self-healing, on restorative energies, and on the means of recovery. The Oedipal crisis was for Erikson "only the infantile or neurotic version of a *generational conflict*"; therefore Oedipal problems "must be evaluated as part of man's over-all development." In contrast to Freud, Erikson was apt to treat the phenomenon of transference as a consequence "of the technical choice of the basic couch arrangement." Despite his hagiographical approach to Freud, Erikson did acknowledge "a significant shift of focus from the classical psychoanalytic outlook to newer perspectives such as my own." And therefore Erikson's special contribution was to emphasize "what, in man's total existence, leads *outward* from self-centeredness to the mutuality of love and communality, *forward* from the enslaving past to the utopian anticipation of new potentialities, and *upward* from the unconscious to the enigma of consciousness."[16]

All the essays in this collection, like everything Erikson wrote, bear rereading; he was one of the foremost psychologists of our era. His essay on youth forms part of his interest in the different stages of the life cycle, and his essay on women attempts to defend his own earlier effort to emancipate his thinking from the constraints of the traditional psychoanalytic view of femininity. For historians, aside from his articles on Freud, the essays of greatest interest will be those on Gandhi. Here Erikson explicitly tried to handle methodological questions concerning the nature of psycho-historical evidence. He did warn the reader, however, about the character of his own involvement with the figure of Gandhi: "my transference to Gandhi no doubt harbored an adolescent search for a spiritual fatherhood, augmented by the fact that my own father, whom I had never seen, had taken on a mythical quality in my early years." Partly Erikson was interested in unraveling in Gandhi the significance for India of a midlife crisis in a political leader. More generally, however, Erikson sought to understand the sources of prejudice, "the human propensity to bolster one's own inner mastery by bunching together and prejudging whole classes of people," and to emphasize how "any group living under the economic and moral dominance of another is apt to incorporate the world image of the masters into its own — largely unconscious — self-estimation. . . . "[17]

Erikson's mythifying came to the fore, however, in efforts to compare Gandhi's *satyagraha* with psychoanalytic technique, as both nonviolent ways of affirming our common humanity. To support this congruence, he reminded us that Freud once fancied going into politics, and Gandhi had thought of a medical career. Erikson can be understood as using Gandhi for the purpose of constructing an alternative image to a cynical view of human nature. The purity of Gandhi's technique lay in its dependence on the recognition of a common humanity: "Gandhi would not even contemplate as an adversary anybody with whom he did not already share a communality in a joint and vital undertaking. . . . "[18]

Erikson's earlier interest in Luther was also stimulated by the changed image of man he inaugurated. Erikson did not reduce Luther's life to the status of a neurotic case; on the contrary, Erikson argued that Luther was great precisely in his struggle to lift his individual problems to a universal level. Erikson believed that the main objective of psycho-history was to relate the particular conflicts of a given leader to the typical needs of his historical time. This task requires an understanding of what was excessive as well as what was typical in any life, taken in conjunction with the social environment. In Erikson's conception of greatness there were "transforming functions of the 'great man' at a certain juncture of history."[19] In understanding the relationship of the individual life to collective history, Erikson proposed that we see how a leader becomes prototypical for his time, fulfilling specific needs in the lives of his followers.

However attractive Erikson's general orientation, in his treatment of specific historical material Erikson often has to seem questionable. Luther himself never mentioned the fit in the choir that Erikson made so much of, nor did Gandhi give any such central place to the strike that forms the "Event" of Erikson's account. As in his essays on Freud, while Erikson functioned as a biographer he was as much a mythologist as an historian. He shrewdly insisted that even the most well-established historical data owe their survival to a past era's sense of what is momentous. The psychologist in Erikson was really more comfortable talking about myth rather than history — two of his most convincing pieces were about the legend of Hitler's childhood and the legend of Maxim Gorky's youth.[20]

Every historical actor, perhaps each individual, needs to develop a myth about himself, and Erikson referred to this process as "historification." In his tolerance for the human need for legend, as in his respect for the quest for heroes, Erikson was at odds with Freud's own negative view of the functions of illusions, and in particular, of religion. Erikson was right in believing that myths can be a means of mastering our anxieties, and of finding external support for our aspirations. And this remains true even if the specific examples of his biographical uses of psycho-history are bound to leave scholars with a good deal of skepticism.

For reasons that remain in good part obscure to me, Erik Erikson's thinking has come to be on the periphery of today's psychoanalysis. The worthy objective of *Ideas and Identities: The Life and Work of Erik Erikson*, edited by RobertWallerstein and Leo Goldberger is to try to establish Erikson more centrally within the profession.[21] I think that Wallerstein is right in being convinced that "no single psychoanalyst [excluding Freud, one presumes] has had a more profound impact on our twentieth-century culture and world than he. Indeed very few analysts have reshaped psychoanalytic perspectives to the extent that he did." After Erikson's death in 1994, when he was nearly ninety-two, Wallerstein organized a San Francisco day-long symposium in 1995 in order to commemorate and celebrate the life and work of Erikson. The proceedings of that symposium made up one issue of the journal *Psychoanalysis and Contemporary Thought*, and has been reprinted here along with four of Erikson's own papers.

Unfortunately it seems to me that Wallerstein's excellent intentions may not succeed in implementing all the objectives that he has in mind, and I will try to explain why I think that. But first a few words about Erikson seem to me in order, and my personal take on him will then help support my general point of view. It appears to me that Erikson deserves to be remembered in his full complexities. He was extraordinarily intuitive and, as Helene Deutsch once remarked, "without elbows"; Erikson may have succeeded in becoming immensely successful, so that he won all sorts of prizes and once even appeared on the cover of *Newsweek*, but he was without customary careerist ambitions. As is probably well known by now, he was analyzed by Anna Freud in Vienna, and continued to practice, especially with children and adolescents, for many years, but Erikson trained relatively few people, and largely sought to exert his influence by means of the impact of his writings themselves. Starting in the 1960s he taught at Harvard for over a decade, yet declined at the time to be a training analyst at the Boston Psychoanalytic Institute. Erikson felt he was bucking the tide of pre-existing psychoanalytic thinking, and did not want to get engaged in any sterile debates about where his ideas did or did not fit into preexisting thinking. Someone like David Rapaport helpfully placed Erikson within the history of ego psychology, for example in his Introduction to Erikson's 1959 *Identity and the Life Cycle*.[22] For all Erikson's directness and capacities for immediacy, his writing could be subtle, elusive, and sometimes hard to follow.

Erikson was trying to be an innovator without drawing any divisions between himself and earlier psychoanalytic thinking which would be unflattering to the past, or cause bureaucratic difficulties with existing psychoanalytic institutions. As a matter of fact, Erikson was so worried about the charge of having merely "Americanized Freud" that he was tempted to mythify some of the links between himself and the Freuds. I remember Erikson's once remarking on the way undergraduates at Harvard took away an unduly pessimistic understanding of Freud's teachings, and I quickly asked whether Erikson had assigned *The Future of an Illusion*. Erikson responded with a wry smile, because of course he was not making use of that anti-religion tract, where Freud was at his most utopian; Erikson was in fact seeking to import into psychoanalysis a set of essentially Christian ethical principles, and his conception of a life-cycle of ego strengths was designed to advance an ethical program as well as explain development. But Erikson was also insistent on the significance of the concept of ego strength for clinical work; people should be characterized not so much by what they repress or deny, but by all the contradictions they are able to unify. In the face of a substantial change like that it was paltry to be accused by people like Kurt Eissler of merely being a therapist rather than an analyst.

Erikson had such a complicated agenda that it can be genuinely difficult to communicate all that he was up to. But he made the situation more confusing by his gentle way of going about things. He had already seen what had happened to someone like Erich Fromm once he published a momentous book like *Escape From Freedom* in 1941.[23] Fromm was assailed by a variety of psychoanalytic big guns (like Otto Fenichel and Karl Menninger) for having aggressively betrayed the purity of the psychoanalytic message, and ultimately Fromm went on to work out an independent and structured view of his own, one which is also not adequately recognized today for what he had tried to accomplish. Erikson might have been relieved that in *Ideas and Identities* the dread name Fromm does not come up more often than twice. Curiously enough, the arch-heretic Jung seems more tolerable in *Ideas and Identities* than Fromm; when Erikson lived in San Francisco he was friendly with the Jungian analyst Joseph Wheelwright, and through his influence Erikson picked up a number of Jungian themes. But Erikson, who in his pre-analytic days was an artist, was uncomfortable with ever drawing hard and fast conceptual lines, and I never could tell whether he was aware or even comfortable with how he fit into previous intellectual history.

My own way of reading *Ideas and Identities* may have been no doubt unusual, but still I can recommend it to others. The first chapter in this collection that I read was Lawrence J. Friedman's contribution; Friedman, an accomplished historian, is Erikson's official biographer, and his *Identity's Architect*[24] has now fulfilled almost everything that one could wish in presenting Erikson's life and ideas. The second chapter that I read was that by Robert J. Lifton, since he was such a close friend and collaborator of Erikson's. Lifton's essay, along with Friedman's, does a first-rate job of giving the reader an over-all idea of Erikson's body of thought, so that the rest of *Ideas and Identities* easily falls in place. Different readers will pick and choose what they want to read first on an individual basis.

The paper of Erikson's on Freud's Irma dream, reprinted here, seems to be the one essay by him that is now securely acknowledged professionally as a classic. It first appeared as long ago as 1954, and yet it still retains its freshness. Although I am not sure that Erikson would have liked to have the public reminded of it, still I think it is a tribute to him that at the time the *International Journal of Psychoanalysis* refused to accept it, so it appeared initially in the *Journal of the American Psychoanalytic Association.* Anna Freud privately wrote how sickening it was to her to have Erikson using her father's material for the sake of Erikson's ideas, and her editorial influence in London was then still powerful. It is a credit to Erikson that he proceeded on his own course, even if he felt pained by his analyst's reaction to his own originality. Erikson's essays on "The Problem of Ego Identity" (1956) and "The Nature of Clinical Evidence" (1958) are also outstanding, and obviously relevant for clinicians. The reader has only to dip into the early paragraphs of each of Erikson's pieces to see how rich the implications of all his thinking are. But I doubt whether Erikson's last essay "The Galilean Sayings and the Sense of 'I'" (1981), which first appeared in the *Yale Review*, will without special help succeed in explaining the relevance of Erikson's Jesus to psychoanalysis.

The other essays in *Ideas and Identities* are of a consistently high caliber. Wallerstein's opening chapter in his introductory overview succeeds in setting the context for Erikson. Marcia Cavell writes about Erikson from a philosopher's perspective, although she does not do enough I think to highlight Erikson's special ethical purposes. Neil Smelser provides another fine essay about Erikson as a social scientist, even if I would have preferred it if he had shown by example how much Erikson had gained from his contact, for example, with cultural anthropology or sociology. Walter Capps appropriately focuses on Erikson's contribution toward understanding religion; still, I cannot ever remember Erikson's having alluded to a forerunner like the Swiss analyst Oskar Pfister, whose views on Christianity and religion were at odds with Freud's own. Erikson was pursuing a tack which was spiritually different from that of most analysts of his day or even ours. Elizabeth Lloyd Mayer contributes a chapter designed to show how Erikson's work on children's play constructions stands up in the light of the latest evidence about gender development. And Stephen Seligman and Rebecca Shahmoon Shanok have a fine piece on how Erikson anticipated today's intersubjective perspective. Doubtless Erikson is not often enough recognized for how he changed the direction psychoanalysis has taken; but by the same token Erikson's current stature should also come from the degree to which his ideas have yet to be adequately accepted.

It is Erikson's own essays, however, which necessarily have the most to teach us. No matter how often I may have read these papers by Erikson, they remain profoundly touching and informative. Erikson liked to say that essentially he had only a way of seeing things to communicate. Those in psychoanalysis who are better logicians, or scholastically more adept, may gain a temporary notoriety; and writers happier with system-building may have their own special interest in reassuring the insecure and people in need of a safe haven. Erikson is partly underestimated today because his voice was so quiet and unpolemical; he was full of original ideas and remained himself as an analytic thinker. It seems characteristic that the messianically motivated in all fields tend to be the more readily acknowledged; those who out of temperamental modesty try to avoid founding schools of their own are too often apt to fall between the cracks. Fanatics, alas, do well because of the life their ideologies assign them, infusing self-confidence.

It remains to be seen how it is going to be best to preserve Erikson's legacy. I think myself that psychoanalysis ought to consider the possibility of opening altogether more doors to social scientists with interdisciplinary concerns; historians (and philosophers) can do something by the way they teach through example. Because outside scholars are not clinicians does not make them any less vital for the future of analysis. Part of Erikson's unspoken agenda was to broaden psychoanalysis's horizons, so when he wrote his life histories of Luther or Gandhi he was partly trying to demonstrate to clinicians the way historical actors succeeded in making constructive use of problems which in others might prove debilitating. Patienthood may be the central concern of practicing psychoanalysts, yet Erikson was trying to get the profession to be more aware of all the aspects of life which could not be exhausted by immediate clinical preoccupations. Childhood was for him only one aspect of the whole life cycle; identity might be a key to certain central developmental tasks, but Erikson thought the goal of "generativity" was no less critical to adulthood. And so one of the points I took away from Erikson was that he was trying to teach that psychoanalysis and social science make a two-way street, each offering the other something precious.

For all its merits I am not sure *Ideas and Identities* succeeds enough in illustrating the full challenge Erikson's life and work amounts to. Lifton seems to me right in saying that Erikson was "the most creative psychoanalytic mind since Freud," and Wallerstein or Goldberger might agree that absorbing what Erikson had to offer is going to take more than any single commemorative volume. The real way of celebrating his life and work lies in the future, when I hope it will prove possible to be more expansive about the varieties of ways on which psychoanalytic thinking can be enhanced by what he wrote. Even though Erikson took pains to dampen down the subversiveness of his thinking, he stood for an immense amount of fresh air, which should be bracing and emancipatory.

Psychoanalysts do not have to be in any way defensive about what might be involved in absorbing the implications of what he had to offer. The generosity and humaneness which Erikson stood for is only a threat to the dry-as-dust codifiers who are interested in hanging on to past routines. To the extent that Erikson continues to inspire new generations of analysts he will have succeeded in being a creative leader of the field. But that may involve acknowledging how much we have to go before his psychoanalytic vision is fulfilled.

Notes

1. Erik H. Erikson, *Life History and the Historical Moment* (New York, W. W. Norton, 1975).
2. *Ibid.*, p. 88, 84.
3. *Ibid.*, p. 19.
4. *Ibid.*, p. 27, p. 136; "The Childhood Genesis of Sex Differences in Behavior," in *Discussions on Child Development*, Vol. III, edited by Tanner and Inhelder (New York, 1958), p. 16; Erikson, *Life History and the Historical Moment*, *op. cit.*, p. 31.
5. *Ibid.*, p. 125.
6. *New York Times Book Review*, March 30, 1975.
7. Erikson, *Life History and the Historical Moment*, *op. cit.*, p. 27, Robert Coles,

Erik H. Erikson: The Growth of His Work (Boston, Little Brown, 1970), p. 13, Erikson, *Life History and the Historical Moment, op. cit.*, p. 27.

8. *Ibid.*, pp. 29, 48.
9. *Ibid.*, p. 77.
10. Roazen, *Freud and His Followers, op. cit.*, pp. 93–94.
11. Erikson, *Life History and the Historical Moment, Ibid.*, p. 76, 77, 66.
12. *Ibid.*, p. 95, 82.
13. *Ibid.*, pp. 90, 92. 91, 95.
14. *Ibid.*, p. 85.
15. *Ibid.*, pp. 56, 29.
16. *Ibid.*, pp. 99, 40, 163, 105, 101, 39.
17. *Ibid.*, pp. 147, 175, 178.
18. *Ibid.*, p. 181.
19. *Ibid.*, p. 47.
20. Erik H. Erikson, *Childhood and Society* (New York, W. W. Norton, 1950).
21. *Ideas and Identities: The Life and Work of Erik Erikson*, edited by Robert S. Wallerstein and Leo Goldberger (Madison, Conn., International Universities Press, 1998).
22. Erik H. Erikson, *Identity and the Life Cycle: Selected Papers, Psychological Issues* (1959), Vol. 1, No. 1.
23. Erich Fromm, *Escape From Freedom* (New York, Holt, Rinehart and Winston, 1941).
24. Lawrence J. Friedman, *Identity's Architect: A Biography of Erik H. Erikson* (New York, Charles Scribner's Sons, 1999); see Roazen, *The Historiography of Psychoanalysis, op. cit.*, pp. 291–94.

10

Jackson Pollock and Creativity

It is easy to suppose that psychoanalysis must have something special to add to the mystery of creativity, and to the psychology of the artist in particular. At least a fairly sizable literature has grown up on this whole subject. Not only did Freud make more than one stab in this direction, but others, both within psychoanalysis and art history, have taken up his lead. Even if this endeavor were to turn out to be a largely mistaken one, the Freudian revolution in the history of ideas has already taken place. It is not just that surrealists in the 1920s, as we saw in Chapter 8 on Lacanianism, had some contact with Freud and his thinking, and countless others interested in art as well, but someone like Jackson Pollock actually underwent psychotherapeutic treatment. A collection of his drawings that he gave to one of his therapists to help pay for the treatment has been displayed at a Museum of Art and are now worth a sizable amount of money, and it is natural to think of psychoanalytic theory in order to help explain what that part of his work adds up to.[1] So, like it or not, by now the ties between psychoanalysis and art are a secure aspect of intellectual history.

For some skeptics it is not immediately obvious what is meant by the term "psychoanalysis," although defining that concept may be easier than coming up with something satisfactory about either creativity or art. Psychoanalysis might for some seem identical to what Freud himself wrote. At least while he was alive Freud was insistent that he alone had the right to decide between that which properly qualified as psychoanalytic and what he regarded as work merely masquerading as part of his discipline. But even if we were to make psychoanalysis coterminous with Freud's texts, the problems we would still confront would not be easy ones.

For although Freud created a coherent and unified system of thought, just as Karl Marx did, the body of Freud's writings is necessarily subject to interpretation. For not everything Freud wrote has the same professional standing. To take one example: should a letter Freud wrote be treated with the same amount of weight as any sentences from one of his most scientific-sounding treatises? It is sometimes tempting to think that a writer reveals himself most tellingly in private communications. Freud's correspondences were vast, and only a fraction of the Freud letters that have survived have been published so far.[2] I think that it matters to whom Freud was writing, what the specific occasion was, and how what he sent squares with the rest of his thinking. Any genius is bound to leave behind quandaries that perplex. Freud's Viennese charm sometimes meant that he privately said things meant for their immediate effect, even if he knew that everything that he was writing would likely get saved and preserved for posterity. North Americans and even Europeans of today are apt to have so much difficulty detecting politesse emanating from the old Austro-Hungarian Empire that I am inclined to think that among contemporaries perhaps only Japanese or other non-Westerns can follow the kind of subtleties that someone like Freud could engage in.

As one examines the corpus of Freud's published works, the so-called canon of his psychological texts, inconsistencies and tensions can be found. Sometimes he is inclined to modest declamations that psychoanalysis must lay down its hands in the face of artistic achievements. Yet at the same time he ventured forth into his remarkable (and hardly cautious) little book about Leonardo da Vinci. He dared to extend psychoanalytic thinking onto some of the most sacred-sounding topics in art history. Just as he thought that novelists, poets, and dramatists could be understood by means of his psychology, painters (and also sculptors) too had to run the risk of being explored by his own kind of reasoning.

Works of creative achievement can never be relegated to a subsidiary aspect of psychoanalytic concern. For even though Freud worked in his consulting room for the sake of combating that which he called neurosis, it ought to be logically clear that one cannot label anything neurotic without a more or less clear idea of its opposite, the healthy. Yet Freud was extremely reluctant ever to get drawn into a discussion of normality, except to indicate that it did not much interest him. Legend has it that Freud once dismissed a patient from treatment on the grounds that the individual in question lacked an unconscious. It was the worst Freud could think of saying about anybody. (The absence of an Oedipus complex would have been to him a sign that the person was not adequately civilized.)

Faith-healers specialize in moralizing about health, whereas Freud sought to overcome the pretensions of traditional ethics to get at the underlying unconscious motivation. Freud did talk about what he called sublimation, and this has to play a key part in the logic of his doctrine. But, even after all the years I have spent studying psychoanalytic theory, I am uncertain about just how to describe what Freud meant by a sublimation. (A cultured Parisian analyst I know has published a book on the subject of sublimation, a premise of which would be that the concept is philosophically complex).[3] Surely examples of creative artistic achievements would be illustrations of sublimations, even if it remains obscure how to account for them.

We do start out, in describing what is meant by psychoanalysis, with Freud; yet even while he was alive there were many famous dissenting voices within the ranks of his pupils. I am not just thinking of such famous theorists as Jung, who I think took a different tack toward creativity than Freud, or Otto Rank, who made art a central part of Rank's post-Freudian psychological constructions. Even within those elements of the psychoanalytic movement which remained firmly loyal to Freud himself, apart from dissenters like Jung and Rank, one finds different approaches to creativity than with Freud himself. For example, the Reverend Oscar Pfister, while respectfully challenging Freud's *Future of an Illusion*, defended religious belief in part by linking it with the artistic creations of sculptors, painters, musicians, and writers.[4] Pfister's *Illusion of the Future*, his answer to Freud, has become almost forgotten, even as we continue to come to terms with the same issues he brought up while Freud was still living.

In the years since Freud's death the theory known as psychoanalysis has changed momentously. Every decade there are new leading thinkers, or at least fresh faces, and they come up with a terminology that sounds novel. But one feature has unfortunately remained constant. When Freud turned to art he often did so with the idea that he was "applying" psychoanalysis; a basis for how he proceeded was that his doctrine was scientific and only needed to be implemented in other cultural areas to demonstrate the power of its insights. In the course of his study of Leonardo, Freud had described the conflict in that great man between his scientific side and his artistic self; it would not be too hypothetical to think that Freud was engaging in a bit of autobiographical inquiry, acknowledging the artistry in his own work. But, as in Freud's thesis of what happened with Leonardo, in the end the scientist triumphed over art, and since Freud's death it has been hard to restrain psychoanalysts from using art as a vehicle for advertising the latest psychoanalytic wares. "Applied psychoanalysis" has meant using psychoanalytic thinking in other areas, rather than, as Erikson had had in mind, trying to broaden psychoanalysis by its contact with humanistic disciplines.

Sublimation has got to be a central part of any aspect of psychoanalysis's attention to art. And yet I wonder whether, since Freud's death, we are not rather worse off than while he was still living. Here is an example of a "sublimation" published as recently as 1991:

> A man in analysis for conflicts that impaired his ability to work had learned to play the clarinet as an adolescent. During one particular summer, he would take his

> clarinet with him when he worked away from home, and on lonely walks he would stop and play where no one could hear him. During the analysis the patient recalled that one of the boys he had lived with that summer distressed him by masturbating at night in such a way that he could be heard. Revolted by this the patient had taken his clarinet and again gone off by himself to play. Later in life he collected recordings by clarinet virtuosos and took great interest in his son's clarinet lessons. When he was a child he was awed by the appearance in his home town of a famous jazz clarinetist and he treasured this musician's autograph. He loved many kinds of music rather indiscriminately and was especially fond of sentimental songs and would often cry over them.
>
> The man was terribly frightened by violent fantasies about competition with male rivals. His clarinet playing proved to offer him a disguised opportunity to express an unconscious masturbation fantasy in which he won the admiration of adoring crowds without risking direct competition with male rivals. In his sexual fantasies he feminized himself so as to avoid competition with male rivals. This was expressed also in a fantasy of stealing his rival's strength by sucking on and then biting off the man's penis, swallowing it, and using it for himself. His mouthing of the clarinet thus allowed him to gratify libidinal and sadistic drive derivatives; it defended him against the danger of retaliation by other men; it allowed him considerable gratification in the sphere of reality as well as the fulfillment of important forbidden competitive sexual wishes related to his father and his son; yet when he played his instrument he felt that he was only a poor imitator of the real man who could really play well, and so he was punished by his failure. This attitude paralleled his chronic self-belittling attitude about his work performance compared to that of other men.
>
> On one occasion the patient had a dream about the clarinet. He was at a dance. The clarinets were all in the front row of the band. One of the musicians was a little black boy who removed the clarinet from his mouth and imitated the sound of the clarinet with his voice. Then a former male teacher appeared in the company of two intimidating women and the teacher waltzed off leaving him alone with one of the scary women.
>
> The dream exactly paralleled his childhood and adolescent experience in which his father repeatedly left him alone to deal with the overwhelming conflicts induced by his mother's seductive and controlling behavior with him. As a consequence he could never feel pleasure in his penis if he touched it. He could only masturbate by rubbing his penis against the bed sheets and then he felt pleasure not in the shaft of the penis but in his perineal area. So in the dream he could only be the little black boy pretending to be a real musician but never allowed to use the forbidden instrument. Both his sublimation and the dream were compromise formations utilizing his musical interest. But there are substantial differences in the comparative structure of these two compromise formations as well as in their duration. The sublimation endured throughout his life and the dream occupied but a moment of his sleeping thoughts.[5]

This clinical illustration is, in my opinion, a laughable example of outrageous nonsense. It was not proposed before World War I but presumably benefits from the latest insights of post-Freudian thinking. We find clarinet-playing belittled, reduced to an infantile set of sexual conflicts. The psychoanalyst-author was writing about an ability that "endured" throughout the patient's life. Yet little appreciation gets shown, I think, for the achievement of being musical. Freud himself made a considerable display of his own lack of musicality, and even gave some reasons, in terms of his own hyper-rationalistic strain of thinking, for his lack of appreciation for music. Yet I recall one highly musical patient of Freud's, also a composer, who reported that after having gone to see a Wagner opera in Vienna, Freud understood more about the performance than the patient had.

If psychoanalysis is understood to be that sort of thinking which led to a risible interpretation of a patient's clarinet-playing, then nobody serious should ever think of using such a doctrine to cast light on the mysterious realm of creativity. One does suspect, in North American training institutes at any rate, that today's candidates are bound to be less cultured than would have once been the case in Europe, and may still be true for certain psychoanalytic centers abroad. A whole school of psychoanalysis in France, originally founded by Jacques Lacan, has worried whether this is a field that can in fact ever succeed in being "transmitted," or whether each person must necessarily think through the subject anew, creating a fresh version of psychoanalytic teaching to suit the individuality of every new practitioner.

So psychoanalysis is more than simply a set of texts, no matter how carefully studied, and even the books themselves, as compared to letters, have to be weighed and assessed to see what they add up to. Freud was often writing with various ideological enemies in mind, so Jung and Rank, for example, continued to play a role in Freud's teaching long after they had both left his fold of students. The oral tradition among psychoanalysts is often richer than the written material, so the regular scholarly way of finding out about psychoanalysis can be misleading in its own right. I know of no psychoanalytic training center where Otto Rank would likely be even mentioned, and to raise the name of Jung would be to trample on the kind of myth-making that implies that Freud must be taught as a separate body of knowledge. To think of any intellectual rapprochement between Freud and Jung would endanger the institutional bodies that have arisen for the sake of conveying psychoanalytic teachings; and so Jung does not get taught at Freudian centers of learning, even though it means an impoverishing of the tradition of thought that Freud can be credited with having helped to initiate.

In studying Jackson Pollock, this narrowness of the traditional way in which psychoanalysis gets learned is bound to have bad consequences. Pollock had more than one Jungian therapist, and the drawings he gave to his first one obviously bear the impact of the ideology of his temporary mentor. Freudian patients have Freudian dreams, and Jungian patients Jungian dreams. To say this should not detract from the standing of psychoanalysis as a body of knowledge. An acquaintance of mine, who was once writing a book on nightmares, reported that his analytic patients produced a phenomenal number of nightmares.

Patients in trouble, and after all there would be no other sound reason for anyone to seek out psychological treatment, are bound to be highly suggestible. In a patient's eagerness to overcome emotional problems, the analyst's predilections are bound to loom enormously large. The impact an analyst has on a patient goes far beyond any spoken words or communicated interpretations. The nature of a consulting room, the taste of the decorations, as well as the meaning that certain artifacts of the analyst's office suggest, are often overlooked as an aspect of the therapeutic process. I think that for an analyst to have an office full of prized possessions, or books, is not any kind of professional indiscretion. On the contrary, the desiccated kinds of consulting rooms that one is apt to encounter in the New World, in contrast to what would be the case on the continent today, for example, say something about what is wrong with the state of our own culture.

In his own treatment Pollock was obviously not "cured," although exactly what a cure might constitute has never been successfully established. He drank a good deal too much. Here, however, it is not at all clear what specific role alcohol plays for writers as well as painters apart from other professions. Thomas Hart Benton, an early teacher and associate of Pollock's, also had a special interest in drinking, although this seems to have been a steadier sort of alcohol consumption rather than the binges in which Pollock indulged. Winston Churchill drank steadily throughout World War II without its being an interference with his extraordinary political performance.

One of Freud's favorite students, Ruth Mack Brunswick, ended her account of the second analysis of Freud's patient the Wolf-Man by writing that his future health would be "in large measure dependent on the degree of sublimation of which he proves capable."[6] But that surely was a tautology; the issue remains what exactly is a sublimation. To say that the Wolf-Man's health depended on his capacity to sublimate would be like saying that the extent of the heat outside depends on the strength of the sun's rays. If Pollock's drinking became dysfunctional, we still have little knowledge about the exact conditions that might account for such a state of affairs.

We do know that symptoms, even the most frightening sorts, can also have a positive function. Jung, and later analysts like R. D. Laing, emphasized the extent to which symptomatology can be a sign of a strong patient's courage to resist the conformist pressures of the outside world. Freud too, as a matter of practice, understood something of this same line of thought. He used to quote Gotthold Lessing: "A person who does not lose his reason under certain conditions can have no reason to lose."[7]

As highly cultured as Freud was, he cannot escape responsibility for much of what has taken place in his name. For example, Freud could write of a patient's emotional conflicts that the "solution" was such and such. Freud seems to have proceeded on the metaphoric assumption that patients represented puzzles that were in principle capable of being solved. Others, such as Jung and Rank, would have been more likely to have insisted that Freud's way of proceeding was falsely scientific, or what is called scientistic. When it comes to any of the great questions of creativity we are obliged to be humble and reticent.

How Pollock could be as disturbed as he was and still make such a momentous contribution to modern art has to remain one of those perplexities that continue to amaze. If one looks at his early drawings, those that he gave to his first Jungian therapist, there is obviously a resemblance to Picasso, but also to Jung's theoretical commitments. Jung then becomes as relevant to understanding those particular drawings as Picasso's own paintings. And this remains true even though it is unclear whether Pollock brought those drawings to his therapist as part of the treatment process in addition to their serving as payment for the therapy he received.

In the end of course Pollock's therapy did not succeed in overcoming his drinking; for lengthy periods Pollock did not drink, and his late and greatest period as an artist seems to have taken place without any alcohol in his life. The car accident in which Pollock died, however, does seem alcohol-related. And yet the therapy Pollock got did not succeed in preventing the later outpouring of his genius. The psychoanalytic drawings that he can have used to pay for his therapy, when collected together for 1992 showings, had to be insured for some two million dollars.

Freud however would not have thought that psychoanalysis as either science or therapy had to rest on its success as an agent of change. When Freud sought to understand Leonardo, he was doing so for the pure joy of what light of understanding psychoanalysis could bring to bear on Leonardo's genius. Freud's impact has been such that few of us can approach any cultural attainments nowadays without some awareness of the childhood of the artist involved.

Freud did think that his most momentous contribution was singling out not just the meaningfulness of dreaming, but the specific significance of the infantile factor in human development. And here some of his followers have made as much a mockery of his spirit as those who have continued to write about sublimation without appreciating the subtleties of all genuinely artistic achievement. The psychoanalytic literature is today filled with vast speculative treatises about the earliest phases of child development. Unverifiable hypotheses about early infancy get trotted out as if something real were being said.

And clinically absurd situations have continued to crop up. In Paris recently

I heard the story of a British mother in London who brought a problem of her two or three-year-old child to a leading Kleinian analyst; the issue was that the child was not yet speaking. The analyst saw the mother and father, but not the child itself; the mother was told that the child was to be brought to analysis five times a week, and then in a year or two the analyst would know what to think. The mother had no bad personal reaction to the analyst, but had another child at home to consider; when the mother explained that the distance between the family residence and the analyst's office meant a great deprivation for the other child, in the amount of time that would be eaten up traveling, the analyst had a decisive answer: "Move." The mother called a child analyst friend in Paris, who reassured the worried woman that many children, especially gifted ones, do not speak on a secure developmental schedule. Without analysis the child did in fact apparently turn out all right.

I wish this anecdote could be confined only to a representative of one extreme wing of psychoanalytic thinking. In the mid–1960s I spent some time as an observer at Anna Freud's Hampstead Clinic, and I remember one therapist talking about a sublimation in a way that still seems to me unforgettable. The issue, this analyst declared, was what happens to the patient when a sublimation gets "taken away"; that was to be the test of the genuineness of the sublimatory process. The person enunciating this doctrine did not seem especially talented herself, and I still feel outraged at the thought that anybody would even think of taking away so precious an achievement as a sublimation.

Anna Freud's school of child analysis was supposed to be at an opposite pole from that of Melanie Klein, and (as we have discussed) they certainly fought against each other, not only as separate parts of the British Psychoanalytic Society but within the international psychoanalytic movement. Yet both Melanie Klein and Anna Freud had more in common than either may have liked to think. In Anna Freud's famous 1936 treatise *The Ego and the Mechanisms of Defense*, sublimation gets treated as a defense "mechanism." Yet if a sublimation were capable of being neurotic, then the whole logic of psychoanalytic thinking has to be flawed. Either sublimation is an alternative to neurosis or it is not; no matter how intimately the two may be connected, in that Freud thought that the worst in us can be connected with our highest accomplishments, sublimation has got to be given a unique status or psychoanalytic theory cannot succeed in getting anyplace.

Pollock at least went on to become the Pollock we all know; his psychotherapeutic treatment did not prove damaging, even if ultimately his drinking contributed to his tragic end. We might know more about his therapy had it not been for the lawsuit that Pollock's wife, also an important painter, launched against the sale of his so-called psychoanalytic drawings. She first consented to having a few of them shown publicly, when the therapist who had once treated Pollock realized the significance of the drawings that he had kept in his files. Selling them off as a unit would have seemed a decent way of preventing them from becoming widely scattered; yet Pollock's widow seems to have taken offense at calling them "psychoanalytic" drawings, and then argued that it was a betrayal of Pollack's privacy to have the therapist proceed to dispose of them.

Once the lawsuit was launched, the therapist was forced to become more circumspect about what he said about Pollock. Although ultimately Pollock's widow failed in her legal case, she did raise a knotty ethical issue. On what grounds can therapists, when their patients become famous, be entitled to talk about the treatment they once oversaw? We have already discussed how the poet Anne Sexton's biographer, with the authorization of Sexton's literary executor, relied on using tape-recorded therapeutic sessions kept by one of Sexton's psychiatrists. There is no doubt that the book was enriched by this therapeutic material, although more interpretations on it might be placed than what the biographer herself chose to make. The Freudian impact on twentieth-century thinking has invaded us all, so that even our most private fantasies, dreams, and wishes are interpretable by a system of thinking that exists in the outside world. Our naiveté has been so compromised that one sometimes thinks that past historical subjects, without the knowledge of psychoanalysis, make better objects of study than today's sophisticates, all too aware of the intellectual structure that Freud created.

It is so easy to abuse psychoanalytic thinking that one does not know exactly what to do. Theories can get transformed into concrete things, and the most creative analysts leave behind themselves ideas that get woodenly invoked. I am thinking, for example, of Donald W. Winnicott, a splendid pixie of a man, whose ideas, at least in North America, are apt now to get tossed around wholly out of keeping with the fluid and unusual way his mind worked. That Melanie Klein, or Anna Freud, can lead to obvious interpretive absurdities does not surprise or especially trouble me. But for Winnicott, despite all his unclassifiable exceptionalness, to get invoked to illustrate the so-called merits of psychoanalysis's explaining away art does seem to me frightening.

E. H. Gombrich, writing for the centenary anniversary of Freud's birth in 1856, could say to analysts that "try as we may, we historians just cannot raise the dead and put them on your couch."[8] But several decades later the situation had radically changed. Artists have gone into therapy, and the issue is what happens when creative works of art encounter psychoanalytic interpretation, not just by the therapists who conducted the treatment but by others as well, with access to some of the same clinical material.

The possibilities for vulgarity have multiplied. The existence of psychopathology is not like having a bad tooth; nobody can, or should be, cured of the human condition. At his best Freud taught that what we achieve draws strength from our weaknesses. And yet so much of what he taught elsewhere also implies that a human being can be purified of conflicts. People enter treatment for the sake of getting help for areas of their life that are troubled; and therefore psychoanalysis has always been stronger in explaining failure than in accounting for successful areas of functioning. (That was one of the central sources of Erikson's devising his own ego psychology.)

Diagnoses can only be relevant for clinical purposes. Even to think of Pollock as a "schizophrenic," as some have done, is to miss the core of his being. A great artist is qualitatively different from a garden-variety psychotic; and although Freud's theories were not designed to deal with psychosis, and someone like Jung, who as we have seen was unlike Freud in being trained as a psychiatrist, was apt to be better at perceiving the capacity people have for being self-healing, no use of psychological terminology can be acceptable as an alternative to the job of genuine understanding.

Psychoanalysis, however we understand it, ought never to become an ally to any demeaning procedure. Using psychoanalysis in the realm of art should evoke the same kind of sacred care that a priest would bring to bear on a needy precious supplicant. People do crave shortcuts, and a sadistic use of psychoanalytic reasoning is all too common, in our general culture and perhaps in clinical consulting situations. I am reminded of an anecdote about Freud in the early 1920s that Abram Kardiner once reported:

> Freud refused to put up with nonsense from his followers. On one occasion a member of the [Vienna Psychoanalytic] Society presented a paper on chess. Freud commented at its end, "This is the kind of paper that will bring psychoanalysis into disrepute. You cannot reduce everything to the Oedipus Complex. Stop!" He was an implacable foe of cant and formula.[9]

It is up to us to stick to Freud's modesty and brush aside the arrogance that can accompany psychoanalytic understanding. Creativity in art should be monumental enough to remind us all of the limits to human understanding and the merits of remaining at sea about how the human soul works. Reinhold Niebuhr, in a paper on "Human Creativity and Self-Concern in Freud's Thought," recalled "the inevitability of the egoistic corruption in all forms of human creativity which has been preserved in the Christian doctrine of original sin." At the same time Niebuhr saw that "that capacity of transcending every social situation and its own self bears within it all the possibilities of creativity."[10] Some mysteries do not need solving and yet their existence should continue to goad us to pursue inquiry.

It still seems compelling that psychoanalysis ought to be able to tell us something about the origins and psychodynamics of creativity. A relatively recent book, *The Origins and Psychodynamics of Creativity: A Psychoana-*

lytic Perspective,[11] by Dr. Jerome D. Oremland, seems to be hobbled by unnecessary references to old arguments once proposed by Freud. Oremland is not able to develop imaginatively Freud's suggestive hints, so that a reader comes away with a distinctly stale taste. The author is a member of the San Francisco Psychoanalytic Society, and his book carries the endorsements of key figures within international psychoanalysis; to criticize this work is not to whip a generally acknowledged tired horse. My own reaction to the text, however, is a mild sense of shock at how bankrupt today's psychoanalytic arguments can be.

To be even more blunt: by what literary right does Oremland feel qualified to say anything critical of Shakespeare's *Richard III*? It is unbelievable to students of the history of psychoanalysis to find Oremland announcing in his Preface: "Creation, be it issue or art, is part of the quest for immortality" without once mentioning the apparently forgotten name of Otto Rank, who put forward just such a thesis about three-quarters of a century ago. It is equally appalling to find Freud's intimate friend Wilhelm Fliess diagnosed here as "psychotic," when one would have thought that it was precisely the creative side of mankind that Oremland was trying to get at. Among the "excellent" psychoanalytic studies of music cited we find a work by Oremland himself.

Although it cannot have been Oremland's intention to impose a Procrustean Freudian bed on creativity, that is what his treatise amounts to. The book contains several "responses" by talented and creative people. (Oremland thinks he has distinguished between talent and creativity, which in my opinion would be a bootless exercise.) But one of these respondents does refer to the interesting work of Arthur Koestler, whose writings do not get mentioned in the book itself. These responses are, I think, weakened by their eagerness to press their ideas into the mold Oremland has offered.

There are a few splendid quotations in Oremland's book, such as Mozart's son Carl's account of going for a walk with his father. Oremland also offers some case vignettes of his own. One has every reason to respect Oremland's seriousness and conscientiousness, but that makes his wooden reliance on the writings of Freud and those organizationally faithful to his school all the more unfortunate. Oremland would have done better to have started from scratch without exposing the hollowness of his conceptual lineage. I hope that Freud himself would not have been pleased to see his own words trotted out after so many years as a substitute for original thinking.

As we have already mentioned, twentieth century psychiatry in Great Britain has developed along a very different course from that which it has followed in America. While Freudian concepts have long pervaded American culture, more old-fashioned attitudes have managed to prevail in England. Freud has been traditionally looked on with a higher degree of suspicion there, and medicine as a whole is accorded nowhere near as high a status as in the United States. Yet, as in the early days of psychoanalysis, the very lack of popular acclaim has meant that in England psychotherapy as a career attracts highly talented practitioners, able to resist conformist pressures.

Dr. Anthony Storr represents the finest of enlightened psychiatric thinking in Great Britain today. Originally a Jungian but for many years an eclectic, he owes more to his broad cultural background than to any ritualistic school of thought. Whatever defects Freud had as a thinker, he was a great writer, and part of his triumph over Jung lay in the latter's difficulties in translating his thought into concise prose.

In *The Dynamics of Creation*[12] Storr has talked about the problem of creativity within the Freudian vocabulary. But while fully aware of the value of this conceptualization, Storr has hit on a shortcoming in the master's thinking and one that long ago Jung was concerned about. The primary inadequacy of early psychoanalysis was its negativism; it could reduce art, for example, to the lowest common clinical denominator. A Storr points out, great art is neither escapist nor defensive, but enriches our understanding of reality.

Freud's devotion to science, as opposed to art, as well as his puritanism about sex, helped account for his success in America. Despite what is generally regarded as a sexual revolution, America has retained its prurient interest in sex, and it has also maintained its faith in medical experts. The puritanism in Freud's thinking led him, and even some of his disciples today, to think of sexuality as an alternative to creativity. The great artist who sublimates does so, according to this view, at the expense of his sex life.

It is a tribute to the power of dogmatic blinders that such a theory could still be maintained. One has only to think of Pablo Picasso to realize the inadequacies of a formulation that contrasts sexual fulfillment and creative work. Despite what Freud sometimes tried to argue, neither fantasy nor play need be pathological in a mature adult. Storr takes the whole issue to a more profound level, for despite all his respect for Freud, in the end he challenges a key assumption of traditional psychoanalysis: the tie between sexuality and human self-realization.

Although the early Freudians were faced with the task of freeing patients from the excessive sexual inhibitions and taboos of their day, Storr argues that unhappiness need not be the equivalent of neurosis. Alongside the notion that creativity is won at the expense of sexual gratification, the early Freudians made too much of the importance of sexual fulfillment as a test of so-called normality. Satisfactory sex can at best alleviate a limited number of human problems, and should not be burdened with more than it can safely sustain. "All the problems in being human are not solved by mature sexual relationships, and once this assumption is abandoned, the work of art does not have to be seen as inevitably a substitute for something else," Storr writes.

Jung has always been attractive to those with an artistic bent, and his theory of psychological types, with his concepts of "introversion" and "extraversion" are by now famous. One of the best aspects of Storr's book is his superb rendering into plain English of characteristic human dilemmas associated with certain personality types. He does not put readers off with unnecessary jargon, nor confuse character with illness. Storr's lucid and well-organized book, filled with fine illustrations of creativity, goes far to fill one of the central inadequacies of contemporary psychoanalytic thought.

Notes

1. Claude Cernushi, *Jackson Pollock: "Psychoanalytic" Drawings* (Durham, N. C., Duke University Press, 1992).
2. Roazen, *The Historiography of Psychoanalysis, op. cit.*, pp. 103–32; Roazen, *Encountering Freud, op. cit.*, pp. 65–80.
3. Sophie de Mijolla-Mellor, *Le Plaisir de Pensée* (Paris, Presses Universitaires de France, 1992).
4. Paul Roazen, editor, with Introduction, Oskar Pfister, "Illusion of the Future," *International Journal of Psychoanalysis*, Vol. 74 (June 1993), pp. 557–79; see below, pp. 239–41.
5. Scott Dowling, editor, *Conflict and Compromise: Therapeutic Implications* (Madison, Connecticut, International Universities Press), pp. 19–21.
6. Quoted in Roazen, *Freud and His Followers, op. cit.*, p. 426.
7. Quoted in Roazen, *Brother Animal, op. cit.*, p. 150.
8. E. H. Gombrich, "Psychoanalysis and the History of Art," in *Freud and the Twentieth Century*, edited by Benjamin Nelson (New York, Meridian Books, 1956), p. 188.
9. Abram Kardiner, "Freud — The Man I Knew, The Scientist and His Influence," in *Ibid.*, p. 50.
10. Reinhold Niebuhr, "Human Creativity and Self-Concern in Freud's Thought," in *Ibid.*, pp. 260, 269.
11. Jerome D. Oremland, *The Origins and Psychodynamics of Creativity: A Psychoanalytic Perspective* (Madison, Conn., International Universities Press, 1997).
12. Anthony Storr, *The Dynamics of Creation* (New York, Atheneum, 1972).

11

The History of Psychotherapy

By the early 1990s the history of psychiatry had entered a fresh professional scholarly phase, and in good part this can be credited to the influence of the pioneering work of Henri F. Ellenberger. This is true even though his 1970 *The Discovery of the Unconscious: The History and Evolution of Dynamic Psychiatry* was so massive and detailed that I doubt if more than a handful of people have ever read it cover to cover. Ellenberger's writings reveal his unblinkered view on many of the most standard controversies, and all of us in the field are indebted in some way to what he accomplished. For example, he notably helped resurrect the work of Pierre Janet; Ellenberger also dissolved many myths about Freud, and took a refreshingly non-partisan approach to Adler and Jung.

Unfortunately Ellenberger did not live to see a volume in his honor appear: *Beyond the Unconscious: Essays of Henri F. Ellenberger in the History of Psychiatry*.[1] This work should do much to help continue stimulating further research. The editor, Mark Micale, has given an excellent overview of Ellenberger's place in the modern history of psychiatric research. Micale offers a sound biographical study of Ellenberger, as well as discusses the central themes in all of Ellenberger's writings. (Although Ellenberger taught for many years in Montreal, it also seems fitting that an Henri Ellenberger Institute has opened in Paris.)

Part One of *Beyond the Unconscious* includes three of Ellenberger's papers: one on Fechner and Freud, another on Moritz Benedikt, and a third on Freud's 1886 lecture on masculine hysteria. Part Two includes Ellenberger on Charcot and his school, Janet as a philosopher, the scope of Swiss psychology, and a fascinating article on the life and work of Hermann Rorschach. Part Three is concerned with "the great patients": psychiatry and its unknown history, the path-breaking 1972 piece demonstrating that Anna O. was a clinical failure, the story of Emmy von N., and the tale of Jung and Helene Preiswerk. Part Four deals with themes in the history of psychiatric ideas: the fallacies of psychiatric classification, the concept of creative malady, and the pathogenic secret and its therapeutics.

A valuable appendix gives a complete account of Ellenberger's writings on the history of psychiatry. Micale has also provided a detailed bibliographical essay running through an examination of most of the relevant literature that has appeared over the last three decades. It is hard to believe that Ellenberger was so unusual in his dedication to scholarship, which for some reason has been slower to grow in psychiatry than elsewhere. But he richly deserved the tribute of this book, and Micale has done a fine job.

When the intelligent child in the fairy tale has the courage to declare that the emperor has no clothes, people are pleased and grateful. Eileen Walkenstein's *Don't Shrink to Fit! A Confrontation with Dehumanization in Psychiatry and Psychology,*[2] in its exposure of conventional psychiatry and psychology, resembles that bright-eyed child. It is a lively volume, and it would be nice to hear that the public had received it with gratitude, but that may be asking too much.

Walkenstein draws on twenty years of psychiatric practice in this much-needed critique of vested interests and self-serving viewpoints in contemporary psychiatry. Sectarianism and dogmatism, she argues, pervade today's therapeutic training programs, and one of the results has been to increase the dependencies of patients. Various therapeutic fads, like the "benign humanism" of growth centers, have been as tyrannical and conformist as classical psychoanalysis. Human beings (not mere ideas) lie behind such failures, and Walkenstein, having known a good many of them, bemoans "that mixture of arrogance and ignorance commonly found, alas, in the average practitioner of psychiatry."

This is a very personal and passionate book. As the author defends the individual's right to selfhood, she relies heavily on vignettes from her own clinical experience. Too many textbooks, by contrast, are not only humanly detached but also misleading, for there tend to be large differences between what therapists write about their practice and what they actually do with patients. Walkenstein attacks the formulas and ceremonies that afflict all schools of psychotherapeutic thought; her aim is to undermine the godlike illusions of therapists. There are power relationships even in the most "nondirective" therapeutic setting. Patients listen too well to what they are told, whereas their psychiatrists may not be listening at all.

Since therapy is hardly an advanced technology, the best therapists have been most aware of their own limitations, and Walkenstein insists on the artistic, poetic character of successful psychotherapy. She emphasizes the inevitable mystery of the human soul — a sense of mystery that should elicit wonder from both patient and therapist. Any human encounter must have its unknowns, and sometimes they are straightforward medical problems. In behalf of her plea for more modesty among psychiatrists, Walkenstein reports how she once overlooked a patient's physical disorder. Humility is essential if we are to sustain the proper awe at life's unfolding.

Walkenstein holds that growth comes out of conflict. She believes that people in general are too eager to please, and that their avoidance of trouble actually causes the evasions that often lie behind a person's psychological problems. Neurotic symptoms, she suggests, can be reminders that we must do something about ourselves. As for therapy, she advocates a mixture of Gestalt techniques and confrontation between patient and therapist; these methods express care to a patient and are capable of establishing a kind of trust that sacharine humanism cannot establish.

Walkenstein also draws on Wilhelm Reich's ideas about body language and proposes that patients be encouraged to be more demonstrative — to show on the outside whatever it is they're feeling. By exaggerating their defensive roles, patients can come to recognize and discard psychological crutches. Walkenstein believes (very optimistically, I should note) that learning patterns can be unlearned; she wants to change behavior, not feelings, and she holds that awareness is the first step in growth.

Yet I suspect that Walkenstein, even as she assaults the various psychiatric establishments, takes her own psychiatric background too much for granted. Throughout her book there are examples of principles — such as the distinction between deeds and wishes — that would be almost inconceivable without the influence of old-fashioned psychoanalytic theory. She tells us that as a therapist she "took chances, aggressively, and followed hunches." Would she recommend the same approach to the psychiatrists she condemns?

Furthermore, she treads sometimes on shaky theoretical grounds. Self-assertion is not the same as aggression, despite Walkenstein's argument to the contrary. Her whole approach, moreover, presupposes a naïve view that, if only people were less inhibited, the best in them would flower. When she tells a patient that he must "undo the past and clean it up," right now, she shares a typical American stereotype that ignores the inevitable limits to therapeutic change. I would think that stoicism could have at least as much to teach as the doctrine that happiness lies within our reach.

Walkenstein also strikes me as being too adamantly opposed to the use of drugs and similar technologies. Whatever the contemporary misuses of tranquillizers, anti-depressants, psychosurgery, and electroshock in American clinical practice, they may still hold the potential of relieving unhappiness, and the relief of suffering is not logically identical with becoming a tool of the status quo.

Walkenstein's central thesis is sound: definitions of normality are tied to social needs, and standardized categories can lead to destructive human labeling. Diagnoses and other classifications put an unfortunate distance between therapists and patients. As such, they can communicate contempt, disgust, or revulsion. She is right in thinking that diagnoses somehow presuppose certain plans for therapy. What's more, different therapists, having made very different diagnoses of the same patient, will tend to bring out contrasting sides of the personality.

Unfortunately, when she isolates the problem of diagnosis from all other possible psychiatric errors, Walkenstein runs the risk of romanticizing deviance. This is a trap that many others have already fallen into. If she wants to protect individuality from the pressures of conformism, then she must, in all honesty, work out a more positive concept of normality that is independent of societies as we know them.

One further point: Walkenstein lists ten criteria by which to choose a therapist. She omits from the list one element that sounds abundant in her own practice, namely humor. She has an excellent sense of humor and her vignettes from the clinic make that clear. Indeed, her illustrations from practice manage to correct some of her exaggerated and even strident assertions. On the whole, I think, this is a good, thorny, useful work.

Gerald Izenberg in his *The Existentialist Critique of Freud: The Crisis of Autonomy*[3] has undertaken an admirable objective: the examination of the existentialist response to Freud's concepts. Not surprisingly for someone so dedicated to the autonomous development of his own ideas, Freud was impervious to the growing challenge to psychoanalysis from within existentialism. But since his death, and the damage to psychoanalysis on the continent inflicted by World War II, existentialism has had a notable impact on European psychiatry. As a profession, however, psychoanalysis has grown narrow. Although in each country different strands of psychoanalytic thought tend to be emphasized in accord with dominant cultural needs, existentialist writings — among other critiques of Freud — have scarcely made a dent at most training centers in Britain and North America.

The merits of the existentialist school of thought lie, as Izenberg points out, in its efforts to get away from the mechanically abstract language of so much psychoanalytic writing. Too rarely do psychoanalysts today present clinical case material, or acknowledge the full influence of the treatment setting on their so-called findings. Moreover, Freud's search for causality implied a positivistic approach which unnecessarily played down the possibilities for individual choice and change. Despite what Freud believed, sequence in time is not identical with a causal connection.

Freud's attitude toward motivation was too biologically oriented, and his version of instinct theory no longer tenable. Problems of self-definition, rather than libido, have gained increasing clinical recognition. Phenomena which Freud saw as bedrock, such as penis envy or sexual perversion, have to be understood in the context of a given culture; even aggression need not be interpreted as a primary, rather than a defensive, drive. Freud's rationalistic means of cure through explanatory reconstructions too often missed the realistic dynamics between therapist and patient. While Freud tried to dodge the normative implications of his ideas, the existentialists insisted on the preeminent significance of concepts like health and authenticity, as they put ethical considerations in the forefront of their thinking.

Many of the defects of this book stem from the comprehensiveness of its objectives. Yet probably the worst chapter is the first, entitled "Freud's Theory of Meaning." Here the author proceeds to violate the best existentialist spirit, for Freud gets presented as an academic-seeming theorist evolving ideas in a personal and historical vacuum. The literature on Freud is now a rich one; it is too late in the game to attribute Freud's weaknesses largely to his acceptance of the assumptions of nineteenth-century science. Intellectual history ought not to proceed so isolated from biographical knowledge. There is, for example, the complicated issue of Freud's self-analysis, and how this interacted with his initial clinical theories.

Larger issues also make one uneasy about this book's conception. If one chooses to study Freud, there should be at least some awareness of the critiques of his ideas that were made while he was alive. Contemporaries of Freud, not to mention former disciples, were aware of many of the defects of orthodox psychoanalysis, and prefigured the contributions of later existentialists. Although this book is filled with hard work, it suffers from a hothouse quality and an arbitrariness in its execution. For why discuss Ludwig Binswanger and Medard Boss so extensively, while just glancing at someone of the stature of Karl Jaspers? And it is unclear what principle of selection underlies the works of Jean-Paul Sartre that get discussed. *The Existentialist Critique of Freud* therefore has an eccentric flavor, and the bibliography shows a similarly capricious approach. Yet one hopes that this book may succeed in helping to broaden the circumference of discourse in which psychoanalysis gets discussed.

Marie Jahoda's *Freud and the Dilemmas of Psychology*[4] is an exceptionally lucid and judicious appraisal of the status of Freud's psychoanalytic psychology. She is up-to-date in scientific methodology; and, while moving across territory which has been land mined with conflicts for the last hundred years, the author does not depart from the detached spirit of impartial inquiry. At times, for instance, when she discusses Freud's theories about women, Jahoda is able to criticize succinctly the master's own conclusions. Yet she somehow appears to hold out the perfectionist illusion of a culture-free psychology. In any event she does not adequately account for the defects in Freud's own social perspectives. Nor can her version of Freud's concept of infantile sexuality help us understand the many valid objections raised by his contemporaries and ex-adherents.

Her general aim is the worthy construction of a two-way street between academic psychology and clinical psychoanalysis. She is right in thinking that too often professional psychologists have restricted themselves to material that can be minutely verified, even at the expense of avoiding discussing the most pressing issues in contemporary life. And she knows that practicing psychoanalysts too frequently have been content to live sectlike existences, so that orthodox Freudians and committed Jungians are apt to know next to nothing about the other's contributions.

As fair-minded as Marie Jahoda is, nonetheless the educated reader cannot expect to find here anything startlingly new. She has herself emerged from within the Freudian school; and it is a tribute to the honest aims of that tradition of thought that she has been able to achieve as dispassionate a position as she has. Yet if she seeks to educate psychologists, through an exposition and appraisal of Freud's work, then she would need even greater distance from her background than she has been able to achieve.

For example, she mentions Freud's voluminous correspondence, without alerting her readers to how much tendentious editing once took place in all of the early editions of Freud's published letters. She is correct in believing that Freud's ideas have been a thorn in the flesh of academic psychology, and that her profession, as well as others, have needed the prod from the founder of psychoanalysis. Yet she restricts the scope of her book too narrowly; for while she acknowledges the moral challenge Freud posed, she does not adequately explore the philosophic implications to the undermining of received wisdom by psychoanalysis.

Even if psychoanalysis were to turn out to be as much an art as a science, one could still conclude that it was hardly insignificant for the understanding of human behavior. But the history of ideas becomes more relevant than the author would like to acknowledge. It is highly likely that Freud deceived himself about the scientific standing of many of his propositions, and that even successful therapeutic results owe more to the power of old-fashioned suggestion than Freud ever realized. Freud's own self-analysis, with its inevitable faults, is a good example of the unconscious blocks to anyone's self-knowledge.

A few factual errors stand out in the book. When Freud treated Gustav Mahler they walked together in Holland, not in Vienna. And it is hardly accurate to describe an experienced analyst like Victor Tausk as "a psychoanalyst in the making"; Tausk was a troubled man who killed himself in

1919, but his sad end should not retrospectively alter his acknowledged professional standing. But Marie Jahoda has been more evenhanded in her discussion of contested issues than many others one can think of who might have attempted a similar book with less success.

Although his name is generally forgotten today, between the world wars Dr. Smith Ely Jelliffe was the psychiatrist of celebrities in New York City — John Barrymore's name stands out amid the people associated with the story of Jelliffe's life. He was a journalist, teacher, and public relations man. Jelliffe appeared in court for some well-known trials, was a prominent editor of a famous medical journal, and co-authored a textbook which was highly influential in its time. He was also a pioneer in the field of psychosomatic medicine, and succeeded in staying on good terms with both Freud and Jung.

John C. Burnham's *Jelliffe: American Psychoanalyst and Physician*[5] is an interesting and important book with two components: the longer part is a historically careful biography. Although it lacks literary artistry, it is a serious contribution to the history of twentieth-century medical thought. Jelliffe had studied in Europe, and became a key source by means of which developments in European neurology and psychiatry came to the United States through the written word. The second section of the book consists of Jelliffe's unexpurgated correspondence with Freud and Jung.

In the past there was a distressing degree of tampering with both Freud's letters and those of Jung. Historians and the family of a great man are likely to be natural enemies. In Freud's case, he was tempted to destroy some of his correspondence, and Jung actually carried out the deed with some of his own letters. As we have seen, up until the publication of Freud's letters to Jung, all the volumes of Freud's published letters had been bowdlerized. The grounds for censorship was not medical discretion but the desire to prop up an idealized pictures of the founder of psychoanalysis. As we have already discussed, Jung's relatives, unlike Freud's, have yet to come to terms with the contradiction between wanting a family member established in history and yet also desiring the protection of privacy.

Within the context of rival ideologies, Jelliffe ranks as unorthodox and eclectic. As a pioneering psychoanalytic psychiatrist, Jelliffe sometimes seems not just an extremist but downright dotty. He once recommended psychoanalysis for cases of senility, even when signs of organic deterioration were already apparent.

All innovators have the defects of their boldness. Jelliffe led the movement that held that the mind and body have to be treated as a single entity. It is hard to deny the merits of intellectual radicalism in contributing to the enduring vitality of the early Freudians. But Jelliffe could go so far as to discuss the psychological background of near-sightedness, interpreting it in terms of castration anxiety. He also speculated about color-blindness, along with more serious-sounding reflections about dermatology, allergies and arthritis. In his enthusiasm, Jelliffe lacked a proper sense of the limits of the new psychoanalytic knowledge, and was led to unfortunate psychological conjectures about Parkinsonianism.

Freud's letters always fascinate, but on the whole the Freud who wrote to Jelliffe is an aging and distant old man. I think that the Jung correspondence here is the more interesting. His emphasis on the need for the analyst to promote the synthesizing capacity in patients fits in with later developments in ego psychology. We have earlier discussed how Jung also understood that infantile conflicts could be used as an evasion and a defense against reality. One of Jung's letters to Jelliffe is remarkable for its subtle bitterness over the accusation started by Freud that Jung was a "mystic."

Jelliffe stands in the broad American tradition of William James. He was open-minded if sometimes credulous — it is wonderful to find him worrying about trying to keep up with European thinkers like Edmund Husserl or Karl Jaspers. Jelliffe, an intellectual as well as a clinician, is part of our heritage from Victorian science and medicine.

Although Freud succeeded in transforming the twentieth century's image of human nature and, at the same time, had a profound effect on the practice of all psychotherapy, academic psychology has been relatively skeptical of his contributions. The great merit of Matthew H. Erdelyi's *Psychoanalysis: Freud's Cognitive Psychology*[6] is that it attempts to find a common ground between experimental psychology and psychoanalysis in order to reawaken that tradition which has long sought to integrate both schools of thought.

Erdelyi is surely correct in thinking that psychoanalysis does not deserve to survive as an independent, dissociated entity, incapable of being challenged by the normal canons of psychological evidence. At the same time, he is also bold, given the usual state of academic opposition to psychodynamic thinking, in insisting that formal psychology, as taught in universities, requires the enrichment that can come from the psychoanalytic perspective.

Although this book serves as an absolutely excellent introduction for students, specialists can find faults with it. From a clinical point of view the citations to the post-Freudian literature will doubtless seem unnecessarily sparse; the author makes no mention, for example, of any work by figures like Bruno Bettelheim, Erik H. Erikson, or Erich Fromm, not to mention writings by so-called deviants like Otto Rank. And the historian will be surprised by many striking biographical omissions; it is a bit odd to read a detailed account of Freud's discussion of the "aliquis" parapraxis without being told that it has been established as an autobiographical exploration on Freud's part. Nonetheless, the strength of *Freud's Cognitive Psychology* lies in the comprehensive scope with which it addresses its objective; it has chapters covering psychoanalytic psychotherapy, the unconscious, models of the mind, twilight phenomena, and defense processes.

Freud was of course the greatest writer in the school of thought he founded, and therefore it makes good sense to use his formulations as the main bridge to academic psychology. Yet one hopes that the time will come when it will also be possible, without any disrespect to Freud's historic achievement, for university psychologists to be equally at home with the thinking of those who have done their best to update his "findings." Clinical experience as well as social and political changes since the turn of the twentieth century have led to legitimate revisionist efforts within psychoanalysis that ought to be of significance to academic psychology.

Among the new generation of Freud scholars that has come of age since I first started publishing in the late 1960s Patrick J. Mahony is outstanding; as both a literary critic and a practicing psychoanalyst, he combines a commitment to the best academic standards of university life with an appreciation for the clinical sides of psychoanalytic work. Mahony's two earlier books, *Cries of the Wolf Man* (1984) and *Freud and the Rat Man* (1986), also make a genuinely important contribution to the literature. *Freud as a Writer*[7] should be read by clinicians as well as scholars.

Mahony has set for himself the worthy task of understanding "the central place of writing in Freud's life." Mahony is highly unusual in that, unlike most earlier literary critics, he seems to have an open mind on old controversial issues. (Nonetheless, the name of Erich Fromm does not appear either in the text or the bibliographies, despite what he contributed to a broadmindedly tolerant view of Freud.) There can be absolutely no doubt, as I have said, that as a writer Freud had no equal among twentieth-century psychologists; and even though many of Freud's positions were, I think, successfully challenged long ago by critics within psychoanalysis, none of them wrote with anything like Freud's commanding style. Freud's full writing powers can be seen in any collection of his letters, when he was working off the top of his head. Freud's virtuosities as a writer have attracted people in literary circles like Lionel Trilling, Steven Marcus, and Stanley Edgar Hyman, to mention only the main literary pundits Mahony cites. But, unfortunately, all too often an appreciation for Freud's linguistic genius has also meant an uncritical acceptance of some of the most dubious parts of psychoanalytic orthodoxy.

In the case of Mahony's *Freud as a Writer*, however, the author seems to me strikingly objective; he rightly appreciates, for instance, the interesting work of François Roustang, who has notably elucidated some of the nuances in Freud's capacities as a rhetorician. But I do have to wonder whether, in any examination of Freud's writing, one can really exclude, as much as

Mahony does here, Freud's actual behavior in practice. *Freud as a Writer* is an expansion of an earlier text, and now that Mahony has taken on the case histories of the Wolf Man and the Rat Man I doubt he would proceed as credulously about Freud's conduct as he once did.

The "Postscript," which Mahony has added to this expanded version of *Freud as a Writer*, seems unusually outspoken. For example, Mahony comments on the absence of critical commentary on Freud's case of Dora, until the appearance of an article by Erik H. Erikson: "If Freud's verbal obtusenesses were remarked by such outcasts as Jung or Tausk or Stekel or Rank or Horney, how many psychoanalysts, under the self-aggrandizing defenses of truth or human sensibility, would have seized the opportunity to write an easy and 'safe' attacking article for one of our journals?" Mahony asks his readers this "leading question" that "they may answer silently to themselves," and then poignantly observes: "The history of silence may also be written."

Mahony rightly insists that too many analysts in North America have resisted the notion that "language is inherently conflictual," and have therefore linked Freud's "prose with the expository discourse of a positive science." Mahony is correct that "argument and struggle are the quintessence of Freud's exposition." Abstracts of Freud's work do reflect an "alienating philosophy," which "does away with Freud's own person and a good deal of his activity." Mahony's boldness has not deterred an analyst like George H. Pollock from writing a foreword to the book. Mahony is hardly flattering about the current state of analysis: "unlike the flattened style of most psychoanalysts, Freud's style embraces multiple perspectives." Mahony, in the tradition of George Orwell, Karl Kraus, and others, ties inadequate language to unthinking orthodoxy, and Mahony objects to "the conservative position of psychoanalytic journals."

My central reservation about Mahony's book, however, derives from my having been personally acquainted with enough of Freud's pupils to have experienced the full impact of the use of the old Viennese charm. Another side of that special tact and kindliness, however, can be described as *schmaltz*. And never once does it appear to have occurred to Mahony to look at Freud's writings with a degree of skepticism about the habitual insincerities of a cultivated gentleman of Freud's era. Often that which Mahony expends effort interpreting literally I found myself placing in the category of whipped cream.

Freud was a great spellbinder, and his capacities as a writer helped ensure his original triumph over, say, Jung and Adler. Their respective weaknesses with language ought not obscure how prescient each of them could be about some of Freud's own central weak points. For the sake of *Freud as a Writer* Mahony sat down and in the course of some six months reread all of Freud; Mahony's diligence as a reader, though, makes me dubious about just how far he has gone in understanding Freud. For myself, I can say that the more I think I have comprehended Freud, the harder it has been for me to reread him, since I find so many things going on in each of his sentences.

Mahony is in agreement with some others who recently have been highly critical of James Strachey's translations. It is worth remembering though that Freud not only personally chose Strachey for the job and was immensely pleased with his work, but in the end actually used in a German text the controversial term, "cathexis," which Strachey had coined. Although in the future it will no doubt be possible to improve on Strachey's renditions, especially as we become more aware of Strachey's own specific biases, I for one remain immensely impressed with the conscientiousness of his literary achievement.

It has taken a long time for the history of psychoanalysis to get beyond the level of partisan propagandizing and crude detraction. The warfare associated with ideological convictions combined with the self-interest of trade unionism still persists, but intellectual historians are now finally succeeding in incorporating studies of Freud into the discourse associated with normal university life. *Freud in Exile,*[8] edited by Edward Timms and Naomi Segal, is an excellent example of the best sort of modern scholarship. It consists of revised versions of papers presented at a 1986 symposium to celebrate the opening of the Freud Museum in London; the publication was timed to coincide with the fiftieth anniversary of Freud's arrival in England.

Part One, the longest and most substantial part of the book, deals with the origins of psychoanalysis. Sander Gilman contributes a fine article on the image of the appropriate therapist; his knowledge of Central European history is matched by his understanding of popular stereotypes and prevalent sexual beliefs. Ivar Oxaal has an interesting piece that reconsiders the Jewish background to Freud's thinking. Oxaal succeeds in elucidating the issue without exaggerating the matter. One of the best articles is by Timms, who concentrates on Freud's London library and his private reading. Freud's marginal notes in the books he chose to take with him into exile in England demonstrate that his cultural interests were an essential constituent of all his creative activity. The annotations in his books establish that Freud did not read literary works, for example, just to relax but applied a working method which reveals a considerable degree of literary sophistication.

Ritchie Robertson addresses himself to *Moses and Monotheism*, the last work Freud completed. Robertson considers it Freud's "most Nietzschean book." Robertson's article deserves attention, especially because practicing analysts are apt to ignore the significance of Freud's thesis in his study of Moses. I was fascinated by all the primary documentation that Murray G. Hall comes up with in describing the fate of Freud's publishing house after the Nazis took over. Hall obviously has his finger on the pulse of old Vienna in his description of the personality of Anton Sauerwald, a chemist, the man whom the Nazis placed in charge of liquidating Freud's business affairs: "Politically speaking, he seems to have been a typical Austrian, keeping all his options open. While wearing the membership pin of the Fatherland on one lapel, he had a swastika on the other." Hall knows that this need not mean that Sauerwald does not deserve full credit for helping to shield the Freuds from the Nazis, and he quotes the full text of Anna Freud's 1947 letter in Sauerwald's behalf.

Part Two of *Freud in Exile* is titled "Reception and Exile," and also contains work of considerable interest. R. Andrew Paskauskas, who edited for publication the full correspondence between Freud and Ernest Jones, has an article about their letters that contains nuggets of important quotations. Pearl King writes about the early divergences between the psychoanalytic societies in London and Vienna. Stephen Bann has an essay on the aesthetics of the Kleinian Adrian Stokes. Not all the articles are equally successful, however, and on rare occasions some authors exhibit the kind of sectarian fanaticism that had hobbled this field of inquiry in the past.

Part Three, "Problems of Translation," contains articles by Malcolm Pines, Riccardo Steiner, Darius Gray Ornston, Jr., Alex Holder, and Helmut Junker. Each of these works has something to recommend it, since every act of translation is also an interpretation, but I would like to raise a point that has hitherto, I think, gone inadequately discussed. To what extent does this concern with issues of translation tend to reinforce rather than challenge fundamentalist sorts of thinking? If we start putting our scholarly resources into refining and correcting James Strachey's *Standard Edition* of Freud's works, will there not be a tendency to slight the issue of the legitimate reservations that ought to be entertained about the substance of Freud's ideas? The new effort to mount a return to the "true" Freud is bound, I suspect, to neglect the fairminded criticisms of his concepts that ought to be considered.

Part Four, "Perspectives for the Future," is the slightest of the sections, but each of the papers repays scrutiny: Ernest Gellner on the anthropological perspective, John Bowlby on changing theories of childhood, Naomi Segal on the question of women, Teresa Brennan on the feminist debate, and Walter Toman on Freud's influence on other forms of psychotherapy. I especially admired the closing piece by David Newlands, the first curator of the Freud Museum in London, which is an account of his labors in creating what is now to be seen at 20 Maresfield Gardens.

Karl Menninger is a giant in the history of twentieth-century psychiatry in the United States; therefore *The Selected Correspondence of Karl A. Menninger 1919–1945*, edited by Howard J. Faulkner and Virginia D. Pruitt[9] is most welcome. Menninger once estimated that he wrote about eighty letters a week. Given that he got his M.D. from Harvard in 1917, and kept still going strong close to his death in 1990, that means his correspondence was immense.

This particular collection provides the basis for the conviction that, if only in terms of the intensity of his activities, the scope of his interests, and the longevity of his career, Menninger deserves to rank as the Winston Churchill of the psychiatric profession in the United States. No one else I can think of compares either with Menninger's output or his impact on the society around him. As a writer of best-selling books and popular as well as professional articles he was tireless; his contribution to humanitarian causes earned him the Medal of Freedom, which he received from President Jimmy Carter in 1981.

By 1920 Dr. Menninger was "head over heels" in his infatuation with psychoanalysis. Like other North American followers of Freud, Menninger was responding to the therapeutically optimistic side of the promise of analysis and became a thorough convert. He and his father founded the Menninger Clinic in 1920, where they were later joined by Karl's brother, William. In 1924 Karl helped establish the American Orthopsychiatry Association, and in 1926 he added a school for disturbed children to the sanitarium he had established in Topeka in 1925.

These letters document Karl Menninger's various enthusiasms, his struggles against the conservative psychiatric establishment, and his participation in a variety of psychoanalytic conflicts. He underwent several personal analyses; the most important in duration and personal meaning were those with Franz Alexander and Ruth Mack Brunswick. Both of these senior analysts were for a time special favorites of Freud. This book concludes with a letter to Anna Freud, with whom Menninger established a secure alliance.

Menninger rightly felt that the contributions of European analysts who immigrated to the United States tended to overshadow the work of native Americans, including himself. To the extent that psychoanalysis was a personal outgrowth of Freud's own life, the master's association, endorsement, and training carried a disproportionate weight. It is certainly true that distinguished American figures who crop up in Menninger's book — Lawrence S. Kubie, for example — are in real danger of being historically ignored.

Quite another side of Menninger's career comes through in these letters. And that is the extent to which he can be held responsible for having oversold the claims of psychiatry. In 1945 we find him writing, "I think every member of Congress, perhaps even every candidate for membership in Congress, and certainly every member of the State Department and every high ranking officer in the Army and Navy, ought to be subject to some kind of scientific psychiatric scrutiny which will be official."[10] Menninger was not then alone as a pioneer in believing that psychiatrists were capable of functioning as modern philosopher-kings; Ernest Jones, whom Menninger here rightly calls a "peculiar, crusty, crabbed guy," agreed with Menninger's political hopes for psychoanalytic psychiatry. Ever since the early 1920s, Menninger chauvinistically anticipated that psychiatrists might be elected to the "supreme council of the world's government."

By the end Menninger turned in a different direction, and in keeping with his earlier boldness he acknowledged the merits of Thomas Szasz's general position. But if Szasz has been on the right track, does that not undermine much of what Menninger earlier so successfully popularized, especially in connection with the law? In 1927 he wrote in a letter that "if a man has a make-up which indicates that he will be antisocial all his life he ought to be in prison all his life without the necessity of his having committed murder."[11] But the idea of punishment without crime would conflict with the most deeply rooted convictions of liberal political theory.

In terms of this book of correspondence, it would seem that non-Freudian psychiatrists like Abraham Myerson, with whom Menninger disagreed at the time while remaining on friendly terms, may deserve a reevaluation. Myerson for instance thought it inadvisable to give psychiatrists more authority in the ultimate councils of the mighty. The immense figure of Adolf Meyer, now virtually forgotten in our general culture, certainly deserves more credit. I suspect that future historians will pay a lot more attention to Meyer, both for his influence and the merits of the point of view he represented, than he has received.

Within the history of psychoanalysis, Karl Menninger's final shifts also make one wonder about the validity of his earlier passionate commitments. I found it a distinctly distasteful aspect of Menninger's letters that he railed against those he considered at the time "traitors to psychoanalytic convictions and principles." Menninger was harsh about both Erich Fromm and Karen Horney, for example, and by reviews of their work helped tarnish their public reputations. In 1940, Menninger criticized Franz Alexander for in any way encouraging "the bastards or the fifth columnists of psychoanalysis . . . .I think you feel that you are tolerant in that respect, and I feel it is a weakness on your part, a neurotic complacency, which in Mr. Chamberlain caused a lot of trouble, as you know. I'm against appeasement."[12] Yet an early footnote to the introduction indicates that in 1985, in a personal communication to the editors, Menninger said, "I think now that Alexander was on the right path and might have saved [us from] the decline of psychoanalysis."[13] This change of heart about Alexander is a concession whose consequences would entail more rethinking than the editors acknowledge. (The editors are unfortunately not highly competent in the history of psychiatry, which is consistent with the lack of support in the field as a whole; the result is a number of editorial howlers. In addition, the book has no index.)

Franz Alexander is by now an extraordinarily neglected figure, while Menninger's old allies, such as Anna Freud, have scarcely ever been rationally assessed within North American psychiatry. As we have discussed, in England, and especially in France, criticism of her work has been savagely telling. If Alexander were ever properly to be established as a central thinker, then the validity of many of Menninger's early commitments, expressed here in his letters, would have to be reconsidered. Menninger led the early fight for psychoanalytic psychiatry in an era when the alternative treatments available were inhumane, but the version of psychoanalytic orthodoxy he preached, unfortunately, may have been all too similar to the harshness of some of the techniques he opposed. His culture did not provide Menninger with enough skepticism toward the early therapeutic claims of psychoanalysis, and his most cynical-sounding critics had some merit on their side all along.

Perhaps Menninger single most lasting contribution will be in the realm of education. If only through those who trained at the Menninger Clinic, aside from the people influenced by his writings, he singularly helped move psychiatric education in the United States onto a new level of professionalism.

Freud, despite all his own reservations about philosophy, has by now earned a secure place philosophically. For some he ranks with modern philosophers of science, and for these people the key question is whether his theorems have been successfully tested, or whether they indeed are capable in principle of being verified. But for others with an equally abstract bent, Freud stands as one of our modern ethical teachers; although he himself never worked out anything like a systematic set of moral convictions, implicit in his whole point of view was a profound challenge to traditional Western morality.

One of the great beauties of Edoardo Weiss's *Sigmund Freud as a Consultant*[14] is that we here mainly find Freud as a practicing clinician. It is hard for some to believe that the man who wrote so many books and articles at the same time was thoroughly dedicated to his clinical practice. And that not only meant that Freud regularly treated over half a dozen patients a day in Vienna, in addition to the many consultations that he agreed to see, but that also he tried, through some of his letter-writing, to keep in touch with the clinical activities of his disciples abroad.

In the instance of Edoardo Weiss, Freud saw in him a central hope for the fate of psychoanalysis in Italy. While at the time Weiss found himself struggling against the Italian opposition to Freud's teachings, and ultimately Weiss abandoned Italy to move to the United States, by our own time the situation in Italy has radically changed, so that today all things connected with psychoanalysis are flourishing there. It is not just that the clinical practice of psychoanalysis has become widely accepted in Italy, even though it has remained a profoundly Catholic country, but that the general ideology of contemporary Italy has been shaped and affected by the message Freud had had to offer.

I believe that it is in its concrete details that *Sigmund Freud as a Consultant* has the most to teach. Weiss's narrative provides the circumstances surrounding the clinical cases he asked for Freud's help about; two of Weiss's sisters were to go for analyses to Freud in Vienna, and they clearly did not hold back from their brother what they had learned, as well as what they considered the major limitations in Freud's approach.

Freud took Weiss into his confidence, and in his discussion of Weiss's patients one can find some of Freud's most characteristic clinical points of view, including Freud's moral biases both in favor of certain cases as well as against other types of human dilemmas. It is worth noting that *Sigmund Freud as a Consultant* contains the only known letter we have in which Freud openly discussed his own analysis of his youngest child, Anna.

By now Weiss, who practiced for many years in Chicago, has succeeded in becoming an honored (if little studied) pioneering figure in the history of the Italian reception of Freud's work. But Weiss's account of his relationship with Freud, as well as the clinical concreteness of Freud's communications with Weiss, will also form a permanent addition to our understanding of the early days of psychoanalysis.

At the beginning of the twentieth century, Freud had published the central texts which formed the basic structure of his system of thought. Freud went on writing until he was eighty-three, and almost until his 1939 death in exile in London, driven to England by the Nazi occupation of Austria, Freud continued to come up with articles and books which upset the apple cart of received conventional wisdom. Still, the basic constituents of Freud's psychological innovations had been laid down in the first decade of that century.

The same early period was also when, starting in 1902, Freud assembled around him allies who were almost entirely former clinical patients of his. They had the appointed purpose of becoming Freud's apostles, promoting his ideas and technique, also supporting him as he came up against criticism. Freud had success in transforming our conception of human nature partly because of the extensiveness of his genuine political talents. He was skilled at promoting his work through the encouragement of his followers.

Phyllis Grosskurth's *The Secret Ring: Freud's Inner Circle and the Politics of Psychoanalysis*[15] offers a valuable vision of Freud's creation, just before the First World War, of the so-called secret Committee, a narrow band of disciples selected among his earlier advocates who were to propagate his thought and preserve the purity of his message. By that time Freud was eager to prevent the kind of opposition from within his own ranks that he had encountered from people like Adler and Jung. Freud wanted nothing more to do with those he deemed backsliders.

Freud gave each member of the secret Committee an antique stone, to be made into rings, for the sake of welcoming them into the inner ranks of his cause. Readers will find these psychoanalysts suffering from human flaws and political conflicts. Various rivalries had to beset these pioneers, as they pressed for Freud's personal favor. The idea of keeping the proceedings of a young scientific movement in any way secret does seem an adolescent concept at odds with the pretensions Freud had that psychoanalysis itself represented a neutral contribution to modern knowledge.

I do wonder whether it is possible to detach the workings of psychoanalytic politics from broader issues of both power and the life of the mind. Whatever surviving letters can be made to sound like, all these early analysts acknowledged their absolute devotion to what Freud stood for. If his underlings had had to choose between ties of old friendship as opposed to the possibility of crossing Freud, they did not hesitate to make their first priority that of continuing to curry Freud's favor. The Committee was a front organization in that Freud always retained the real authority, even after he had fallen ill with cancer of the jaw in 1923.

He used his political savvy in behalf of his organizational objectives, but such maneuvering should come as no surprise. The Committee itself was hardly kept secret, and Freud had a photograph of its members on a wall of his consulting room. Freud could be, as Grosskurth says, two-faced, but this kind of careerist hypocrisy needs to be understood, if not excused, by the prevailing general standards of old-world culture of that time. It should be enough to say, without accusing Freud of being a schemer, that he functioned as an enlightened despot over his following.

Individual trees growing in the history of psychoanalysis can be mistaken for the general woods of the tale. For in the end none of the controversies we associate with the story of Freud's discipline would matter were it not true that he made a central contribution to our understanding of emotions like love and hate. Despite all Freud's human frailties, which are bound to get highlighted under microscopic inspection, he remains in my view a central figure in modern Western literature.

Feelings of euphoria as well as worthlessness have been experienced in fluctuating sequences by some of the world's most talented writers and artists, and the occurrence of mood disorders among such articulate people makes a compelling story. *Touched With Fire: Manic-Depressive Illness and the Artistic Temperament*[16] by Kay Redfield Jamison is full of fascinating accounts of the stormy ups-and-downs known to Lord Byron and numerous others. The high rates of hospitalization and suicide for so many of our most creative figures has to make for a sober reconsideration of the price of artistic achievement.

In addition to providing enthralling anecdotes, especially about great poets, Jamison has exhaustively examined the latest scientific evidence about the incidence and treatment of manic-depressive problems. The extremities of highs and lows no longer have to be as detrimental to family life and loved ones as once was the case. Modern pharmacology has invented a wide variety of drugs, such as lithium, to help dampen the worst ravages of destructive mood swings. There is, however, a risk of the baby going out with the bath water. Many highly talented individuals have resisted treatment on the grounds that it might hamper their ability to concentrate on their work.

While this resistance to modern science may be irrelevant to the worst instances of "bipolar" human suffering, it is still an open question about the circumstances in which medication should be used. One of the central problems with modern psychiatry is that the different ideological schools fail to listen to each other. So orthodox analysts have been known to treat patients for decades without turning to any use of drugs. And at the other extreme there are biological psychiatrists who prescribe heavy-duty pills seemingly at the drop of a hat.

If there is one central weakness to *Touched With Fire*, I think it has to do with a failure to examine the role of the environment in setting off mood changes. Creative people are not just prisoners of biological clocks, but individuals who must cope with a variety of pressures. And the dilemma of how to differentiate between the multiple sources of human troubles ought not to be swept under the rug.

Fascinating work is going on in the history of psychoanalysis. Above all, Freud's correspondence is coming out at a steady pace; and earlier editions of Freud's letters, such as those to Abraham, are scheduled to reappear in an unexpurgated version. It will take at least another generation before we have all Freud's missives in print, and in the end they should surpass in size Strachey's *Standard Edition*. Furthermore, the success of Freud's influence has meant a proliferation of alternative schools of thought. In France today, we have a wholly independent use being made of Freud's teachings; as we have seen, Lacan succeeded in putting psychoanalysis on the map of French intellectual life. And in Britain — partly due to the effects of the so-called British School, initiated by Klein — analysts have been thinking along lines that are refreshing from a North American perspective. In 1989 Judith M. Hughes published *Reshaping the Psychoanalytic Domain*, highlighting the contributions of Klein, W. R. D. Fairbairn, and Donald W. Winnicott.

In the context of her excellent earlier work, Hughes's *From Freud's Consulting Room: The Unconscious in a Scientific Age*[17] comes as a disappointment. She starts off with a promising first paragraph:

> Over the past twenty-odd years a shift has taken place in writing the history of psychoanalysis. What had generally been considered the private preserve of the

> analytic profession, despite poaching on the part of intellectual historians and critics, literary and social, has become a topic for historians of science. It is under the rubric of the history of science, broadly conceived, that my study falls.[18]

Unfortunately, this admirable ambition does not, in my opinion, achieve fulfillment in the course of *From Freud's Consulting Room.* Hughes is enormously conscientious, and her book is full of hard work. And the prose is smooth. What is missing are all the jagged edges that have piled up over the last century of psychoanalytic historiography. For example, she begins, and then ends, by comparing and contrasting Freud and William James — but if she had cited a few of James's critical remarks after he met Freud personally, in contrast to how James reacted to Jung, we might feel reassured about getting a balanced account. (Earlier I noted a similar omission in Linda Donn's work.)

As it is, Hughes would seem to have put aside what she learned from writing *Reshaping the Psychoanalytic Domain.* It surely cannot do at this late stage to be citing Freud himself uncritically. It would seem that she has been so taken in by Freud's great capacities as a writer that she does not stand back and challenge his account of things. She tells us that she has now become a clinical associate at the San Diego Psychoanalytic Institute, and that this took place "roughly half-way through the writing"[19] of this new book. It is unfortunately the case that American training institutes have been notoriously unwilling to foster critical thinking, and I hope that in Hughes's future writings she will be able to emancipate herself from the comforts of associating with like-minded people. Without seeming to know it she has exemplified some of the characteristic failings of what she called "the private preserve of the analytic profession," without adding enough to the history of science itself.

Master Clinicians on Treating the Regressed Patient, volume 2, edited by L. Bryce Boyer and Peter L. Giovacchini[20] is an interesting collection of papers on the extension of psychoanalytic therapy to patients with borderline personality disorders or psychosis. The authors are all brave and steadfast in their attempt to cope with the frustrations connected with so-called regressed patients. Although the contributors to this volume come from a variety of different national cultures and a pluralistic set of ideological viewpoints, the focus of their inspiration seem to be L. Bryce Boyer's Center for the Advanced Study of the Psychoses in San Francisco.

Freud designed his system of treatment for neurosis, which presents a very different set of clinical problems than are dealt with in *Master Clinicians on Treating the Regressed Patient.* The clinical workers in this book start with the premise that Freud himself had "constricted horizons of the therapeutic process," although they realize that in many instances Freud's patients may have been "suffering from much more serious psychopathology than he suspected."[21]

One central theme that comes up concerns the issue of how therapists should make use of the phenomena of counter-transference. It has long been apparent that Freud's early view of counter-transference as an impurity endangering the therapeutic process is an inadequate point of departure. Disciples of Melanie Klein in particular have stressed the desirability of what can be learned through the therapist's own emotional reaction to patients. Although the writers in this collection seem unaware of it, Helene Deutsch in 1926, as I have noted before, was one of the first analysts to write about the positive uses to which counter-transference can be put.

It is hard to be in any way critical of therapists who are obviously laboring in behalf of such a humanitarian cause, and being self-critical to boot. At several points in this book writers dismiss past dogmatisms that have arisen within their own schools of psychoanalytic thought. *Master Clinicians on Treating the Regressed Patient* is admirably eclectic and open-minded. The accounts of patients are thoroughly engrossing. Some of these patients, however, have been in treatment for years and years, and it is unclear how the authors think the recent advancements on the pharmacological front should be absorbed within modern practice. I recall at least one patient in this volume having been treated by drugs, and yet the reader does not come away with a confident conviction of what role the authors think that medication should play.

Over fifty years ago the pioneering analyst Sandor Rado began to talk about the legitimacy of biochemistry and the importance of studying genetics. Freud's view was that the most seriously disturbed patients, those whom he did not want to treat himself, were suffering from deficits that no amount of psychological treatment could make up for. In practice, we know that Freud was capable of accepting for analysis even patients whom he diagnosed as "schizophrenic," but then he, like other pioneers, was pushing forward the frontiers of knowledge.

Today, given that a great deal is known about how to approach "regression" with the aid of pharmacology, I think it behooves psychoanalysts to grapple with the issue of how their practice needs to change in the light of what is now understood. There are still too many barriers between those who take a strictly so-called biological view of mental suffering and the various schools of psychoanalysis as represented in this volume. The book is superb as far as it goes; old-fashioned psychoanalytic thinking gets a good going-over because the authors are aware of weaknesses in the outlook of the early analysts. Still more bridge-building needs to be done, however, and I think a still further volume of papers, one that explicitly addresses the problem of the therapeutic role of drugs within the framework of a treatment modality that remains humanistic, would do an important service in advancing today's therapeutic science.

Despite all the well-meaning efforts to establish links between social science and medicine — and there is an interesting story about the repeated efforts throughout this past century to make sure that these two fields remain in contact with one another — I think that at the present time the existing linkages are about as fragile as they have ever been. It is true that there is a fascinating new interest in the history of psychiatry, and professional historians are working in this area in an unprecedented way. By and large, though, the whole topic of culture and medicine remains a subject that attracts rare attention.

Within psychoanalysis the situation has not been too promising. As I have already pointed out, Freud started out with the belief that there was something that he called "applied psychoanalysis"; but implicit in that concept was the idea that psychoanalytic so-called truths already existed, waiting to be confirmed through social research. Freud himself relied on nineteenth-century style anthropology, for example, and seems never to have understood what modern field work could be like. As a result, his own writings in this area, and the kind of work he sanctioned, were of a far grander and more speculative nature than is apt to prove attractive to today's working social scientists. It is true that his perspective meant that the most general philosophical questions would be, if not explicitly approved by Freud, matters that others could readily seek to explore.

The problem is that Freud, and the early analysts in general, did not see the relationship between psychoanalysis and society as a reciprocal one. Social science has something important to add to our understanding of depth psychology, and yet there are, as far as I know, no preexisting institutions that educationally encourage people to be interested in both psychoanalysis and social science. Those people who have made a notable contribution in this area have had to do so out of their own individual initiative and without adequate professional backing.

In the meantime, it is well known how psychiatry has been moving in a positivistic direction, and biological discoveries have made psychoanalytic concerns seem to be little more than an irritating distraction. Classification, just as at the beginning of the twentieth century, has once again come to seem a critical matter, and exact-sounding diagnoses, along with pharmacology, have attracted some of the greatest prestige.

Scientism, a false kind of knowledge, is as much a threat now as ever. It is too easy to forget how diagnoses can be a response to mental categories as opposed to clinical so-called realities. There seem to be more psychiatrists in North America than in the rest of the world combined, which means that most of mankind's experience is beyond the ken of our own most fashionable preoccupations. The phenomena of anorexia nervosa, to take only one syndrome, seems not widely known outside the Western countries. With all the universalistic-sounding rhetoric that modern psychiatry has helped to promote, it is important to recall just how embedded in particular cultures human distress actually is. Psychiatry has to do with healing, and therefore the life histories of patients have to be understood; but these complexities are not conceivably going to be adequately dealt with apart from our ability to understand idiosyncratic social norms.

It is in this context of how medicine and social science have stayed too far apart, even though they are essential to one another, that Edward Shorter's work seems to me important. His *From the Mind Into the Body: The Cultural Origins of Psychosomatic Symptoms* follows up on his earlier, admirable *From Paralysis to Fatigue*.[22] Here he continues the story, giving concrete illustrations of the play between biology and culture. His book is based on "the premise that biology and culture interact in the production of psychosomatic symptoms."[23] The high point of psychoanalysis's concern with psychosomatic matters may have come after World War II; regrettably no adequate study has ever been done of Franz Alexander's contributions. Even though many of the pioneers in this area may turn out to have been mistaken and gone in directions that can no longer be maintained, it is striking how little attention is paid now to someone like Alexander, who in his career did so much to breathe life not just in this one field, but within psychiatric education as a whole. (In his lifetime, Alexander became highly controversial, and it is a sign of his impact in Chicago that ever since he left in 1956 analysts there have been so fearful of the charge of unorthodoxy that Alexander's name almost never is cited by the people one might most expect.)

Shorter's *From the Mind Into the Body* is the work of an imaginative professional historian who offers specific examples of the way cultural forces and biological predispositions come together to form symptomatology. Some may find Shorter is too daring in concluding that fibrositis or chronic fatigue syndrome are properly to be considered "media-spawned plagues."[24]

Shorter provides an altogether admirable account of the chronic illnesses that bother middle-class patients who enjoy a lot of leisure. The diagnosis of "neurasthenia" has long since been abandoned in North America, where the term first originated, and yet in China today that terminology is still being used. If bed cases and invalidism have evaporated in our society, Shorter thinks that one explanation may be that there was relief to be found "in the surgeon's knife." Both "the bed cases and the polysurgical patients represent extreme forms of culture-bound behavior."[25]

Shorter explores the role of gender and ethnicity in symptom-formation, and has an especially rich chapter on "the cultural face of melancholy." He also discusses the specific problems of youths. Shorter has some wonderful case histories to illustrate that both nature and nurture go into making up psychosomatic problems. He is one of those exceptional people whose work bridges medicine and social science, and on a subject relevant to the history of psychoanalytic ideas.

The interesting papers in *100 Years of Psychoanalysis*, edited by Andre Haynal and Ernst Falzeder,[26] were presented at a symposium that took place in Geneva on Sept. 17 and 18, 1993. It is hard to know whether as a field psychoanalysis is stranger than any other. But I am not familiar with any subject in which papers in journals so regularly appear that start out with what purports to be a historical survey of the literature; these pieces are usually written by busy practicing clinicians, and they necessarily rely for their citations on the educational background they have received at the various training institutes that exist. Yet there are no psychoanalytic centers where, as far as I know, the study of the history of psychoanalysis matches anything like what a university-trained person would expect. Within universities there are an increasing number of people interested in raising the level of understanding of the past of psychoanalysis to a level that would be academically respectable.

This particular collection of articles is admirably open-minded and non-doctrinaire, and there is something to be learned from each essay. Andre Haynal deserves to be congratulated for having orchestrated such an admirable symposium. My reaction to the chapters may be idiosyncratic, but I will discuss them more or less in the order I read them. Right at the outset I dived into Ernst Falzeder's "The Threads of Psychoanalytic Filiations Or Psychoanalysis Taking Effect"; I had heard Falzeder present some of this material at a lecture in London, and I was eager to get all the details straight. Falzeder is concerned with who analyzed whom, and there is a large pullout at the back of the book called "Spaghetti Junction" with the lines of influence, which Falzeder calls "apostolic succession," made clear. I do not think Falzeder is always correct in this attempt at constructing a family tree, and it would have had to be twice the size for me to be able to follow it all, but he has performed a ground-breaking service in making this attempt.

Albrecht Hirschmüller, the careful German biographer of Breuer, has come up with some seven new letters from Breuer, and one of Freud's; it may be my own cultural ignorance, but I was amazed to find Breuer in 1907 writing to Freud as "Dear Professor." Jean Starobinski, trained as a psychiatrist but also one of the world's great men of letters, an expert on Rousseau and Montaigne, has a scholarly piece on the word "abreaction." John Forrester from Cambridge University delivered a chapter on "The Balance of Power Between Freud and His Early Women Patients"; in keeping with Forrester's commitment to French psychoanalysis, he has some unexpected insights. Carlo Bonomi from Florence contributed an altogether remarkable piece about the relevance of Freud's pediatric training to psychoanalysis.

Patrick Mahony from Montreal gave "Psychoanalysis — the Writing Cure," which pursues Mahony's interest in Freud as a writer. Peter Rudnytsky writes informatively about Freud's representation of female sexuality in the case of Little Hans. Peter Loewenberg, an historian and psychoanalyst from Los Angeles, pursues the problem of Freud's psychosocial identity, and reminds us of Thorstein Veblen's great essay on the marginality of Jews as a basis for their intellectual preeminence. And Haynal, with his special concern for philosophy, traces Freud's relationship to Brentano, Schopenhauer, and Nietzsche; Haynal is also at home with the history of biology, so he can follow Freud's roots there as well.

The final section of the book is devoted to Freud's intimate relationship with Ferenczi. Judith Dupont's discussion of "The Notion of Trauma" seemed to me outstanding, and her account of Ferenczi reminded me of Victor Tausk. (Dupont, a niece of Michael Balint, has been the moving force arranging for the appearance of the editions of the Freud-Ferenczi correspondence). Christopher Fortune pursues his interest in the intriguing American patient of Ferenczi's, Elizabeth Severn, with whom Ferenczi tried "mutual analysis." Andrew Paskauskas, the editor of the Freud-Jones letters, provided a chapter suggesting grounds for thinking that Jones "unconsciously hated" Ferenczi. Arnold Rachman from New York has a rich paper on Ferenczi's "The Confusion of Tongues" speech, which is part of a much larger treatise about Ferenczi. The Bostonian Axel Hoffer discusses Ferenczi's 1926 offer to analyze Freud, and Judith Vida from Los Angeles looks at how Ferenczi's work has been a pioneering part of modern psychoanalysis. The Swiss analyst Olivier Flournoy concludes with an overview of the history of psychoanalysis.

100 Years of Psychoanalysis will be welcomed by all serious students of the historiography of this field. The book promotes no party line, but the authors are trying to fill some of the gaps in the existing literature. Helping to reestablish Ferenczi, for example, does not in any way detract from Freud's own standing, although curiously enough even in Ferenczi's native Hungary his work has been relatively neglected. The practice of psychotherapy in the future, and our knowledge of the twists and turns psychoanalysis has taken over the last 100 years, can only be enhanced by this sort of new striving for objectivity and fairness.

No summary can hope to do justice in covering the huge overview of the field provided by *Companion Encyclopedia of the History of Medicine*, volumes I and II, edited by W. F. Bynum and Roy Porter.[27] The editors are both leaders at the Wellcome Institute of the History of Medicine in London, England, and have been in the forefront recently of tirelessly expanding the discipline. Although those with an interest in psychoanalytic matters cannot be expected to be concerned with the full range of the topics covered in these books, I will try to point out essays that seemed to me particularly compelling or pertinent.

In Volume I, Arthur Kleinman, who has done outstanding work linking anthropology (especially in China) and psychiatry, has a solid essay on "What Is Specific to Western Medicine?" Arthur L. Caplan contributes a chapter on "The Concepts of Health, Illness, and Disease" as he contrasts the normative with the purely empirical approach. Theodore M. Brown writes on "Mental Diseases," with a special concern about psychosomatic problems. Roy Porter has a chapter in "Diseases of Civilization," which includes references to Freud's work as well as to the writings of Wilhelm Reich.

Volume II has pieces also of critical conceptual interest to students of psychoanalysis. Edward Shorter examines a specialty of his, "The History of the Doctor-Patient Relationship." Sander Gilman discusses "Psychotherapy" with direct attention to the psychoanalytic movement. Jan Goldstein treats "Psychiatry," which includes reference to twentieth-century American responsiveness to psychoanalytic teachings. And Roy Porter's "Religion and Medicine" discusses the ways in which traditional beliefs have had a bearing on all issues connected with the state of the soul.

Doubtless serious-minded readers will find even more of interest here for those with a special preoccupation with psychoanalysis. The editors have exhaustively succeeded in their objective of taking stock of the current state of the art and science of medicine.

Howard Book's *How to Practice Brief Psychodynamic Psychotherapy: The Core Conflictual Relationship Theme Method*[28] is an interesting manual on how to conduct brief psychodynamic psychotherapy along the lines proposed by Lester Luborsky, who has written the brief foreword. The idea of the method is that it is possible in the course of an initial evaluation and socialization phase to isolate a core conflict that will be the focus of therapy. According to this technique, it is efficacious to identify the core difficulty, as it interferes with the patient's well-being, and then illustrate, over the course of sixteen therapeutic sessions, how the core conflict constitutes an interpersonal hindrance.

Howard Book sets out by means of a clear conceptual roadmap the different phases of this sort of treatment. He also illustrates his argument with brief clinical vignettes. Book is aware of the history of brief psychodynamic psychotherapy as well as the need to establish clear criteria for the kinds of patients that stand to benefit from this approach. Throughout he is sensitive to the value of traditional psychoanalytic concepts; he cites how countertransference on the therapist's part can prove harmful to the patient and interfere with the success of the whole focus-orientation.

More than half of the book is taken up with the case of one particular patient, and readers will find this discussion perhaps the most enlightening aspect of the volume. Book willingly admits his mistakes, even in the course of this successful treatment; for example, he says he was not sensitive enough to a secondary core conflict that existed besides the one he chose to concentrate on initially. Book does not believe that the method he is advocating is a panacea for all possible difficulties. He is open to the advantages and uses of long-term psychotherapy and psychoanalysis as well as medication. This is a conscientiously detailed account of a special method especially suitable for a limited number of psychologically minded and highly motivated patients. In a time when decreasing therapeutic resources coincide with increasing demand for treatment, the core conflictual relationship theme method is designed to improve access to psychotherapy.

It is impressive to me how Book has been able to rely on the whole tradition of psychoanalysis in order to illustrate a technique that is substantially at odds with Freud's own technical recommendations and practices. One hopes that in the spirit of scientific tolerance, the approach that Book illustrates in this manual will seem welcome to practitioners of a variety of different schools of thought.

It is heartening to see just how much change has quietly been taking place within clinical psychoanalysis. For Richard Brockman's *A Map of the Mind*[29] is full of lively stories about patients which he has either treated himself or supervised, without any excessive theorizing or genuflecting toward old doctrinal orthodoxies. Nor is it necessary for him to scapegoat rival ideologies. Each of the cases he describes was seen in face-to-face encounters, and he recounts his own efforts to arrive at some cautious generalizations from the clinical situations.

For Brockman an important constituent to every case has to be the therapist's own counter-transference feelings. Brockman does not trot out the concept of counter-transference as a last resort, or as the result of a clinical stalemate, but rather he assumes as a given that psychotherapy is a genuinely human transaction between people capable of mixed, confusing, and only partly rational affects. Although he does not himself provide any examples of outstanding clinical failures, reading *A Map of the Mind* reminded me of just how brave Freud had been in telling the world about his own frustrating therapeutic experience with the woman he named "Dora." But Brockman does not himself proceed on any grandiose assumption that the therapist is in any way omniscient.

Brockman takes for granted the significance of the alleviation of distressing symptomatology, and he also quietly endorses the utility of pharmacological medication. It is, I think, a tribute to the tradition in which Brockman works that he does not engage in any empty search for precise-sounding diagnostic classifications. His main achievement, and it is a considerable one, is to demonstrate the influence and role of emotions connected to transference feelings on the conduct of the therapy.

A Map of the Mind communicates, in its concrete illustrations, the rare kind of intimacy that takes place in the course of psychotherapy. Ideally the time should come when psychotherapists like Brockman will discuss at length under what circumstances they recommend which sorts of drugs, just as hopefully biological psychiatrists will be able to spend more time in describing the human interactions with the patients they treat. In the meantime, and without awaiting the arrival of a utopia in which students of the mind and experts on the body will be able readily to converse with one another, *A Map of the Mind* to me represents an admirable bringing together of humanistic and strictly scientific perspectives.

Although there is little in psychoanalytic theory to prepare one for it, different countries continue to have separate national psychotherapeutic traditions. When one thinks of France the name Lacan comes to mind even more immediately than that of Klein or Winnicott crops up in connection with Britain; in turn, the Americans have had ego-psychology as well as Kohut's thinking about the self. And the Italians are notably receptive and open to a wide variety of different ideological strains. But the Germans — here one is apt to pause in uncertainty about what most characterizes psychoanalysis there today.

The collection of essays called *The Future of Psychoanalysis* should help get us started about the nature of some of the most interesting German psychoanalytic thinking. The editor, Johannes Cremerius, opens with a blistering piece that deals with the authoritarian and hierarchical structure of the International Psychoanalytic Association (IPA). He has assembled a variety of arguments, all unfortunately true, about how training at institutes bears too many analogies to the religious instruction of an organized Church. Psychoanalysis, he holds, is threatened by its failure to keep in touch with the broadest philosophical, political, and social questions. Above all, the crisis in psychoanalysis can be traced to its unwillingness to cease to be a "movement" and its hesitancy to fulfill Freud's hopes of having created a science.

An unspoken part of Cremerius's thesis is the extent to which the bulk of German psychoanalysts have seemed by and large identified with the powers-that-be in American psychoanalysis. Perhaps such links were inevitable, given the post-World War II role of the States in helping with the reconstruction of Germany. But the present-day gloom within American psychoanalysis has afflicted the German analysts as well; unlike in France, for example, where Lacan managed to keep analysis vital by being in touch with philosophy, literature, and university academic life in general, the Germans allowed themselves largely to become more narrowly concerned with the middle-class appearing aspects of therapy itself.

And now that the public health insurance is cutting back on its previous generosity to analysts, German analysis is suffering in an acute way. Various of these essays refer in passing to the problems of public payments, and how the decreasing frequency of mandated paid sessions each week conflicts with traditionally accepted expectations. One wishes that one of the eight interesting writers in *The Future of Psychoanalysis* specifically addressed themselves to the problems unique to Germany.

German analysts of course have to deal with a special and ghastly divide in their history associated with the Nazi era. Exactly who in the past of rival organizations can be considered guilty of collaborating in an unsavory way would make for an immensely complicated story, and perhaps finger-pointing about which ancestors did what would be endless. But political events of this past century make it impossible for Germans to enjoy the luxury of entertaining continuities the way the American or British can. This is particularly striking in that although the Berlin Training Institute was the first one to be established after World War I, the name of its founder — Karl Abraham — does not once come up in *The Future of Psychoanalysis*.

Yet the level of thought throughout all the essays here is unusually high. Names like Adorno, Horkheimer, Fromm, Mitscherlich, and Habermas keep turning up; the ideas discussed are cosmopolitan. The authors in *The Future of Psychoanalysis* are aware of the dangers of false scientism as well as the perils associated with North American pragmatism. These writers are justifiably harking back to an era of psychoanalytic intellectuality, and to a clinical approach which takes for granted the values of civilized stoicism. Psychoanalysis arose a hundred years ago inextricably as part of the best in Western culture, and if the writers in *The Future of Psychoanalysis* are in any way representative, they demonstrate that analysis in Germany appears to be alive and well.

Notes

1. *Beyond the Unconscious: Essays of Henri F. Ellenberger in the History of Psychiatry*, Introduced and edited by Mark S. Micale (Princeton, N.J., Princeton University Press, 1992).
2. Eileen Walkenstein, *Don't Shrink To Fit! A Confrontation with Dehumanization in Psychiatry and Psychology* (New York, Grove Press, 1977).
3. Gerald N. Izenberg, *The Existentialist Critique of Freud: The Crisis of Autonomy* (Princeton, N.J., Princeton University Press, 1977).
4. Marie Jahoda, *Freud and the Dilemmas of Psychology* (London, Hogarth Press, 1977).
5. John C. Burnham, *Jelliffe: American Psychoanalyst and Physician* (Chicago, University of Chicago Press, 1984).
6. Matthew Hugh Erdelyi, *Psychoanalysis: Freud's Cognitive Psychology* (New York, W. W. Freeman & Co., 1985).
7. Patrick J. Mahony, *Freud as a Writer* (New Haven, Conn., Yale University Press, 1987).

8. *Freud In Exile: Psychoanalysis and Its Vicissitudes*, edited by Edward Timms and Naomi Segal (New Haven, Conn., Yale University Press, 1988).
9. *The Selected Correspondence of Karl A. Menninger, 1919–1945*, edited by Howard J. Faulkner and Virginia D. Pruitt (New Haven, Conn., Yale University Press,1989).
10. *Ibid.*, p. 428.
11. *Ibid.*, p. 76.
12. *Ibid.*, p. 334.
13. *Ibid.*, p. 6.
14. Edoardo Weiss, *Sigmund Freud As A Consultant* (New Brunswick, N.J., Transaction Publishers, 1991).
15. Phyllis Grosskurth, *The Secret Ring: Freud's Inner Circle and the Politics of Psychoanalysis* (Toronto, Macfarlane Walter & Ross, 1991).
16. Kay Redfield Jamison, *Touched With Fire: Manic-Depressive Illness and the Artistic Temperament* (Toronto, Macmillan, 1993).
17. Judith M. Hughes, *From Freud's Consulting Room: The Unconscious in a Scientific Age* (Cambridge, Mass., Harvard University Press, 1994).
18. *Ibid.*, p. 1.
19. *Ibid.*, p. vii.
20. *Master Clinicians on Treating the Regressed Patient*, vol. 2, edited by L. Bryce Boyer and Peter L. Giovacchini (Northvale, N.J., Aronson, 1993).
21. *Ibid.*, p. 85.
22. Edward Shorter, *From the Mind Into The Body: The Cultural Origins of Psychosomatic Symptoms* (New York, Free Press/Macmillan, 1994); Edward Shorter, *From Paralysis to Fatigue: A History of Psychosomatic Medicine in the Modern Era* (New York, The Free Press, 1992).
23. Shorter, *From the Mind Into the Body, op. cit.*, p. ix.
24. *Ibid.*, p. 18.
25. *Ibid.*, pp. 41, 54.
26. Andre Haynal and Ernst Falzeder, editors, *100 Years of Psychoanalysis* (London, Karnac, 1994).
27. W.F. Bynum and Roy Porter, editors, *Companion Encyclopedia of the History of Medicine*, Volumes I & II (London/New York, Routledge, 1993).
28. Howard Book, *How to Practice Brief Psychodynamic Psychotherapy: The Core Conflictual Relationship Theme Method* (Washington, D.C., American Psychological Association, 1998).
29. Richard Brockman, *A Map of the Mind: Toward A Science of Psychotherapy* (Madison, Conn., Psychosocial Press, 1998).
30. Johannes Cremerius, editor, *The Future of Psychoanalysis*, translated by Jeremy Gaines (London, Open Gate Press, 1999).

12

Public Scandal

Before getting to some of the most painfully contentious of the public squabbles in the history of psychoanalysis, I would like to start with one of the least known and most harmonious examples of a key difference of opinion that got into print. Oskar Pfister (1873–1956) was a pastor living in Zurich when in 1928, while practicing as an analyst, he published a respectful reply to Freud's *The Future of an Illusion.*[1] According to one of the letters from Freud to Pfister that have so far appeared in print (their published correspondence is one of the more incomplete ones), Freud's *The Future of an Illusion* "had a great deal to do with" Pfister. Freud also said that he "had been wanting to write it for a long time, and postponed it out of regard" for Pfister.[2] Assuming that it remains true in all questions of intellectual history that in order to understand a text we must appreciate the opponents that a thinker had in mind, then to grasp the context of Freud's argument in *The Future of an Illusion* we have to know more about Pfister's own position, against which Freud said he was reacting.

Pfister's reply to Freud, "The Illusion of a Future: A Friendly Disagreement with Prof. Sigmund Freud," did not appear in English until 1993. This has to be striking, since so much attention in recent years has been devoted to the problem of psychoanalysis and religion, and to the issue of the ways in which Freud might have been unduly biased against religious convictions.[3] Pfister's "The Illusion of a Future" appeared in Freud's journal *Imago*, and is a sign of Freud's willingness to tolerate disagreement within his movement. (I originally found the draft of an English translation of "The Illusion of a Future" among Anna Freud's papers at the Library of Congress; but she obviously did not share Pfister's views, and evidently failed to try to forward the publication of Pfister's piece, which was about the same length as Freud's own little book.) Freud's lack of defensiveness in his reaction to Pfister may be the proverbial exception that proves the general rule of Freud's intolerance of dissent.

It is not often seen how Freud did not always stick to the anti-religious thesis as eventually expressed in *The Future of an Illusion.* In his case history of the Wolf-Man, for example, Freud had sounded quite differently disposed:

> Apart from these pathological phenomena, it may be said that in the present case religion achieved all the aims for the sake of which it is included in the education of the individual. It put a restraint on his sexual impulsions by affording them a sublimation and a safe mooring; it lowered the importance of his family relationships and, thus, protected him from the threat of isolation by giving him access to the great community of mankind. The untamed and fear-ridden child became social, well-behaved, and amenable to education. . . . So it was that religion did its work for the hard-pressed child — by the combination which it afforded the believer of satisfaction, of sublimation, of diversion from sensual processes to purely spiritual ones, and of access to social relationships.[4]

So, in a clinical context, Freud could be far more religiously receptive than the clear-cut rationalistic line of argument in *The Future of an Illusion* may make him sound. However complicated Freud's outlook on religion should be taken to be, the particular stand he took in *The Future of An Illusion* is consistent with an important strand in his outlook as a whole. In Freud's 1927 critique of religion he was countering not only what he thought of as Pfister's position, but he was also continuing to settle the differences between himself and the line of thinking which Jung had represented within psychoanalysis.

When the full difficulties between Freud and Jung broke out, Pfister had been exceptional among the Swiss in sticking by Freud's side. There are still enough letters to come out between Freud and Pfister that it cannot be safe to make any secure generalizations about their relationship. We do know that in 1919 Pfister helped found a new Swiss Society for Psychoanalysis, and then in 1928, when Dr. Emil Oberholzer set up a separate Swiss Medical Society for Psychoanalysis, Pfister continued to be a leader in the Swiss Society for Psychoanalysis, which retained the only Swiss link with the International Psychoanalytic Association (IPA). Oberholzer's group, evidently founded in opposition to Freud's position in behalf of lay analysis, did not survive World War II.

Pfister's personal and organizational loyalty to Freud only serves to make more apparent the seriousness of his differences with Freud as expressed in "The Illusion of a Future." For Pfister was not just a man of God who felt compelled to speak out against atheism; Pfister's thesis on religion is closely intertwined with his views on both morality and art. These subjects have in recent years given rise to a good deal of psychoanalytic reexamination. We know now, for example, that although in his later years Freud made a display of his own distance from formal philosophy, as a young man he was far more involved with it than we had ever realized before.[5] So that when Pfister finds analogies between Freud's position in *The Future of an Illusion* and the reasoning of Ludwig Feuerbach, it is striking how Freud's own early reading of Feuerbach could lie behind his ultimate thinking.

Freud's approach to religion has to be a central part of understanding his work. For he went after not just the kind of position that Pfister stood for, but was also aligning himself alongside Nietzsche in attempting to overturn many aspects of traditional Western ethics.[6] In *The Future of an Illusion* Freud was speaking as a sustained Enlightenment *philosophe* who believed in the overwhelming merits of science and progress. Pfister's 1928 reply is bound now to seem almost prophetically telling. For Pfister was articulating some of the central inadequacies in Freud's whole approach to ethics, art, and philosophy, as well as, implicitly, the practice of psychotherapy. When I made possible the belated appearance in English of Pfister's "The Illusion of a Future" I was hoping to help further healthy debate within psychoanalysis.[7]

During the winter of 1983–84 Janet Malcolm's *In the Freud Archives*[8] created a sensation when it appeared first as two long articles in the *New Yorker.* Earlier she had published a sparklingly written *Psychoanalysis: The Impossible Profession.*[9] (Although the dazzle of her prose partially disguised the fact, at bottom Janet Malcolm was engaging in a fundamentalist defense of orthodox psychoanalytic apologetics.) *In the Freud Archives* did not mention that many donors of material to the Freud Archives had no intention of its being locked away. Selective access to the Freud Archives has compounded the scholarly sense of frustration about them. For the Archives has allowed certain arbitrarily chosen individuals to use documentation that has remained barred to researchers at large.

The basis for Malcolm's *In the Freud Archives* was a hubbub that originated in the *New York Times.* In 1980 Eissler, the creator of the Freud Archives, had appointed a successor, Jeffrey M. Masson, to be Projects Director. Masson was apparently so devoutly faithful a Freudian that Eissler (and also Anna Freud) neglected to be adequately concerned about Masson's longstanding obsession with the significance of the sexual seduction of children.

In 1981 Masson gave interviews to a *New York Times* reporter (Ralph Blumenthal) in which he alleged, supposedly on the basis of what he had seen in the Freud Archives, the legitimacy of Freud's pre–1897 conviction that neurosis arises from childhood sexual abuse. (Masson's interviews and the publicity that followed helped to promote the revival of the whole discussion of seduction which we discussed in chapter 1.) To add further fuel to the flame of controversy, Masson maintained that by the 1980s psychoanalysis had deteriorated into a hopelessly sterile discipline.

Masson further charged that Freud only abandoned his early belief about the key importance of seduction because of his cowardice in the face of Viennese professional criticism. Masson had at once made himself a public embarrassment to organized psychoanalysis, and Eissler fired him from his position at the Archives. Masson retaliated with a thirteen million dollar law suit and eventually accepted a financial settlement of $150,000.

By means of *In the Freud Archives* Malcolm painted a sympathetic portrait of Eissler as a fanatical defender of the sealed archives. Yet she completely failed to document how many earlier wars he had fought on behalf of his idealized image of Freud. Nor did she question Anna Freud's cooperation in helping to construct the situation Masson was able to exploit.

Malcolm's success as a publicist came from a skillful manipulation of the story of the personalities involved in the 1981 falling-out between Eissler and Masson. In the course of describing Masson's quest for publicity, we learn about his background as a Sanskritist (he once taught at the University of Toronto) and his compulsive womanizing. Malcolm chose to give space to one other figure, Peter Swales, on the grounds that he had had his own difficulties with both Masson and Eissler. Malcolm, despite the title of her book, revealed no new information about primary Freud documents. And she made no effort to explore the reasons why Freud should inspire such devout sectarianism.

In the end, Malcolm managed to give an immense amount of coverage to Masson's own hobbyhorse connected to seduction. When his book *The Assault on Truth: Freud's Suppression of the Seduction Theory*[10] appeared in 1984 the news media afforded it an altogether disproportionate amount of attention. Serious observers rose to denounce Masson's fabricated historical constructions about Freud. Yet once Masson had gained his public platform, some were bound to be taken in by his tendentiousness; in particular, a few feminists mistakenly thought that his work lent support to their own cause.

The whole story about the Freud Archives is ironic in that Freud himself sought to be such a relentless truth-seeker. We have already touched on how historians and the families of great men are likely to be, by nature, antagonistic and at odds. Freud had expressed reluctance about an authorized biography, and was tempted to destroy some of his correspondence.

Yet it is doubtful if Freud knew how credulous the public can be. At the time *In the Freud Archives* appeared, with one exception all of the volumes of Freud's published letters had been bowdlerized; although Malcolm discussed none of this, the grounds for censorship had nothing to do with medical discretion. Freud felt disdain and contempt for American life, even if — and partly because — in his last years Americans were his most lucrative patients. It is hard to know whether he would be amused or feel his cynicism vindicated by Malcolm's installment about the fate of his papers in America.

Those two stylistically dazzling articles by Janet Malcolm which were written for the *New Yorker* in late 1983 alleged that Masson had behaved self-destructively in losing his job at the Archives; yet this incident became an essential constituent in helping launch Masson's public career. She had dwelt on the background and circumstances connected with his being dismissed, after his year as project director, once he told that *New York Times* reporter about his thesis that Freud had, in 1897, lacked the courage of his convictions about the origin of neurotic suffering coming from childhood sexual seduction. To repeat: Masson claimed that documents he alone had seen proved that Freud had invented his theory of the Oedipus complex, and hypothesized the role of fantasy — as opposed to the external reality of child abuse — to curry favor with the Viennese medical establishment.

When Masson sued the Freud Archives, as well as their ally the wealthy Muriel Gardiner (model for Lillian Hellman's *Julia*), it was because he had given up his tenured position at the University of Toronto to go to the Archives. Eventually a settlement was worked out, which in addition to the money allowed Masson to edit Freud's correspondence with another medical pioneer, Wilhelm Fliess, which appeared in 1985. That volume of letters was carefully sanitized of Masson's pet theory about the key importance of linking neurosis to the sexual seduction of children, which had created a temporary sensation when it appeared in Masson's 1984 book *The Assault on Truth.*

Ever since the 1983 *New Yorker* articles, Masson claimed that Janet Malcolm's articles had invented damaging words to put into his mouth. Malcolm denied this, offering as proof her tape recordings. The litigious Masson sued her and her publishers for libel, asking ten million dollars in damages.

It turned out that an examination of Malcolm's tapes do not sustain all her Masson quotations, and although two lower courts dismissed Masson's suit, the U. S. Supreme Court agreed to hear an appeal. Insiders suspected that the high court would not have accepted the case on appeal unless it were tempted toward a reversal, and in fact the Court did send the case back for a jury trial. Then two jury trials, both attended with an immense amount of New York newspaper publicity, followed; the first, in 1993, ended inconclusively. The second jury found against Masson in 1994.

One of the most striking aspects to Masson's 1990 *Final Analysis: The Making and Unmaking of a Psychoanalyst*[11] is that he made no mention whatever of Janet Malcolm. He stopped his narrative before Janet Malcolm's *New Yorker* pieces appeared. This became especially interesting because in a 1989 series of pieces in *The New Yorker*, Malcolm, also without once mentioning Masson's suit against her, made a similar accusation of a double-cross against the writer Joe McGinnis, saying McGinnis had, in his book *Fatal Vision*, betrayed his subject, Dr. Jeffrey MacDonald, about the savage murder of MacDonald's family. The pervasively repeated theme of the perfidy of disloyalty seemed to engulf both Masson and Malcolm.

It is hard to agree with Malcolm's assertion that all journalists are confidence tricksters, but the distortions and misstatements in *Final Analysis* do make one think that there are more such creatures around than one might imagine. *Final Analysis* is mostly concerned with Masson's training as an analyst in Toronto. For a decade Masson had been living in Berkeley, California, and was writing *Final Analysis* for America and the world, but anyone friendly to Canada could hardly read *Final Analysis* without feeling insulted. It is not just that he treats Toronto as a hick town, but he also talks about "the provincial" nature of Canadian intellectual life. It would have been wiser if Masson had at least spelled the novelist Margaret Laurence's last name correctly when calling on her vision to describe a Canadian incident.

Perhaps no one outside Ontario would be able to zero in on some central defects in Masson's argument. Psychoanalytic training has its many problems, and a large literature on it has grown up, but Masson writes as though he were the first ever to have been excommunicated by the faithful.

What was bound to be striking to Torontonians were the specifics of Masson's case against his training analyst. He named him, Dr. Irvine Schiffer, as had Janet Malcolm, and Masson tried to make it appear that he had made a great sacrifice in his five-year training analysis, repeatedly telling us how much money it cost him. Masson said that between 1971 and 1976 he paid seventy-five dollars an hour, five days a week, an astronomical sum, and mentioned only in passing that "the government did pick up part of the tab."

Though too many analysts have extra-billed for so-called uninsured services, that fee did not, even in 1990, run to seventy-five dollars an hour. In the early seventies, OHIP (Ontario Health Insurance Plan) covered almost the whole shot, and although there can be no certainty that Masson fully availed himself of OHIP assistance, it is troubling that his allusion to the existence of OHIP is a misleading reference.

"In Canada," he writes, "medical insurance, which is universal, pays for at least 60 per cent of an analysis." While there is federal legislation about medical insurance, the specific arrangements differ from province to province. I dwell on this because it is telling about the unreliability of everything else in *Final Analysis*; also, Masson has bitten the hands that fed him. Masson was essentially arguing, from his Toronto experience and his contacts with the highest levels of international psychoanalysis, that the profession is a racket.

If he felt victimized during his analysis, as he alleges, then why did he not just walk out? If he subconsciously wanted to be abused, then was he telling us something about his own peculiar psychology, and perhaps a bit about his childhood?

Janet Malcolm never reported, in her celebrated *New Yorker* articles on the Freud Archives (which subsequently appeared as a book), having asked Masson the obvious question of whether his interest in sexual seduction had an autobiographical basis. In *Final Analysis*, Masson pretended that the subject gradually came up in the course of his historical research — though anyone who knew him at the time was aware that it was a subject that concerned him intensely all along. As I have pointed out before, that Anna Freud and her ideological allies, among them Eissler, could not spot Masson's obsession before appointing him to the Archives in 1980 tells us something about their own short-sightedness.

It has to be one of the curiosities of one branch of feminism (*Final Analysis* came with an endorsement from Kate Millet) that a man like Jeffrey Masson, who claims to have slept with a thousand women, became an ally in the struggle for female emancipation.

Frederick Crews is a literary critic whose essays in his collection *Out of My System: Psychoanalysis, Ideology, and Critical Method*[12] had already been prominently published. He is noteworthy for his interest in the uses of Freudian psychology, and for having sought out the bases in society for what might appear to be purely artistic positions. Crews possesses a formidable polemical command of English. While he tells us here that his "vocation" has been "to be forever deciding that I would rather not be a fanatic of one sort or another," his various self-righteous attacks on others leave the impression that despite his disclaimer he remains a true zealot.

In the opening essay, first written in 1966, Crews systematically dismisses possible objections to his own proposed critical methods, yet by the end of this volume his essays have implicitly repudiated his earlier expressions of Freudian fundamentalist faith. Crews has been honest enough to leave an account of his shifting examples of belligerence. He has printed his essays in their order of composition, and left them "substantially unchanged." He denounces, in turn, such different writers as Norman O. Brown, Northrop Frye, Herbert Marcuse, Wilhelm Reich, among others; but while claiming to aim at "rational, non-sectarian discourse," Crews fails to provide an account of what evidence had led him to change ideological points of view. His newly expressed skepticism "about closed interpretive systems in general" does not justify, or befit, his own continued dogmatic practices.

Crews now acknowledges that "psychoanalysis is less a science than a world view," at the same time as he identified himself with "the naked daring of the original Freudian vision." It is hard for anyone to become well-versed in the history of psychoanalysis. We have seen how sectarianism has meant that each rival school of depth psychology ignores the contributions of the others. Although Crews can concede that at the outset of his work he made "scant allowance for psychologies other than orthodox Freudianism," he still dismisses Carl G. Jung as a "neo-Platonist" in contrast to a supposedly reliable "psychologist." Crews dislikes "excommunicative hairsplitting" while participating in it himself. He chooses to cite second-rank psychoanalytic thinkers who belatedly arrived at a perspective held by Jung around World War I.

Still, Crews's credulity is understandable. Freud was not only a great psychologist but a fascinating writer; and he was philosophically more cosmopolitan than his revisionist successors. But a gulf has long existed between psychoanalysis's individualistic theory and its all-too-often conformist practices. Even if one can see the autobiographical element in everything Freud wrote, it need not dim an appreciation of his stature in the history of ideas. Freud was in fact a more interesting figure than the Master whose myth now supports the needs of a bureaucratic movement.

Crews does at least not last long as an advocate of any orthodoxy. Although during the Vietnam war he turned against Cold War assumptions, he has already trenchantly criticized "New Left" convictions. And while in this volume he repeatedly writes in praise of fashionable ego psychology, and in particular of Erik H. Erikson's work, simultaneously with the appearance of *Out of My System* was a severe critique of Erikson by Crews in the *New York Review of Books*. By the mid–1990s Crews would be lambasting Freud not only in the *New York Review* but in subsequent books. Crews has become keenly aware of the place of ideology in the life of the mind, but even in *Out of My System* he exempts psychoanalysis from an examination of the bourgeois character of its so-called findings.

In the course of this collection Crews reprints an essay rejecting the suggestion that the appeal of Conrad's *Heart of Darkness* lies in its ideas. Crews admires Conrad yet dislikes his conservative side, and treats the plot as if it were a dream recounted to a psychoanalyst; for Crews the interpretation of the story is "beyond doubt" an expression of primal scene material. Yet in a later essay Crews argues against the same reductionist emphasis on infantile factors in art.

It is not surprising when practicing analysts support myths about Freud on behalf of the occupational security of their status quo. If a cultured intellectual is capable, even temporarily, of swallowing such a party-line, however, there is ground for distress. Crews's recurrent fanaticism does yield telling individual points. As John Stuart Mill observed in urging tolerance for "one-eyed men" like Jeremy Bentham, the key issue is whether such great thinkers succeed in being followed by those able to correct the imbalance of creative distortions. Freud can be excused many mistakes by virtue of his originality and genius. His followers and their critics, however, must share the more standard tests that the rest of us try to live by.

Unsavory professional notoriety now surrounds the name of Masud Khan, who died in 1989. For many years he functioned as a powerful leader within the British Psychoanalytic Society; he was known as a favorite disciple of

Donald W. Winnicott's, and, in addition, Khan had been politic enough within the British Society to be on good terms with the followers of both Anna Freud and Melanie Klein. (Khan had had the foresight to pick them both as supervisors during the final years of his training.) In organizational terms Khan was considered thoroughly "reliable"; he became a key insider within the International Psychoanalytic Association (IPA). Then he got cancer, and according to one version of his story, this affliction released sides of Khan that were undreamt of; he had an affair with a patient, which ruined him within the British Society. His final break with his British colleagues came over the anti-Semitic passages contained in *The Long Wait: And Other Psychoanalytic Narratives*[13]; thereafter he ceased even being a member of the British Society. Precisely because previously he had been the author of many and much-admired books and technical papers, as well as an editor, Masud Khan's fall from grace was widely known and much lamented.

My own view of matters connected with Khan is different. When I first met him, in 1965, I found him extraordinarily difficult; the word arrogance does not begin to cover the imperiousness of his manner. That he came from an extraordinarily rich Pakistani background did not, in my view, make his conduct any more tolerable. As I recall our first meeting, he went on for at least half an hour with a bitter denunciation of all things American; after I withstood that assault, he mellowed, and I found him capable of being delightful and brilliant. At the time, I did not realize how unctuous he was capable of being toward the powers-that-be, but in later years, when I read his correspondence with Anna Freud, I was astonished at what a flatterer he could be. I would never have thought of him as a Uriah Heep. It is true that once I began to publish my books, Khan showed signs of being opposed to everything that I was writing, but I was so naïve as not to realize how he was working against me within the inner sanctums of the international psychoanalytic movement.

So, for myself, I see no great transformation in Khan; he was always more or less impossible, and that he turned on his former allies seems to me not out of keeping with the man I knew. At the same time, I found *The Long Wait* a fascinating book. I would not have expected him to be so artistically talented. I do not know whether the clinical cases it recounts are reliable; I would feel more confidence in his approach if he gave an example of a mistake on his part or a therapeutic encounter that went badly. Even an illustration of a clinical stalemate might lend more credibility to his reported approach. But whether *The Long Wait* is fiction or fact, I found it absolutely compelling reading, almost impossible to put down. Although I am Jewish, the anti-Semitism it contains seemed to me mild amid all the other of his prejudices he was willing to expose; his Francophilic convictions struck me as no less eccentric than what he said about Jews.

The first clinical vignette, "Prisons," makes an engrossing beginning. Written in 1984, it concerns a patient Khan treated for about a decade. British analysts do not think long-term treatment unusual; Khan was in contact with the man for some thirty years. That patient was having difficulties with a homosexual perversion that I am not at all sure I understand, but I know that Khan also wrote some elaborate theoretical papers about this patient's particular problem. What struck me right away in his clinical report was that Khan is willing to give a verbatim account of his own reactions to the patient's associations. Khan sometimes kept notes because, he tells us, " it is useful to keep alert, when nothing is happening clinically."[14] Although Khan was widely read in the psychoanalytic literature, the citations in connection with Winnicott are obtrusive. Equally striking are some of Khan's silences; although he invokes, from a French source, Helene Deutsch's concept of "fate neurosis," and in later portions of the book uses her concept of the "as if" character type, Khan never once mentions Helene Deutsch's name.

The book contains illustrations of what I regard as clinical wisdom. Khan had learned, he tells us in "Prisons," "never to be in a hurry to 'cure' symptoms," and also "to respect the self-protective and self-curative value of a patient's psycho-sexual pathology. . . . "[15] Despite what some defenders of analytic orthodoxy might now like to think, I doubt that Khan's clinical practices changed very much; whatever the particular dates associated with the case histories in *The Long Wait*, he consistently sounds like the man I first met in 1965.

"When Spring Comes," dated 1986, is as much concerned with Winnicott's clinical behavior as it is with the woman he referred to Khan for treatment. As a result, the chapter tells a good deal about Khan's relationship with Winnicott. Again, on the basis of my own brief personal knowledge of Winnicott, it sounds to me a credible version of how they got on. One could not imagine two people more apparently different: Winnicott was untutored about the printed literature, charming and whimsical, and liked to think that Khan had read absolutely everything; Khan could not only prepare an index for a Winnicott book, but also "rewrite" his papers. Winnicott, in his last years, sounded worried about how Khan would be without him, but Khan made plain that he expected to turn (as he did in fact do) to Anna Freud for later help. "The real purpose of writing this chapter is to share with the reader my joyous experiences, so very strict too, of 'working with' D. W. W. on living cases."[16]

"Empty Chairs, Vast Spaces" (1986) concerns Khan's highly unusual treatment of an American woman. Among other things he reports having told her was, "In America most, if not all, of the 'lay analysts' are militant charlatans."[17] I hear echoes of Freud's reporting that the Rat Man was fed during treatment when Khan tells us, "Tea was brought to the consulting room."[18] It is in connection with this case history that Khan wrote a paragraph that has gained infamy:

> By starting on a new style, and scope, of clinical work with a patient/person, and his/her total environment, as was appropriate to the patient's needs, I was freeing myself of the rigid Yiddish shackles of the so-called psychoanalysis. I say "Yiddish" because psychoanalysis, for better or worse, is not only Judaic in its inherited traditions, but also Yiddish and Jewish. The three are quite distinct in my experience. Even though only two Jewesses played an important role in my education (Melanie Klein for a short while, and Anna Freud mutatively and for much longer), the impact of the Judaic-Yiddish-Jewish bias of psychoanalysis was neither small nor slight on me. If it undoubtedly nurtured me, it has also cramped my personal and ethnic styles. It was an ego-alien ferment, as well as an increment, in my totality of experiences. In the year 1974 (when this clinical work took place) I was to be fifty years of age. Time to be my own person.[19]

Khan also included a copy of a letter he wrote in 1974 to the patient's lover (the letter was also shown to the patient). Khan complained of the "gathering power" of the Kleinians, spoke of the practice of caring towards his peasants he had learned back home, and expressed his annoyance at "those miserable creatures, the neurotics, addicted to being analyzed."[20] We learn that among the servants Khan had at his London flat were a houseboy, a secretary, and a chauffeur.

"A Dismaying Homosexual" (1987) contains Khan's unabashed account of how he lost his temper with a Jewish patient.

> One more personal remark about me, my wife, my staff or my things, and I will throw you out, you accursed nobody Jew. Find your own people then. Shoals of them drift around, just like you. Yes, I am anti-Semitic. You know why, Mr. Luis? Because I am Aryan and had thought all of you Jews had perished when Jesus, from sheer dismay — and he was one of you — had flown up to Heaven, leaving you in the scorching care of Hitler, Himmler and the crematoriums. Don't fret, Mr. Luis; like the rest of your species, you will survive and continue to harass others, and lament, and bewail yourselves. Remarkable how Yiddish/Jewish you are.[21]

Actually Khan's account of his anger shows him to have been rather more fluent in his prejudices than I suspect he was in reality. It is in keeping with the man I fleetingly knew that he would observe that "the USA is the first nation known to *homo sapiens* that has created a scatter of civilizations, spread all over America, without creating any culture of any sort."[22]

"Outrage, Compliance and Authenticity" (1984) is both an account of a patient who found outrageousness "ego syntonic and a social asset" and a defense of Khan's own manner of proceeding in life. Khan reports that he regularly kept new patients waiting for five or ten minutes. Khan was grandiose not only about himself but those he was associated with. He tells of the special care that the analyst J. B. Pontalis in Paris had extended toward him during his illness with cancer: "Such care and holding by a colleague of the same generation is, I believe, rare in the history of psychoanalysis; except for the friendship between Anna Freud and the American millionairess, Dorothy Burlingham."[23] In this case history we hear about Khan's butler and housekeeper, as well as his estates back in Pakistan.

In "Thoughts" (1986) Khan tells us about himself as "an aristocrat"; the word dictator would seem to me equally appropriate. Khan sounds proud to be described by others as "a maverick among analysts." He somehow was able to think that he could claim without fear of obvious contradiction that "self-cure is a concept I have introduced. . . . "[24] Khan nonetheless spoke relatively favorably of the work of both Erik H. Erikson and Sandor Ferenczi.

"The Long Wait" (1987) is the account of the treatment of a Muslim aristocrat like him. His approach with her was highly idiosyncratic, even for Khan. But it gave Khan a platform by which he could both criticize Freud's procedure as one-sided and condemn most of Freud's followers for lacking "his guts and strength." The single person in analysis who emerges entirely unscathed in the course of Khan's book is Anna Freud: "Freud's had been a haunted life; only at the end did he find true love in his Antigone-Anna. Freud died a man in grace." One wonders, though, whether "Miss Freud" would have whole-heartedly and without any qualification agreed, had she lived to read his 1987 "Afterward" in *The Long Wait*, with the merits of the proposition that "the assumed anonymity of most analysts can provoke unnecessary infantile attachments and attitudes in the patient which analysts then interpret as the patient's transference." Khan thought that although his own "clinical approach creates its own demands for both analyst and patient, it also facilitates that mutual sharing which is fundamental to my way of working."[25]

In my opinion far too much of the psychoanalytic literature is taken up with theoretical abstractions, and too few actual clinical illustrations are to be found. One reason that Khan's book is so readable is that he presents real-sounding patients, and he himself emerges as a therapist working with an individual style of his own. Around the time *The Long Wait* appeared I met an analyst/analysand of Khan's who calmly supported the idea, even then, that Khan was clinically astute. It is beyond my competence to weigh further the pros and cons of Khan's approach; I would think that one would have to have been pretty stouthearted to be able to stand up to him. Yet there is, I feel, undoubted merit in some of his criticisms of the more conventional rigidities of his "classical" colleagues.

Still I have to be once again reminded of how power can be abused therapeutically. Khan was one of the best-trained analysts in London, and I do not believe that his behavior in these clinical encounters, acknowledged by himself to be outrageous, was entirely new to him thanks to changes due to his sustained bout with cancer (and alcoholism). But what checks can there be on any analyst's conduct? Even the "nebbish"[26] that Janet Malcolm praises in contrast to Khan can abuse his position manipulatively; classical analytic power can be more insidious and harder to combat than Khan's obvious overbearingness. Other professionals, at least, have some counterbalances to their effects on their clients. University teachers, for instance, run into limits on the extent they can suggestively influence their students because the pupils are simultaneously under the spell of other mentors as well. In any therapeutic interaction there are unique possibilities for the abuse of power, and the example Khan presents us with in *The Long Wait* is only one chilling reminder of what can happen.

Aside from the simple historical statement that Freud's psychoanalysis is now over a century old, there is little likelihood of widespread agreement about anything else that could be said on the subject. Right from the outset, in the world of Old Vienna, some dismissed Freud as a crank. Even if his genius as a writer were acknowledged, critics worried that the therapeutic procedure he proposed might prove dangerous. Freud, in fact, had an ambitious moral agenda, beyond therapy and science, aiming to transform the values of world culture. By 1910 he had succeeded in attracting an international following, some of his adherents becoming blind proponents.

In spite of his difficulties with Adler and Jung, by the early 1920s Freud was world famous, even if still the focus of heated disagreements. Though he has been dead since 1939, little consensus about his standing has emerged. Frederick Crews published celebrated polemical articles on Freud in the *New York Review of Books* in 1993–94, displaying his complete loss of confidence in Freud. Crews believed that Freud "has been the most over-rated figure in the entire history of science and medicine — one who wrought immense harm through the propagation of false etiologies, mistaken diagnoses and fruitless lines of inquiry."

At the same time that such disparaging views were being prominently aired, aspects of Freud's theories have become a secure part of contemporary common sense. Thanks to Freud's influence, slips of the tongue, dreams, and neurotic symptoms are all considered meaningful, despite a variety of theories to account for them. The literature about Freud continues to proliferate, and for some years he has dominated intellectual life in France.

John Forrester's *Dispatches from the Freud Wars* is not a general account of scholarly debate.[27] Forrester is an English don sympathetic to Freud's objectives, and these complex essays represent both work in progress that builds on Freud and a final chapter dealing with some of the best known of Freud's recent "detractors." It is unfortunate that the response to Freud still seems to be so much all-or-nothing. Forrester, interestingly, uses Freud's thinking to reconsider such subjects as the links between envy and justice, and the nature of discretion as opposed to transgression.

Since at least 20,000 of Freud's letters have survived, each time a new volume of his correspondence comes out scholars are forced to reconsider what has been newly learned. Freud's clinical practices shed light on his most abstract principles, and if only because so much of what he proposed came from autobiographical sources, Forrester and others are rightly concerned with expanding our understanding of Freud's life. That Freud could himself be self-deceived, betrayed by the undercurrents of his own unconscious motives, only dramatizes the significance of the position he had staked out about how inevitable it is that we lie to ourselves.

Gordon Warme's *The Psychotherapist* is a wholly different kind of book, in that he is a practicing clinician.[28] It would be hard to imagine a more balanced introduction to what psychotherapy is about than what Warme has come up with. While Forrester can sometimes get caught up in abstruse debates only intelligible to academics, Warme is consistently down-to-earth about what therapists and their clients are engaged in. He is at home with great literature, and uses literary insights to advance his argument. His text illustrates how far psychoanalysis has moved away from Freud's early interest in reconstructing isolated traumas from early childhood. Warme shows that in the hands of the best modern therapists, irony, sensitivity, and a subtle understanding of human interactions are essential aspects of clinical engagements.

Oddly enough, however, Warme has little to say about psychopharmacology, although it is well known that pills are far more important to psychotherapeutic practice than they were only a generation ago. Although analysts like Warme may be aware of the dangers of the misuse of therapeutic power, the increased reliance on medication should reopen the question of the possibilities of authoritarianism. People in trouble are highly suggestible, and it can be harder to check the validity of a therapist's interpretations than one might suspect. When drugs are added into the situation, and diagnoses themselves shaped by the demands of insurance systems, it is even more necessary to be wary of therapeutic abuses. Perhaps someone as enlightened as Warme will undertake to follow up on the ethics of biological psychiatry.

While Forrester's book is consistently challenging and Warme's account both humane and wise, Margaret A. Hagen's *Whores of the Court: The Fraud of Psychiatric Testimony and the Rape of American Justice* makes for a hard read.[29] She is correct to be concerned about what sort of experts clinicians are, and dubious about the legal implications that the use of psychological influence can have. But Hagen is so combative, for instance in her title of the book, that she unknowingly undermines the case she is trying to establish.

Hagen is an experimental psychologist who thinks that other kinds of psychologists are engaged in "junk science," menacing liberties through their influence on courts and weakening the ideal of individual responsibility. She has caught hold of a genuine dilemma, and it would be folly to suppose that there are not genuine problems in building bridges between law and psychology. To the extent that legal rules rely on assumptions about human intention, not to mention the vagaries of diagnoses and the whole field of family law, any modern system of justice must come to terms with the kind of evidence modern psychology can offer. In an adversarial legal contest, each side will hire its own experts, but that does not necessarily mean the prostitution of psychological knowledge, any more than for adversarial lawyers.

Hagen does call attention to the appalling recovered memory movement, which has gotten away with charging people for crimes long after one might have thought statutes of limitation had expired, and on the basis of dubious evidence which others besides Hagen have linked to the Freudian theory of repression. Since Freud has become, as W. H. Auden announced in a poem at Freud's death, "a whole climate of opinion," he can be blamed for all kinds of reasoning he never can have imagined possible. Hagen has a field day pointing out examples of what looks like groundless legal reliance on psychological specialists.

No matter how easy it can be to score points at the expense of therapists brave enough to withstand the withering criticism that can be expected in a courtroom, there is no possible way of going entirely without the psychological thinking that Freud pioneered. Freud changed our conception of what it means to be a person, and that revolution is not readily undone, certainly not by the kind of advertising copy embodied in Hagen's unfortunate book. As long as we believe it is not ethical to blame people for acts beyond their control, the law must adjust to changing psychological concepts.

The issue is often not whether to make use of psychology, but how to do so without undue credulity. It would be grandiose to think it possible to reverse the effects of the past 100 years of intellectual history. As I have tried to argue, the inadequate legitimacy given to dissenting opinion is a central source of the bitterness surrounding the controversies connected with psychoanalysis. It ought to be possible to challenge aspects of Freud's system without being considered the enemy; and different points of view should get acknowledged as legitimate, without being dismissed as Freud-bashing. Perhaps it is precisely because this sort of psychology has usurped so many of the traditional functions of religious belief that the quarrels have been as heated and sectarian. An appreciation of the best spirit of Freud should remind us of the inevitable mystery of the human soul, and how little we still know about motivation.

Mikkel Borch-Jacobsen, a philosopher who is an expert on French psychoanalysis, has written a fascinating little book, *Remembering Anna O.*,[30] on Josef Breuer's famous patient Anna O. (Bertha Pappenheim). Although there were subtle hints in the literature beforehand, ever since the momentous publication of a paper by Ellenberger in 1972, already referred to, we have definitively known that despite Freud's claims to the contrary Breuer's treatment of Anna O. was neither a therapeutic success nor an example of catharsis. Ellenberger came up with sanatorium records that showed that after the treatment by Breuer Anna O. was addicted to morphine and chloral. Subsequently she recovered and went on to be a pioneering German social worker. Later Albrecht Hirschmüller, in his Germanically exact biography of Breuer, unearthed even more primary documentation. Jung was verbally making the point about Breuer's failure with Anna O. as early as the 1920s, so Freud must have privately revealed the truth to the man he had once chosen to be his successor.

Borch-Jacobsen has highlighted the way the record has been mystified. In the light of what we know now, it becomes more understandable why Breuer was reluctant to publish the results of his work with Anna O. It would seem that not only was Freud using Breuer as a reputable model behind whom it was safe to appear to follow, but it may also have been that Freud was willfully entangling Breuer in a myth about the origins of psychoanalysis. Although Freud was so enduringly bitter about Breuer that he was capable of cutting the old man on a Viennese street, Breuer's death called forth from Freud both a condolence letter to the family as well as an obituary.

A close examination of this early case history leaves in a shambles one of the most long-standing legends of psychoanalysis's beginnings. The French publication of *Remembering Anna O.* received favorable reviews, but also the denunciation of Andre Green, one of French psychoanalysis's leading spokesmen. It seems to me that Borch-Jacobsen has correctly shown what some of Freud's earliest clinical critics were most alarmed about — the extent to which psychotherapists might stumble over the suggestibility of their patients. Although Borch-Jacobsen confines himself to hysteria, all therapeutic outcomes can be enlightened by the logic of his thinking.

Remembering Anna O. can easily and enjoyably be read at one sitting, but it is important enough to bear rereading. It will be discomforting to those of us who have hoped for an end to research that fuels assaults on Freud. The scholarly pendulum continues to swing away from idealizations of Freud toward efforts at debunking, and there seems no early end in sight to Freud's being enduringly controversial. Borch-Jacobsen's relentless and illustrious reasoning will enhance the historiography of psychoanalysis, and defenders of orthodoxy should be worried about when the next shoe will drop.

Censoriousness is not an attractive quality, even though it can have short-term advantages, including gaining readers and converts. Edward Dolnick, a professional journalist, has written *Madness on the Couch: Blaming the Victim in the Heyday of Psychoanalysis*[31]; it is an excellent book about some of the key missteps, mainly in the last half-century, which led a large group of psychoanalytic writers to blame patients and bash families. Paradoxically Dolnick's own moralism leads him to start off by being so harsh about Freud that I suspect many might be put off by the first section of his book. Dolnick does not mention the existence of Freud's spittoon, but there is not much else unattractive that he overlooks.

The book has so many merits that it is unfortunate that Dolnick could not restrain himself from some easy potshots. We are not living in an era when, at least in America, psychoanalysts are wielding major psychiatric power. As Dolnick points out, biological psychiatry is now clearly in the saddle. While Lord Acton's famous aphorism about the corrupting possibilities of power helps explain what went wrong among analysts, Dolnick does not seem adequately aware of the need also to challenge some of the dangers inherent in present-day psychiatric thinking.

Instead Dolnick does a trenchant job of showing, especially in the areas of schizophrenia and autism, how analysts missed the boat in the period after World War II. I do find it unfortunate how Dolnick has chosen to single out for blaming some of the pioneers (if not heroes) of the treatment of schizophrenia. I am more familiar with the writings of Paul Federn (whom Dolnick skips) than those of Frieda Fromm-Reichmann, but it seems to me unfair to reduce her down to the promotion of the concept of "schizophrenogenic" motherhood. She died in 1957, and as late as the mid–1960s Donald Winnicott was denying that schizophrenia was organic or biochemical but rather an "environmental failure." Dolnick does not seem to realize that he has been trashing some of the most enlightened figures in twentieth-century psychiatry — Harry Stack Sullivan, Harold Searles, Gregory Bateson, among others, even Hilde Bruch.

Dolnick does, by his chapter 8 on "Ice Picks and Electroshocks," discuss the alternative school which started from reasoning about the brain. Lobotomies were being performed at the rate of 5,000 a year from 1949 to 1952. Brain surgery is still around. I do not see the point of ridiculing those analysts who, in the midst of therapeutic and scientific darkness, were struggling as best they could to deal with patients in the most acute sorts of misery. At the end of the book Dolnick concedes, "To hold a sick person's hand is a good deed; to go on to proclaim hand-holding as a cure is something else entirely." And Dolnick concludes the book by quoting Robert Frost's definition of tragedy: "something terrible happens and nobody is to blame."[32] If only Dolnick's entire book had been infused with such compassionate feelings he might have avoided the polemicism that mars too much of his text.

Still for those who are struggling to catch up with the latest in biological psychiatry, Dolnick does much to outline some of the main lines of genetic studies, the growth of antipsychotic drugs, and comparisons with the results of psychotherapy. One wishes there were some way magically to rearrange things so that there would be much less of a divide between those who know about brain chemistry and the experienced clinicians with their savvy about the strengths of psychotherapy. Dolnick does mention a dissenter like Lauretta Bender (who married Paul Schilder) as a proponent of autism being organic, although Dolnick neglects Sandor Rado as a psychoanalytic advocate of the significance of genetics. Therapeutic hopefulness arises from biological as well as psychological premises; and arrogant self-assurance can originate from both sides. Freud did sometimes exaggerate his claims, although he also published his case of "Dora" acknowledging a therapeutic stalemate. Dolnick touches on the problem of obsessive compulsiveness, without linking it enough, I think, to schizophrenia. *Madness on the Couch* has an immense amount to teach. Freudians can be compared not just to Communists (as Dolnick does) but to Keynesians as well; it is not hard to be self-deceptive for idealistic motives. Dolnick's book is largely a work of dismantling, and at times he appears (as on autism) to be beating a dead horse. While Dolnick has provided invaluable guides to the future of psychiatry, zealotry in behalf of any school of thought is likely to produce a new set of follies.

Notes

1. Hans Zulliger, "Oskar Pfister: Psychoanalysis and Faith," in *Psychoanalytic Pioneers*, edited by Franz Alexander, Samuel Eisenstein, and Martin Grotjahn (New York, Basic Books, 1966), pp. 169–79.
2. Sigmund Freud, *Psychoanalysis and Faith: Dialogues with the Reverend Oskar Pfister*, edited by Heinrich Meng and Ernst L. Freud, translated by Eric Mosbacher (New York, Basic Books, 1963), p. 109.
3. See, for instance, Erik H. Erikson, *Gandhi's Truth: On the Origins of Militant Nonviolence* (New York, W.W. Norton, 1969); Erich Fromm, *Psychoanalysis and Religion* (New Haven, Conn., Yale University Press, 1950); W. W. Meissner, *Psychoanalysis and Religious Experience* (New Haven, Conn., Yale University Press, 1984).
4. "From the History of an Infantile Neurosis," *Standard Edition*, Vol. 17, pp. 114–15.
5. Paul Roazen, *Freud: Political and Social Thought*, third edition, with a new Introduction (New Brunswick, N.J., Transaction Publishers, 1999), pp. 101–10, 126; *The Letters of Sigmund Freud to Eduard Silberstein, 1871–81*, edited by Walter Boehlich, translated by A. J. Pomerans (Cambridge, Mass., Harvard University Press, 1990).
6. Roazen, *Political Theory and the Psychology of the Unconscious*, *op. cit.*, Part I, Ch. 2, pp. 28–48.
7. Oskar Pfister, "The Illusion of a Future: A Friendly Disagreement with Prof. Sigmund Freud," edited by Paul Roazen, *International Journal of Psychoanalysis*, Vol. 74 (1993), pp. 557–79.
8. Janet Malcolm, *In the Freud Archives* (New York, Alfred A. Knopf, 1983).
9. Roazen, *Encountering Freud*, *op. cit.*, pp. 48–51.
10. Jeffrey M. Masson, *The Assault on Truth: Freud's Suppression of the Seduction Theory* (New York, Farrar, Straus & Giroux, 1984).

11. Jeffrey M. Masson, *Final Analysis: The Making and Unmaking of a Psychoanalyst* (New York, Addison-Wesley, 1990).
12. Frederick Crews, *Out of My System: Psychoanalysis, Ideology, and Critical Method* (New York, Oxford University Press, 1975).
13. Masud Khan, *The Long Wait: And Other Psychoanalytic Narratives* (New York Summit Books, 1989).
14. *Ibid.*, p.4.
15. *Ibid.*, p. 9.
16. *Ibid.*, p. 47.
17. *Ibid.*, p. 54.
18. *Ibid.*, p. 60.
19. *Ibid.*, p. 62.
20. *Ibid.*, p. 64.
21. *Ibid.*, pp. 92–93.
22. *Ibid.*, p. 113
23. *Ibid.*, pp. 118, 123.
24. *Ibid.*, pp. 144, 150, 155.
25. *Ibid.*, pp. 196, 200.
26. Janet Malcolm, "Review of *The Long Wait*," *New York Times Book Review*, April 9, 1989, p. 25.
27. John Forrester, *Dispatches from the Freud Wars: Psychoanalysis and Its Passions* (Cambridge, Mass., Harvard University Press, 1997).
28. Gordon Warme, *The Psychotherapist: Use and Abuse of Psychological Influence* (Northvale, N.J., Aronson, 1997).
29. Margaret A. Hagen, *Whores of the Court: The Fraud of Psychiatric Testimony and the Rape of American Justice* (New York, Harper Collins, 1997).
30. Mikkel Borch-Jacobsen, *Remembering Anna O.: A Century of Mystification*, translated by Kirby Olson in collaboration with Xavier Callahan and the author (New York, Routledge, 1996).
31. Edward Dolnick, *Madness on the Couch: Blaming the Victim in the Heyday of Psychoanalysis* (New York, Simon & Schuster, 1998).
32. *Ibid.*, pp. 289, 294.

13

Sandor Rado

Sandor Rado (1890–1972) was one of the most brilliant of the early analysts, all of whom were by today's standards highly educated and cultured. In 1913 he became, with four others, a founding member of the Hungarian Psychoanalytic Society. He first met Freud before World War I, thanks to a letter of introduction from Rado's mentor in Budapest, Sandor Ferenczi, who, as we have seen, was once such a special favorite of Freud's. (Rado's first known letter to Ferenczi, dated July 23, 1911, is included here — thanks to the generosity of Dr. Judith Dupont — as an appendix at the end of this chapter.) Rado ultimately went on to become known as an outstanding theoretician in the movement, and in Europe he analyzed figures of the stature of Wilhelm Reich, Heinz Hartmann, and Otto Fenichel. Rado was not only the first director of the Institute of the New York Psychoanalytic Society, but after his falling-out with the orthodox leaders of that group he was the most important figure in setting up a Psychoanalytic Institute at Columbia University's medical school. Despite his break with the orthodox movement, he continued to attract a range of remarkable patients: people like the musician-composer Leonard Bernstein, the pediatrician Dr. Benjamin Spock, and the writer Mary McCarthy went to him as an analyst.

Professional fields are apt to have poor memories, so although the name of Sandor Rado was once famous within psychoanalysis, and he remains remembered by a certain select group of practitioners,[1] the educated general public has little basis for being aware of him today. It was my hope that the publication of a condensed version of Rado's interview for the Columbia Oral History project, along with the existing thirty-six letters from Freud to Rado, would by itself help to reestablish Rado's proper historical standing.[2] But the descendants of such mavericks are not apt to want to be reminded of their controversial origins. And so, just as the Washington Psychoanalytic Institute's great but troublesome Harry Stack Sullivan left younger analysts there unfortunately eager to "live down" the memory of their pioneering leader, so the Columbia Psychoanalytic group has not been eager to advertise its beginnings in one of American psychoanalysis's major splits.

Entirely aside from the desire of the psychoanalytic organization to bury one of the titanic conflicts that were once so prominently associated with Rado, reasonable explanations can also be found to account for the striking omission connected to his name within historiography. Following his schism from the New York Psychoanalytic Institute Rado authored a number of remarkable technical papers, yet towards the end of his life he was expressing himself within a specialized vocabulary which is unlikely to be accessible to many today.[3]

In contrast to the hermetic way in which he came to express his ideas, while he had been still writing as a member in good standing within orthodox psychoanalysis his articles from then remain readable now; some of his papers from the 1920s, on melancholia and drug addiction, for example, continue to seem outstanding. Freud's original terminology, which Rado then shared, has so succeeded in becoming popular with the contemporary intelligentsia that even such old essays by Rado can now be more or less readily understood. This has to be paradoxical, since what came to be Rado's attempt to replace Freud's metapsychological thinking with a new set of fundamental hypotheses led to such an idiosyncratic set of categories and formulations that these terminological innovations have now more or less fallen by the wayside. And this remains true, even though, as we shall see, many of his central criticisms of what once was the core of psychoanalytic orthodoxy have more or less been generally accepted today as valid.

As has happened before in the history of psychoanalysis, the ideas of even the most stridently "deviant" rebels could quietly get absorbed within today's accepted psychoanalytic thinking. Rado, as one of his organizationally loyal Hungarian compatriots explained to me in the mid–1960s, had "not been able to wait," and for that reason he ended up walking into the line of psychoanalytic "traitors" inaugurated by Adler and Jung. Like Melanie Klein, however, Rado remained an analyst in good standing, but, as we shall see, he failed to inspire disciples of his own to carry on the work he started with his name prominently associated with it.

When the New York Psychoanalytic Society was establishing in 1931 its first Training Institute, the local consensus was that Dr. A. A. Brill, an analyst who practiced in New York and was also one of Freud's first translators, would not be up to the job of creating a modern scientific center of learning and instruction. (Brill had raised the money for the Institute.) The Berlin Psychoanalytic Institute was then considered the most successful training facility, and Rado was a prominent teacher there. After Otto Rank, who had once been a great personal ally of Freud's, experienced his own falling out with the creator of psychoanalysis,[4] Freud appointed Rado to succeed Rank as editor of the German language journal the *Internationale Zeitschrift für Psychoanalyse*, then the most important international psychoanalytic publication, and Rado also became an editor of Freud's *Imago*. Later in 1926 Rado had edited two volumes of essays written specifically in honor of Freud's seventieth birthday. When Rado organized a famous symposium on the subject of lay analysis, he did not himself contribute, since he could not share Freud's own viewpoint and yet did not want to disagree with him publicly.

Rado felt that there had been a series of early sources of his difficulties, with Anna Freud in particular, whom Rado felt exaggerated her father's dislikes, which could, in any case, be pretty sharp and lasting. When Ferenczi died in 1933, Rado wrote an obituary of his old teacher which Anna considered too warm and appreciative of Ferenczi, who was then in Freud's bad graces. As we have seen, historically Ferenczi's name was to become a stalking horse for psychoanalytic liberalism. The pros and cons over Ferenczi tended to mirror the spectrum of psychoanalytic beliefs from the most liberal to the most conservative. To Rado, Ferenczi was the movement's poet, and even though Rado could not go along with many of Ferenczi's ideas, Rado had no use for the heresy-hunting which people like Jones had gone in for.

After Rado had moved to the States, he spent each of the next summers in Europe, visiting Freud every time, until in 1935 a central crisis finally arose between himself and Freud. Rado thought that the Viennese analysts around Freud constituted a palace guard of advisors, a "camarilla," and that they had long envied Rado's special position within the movement. Freud himself was known to have resented the way Rado had been successfully helping so many analysts to leave the European continent for the United States. In the long run, Rado's efforts helped psychoanalysis survive the damage that Hitlerism inflicted on Freud's movement. In the short run, however, Freud was blaming Rado for what he feared was the increasing isolation of psychoanalysis in Europe. Rado had opposed Freud's plan to build a new international institute in Vienna after Hitler had come to power in Germany; Freud allowed himself to entertain such an unrealistic project even though others assured him it was politically impractical.[5]

The turning point which took place between Freud and Rado in 1935 was occasioned by a critical review published in the *Zeitschrift* of one of Rado's monographs; it was written by Jeanne Lamp-de Grout, a wealthy Dutch analyst who was then a current analytic patient of Freud's.[6] The problem was that the negative review appeared to be published with Freud's tacit endorsement; Lampl-de Groot had expressed not only her own opinions but also critical comments raised at a meeting of the Vienna Psychoanalytic Society. Rado was deeply offended at what he considered the insult, and Rado never saw Freud again. One 1938 patient of Freud's reported in a diary that Freud had commented about analysts in the New World that "'The American group is largely Jewish, dominated by Rado . . . while the Americans' — meaning the Gentiles — 'do not seem much better.'"[7]

Rado continued as education director of the New York Psychoanalytic Institute for a total of ten years. But at the same time that he had run into trouble with Freud and prominent analysts in Vienna, he found himself being criticized on a different front by Karen Horney. She could not agree with many aspects of Rado's reasoning in one article; when she teased out from his thinking "the underlying premise that the awareness of the possibility of a major pleasure definitely destroys the enjoyment of an attainable pleasure that is considered inferior to it," she allowed herself to wax sarcastically:

> How does this assumption coincide with the data of everyday life? It would imply, for instance, that a man who thought Greta Garbo more attractive than other women, but had no chance of meeting her, would as a result of the "discovery" of her superior charms lose all pleasure in having relations with other women available to him. It would imply that one who is fond of mountains would find his pleasure in them utterly spoiled by imagining that a sea resort might offer a greater pleasure . . . The principle applied by Rado is certainly not the pleasure principle, but might better be called the greediness principle. . . . [8]

One can well imagine that Rado, who was present when Horney read her paper, was displeased. (He happened to love the seashore, and took special pleasure in good food.) However Rado and Horney were temporarily at odds, it was to be ironic that not long after Horney had been demoted from instructor to lecturer by the governing Education Committee of the New York Psychoanalytic Society, the occasion for her resigning with a few other analysts to set up a new Institute, Rado himself was deposed as educational director.

In 1944, just as Rado was about to conclude the negotiations to found the new Psychoanalytic Clinic at Columbia University's College of Physicians and Surgeons, he was thrown out of the New York Psychoanalytic Society's Institute as a training analyst for future candidates. Starting in the late 1930s Rado had been going off on a different tack, so that even before 1944 he was viewed as a psychoanalytic Benedict Arnold. Freud's expressed view that by 1938 Rado had in some way come to "dominate" any group of American analysts would have been an exaggeration of his power, although Rado was a remarkable teacher. Freud's distaste for all things connected to America was notorious, and he repeatedly thought that America — the most lucrative source of rich patients in Vienna — had been capable of seducing followers of his, such as Jung, Rank, and Ferenczi, into the land of psychoanalytic heresy.

In 1970 Herman Nunberg, who had remained a leading staunch orthodox analyst, referred to those who had supposedly abandoned psychoanalysis: "Rado had moved farther and farther away from psychoanalysis, had even given up its basic tenets and yet still called himself a psychoanalyst." Nunberg was specifically classing Rado with the more famous dissidents in psychoanalysis by referring to "what has amounted essentially to the abandonment of psychoanalysis (for example, Adler, Jung, Rado, etc.)"[9] Rado had looked to many as a "traitor" to "the cause" which Freud had championed, and could in that way be seen as following in the direct line of Adler, Jung, Rank, and Horney. Unlike with the other "dissidents," who chose to make their appeal to the general reading public, Rado wanted to go deeper into university medicine; he was seeking to get away from the orthodoxy and traditionalism that he felt had "cursed" psychoanalysis for too long.

Rado had been publicly put into the general bin of being a psychoanalytic heretic at the same time as he was organizing the Columbia Psychoanalytic Clinic, an institution which has survived and continues notably to function today. Rado had been from the outset of his career at the Berlin Psychoanalytic Institute in the 1920s especially concerned with establishing standards of education and training within the field. So even when he was becoming notorious as a "deviant" in Freud's movement, Rado was simultaneously successful in helping to bring psychoanalysis within university life, and therefore he raised the standards of research and practice in the field. Rado's commitment to science seemed to him to preclude his writing for the lay public.

As time went on Rado, like other so-called deviators in psychoanalysis, worked out new terms for old concepts, as he sought to express an individual point of view. Yet Rado was not some sort of isolated eccentric. For some years he was a member of the New York State Mental Hygiene Council, and both governors Averell Harriman and Nelson Rockefeller supported his work with grants from the New York state budget. Rado stayed on as director of the Center for Psychoanalytic Training and Research at Columbia University until 1956, and retired from Columbia in 1965 as required when he reached the age of sixty-five, after which he helped to create the New York School of Psychiatry at the State University of New York, where he was director for ten years. (That institution proved "relatively short-lived."[10])

It would be widely acknowledged among analytic professionals that Rado had once authored many classic papers within psychoanalysis, although it is more difficult to establish how after his falling out with the ranks of orthodox psychoanalysis his independent thinking led him to develop a theoretical system of his own. For example, he became opposed to the idea that the removing of repressions, and the emergence of buried memories, can be expected to have good therapeutic effects; and he thought that the deliberate provoking of transference was a clinical mistake, since it undermined the patient's capacity for autonomy and self-reliance. In addition, Rado was prescient enough to have emphasized the significance of the study of genetics, as well as biochemistry, for the future of psychoanalytic psychiatry. Further, Rado dissented from Freud's theory of bisexuality as well as Freud's orientation toward the drives. On all these points Rado was way ahead of his time, and today's analytic practitioners would have little difficulty agreeing with the substance of his early dissents (even if there would be only the rarest occasion for anyone to point out Rado's pioneering on these points).

Admittedly, Rado's later writings can be hard to follow. I have little doubt that if he had chosen to do so, he could have learned the talents that go with good journalism. From Rado's point of view, Horney, as well as Erich Fromm, had been immensely successful in this line of endeavor as popularizers. But Rado disdained what seemed to him too close to public relations, and put his faith instead in medical science. The future, he believed, would redeem him, even without his stooping, in his lights, to appeal to the public at large. He did help to see to it that the Association for Psychoanalytic Medicine got started, and he was also one of the founders of the eclectic American Academy of Psychoanalysis.

All the outstanding "dissidents" in the history of psychoanalysis have fared less well than the so-called mainstream in the field. But Jung and Lacan, whose students created organizations that by now are successful on a worldwide basis, were the two great exceptions to the marginalization that affected most of the various remaining minority voices. Freud was himself such a great writer that he was his own best spokesman, and he has succeeded against his contemporary opponents largely by virtue of his capacities to express himself clearly and persuasively. More literary critics have continued to be drawn to Freud's side of things than to any of the alternative rivals among psychologists, and these humanists have continued to be a potent source of Freud's continuing power. The irony is that some of Freud's relatively minor pupils are today better known, as they bask in Freud's own reflected glory, than a few of Freud's most brilliant critics. It therefore can often be hard to know where Freud was going wrong because of his capacity to make so plausible a case in his own behalf.

There has been such an explosion of interest in the whole history of psychoanalysis that Rado's current neglect becomes more noteworthy:

> It is remarkable that Rado has faded into near complete obscurity in both psychoanalytic theory and historiography. Rado's erasure from psychoanalytic history has been far more complete than that of his lifelong friend Ferenczi, or that of Adler, Rank, or Reich — all of whom have undergone (or are undergoing) subsequent reappraisals. Furthermore, Rado was consequential in terms of the interface be-

> tween psychiatry and psychoanalysis, in their theoretical, institutional, and political relationship to each other. He not only founded the first psychoanalytic center within the American Psychoanalytic Association that was part of a university and a department of psychiatry, but himself predicted some of the far-reaching consequences of the inadequate integration of psychoanalytic organizations into academic, medical and research institutions, resulting in the attenuation of both.[11]

Perhaps Rado's standing today says something in general about the poor state of how the psychiatric past gets recalled. Medical schools are traditionally focused on the practical problems associated with the training of fresh practitioners; so the history of medicine in general, of which psychiatry itself is of course only a part, gets little attention. One of the more fascinating passages in Rado's Columbia Oral History memoirs concern perhaps the most notable and influential figure in the history of twentieth century North American psychiatry — Johns Hopkins's Adolf Meyer. Yet Meyer, not a good writer, is not well known today.[12] I cannot ever forget a book review written by the justly celebrated literary critic Elizabeth Hardwick which once appeared in the *New York Review of Books*; she was talking about a biography of Zelda Fitzgerald, and mentioned in passing that Zelda's husband Scott had once taken Zelda in Switzerland to "a certain" Dr. Bleuler. Although Elizabeth Hardwick is one of the great American women of letters, and had once been married to Robert Lowell, a poet with his own psychiatric troubles, she did not need to know how Bleuler was one of the central figures of modern psychiatry. So if Rado has gotten the short end of the historical stick he is hardly alone.

The interviews which Bluma Swerdloff had the foresight to conduct with Rado for the Columbia Oral History Research Office made it easy to help rectify the scales in his behalf. She also interviewed a number of other leading psychoanalysts, and the full transcripts are on file at Columbia.[13] Yet when I read them through, the set with Rado stood forth and I thought cried out to be made into a book, which ultimately became *Heresy: Sandor Rado and the Psychoanalytic Movement.*[14]

It took remarkably little ingenuity to make Rado's interviews comprehensible to a general reader. Like Freud himself as Rado described him there, Rado was a spellbinder who spoke like a book. (One of Rado's youthful characteristics had been that he had a photographic memory; Ferenczi was described by Rado as "beside himself" when he realized that Rado could remember page numbers in books, and therefore exactly where Freud had said things.) Even the themes Rado dealt with in each of his interviews had a certain inherent coherence to them. I did have to cut redundancies from one interview to the next, which took place over a fairly extended period of time; I also had to reorganize everything into individual chapters, and I smoothed out the grammar. Repetitions were meaningful to me in underlining what Rado thought was most important, but they had to go for the sake of making up a published volume. Sometimes Rado made flip or excessively polemical judgments which I do not think he would want to stand the test of time, so I exercised my own judgment in omitting what I thought did not deserve to be preserved in public. (Originally Rado had marked certain passages of these interviews to be closed until later dates, but all such restrictions had long since expired by the time I got to my editorial job and everything he had to say could be freely examined. Still, Rado's initial hesitations about revealing certain points was in itself telling.) I would suggest that specialists might want to consult for themselves the original transcripts, which are readily available for inspection. I wish I could be clearer about my standards of selection from the whole manuscript that runs to some 317 typed pages, and got reduced down to 172 printed pages. I tried to include everything that I thought would be permanently interesting in what Rado had to say.

These Columbia interviews were given between 1963 and 1965. As it happens, I also, entirely on my own initiative, interviewed Rado twice in 1966 and 1967. Some of the same subjects came up, but different issues did as well. I used no tape recorder but relied on pen and paper, as well as my memory. I can never forget that at one critical point Rado ordered me not to write something down; although he was by then supposedly an established heretic, he still remained so imbued with the traditionalistic ethos of early psychoanalysis that he had to mind ever being accused of disloyalty and indiscretion even then. (He also refused to reveal what he was also proud of having understood, based on his reading of Freud's *The Interpretation of Dreams*, about Freud's dream life.) It was my practice always to rewrite and amend my notes after all my interviews, with Rado as well as other early psychoanalysts, so his temporarily losing control while I interviewed him only meant that that particular issue, connected as it happened with his version of Freud's daughter Anna (and her rivalry with other female pupils of Freud's), was to be indelibly embedded in my mind.

Blum Swerdloff did an excellent job of getting Rado going with his reminiscences, and her particular set of questions elicited the material that eventually appeared in the transcripts. Inevitably there are also gaps that remain. Rado had had an early wife who had been personally analyzed by Freud during World War I, but that matter never came up in the interviews. (Patients Freud had analyzed came up in my own interviews with Rado.) Rado was not pressed by Swerdloff on the origins of the difficulties between Freud and Ferenczi, although Rado touched on what had happened. Nor did Jones's biased treatment of Ferenczi get challenged in these pages.[15] It was my own experience that almost any substantial query set Rado off on a unusually sequential set of comments. That he had his own prejudices and blind spots would have to be inevitable, and it should go without saying that nobody should assume more than that *Heresy* represents Rado's side of the story. He alluded there to letters from Freud to him, written in an irritable mood, that no longer seem to survive; if Rado destroyed them, as others similarly situated may have, we are lucky that Rado saved as much as he did. Rado's other correspondences, and what one would expect to be his vast files, have simply vanished. (Rado had Alzheimer's disease at the end of his life, and his family destroyed his appointment books.)

In my opinion the informality of the presentation of Swerdloff's interviews in *Heresy* has something unique of its own to teach. Here we have Rado talking off the top of his head; that he had a powerful mind was evident to anyone who knew him. Freud, and before him Ferenczi, were both quick to spot Rado's many talents. All the extant letters from Freud to Rado were included there; they are mainly concerned with business matters associated with the publication of the *Zeitschrift* and are testimony to Rado's standing in Freud's world. Rado told me how quietly proud he was of Freud's 1927 words: "you who are perhaps the one among us who does the most work for the common good. . . . " Another has to be telling about what in contrast Freud thought of his American following: "The Americans transfer the democratic principle from politics into science. Everyone has to be president [of a psychoanalytic society] once, no one may remain president, no one may distinguish himself from the others, and thus they all learn and produce nothing, one and all."[16] Rado took a different tack toward the States, even if it helped cost him Freud's support.

While Rado's historical role has been generally neglected, that does not mean that we now have to endorse everything he believed or had to say. For example, I think that he underestimated Freud's positive contributions to the humanities, and Rado was too intolerant of the significance of psychoanalysis for philosophy and the social sciences. At the same time I think Rado had some telling points to make about where Freud had gone wrong. And within psychiatry itself, Rado may well turn out to have been prophetic about the future of biology. It is all too easy for those of us in the cultural sciences to appreciate the part society plays in human dilemmas. No one reading the pages of *Heresy*, which help recreate the different world in which Rado grew up, can fail to appreciate just how sophisticated a European man of letters he was. At the same time developments within psychiatry have confirmed Rado's prescient convictions about the future importance of genetics and biology for psychiatric knowledge.

Although Lacan (who started off in psychiatry and moved toward the cultural sciences) was to develop in a very different direction from Rado, Lacan like Rado proceeded under the banner of a "return" to Freud. Melanie

Klein too, in her own separate sort of thinking in Britain, liked to think of herself as being more Freudian than Freud. Wilhelm Reich also claimed to be recovering parts of Freudian thinking, connected to the primacy of instinctual life, that Freud had unnecessarily jettisoned. And so Lacan, Klein, Reich, and Rado repeatedly were to single out as of preeminent status aspects of Freud's early work which they each themselves wanted to stress in an effort to stick to some special starting point in Freud.

Psychoanalysis remains a curious field in which individual thinkers can remain strikingly isolated from one another. Rado belonged to the radical Left within the history of psychoanalysis, but it has remained a fragmented tradition of so-called dissenters. Although Rado was for a time allied at Columbia with New York City's original and prolific Abram Kardiner, and Rado's work on therapy was also similar in many ways to the ideas of his fellow-Hungarian Franz Alexander, these critics of traditionalism have rarely been able to establish any coherent line of intellectual descent. Horney wrote harshly about Rado, as we have seen, and Alexander wrote critically about Horney; Erich Fromm even attacked Rank's ideas as sounding fascistic. (In fact, Rank's concept of "will" was central to his thinking, but quite unlike anything politically authoritarian.) None of these people on the psychoanalytic Left would have dreamt of citing approvingly any of the earlier so-called heretics in psychoanalysis, such as Adler or Jung. Even though these nonconformists were the ones with the most original ideas, their position has not so far won them adequate recognition within intellectual history.

I have argued that it is so hard to become well educated in the real story of psychoanalysis because of the sectarianism that has over the years afflicted the movement. Those who founded no schools of followers, whatever the substantive merits of their contributions, are likely to be even more neglected than even Rado. So it has been the most gentle ones who have tended to be neglected. Rado knew how to fight, and although he was successful in institutionalizing his ideas, succeeding generations who belonged to the organizations he had created found it more opportune to join up with the "mainstream" itself. Splinter tendencies have tended to be long-run failures, even though at the time they first arose they may have established certain key principles. There has been a realistic fear of getting "lost" apart from the ongoing psychoanalytic "movement" as a whole. Some of today's most persuasive critics of Freud are now only reinventing concepts that were first advanced many years ago but whose origins have been forgotten.

Just as too few people among our contemporaries seem able to be open minded about appreciating both Freud's accomplishments as well as his limitations, so it is hard for practitioners to be sensitive to both the strictly psychological side of the interaction between patients and therapists as well as to the fundamental biochemical nature of the physiology of our being.

Different schools of psychotherapeutic thought are apt to live existences independently of each other, and there seems little support for encouraging a tolerant understanding of contrasting points of view. Rival perspectives in this whole area tend to be held with an uncharitable and a religiously intolerant kind of fervor; and catholicity of understanding is rare.

For example, my own limited perspective necessarily had to play its part in shaping the narrative that appeared in *Heresy*. I should add that Rado did read the original transcripts through and made minor corrections and emendations. These were sometimes telling and informative, as well as what he chose to leave alone. What got put into *Heresy* was taken from a transcript of the written word; yet I hope it will be agreed that that book can add some rare insight into the story of the growth of Freud's school, and that Rado's voice is acknowledged as one that is still deserving of being heard. Intellectual history should consist of a set of alternative points of view which do not necessarily lead in a unilinear direction, but still cross-checking is something that ideally should take place.

Appendix

Sandor Rado's first letter (from Bonn, Germany) to Sandor Ferenczi, July 23, 1911. Rado was, at the age of twenty-one, about to finish his political science degree, although already enrolled as a medical student. This letter illustrates what a prodigy he was.

Highly honored Herr Doctor,

As I was setting out to write to you, I felt a remarkable urge to use the German language. Repeatedly unsuccessful attempts at bringing forth so much as one single Hungarian sentence, force me to do justice to this interesting stirring of desire, especially since I would like to postpone its analytic revelation on account of time considerations. If this should bring about flagrant violations of your feeling for the language, I ask your kind forbearance — in philological matters I will be an anti-talent all my life.

The short summer semester is already nearing its end, without my having managed to cope with all the material I had planned to. Nevertheless I believe I may assign a considerable value to this excursion into natural sciences, for it has given my whole thinking enormously deeper and firmer foundations.

The abundance of new facts and thoughts has first of all, increased in an almost unbearable manner the need for a dynamic theory of the whole of mental life, in accord with the teachings of Pikler and Freud. Thus all my striving is directed towards the construction of such a "synthesis," although the latter would possibly turn out to be quite incomplete as a consequence of my inadequate knowledge of natural science. Yet I cannot help doing it; a hypothesis, however primitive, even if for my own use only, about the nature and the biological functions of consciousness (the discovery of which Pikler was not capable of at all); a revision of Pikler's doctrine of the material correlate of pleasure and pain and the purposeful selection of all movements — this I must bring about not only as the longed-for intellectual satisfaction, but also as the fundamental condition of all future intellectual activity.

Not without melancholy I have just read Rosenstein's article in the *Zentralblatt* — it is a highly successful treatise, but contains not a single thought that I have not from time to time expressed in my circle of friends, only that it didn't get written down. The credit must remain his alone for having first drawn the psychoanalysts' attention to the identity in character of the two doctrines; it is a pity that his correct explanations are lacking that very power of inmost conviction which permeates the writings of Pikler and the psychoanalytic authors.

Of course, my efforts have led to results far beyond what is shown in this sketch — after all, it was essentially further goals that I had set myself. If I should succeed in bringing my attempt to a conclusion, it will in any case have to pass your esteemed criticism.

On August 1st I unfortunately have to travel home, and until *Rigorosen* are finished, I will not be able to think about any other work. My father has made the doctorate the *sine qua non* of everything further, and I must admit he's right.

In reading Harnik's report on suicide etc. (in the 20th . . .) I must regret that I have no detailed orientation in the matter, and especially I have not read Adler's study about organ inferiority. But I believe that in the analytic literature known to me I have not found any indication at all of a quite obvious fact which seems especially important in this connection. (If there should already exist such trains of thought, please do not take the following remarks amiss.)

The appropriate/purposeful selection of consciousness-contents, present and capable of being present, as they are carried out by means of forgetting and repression (in the negative sense, through action, and positively, through illusion) is an indispensable condition of life. But a failure of this function is possible not only in the sense that we forget and repress more than is normally necessary (or we do this in an incomplete way, with symptom-substitution), but also in the other direction, i.e. that we are quite incapable of forgetting and repressing in the necessary degree (and also do not manage to make any symptom-substitution).

If hereby consciousness-contents with an accent of reluctance are constantly brought into actuality (even if these are in fact true, such as: we have to die; all life on earth will one day be extinguished, etc.), and if we further do not succeed in the elimination of the inferior conflicting drives (not even in the form of hysteria and neurosis), this must bring about a life-weariness, and, depending on its intensity, lead to melancholy, criminality — suicide.

In this, I believe, the mechanism of these phenomena should be discerned, and only after we have recalled these should we proceed to the determination of those motives which have as their consequence a process of more or less forgetting and repressing. Also, from this insight one immediately arrives at fruitful suppositions concerning these motives.

In any case, therapy or prevention in these cases — in whatever way, perhaps through analysis and overcoming of the conflicting consciousness-capability of various complexes in various kinds of criminals, — this is an area which I would like to investigate in the future with my modest capabilities.

Unfortunately there has not yet been any opportunity here for practical analysis. On the other hand, the analysis of my own dreams and neurotic phenomena had brought to light some quite striking childhood memories from my 4th to 6th years of life, and thus had led to the deepest crises of my former breathing difficulties. The mechanism of the origin and development of this neurosis is of such astounding beauty that it should convince and convert even non-believers. On the occasion of our next personal meeting, I will be so bold as to submit this analysis to your highly valued criticism: to communicate it in writing would take too much room and space.

While leafing through "Psychopathology etc." I was recently reminded by the "Déjà vu" phenomenon, of a similar experience in Budapest which provides, besides the confirmation of the information given by you about the origin of night-time dreams, the most cogent proof of Freud's views, and what is more, of the whole of Piklerian psychology. Remarkably, I missed a chance to tell you about this matter back in Budapest, so here I would like to make up for a lost opportunity.

In my father's business, there was a Herr B who was employed as a bookkeeper from my fourth to fourteenth year (1894–1904), he was a poor beggar and unlearned young fellow who had been taken in only out of sympathy, and had totally to thank my father for his education and existence. After a few years the man, who had originally been competent and hard-working, began to become lazy and useless, but because of my father's kindness he was able for the time being to keep his position. But finally, dishonest acts began to occur — he got his fingers into the cash. He was quickly and unceremoniously thrown out.

In the years that followed he was a constant figure of my dreams, of which of course I had no understanding at the time. Now I can state that he was an extremely important personality of my childhood years, since it was he that kept supplying me with most precious objects of that period: pencil, ruler, etc., and was always striving to bring me joys in other ways as well. In the meantime I had not seen him.

Now, in the middle of December, he approaches me on the street in Budapest. Dirty, tattered, with all the marks of moral and financial depravity. Deeply moved, I engage him in conversation, but he doesn't recognize me. Then, when I tell him who I am, he cries out in astonishment: "*Du bist de Sany*!" You (using the familiar form) are Sanyi!" (He had never used the familiar form with me) — and he is in the utmost embarrassment. Then, stuttering somewhat, he says: "That story back then — that wasn't quite how it was — I have something more to tell you about it" — but he has no address to give me, and so we part until the next chance meeting.

I had violent feelings of sympathy for the poor wretch, and felt a grudge toward my father for his fate, who had treated him so unceremoniously back then. I thought about the inhumanity of letting him sink so low, and I decided as best I could to let my father know about the encounter; perhaps something could be done.

The next day I wrote home, but in the meantime I had forgotten without a trace the whole stormy incident, as well as my resolution.

Our paths crossed again in about two weeks. At the sight of him, I felt surprise; the feel of the unexpected expresses itself in the thought: "What, is this man still here, in this condition?" — shortly after, however, I muse to myself, much as one catches oneself at fantasies: — "This though was quite senseless, and reasonably, I could not have expected anything but what reality presented me with." And yet — I had almost believed that he was again employed at our place in Kisvarda. A memory which suddenly surfaced lays the foundation for this expectation: the scene is hovering in plastic form before my eyes, and I see him again seated at his old desk. At the old desk, in the old office, from which we had moved away six years earlier, — and so I am beginning to reject the stubborn memory as an illusion, when suddenly the thought flashes that it has its origin in a dream situation.

After this idea, a whole mass of memories comes crashing in, and all at once everything become understandable and clear:

In the night following the day of our first encounter I had a dream of thoroughly infantile character. Among other things I saw B in a situation which fulfilled all my wishes: in his old place, clean-shaven, in an "elegant" scottish-plaid suit. Thus, my expectation rested upon this dream.

It is clear that this unreal satisfaction of a wish, secured by quick repression, was brought about by a conflict with powerful needs. Piklerian psychology furnishes a profound understanding of this process:

Unreal experiences (dream, hallucination, sometimes daydream, etc.) leave behind the *same* dynamically effective expectations of certainty, as the normal, real, experiences of reality. We only come to a realization of their unreality through the experience of the contrasting reality, the expectation of reality which corresponds to them is conquered only by the contrasting expectation of certainty which has its origin in reality. When, awakened from my sleep, I remember my dream, the expectations of certainty created by the dream — dynamically effective forces directed toward the future — are conquered by the experience of the opposing reality, and these expectations of certainty, originating in the experience of reality, will pass over into a "constant phenomenal stock of expectation." But if the dream is forgotten, repressed, i.e. held in that deeper mental channel whose experiences are beyond comparison with the higher consciousness — (obviously, mutual influence can only take place between conscious experiences or those that have become conscious.) — thus the expectations of reality which correspond to its content pass into a constant phenomenal stock of expectation, and represent, although they have originated and *remained* unconscious (secured against conquest), the same expectations, directed toward the future, the same constantly (unconsciously) effective forces as those that come from real and conscious experiences. Our "constant phenomenal stock of expectation," as Pikler calls the mentally effective forces, including the unconscious ones, must thus contain an enormous mass of expectations of certainty coming from unreal experiences.

Only in this way is it comprehensible and possible that the "unconscious" is such a powerful and dangerous factor of our psyche. Dangerous: the unconsciously arising and repressed "expectations of certainty" are withdrawn from all refutation (which can only take place in consciousness), and yet they are every bit as effective as those forces which come from consciousness. It is obvious that everything which we call mood, feeling, hunch, and moods which are incomprehensible to the conscious, are fragments of *unconscious* "expectations of certainty" which have been released from repression and made their way into consciousness.

In the case above, I was running around with the unconscious, victorious expectation of certainty, the thought that B was fully taken care of: I experienced the opposing reality as a "surprise" (compare Pikler), and I conquered and supplanted the previous, opposing expectation of certainty, which on this occasion had become conscious, with the expectation of certainty which corresponded with this experience.

In all cases where we make a selection between opposing "wants" in favor of the more valuable — and this is the case without interruption — the inferior one is satisfied in an unreal manner instead of with action. The "protection" of this satisfaction is repression whose depth is determined by the value-factor. However, all this, which we dispose of in an "unreal" manner, figures in our psyche in exactly the same way, with the same power of expectation directed toward the future, as if we had acted in a real manner. Only in this way is it possible to fob off desires in this manner, and comprehensible how our consciousness is determined so tremendously (and so disguisedly) from the direction of the unconscious.

It appears as one of the most beautiful and fruitful tasks, to create the dynamic — psychological basis, in Pikler's sense, for the facts of the unconscious (the dream) as found by Analysis.

To complete the above analysis, I would like to mention the reasons that caused the elimination of the B matter.

At the time, I was just about to make greater demands of my father. In the interest of his consenting to my medical studies, an analytic cure with you, the payment of a soon-to-be-expected bookseller's bill, the prevention of the possibility of my failing my dreaded upcoming examinations, as well as many other matters — I was very eager to keep my father in the best possible mood by sending him the right kind of letters. The planned communication would have (for all his well-known goodness of heart), provoked in him self-reproach, but in the final instance it would have turned his mind against me. Even though this collision escaped me in the excitement produced by the encounter (the welling-up of the infantile affects, etc.), my more calm and collected unconscious knew how to prevent the disaster.

Furthermore it is clear why I have always forgotten to tell you about this matter. I was not able to get everything from my father at that time, among other things the analytic cure had to be dropped. Thus my neuroses, useful to me as self-reproach, put up resistance against the communication of this matter, which was connected with the dropping of the cure, and only now, after I had reported to you the above about the successful analysis of my last symptom, it "strangely" occurred to me to communicate this matter to you.

Even if I hope that my primitive account and my use of German language (which has in the meantime been analyzed) have not made my report totally unbearable to you, nevertheless I would like to beg your pardon if I have perhaps misused your kind invitation by making a so much larger claim on your time and patience.

I also have the mitigating hope that you will receive this letter forwarded to you in your summer vacation.

Yours faithfully you obedient servant,

Alexander Rado[17]

Notes

1. See Franz Alexander, "Sandor Rado: The Adaptational Theory," in *Psychoanalytic Pioneers*, edited by Alexander, Eisenstein, and Grotjahn, *op. cit.*, pp. 240–48; Franz Alexander and Sheldon Selesnick, *The History of Psychiatry* (New York, Harper & Row, 1966), pp. 327–29; *Bulletin of the Association for Psychoanalytic Medicine*, Vol. 12 (Feb. 1973); Howard Davidman, "The Contributions of Sandor Rado to Psychodynamic Science," *Science and Psychoanalysis*, Vol. 7 (New York, Grune & Stratton, 1964), pp. 17–38; David Forrest, "Sandor Rado's Contribution: A Poll," *Academy Forum*, Vol. 32, No. 1 (Spring 1988), pp. 10–12; John Weber, "Sandor Rado," *International Encyclopedia of Psychiatry. Psychoanalysis, and Neurology* (New York, Aesculapius, 1977), pp. 355–56; Craig Tomlinson, "Sandor Rado and Adolf Meyer: A Nodal Point in American Psychiatry and Psychoanalysis," *International Journal of Psychoanalysis*, Vol. 77 (1996), pp. 963–82. See also Rosalind Baker Wilson, *Near The Magician: A Memoir of My Father, Edmund Wilson* (N.Y., Grove Weidenfeld, 1989), pp. 102–109.
2. Paul Roazen and Bluma Swerdloff, *Heresy: Sandor Rado and the Psychoanalytic Movement* (Northvale, N.J., Aronson, 1995).
3. See Sandor Rado, *Psychoanalysis of Behavior — The Collected Papers*, Vols. I & II (New York, Grune & Stratton, 1956–62); Sandor Rado, *Adaptational Psychodynamics: Motivation and Control*, edited by Jean Jameson and Henrietta Klein (New York, Science House, 1969).
4. Roazen, *Freud and His Followers*, *op. cit.*, Part VIII.
5. Anna Freud would seem to have echoed her father's hopes. See Young-Bruehl, Anna *Freud*, *op. cit.*, pp. 200, 277.
6. Roazen, *Freud and His Followers*, *op. cit.*, pp. 507–09; Roazen, *Helene Deutsch*, *op. cit.*, pp. 281–84.
7. Smiley Blanton, *Diary of My Analysis with Sigmund Freud* (New York, Hawthorn Books, 1971), p. 117.
8. I am indebted to Professor Bernard Paris for bringing this passage to my attention. See Karen Horney, *Feminine Psychology*, edited by Harold Kelman (New York, W. W. Norton, 1967), p. 219.
9. Herman Nunberg, *Memoirs: Recollections, Ideas, Reflections* (New York, The Psychoanalytic Research and Development Fund, 1969), p. 46.
10. Tomlinson, "Sandor Rado and Adolf Meyer," *op. cit.*, p. 964.
11. *Ibid.*
12. Roazen and Swerdloff, *Heresy*, *op. cit.*: Ch. 13; Paul Roazen, *Canada's King: An Essay in Political Psychology* (Oakville, Ontario, Mosaic Press, 1998), Ch. 2, pp. 21–40; Tomlinson, "Sandor Rado and Adolf Meyer," *op. cit.*
13. See Bluma Swerdloff, "A Historical Portrait of Sandor Rado," *Bulletin of the Association for Psychoanalytic Medicine*, Vol. 25 (Spring-Summer 1986), pp. 118–25; Bluma Swerdloff, "Oral History Among Psychoanalysts — A Personal Experience," *Bulletin of the Association for Psychoanalytic Medicine*, Vol. 19 (Jan. 1980), pp. 44–49.
14. Roazen and Swerdloff, *Heresy*, *op. cit.*
15. Roazen, *Freud and His Followers*, *op. cit.*, pp. 363–71.
16. Roazen and Swerdloff, *Heresy*, *op. cit.*, pp. 162, 156.
17. I am grateful for Tom Taylor's translation.

Conclusions

A Plea for Toleration and the Future

The history of psychoanalysis is so full of acrimony that it seems to some outsiders that nothing connected with this field can be held to be securely established. My own belief, however, is that those disputes can also be seen as a sign of vitality. What has held my interest in this subject over the last four decades has been precisely the significance of the contests between rival points of view. Although it has been tempting to reduce differences of psychoanalytic opinion down simply to questions of clashes between personalities, as well as the mundane organizational desires to promote power and influence, I do believe that one of the most enduringly important features to psychoanalysis's controversies is the extent to which they embody rival ideas of how the good life should be led. Moral and ethical convictions underlie almost every aspect of the world of psychoanalysis.

Freud at times had liked to think he had created a neutral science, and that the subject of philosophy was alien to what he had attempted to accomplish. But, as I mentioned in the preface, right from the outset of the pre-World War I difficulties, for instance with Adler, Adler's socialist convictions helped drive him into being publicly repudiated by Freud; Adler proceeded to set up his own school of thought. And Jung, a psychiatrist who was the son of a Protestant minister, took different views of religion and therapy from those of Freud. As Freud denounced Adler and Jung he often invoked clinical categories of psychopathology to explain their "deviations," but such name-calling should not obscure the extent to which these earliest "heretics" were bent on promoting world views and values different than those of Freud himself.

I have begun with these preliminary remarks in order to set the stage for the problem of evaluating, for example, ego psychology as opposed to the ideas of Lacan. There are so many myths about ego psychology in France —

one of the liveliest centers of psychoanalysis today — that it is hard to know where to begin in clearing up all the confusion. Although I do not think anyone has dared yet to put the following point in print in connection with this particular controversy, one has to deal first of all with the problem of anti-Americanism. The twentieth century witnessed an unprecedented rise in America's political power, at the same time that the role of the French, as well as the British, has dwindled. Such a shift of political fortunes is bound to be accompanied by cultural influences as well, and on both counts one can expect that bitter resentments will be left in its wake. While Americans felt reluctantly forced into European and then world affairs, it has not been hard for the beneficiaries of America's new imperial position to feel resentful of their dependent need for military American help, which has also extended to cultural matters as well.

In France, the situation has been complicated by the extent to which psychoanalysis has been of concern mainly to the traditional political Left. It can be truly scandalous to look closely at some of the past ideological commitments of France's greatest intellectuals. A wonderful writer like Jean-Paul Sartre allowed himself to utter political nonsense that one does not even want to look up.[1] Dictators like Stalin and Mao attracted the support of an appallingly large array of French thinkers. The collapse of the Soviet Empire, leaving the United States the undisputed world giant, has only fueled the anger of many French intellectuals against the increasing influence of America; and the decline of Marxism has helped promote the cause of psychoanalysis. Such deep-seated emotions as anti-Americanism are of course ambivalent, and get accompanied by feelings of admiration, even if these positive views are less likely to be openly expressed. As Lacan's ideas have spread outside France itself, these particular considerations should no longer be so important; but in any system of ideas the founding legends attract a life of their own, and it would be impossible to divorce Lacan from French intellectual currents as a whole.

One way of getting through to the roots of the problem of ego psychology in the context of the French intelligentsia is to question just exactly whose form of ego-psychology we are talking about. Is it that of Freud, or of the neglected Viennese Paul Federn?[2] Are we dealing with the work of Anna Freud, or Heinz Hartmann, or Erik Erikson? There is a surprising degree of differences between these various proponents of ego psychology, even though they can be lumped together for the sake of polemical purposes.

Lacan's success in establishing psychoanalysis in France came relatively late in terms of twentieth-century intellectual life. As in everything connected with analysis, the personal element plays an inevitable part. As we have discussed, Lacan had been analyzed by Rudolph Loewenstein, and their relationship remained at best an ambivalent one. In the French literature on

Lacan, it is often stated that Loewenstein is considered one of the founders of ego psychology. In fact, Loewenstein has to be ranked, as I have already indicated, one of the minor figures in the development of psychoanalytic thinking, even though, along with Ernst Kris, Loewenstein did co-author some once famous papers with Hartmann.

As we have seen, Lacan liked to think, along with such different figures as Klein, Reich, and Rado, that he had accomplished a reversion to the so-called true Freud. (In different ways, Erich Fromm and Erikson also maintained their utter faithfulness to Freud's basic intentions.) But it has to be awkward for Lacan's position that it was Freud who initiated the movement of thought known as ego psychology, even though Freud admitted he could not follow the reasoning of another pioneering ego psychologist, Federn. Anna Freud was responsible for giving ego psychology a boost, in her *The Ego and the Mechanisms of Defense,*[3] even though what she had in mind was different from what later flourished in America. (In a book review of that 1936 text, Ernst Kris had no doubt that "many well-known critics" of psychoanalysis would now find that it was "becoming Adlerian."[4] Freud had reproached Adler for extending psychology beyond psychopathology to cover normality as well.) We have seen how since Anna Freud led the effort to exclude Lacan from membership in the International Psychoanalytic Association (IPA); by not allowing him to continue to train if he stayed in, her ideas became a ready target in France. In my own view, Anna Freud's influence, much greater in the United States than in Britain, has not received enough critical examination in the States. Her ideas about continuity and child custody, worked out with allies at the Yale Law School, have become too readily a part of North American legal thinking. So it can be gratifying to find her work dissected and contested in France, while in America she seemed to reign unquestioningly by virtue of being Freud's daughter.

Although Freud's concept of the death instinct has attracted a great deal of attention in France, elsewhere it never gained the support of more than a small handful of clinicians. Ego psychology itself arose out of the need to try to get some sound horse-sense into the practice of analysis. A notion like that of a "negative therapeutic reaction," put forward by Freud to account for clinical failure, was I think a dangerous way of denying the analyst's responsibility for what might have gone wrong in the treatment situation. Freud was an immensely hard-working clinician, even if his real practices do not get adequately reflected in the rules he initiated for beginners. He always wanted therapeutic success, no matter what he wrote about psychoanalysis as a science and the dangers of therapeutic fervor. Ego psychology was designed not just for theoretical neatness, but to promote better clinical results.

An anecdote can underline the contrast between the Old World culture and that of the New: I once invited a sophisticated French analyst to present a paper at my local psychoanalytic institute. She was an embodiment of the best of continental culture, and at one point in her talk happened to mention the critical matter of tact. I felt mortified when a candidate in training put up his hand to ask the question: "What is tact?" To have raised such a point meant that he had missed the essence of the model before him that the Parisian had presented, and also had betrayed how callously crude North American practice can be.

This same French analyst once said to me how "indiscreet" her own consulting room was. It was filled with lovely artifacts from her native land, and also gave away her scholarly inclinations. I replied to her that I did not think there was anything at all wrong with her beautiful consulting room, and that it is good for patients to have the support of the analyst's reality. She then told me that although she liked one particular American analyst, she could not fathom how he could see patients in his own consulting room, which evidently had only one plant and a picture or two. To her that was a barren context in which to try to help people.

No concepts can by themselves have enough life in them to counteract the influence of the general national culture on how analyses are conducted. Erikson's ideas about ego psychology, for example, were designed to counteract the negativism that can be detected in Freud's writings. As we saw, one of his most famous clinical papers was a reanalysis of Freud's Irma Dream, in ways for example which show I think the influence of Jungian ideas on Erikson. Lacan referred to this particular paper of Erikson's, yet Erikson has never made much of an impact in France, in part because of the gently evasive way he had of expressing himself. Lacan is reliably said to have considered Erikson the most dangerous, because the best, of the ego psychologists.

Erikson and Hartmann had entirely different ways of expressing themselves. Hartmann sought logical precision and theoretical structure, while Erikson retained his artistic commitment to a more elusive way of expressing himself. We ought not, Erikson insisted, to assess someone only in terms of symptoms, or of what has been denied or cut off, but rather Erikson proposed to look at people in terms of how many contradictions and tensions are capable of being unified constructively. The ego was meant by Erikson to be not only a key agent of inner integration, but a means by which people draw support from social institutions, like religion for example. Erikson's version of ego psychology tried to highlight the positive. Anna Freud expressed her own reservations about the work of her former student by saying that she found much of Erikson's writings incomprehensible, exactly the same way Freud would describe work which he disliked.

There is little doubt in my mind that Erikson did, in fact, wind up in a generally conservative position; his occasional social and political comments betray the extent to which he sought social acceptance for himself and psychoanalysis, even if it meant at times advocating conformism. But such a weakness, which would be eagerly seized upon by followers of Lacan, cannot justify leaving intact the sometimes shocking abuses of power implicit within old-fashioned analytic therapy.

In the mid–1960s, I interviewed a famous Kleinian analyst in London. When I cautiously asked what could justify her proposal that all analyses should last, as a matter of principle, for ten years, the answer I got was one word: "research." A genuine side of Freud got reflected in what I regard as a clinician's hubris. The founder of psychoanalysis did aim to overturn many elements of traditional Western culture, including Christianity. And his moral challenges have been one of the sources of his cultural successes. But to treat patients as guinea pigs is objectionable to me. And for this same Kleinian analyst to throw at a mother an outrageous demand that a woman move her family for the sake of learning what the analyst thought about her young child does not seem to me an attractive aspect of Freud's legacy. Yet when I once told this story about early Kleinian intransigence to a prominent Lacanian in Paris, he agreed with the suggested Kleinian clinical approach. An analysis should be, he held, a serious human disruption. In this case, however, it was the mother and the rest of the family who were being threatened with being unsettled. (I have sometimes speculated about the bases for the impact of Klein in France.)

Now Lacan not only established psychoanalysis within the heart of French intellectual life, but he brought together philosophizing and analyzing in a way which represents, I think, a genuine return to one of the best parts of Freud's original intentions. He may have disdained formal philosophy, although he studied it as a young man, but he appreciated it when his followers showed signs of broad cultural interests. I have said that we can find in Paris today analysts who are cultivated in a way reminiscent of the early Freudians. But how can patients be protected from the human propensity for cruelty, if not sadism? Ego psychology, as represented by Federn and Erikson, was designed to help cushion the impact of a fallible analyst on weak and suggestible patients. As one famous French analyst once put it to me, if you hit patients over the head (metaphorically) they are likely to respond with a thank you. But that is testimony to the almost infinite human propensity for credulity and masochism.

Ego psychology is not another name for egotism, although I have encountered people in France who seem to think that ego psychology is a way of promoting self-involvement if not selfishness. A successful analysis, I think, has to involve implicit human supportiveness by the therapist. This can be accomplished by a wide variety of means, like Freud's hand-shaking before and after analytic hours, or Lacan's own deep cultural erudition. A reference to a philosopher, or even a book, can help bridge the inevitable gulf between patient and analyst. A patient's problems may well be encapsulated within his ego, and Freud did expect that people overcome their dilemmas. Change is indeed likely to be painful, but that does not mean that the analyst is justified in maximizing suffering.

At his best, Freud knew that the analyst must accept inevitable human limitations. As Helene Deutsch once put it to me, analysis should teach people where to compromise. Such a humble principle is safer than the utopianism exemplified in some of Freud's messianic disciples. Although I have singled out one British Kleinian as a frightening example of how much untrammeled power an analyst can try to wield, there is a tradition within Freud's thinking that supports such intrusiveness.

Notable weaknesses are not hard to spot in each different strand in psychoanalytic thinking; within ego psychology, for example, Hartmann did not choose to illustrate his reasoning with clinical examples. His work has not been thriving in North America since his death[5]; instead, the movements of self-psychology and object relations have been in the vanguard of progressiveness within analysis. But one of the worst aspects of sectarianism in psychoanalysis is that the wheel seems constantly to be reinvented. Jung made many sound clinical points, although it would be heresy to cite him in many analytic publications.[6] And I am told that too many references to Lacan in a clinical paper would lead to rejection by the most prestigious American analytic journals.

Lacan is only the most recent of the great heretics of analysis, and in some sense that has to be considered a real achievement on his part. He found himself as a Catholic excommunicated from a Jewish church, and any such fate has to be painful to endure. His originality is unquestionable, although it is not necessary to endorse either all his ideas or his every clinical recommendation. Just as Lacan should be of interest to intellectual historians, so should ego psychology itself be a fascinating subject. I am not proposing the jejune idea that there is a bit of truth in everything, or that what is needed now is some artificial rapprochement between Lacan and ego psychology.

Although it may not be evident on the surface, and some of Lacan's atheistic followers would deny it, I have found in his work an eloquent restatement of some fundamental Catholic teachings. As I have discussed earlier, when I interviewed Lacan's brother, a Benedictine monk who was familiar with all Lacan's ideas, he was able to restate them within Catholic theology. And in Erikson too there was an implicit desire to bring Christianity within analysis. Oskar Pfister was not the only analyst in Freud's lifetime to try to import Christian principles within the practice and thinking of analysts.

Unfortunately it has been the dogmatists who have succeeded in having the greatest influence within analysis. The most gentle souls are apt to be forgotten. Otto Rank, whose ideas we have scarcely touched on here, once powerfully suggested that Freud's concept of latent homosexuality was designed to tyrannize over humanity. It needs to be reiterated that tolerance, compassion, charity, and generosity are important ideals, not to be ignored in a natural enthusiasm among intellectuals for system-building. Fanaticism is too easy, and I deplore all varieties of fundamentalism. The simple desire to help patients need not be a result of some malignant craving. Humanitarianism is not only, despite what Freud once held, a sublimation of homosexuality.

Although earlier Anna Freud admired Heinz Kohut, in the end she deemed him "antipsychoanalytic." I recall with genuine horror how Karl Menninger could once denounce Erich Fromm. As we know, Ernest Jones tried to establish that Sandor Ferenczi's differences from Freud reflected Ferenczi's supposed insanity. I have already mentioned how even a liberal like Franz Alexander (himself later denounced in an article by Eissler[7]) could repudiate Karen Horney's work. Fromm wrote critically against Rank, and Jung as well. Up to a certain point, these controversies are invigorating, but too many of the more sorry aspects of these episodes keep reappearing.

I think that the ego psychology which was once so prevalent in America, and which now has been followed by more fashionable schools of thought, ought not to be dismissed out of hand. There was a time when Hartmann was considered the prime minister of world psychoanalysis, although nowadays he is much less apt to be cited any more. Hartmann briefly lived in Paris, after leaving Vienna, and in New York he was a representative of a broadly educated generation of analysts. I have spent my whole career trying to preserve endangered reputations in the history of analysis (including Freud's standing as a political theorist), and maybe it is time now to reconsider the neglected merits of Hartmann's thinking. (Victor Tausk was responsible for originating the concept of ego boundaries, which his friend Paul Federn took up.)

At the same time, now that Lacan has become such a powerful influence within analytic thinking, it would be frightening to think that past patterns of wholesale acceptance of certain approaches are going to be unthinkingly persistent. Lacan's work needs to be critically scrutinized in order to absorb the full benefit of what his teachings have to offer. I once tried to explain to Erikson that I thought there were some similarities, connected with their attitudes toward religion, between his work and that of Klein, but he had closed his mind to her writings. Since Winnicott told me that time that the one analyst whose books he envied not having written himself were those by Erikson, I had to be surprised when that book on Winnicott appeared without a single reference to Erikson.[8]

It is up to historians of ideas to try and keep in touch with all branches of analysis, and in the end it may turn out that there are more parallels between Lacan and ego psychology than any of the active proponents in an old controversy ever realized. Analysis will only thrive if we take nothing on faith. Biological psychiatry has been getting pretty much a free ride in America, but there is increasing evidence that all nosology and diagnoses reflect ethical and social preoccupations. Think how things have changed on the one issue of homosexuality, and how family life has altered. It is important that as students of the life of the mind we do nothing to fan the flames of intolerance, but instead try to come as close as possible to the standard of impartiality which we know ahead of time we will be incapable of accomplishing.

Toleration should not be considered a lack of intellectual ability, but rather become an active energizing ideal. Being tolerant can be more difficult than one might expect. Not being too sure that one is right is a mark of having a civilized intelligence; allowing for give and take is part of fair play. The possibility of being wrong would minimize the occasions for denouncing others. None of this means that proper standards should not be vigorously maintained. But any approach which proclaims "the poison of eclecticism"[9] needs to be rejected. Legitimate doubt should mean the sort of skepticism that is able to put up with basic uncertainties. Credulity is psychologically tied to intolerance, and overall skepticism would minimize the kinds of ideological battles that have marked the history of psychoanalysis. As the great judge Learned Hand once maintained: "all debate, all dissidence, tends to question, and in consequence to upset, existing convictions: that is precisely its purpose and its justification."[10] Even if it is probably true that countries will always pride themselves on the supposed inferiorities of others, genuine intellectuals ought to try to avoid promoting such false identities.

One of the ways intolerances have succeeded in being perpetuated within psychoanalysis has been by means of different schools of thought having had their ideas quietly assimilated by successive streams of thought. The continuities, as well as the discontinuities, within psychoanalytic thought deserve attention. From the perspective of the history of ideas it is apparent that today's so-called mainstream has successfully incorporated many of the points of view of writers who were once actively despised. But as I have said, the very notion of a "mainstream" seems to me to have authoritarian implications of its own, including the suggestion that there are fringe groups which are less deserving of respectful attention. One of the attractions for intellectual historians in studying psychoanalysis is the number of earlier writers who have been for one reason or another fallen by the wayside and therefore been neglected.

At any point in time there has been an orthodoxy in force, even though the content of what is most fiercely defended has changed from decade to decade. As we have seen, literary popularizers and outside acolytes have often been more likely to defend the "mainstream" than more knowledgeable insiders who are more aware of clinical subtleties. When scholars become practicing analysts themselves they should have the security to take along with them the standards they are used to in normal university life. But in the nature of the case clinical work does involve evidence which is unusually difficult to replicate; and all the insecurities of pursuing these sorts of psychological investigations have been likely to involve a lack of respect for differences of opinion that one has come to expect in other academic disciplines.

It is unusually difficult in psychoanalysis to find different perspectives being entertained with comfort; too often disagreements have been temporarily settled by fiat, which can take the form of excluding some from the ranks of legitimate psychoanalysis. (The expulsion, or secession, of Adler and Jung set an unfortunate pattern for later divergences.) All of these sorts of conflicts have come to seem like mini-wars of a quasi-religious nature. Marxism too has had its own share of sectarianism. The future of psychoanalysis would, I think, be more secure if we could count on a decent respect for the motives of those who differ from ourselves even in the most basic sorts of ways. Genuine diversity of opinion requires an enormous degree of respect for divergent points of view; and this means, for those of us who see ourselves as middle-of-the-road types, that we must put up even with a degree of partisanship which can grow to distinctly unpleasant proportions. (To answer accusations should not make one party to the guilt of sectlike intolerance.) But of course it is only human to see ourselves as moderate and others as extremists. Even so, the ideal of toleration should command adherence if psychoanalysis is to deserve to have a secure prospect of making as much of a mark in the present century as it did in the twentieth. It can be possible to be principled in defense of plural outlooks. If there were arguments within the context of normal rules of debate it would only enhance, I believe, that the future will consider this form of psychoanalytic reasoning as a legitimate contribution to human thought.

In America recently there has been a rash of scientistic assaults on Freud's way of thinking, so that it is apt to be widely assumed that psychoanalysis has permanently collapsed, and that the well-known advances in biological psychiatry, with all the new medications available, have succeeded in rendering every branch of Freud's teachings irrelevant. Yet as one travels, in France, Italy, Great Britain, and Latin America, for instance, one gets some idea of how alive the ideas Freud first advanced remain. I am not referring to this or that technical therapeutic recommendation Freud proposed, much of which has proved invalid for today. But outside America psychoanalysis has succeeded in remaining attached to philosophy, despite Freud's insistence that the two areas be kept separate. And so, again in striking contrast to what has happened in the States, elsewhere psychoanalysis has become an increasingly secure part of university life. In France, and also Argentina, for example, one does not have to intend to become a practicing analyst in order for students to take seriously the implications of Freud's work for the life of the mind. Even in Boris Yeltsin's Russia psychoanalysis was legitimized as an aspect of a university curriculum.

I remain optimistic about what the next phase in the story of psychoanalysis might be like. I have suggested that in the United States clinicians will no longer be attracted to the field for the sake of mere careerist considerations; since departments of psychiatry are so hostile to all psychodynamic thinking, those who go into the field will have to do so for some of the idealistic purposes that Freud's original followers had. People who are natural outsiders are bound to be more creative than those motivated by the conformist pressures that in the 1950s and 1960s were so striking in American analysis. Further, in countries like Italy the established psychiatrists, eclectically oriented to a wide range of different psychoanalytic schools of thought, are aware of the way in which psychoanalysis was once oversold as a therapeutic remedy in the States, and these Italians are determined not to make the same mistake themselves.

In Great Britain there are more than a dozen psychoanalytic centers attached to the newer colleges, although both Oxford and Cambridge remain as stubbornly resistant as ever. At many of these psychoanalytic units, part of normal British institutions of higher learning, the students also do intend to enter upon therapeutic practice someday. Only in America was the medical monopoly on psychoanalysis able to be largely successful, which is partly why Freud was so disdainful about the New World reception to his work. I have wondered, thinking about the rise and fall of analysis in America, whether a key aspect of the situation has not been medical narcissism, and the difficulty in analyzing such a set of emotions in the course of training by therapists who are also themselves physicians. Now that American psychologists have won their suit against the branches of the IPA, the numbers of nonmedical people getting psychoanalytic certification has notably risen.

Even though psychoanalysis has been in existence for over a hundred years now, as a whole physicians are still relatively unaware of the significance of Freud's teachings. One can wonder how many surgeons, for example, take adequate preparations for the mental complexities of their patients, or even understand the key significance of the whole relationship between patient and surgeon, which can be a key component to the success of the treatment procedure.

In my own special field, political thought and the history of ideas, I am acutely aware how little psychoanalysis has managed to achieve in changing the more traditional outlook on what constitutes rational conduct. It sometimes seems to me that all the indictments of Benthamite reasoning, levelled by thinkers as diverse as John Stuart Mill, Nietzsche, Dostoevsky, and even Charles Dickens, have fallen on deaf ears.[11] Although public figures have been eager to make use of psychoanalytic thinking for propagandistic purposes of electoral manipulation, the academic study of political science has never accepted the legitimacy of Freud as a pioneering figure.

If one looks at a street-side bookstall in Buenos Aires or Mexico City, where daily newspapers can be bought, there will be available, for approximately ten dollars, a hardcover edition of Rousseau's *Social Contract* along with a similarly bound first volume of the Spanish edition of Freud's complete works. To me that is a fulfillment of my dream that Freud be understood as a great social philosopher.

As someone who has written critically about many flaws in a variety of psychoanalytic thinking, it may seem surprising that I am so hopeful about the future of psychoanalysis. But as long as orthodoxy, sectarianism, and fundamentalism can be kept at bay — which is by no means easy — psychoanalysis has immense possibilities for expanding the horizons of laymen, physicians, as well as academics. Too often historians, to take just one profession, do not realize the extent to which psychological premises are built into the way they go about their thinking.

It is never wise to rest on one's laurels, and for all the success of psychoanalysis over the past century now is no time for complacency. If open-mindedness and tolerance could become key components at psychoanalytic educational centers, then the religiously tinged heresy-hunting of the past need not be repeated, and the implications of what can be meant by unconscious thought processes will succeed in continuing to transform how we think about how we think.

Notes

1. Tony Judt, *Past Imperfect: French Intellectuals 1944–1956* (Berkeley, University of California Press, 1992).
2. Roazen, *Brother Animal, op. cit.*, pp. 187–91; Roazen, *Freud and His Followers, op. cit.*, pp. 304–10.
3. Anna Freud, *The Ego and the Mechanisms of Defence, op. cit.*
4. Ernst Kris, "Book Review of Anna Freud, *The Ego and the Mechanisms of Defence*," *International Journal of Psychoanalysis*, Vol. 19 (1938), p. 142.
5. Martin S. Bergmann, *The Hartmann Era* (N.Y., Other Press, 2000).
6. John Beebe, Joseph Cambray, and Thomas B. Kirsch, "What Freudians Can Learn From Jung," *Psychoanalytic Psychology*, Vol 18, No. 2 (Spring 2001), pp. 213–242.

7. K. R. Eissler, "The Chicago Institute of Psychoanalysis and the 6th Period of the Development of Psychoanalytic Technique," *Journal of General Psychology*, Vol. 42, First Half (Jan. 1950), pp. 103–57.
8. Adam Phillips, *Winnicott* (London, Fontana, 1988).
9. Kurt R. Eissler, *Medical Orthodoxy and the Future of Psychoanalysis* (New York, International Universities Press, 1965), p. 84.
10. Quoted in Gerald Gunther, *Learned Hand: The Man and the Judge* (Cambridge, Harvard University Press, 1995), p. 591.
11. Paul Roazen, *Political Theory and the Psychology of the Unconscious, op. cit.*

Index